Unfolding Mallarmé

The Development of a Poetic Art

ROGER PEARSON

CLARENDON PRESS · OXFORD

This book has been printed digitally and produced in a standard specification
in order to ensure its continuing availability

OXFORD
UNIVERSITY PRESS

Great Clarendon Street, Oxford OX2 6DP

Oxford University Press is a department of the University of Oxford.
It furthers the University's objective of excellence in research, scholarship,
and education by publishing world-wide in

Oxford New York

Auckland Bangkok Buenos Aires Cape Town Chennai
Dar es Salaam Delhi Hong Kong Istanbul Karachi Kolkata
Kuala Lumpur Madrid Melbourne Mexico City Mumbai Nairobi
São Paulo Shanghai Taipei Tokyo Toronto

Oxford is a registered trade mark of Oxford University Press
in the UK and in certain other countries

Published in the United States
by Oxford University Press Inc., New York

ISBN 0-19-815917-X

Antony Rowe Ltd., Eastbourne

une approche contient l'hommage.
                              ('Solitude')

Ecrire—[...] Ce pli de sombre dentelle, qui retient l'infini, tissé par mille, chacun selon le fil ou prolongement ignoré son secret, assemble des entrelacs distants où dort un luxe à inventorier, stryge, nœud, feuillages et présenter.

Avec le rien de mystère, indispensable, qui demeure, exprimé, quelque peu.

('L'Action restreinte')

Lire—

Cette pratique—

Appuyer, selon la page, au blanc, qui l'inaugure son ingénuité, à soi, oublieuse même du titre qui parlerait trop haut: et, quand s'aligna, dans une brisure, la moindre, disséminée, le hasard vaincu mot par mot, indéfectiblement le blanc revient, tout à l'heure gratuit, certain maintenant, pour conclure que rien au-delà et authentiquer le silence—

('Le Mystère dans les lettres')

je ne suis pas obscur, du moment qu'on me lit pour y chercher [...] la manifestation d'un art qui se sert [...] du langage; et le deviens bien sûr! si l'on se trompe et croit ouvrir le journal.

(Letter to Edmund Gosse, 10 Jan. 1893)

Ce que l'hymen déjoue, sous l'espèce du présent (temporel ou éternel), c'est l'assurance d'une maîtrise. Le désir critique—c'est-à-dire aussi bien que philosophique—ne peut, en tant que tel, que tenter de l'y reconduire.

(Jacques Derrida, *La Dissémination*)

Acknowledgements

IN writing this book I have been indebted not only to the extensive and distinguished body of critical literature devoted to Mallarmé but also to the many students at Oxford with whom I have been able to share my interest in Mallarmé's poetry and by whom I have been led, in the course of discussion, to several of the interpretations proposed here. I am also especially grateful to Malcolm Bowie, Ian Maclean, and Clive Scott for their helpful advice; and to the Provost and Fellows of The Queen's College, Oxford, and the Board of the Faculty of Medieval and Modern Languages at Oxford for enabling this book to be written by granting periods of sabbatical leave and providing financial assistance towards the costs of research.

Contents

Note on References

The following abbreviations have been used in the footnotes.

Corr.   *Correspondance*, ed. Henri Mondor and Jean-Pierre Richard (vol. i),
           Henri Mondor and Lloyd James Austin (vols ii–xi) (11 vols, Paris,
           1959–85)

DSM   *Documents Stéphane Mallarmé*, ed. Carl Paul Barbier *et al.* (7 vols,
           Paris, 1968–80)

Larousse   *Grand Dictionnaire universel du XIXe siècle*, ed. Pierre Larousse (15
           vols, Paris, 1866–76; 1st Suppl. 1877; 2nd Suppl. [1890]; reprinted by
           Slatkine, 17 vols, Geneva, 1982)

Littré   *Dictionnaire de la langue française*, ed. Paul-Émile Littré (4 vols, Paris,
           1863–72; Suppl. 1877)

OC   *Œuvres complètes*, ed. Henri Mondor and G. Jean-Aubry (Bibliothèque
           de la Pléiade) (Paris, 1951)

OC (BM)   *Œuvres complètes*, vol. i: *Poésies*, ed. Carl Paul Barbier and Charles
           Gordon Millan (Paris, 1983)

Robert   *Dictionnaire alphabétique et analogique de la langue française*, ed. Paul
           Robert (9 vols, Paris, 1985)

'Devant la lettre': On Reading Mallarmé

J'abomine les *préfaces* issues même de l'auteur, à plus forte raison
trouvé-je mauvais air à celle ajoutée par autrui. Mon cher, un vrai livre
se passe de présentation, il procède par le coup de foudre, comme la
femme envers l'amant et sans aide d'un tiers, ce mari.

(Letter to Charles Guérin, 24 Dec. 1894)

This study has two principal aims: to propose new meanings in Mallarmé's
poetry and to present the development of his poetic art as a successful search
for linguistic and textual mastery.

Poetry for Mallarmé was first and foremost an art of language, and
Derrida's brilliant essay in *La Dissémination* takes us to the centre of the
Mallarméan experience of language. As the Derridean analyses of the
'antre/entre' and the 'hymen' demonstrate, meanings spill out of words
like peas from a dehiscent pod: language is forever contradicting itself,
repeatedly gainsaying the message which it is complacently intended or
understood to convey. Meaning is 'indécidable'. For Derrida, to speak of
'polysemy' in this context would imply semantic richness and the multiple
'presence' of meaning: he prefers to speak of 'dissémination'[1] and to char-
acterize Mallarmé as a writer who displays language, with increasing know-
ingness, as a place of proliferating non-meaning. Whereas Derrida envisages
Mallarmé's loss (or abdication[2]) of authorial control over language princi-
pally at a semantic level, Julia Kristeva sees it more at the phonological and
morphological levels (in her readings of 'Prose (pour des Esseintes)' and 'Un
coup de Dés' respectively).[3] But, like Maurice Blanchot before them,[4] both
champion Mallarmé for his 'revolutionary' displays of linguistic powerless-

---

[1] 'C'est à ce concept herméneutique de *polysémie* qu'il faudrait substituer celui de *dissémi-
nation*.' Jacques Derrida, *La Dissémination* (Paris, 1972), 294.
[2] See *La Dissémination*, 254–5, where the question of 'intention' is neatly finessed.
[3] *La Révolution du langage poétique* (Paris, 1974), 205–91.
[4] See in particular 'Le Mythe de Mallarmé', in *La Part du feu* (Paris, 1949), 35–48;
'L'Expérience de Mallarmé', in *L'Espace littéraire* (Paris, 1955), 30–41; and 'Le Livre à venir',
in *Le Livre à venir* (Paris, 1959), 303–32.

ness and 'failure' rather than for any mastery by which he might be seeking to harness and exploit the 'disseminating' tendencies of language in his pursuit of poetic beauty.

Post-structuralist readings of Mallarmé revealed, if nothing else, the poverty and misdirection of so many traditional attempts to recuperate his difficult poems as 'intentional' representations of the real world. All readers of the critical material devoted to the *Poésies* are familiar with the absurd debates about the possible referents of 'ptyx' in the 'Sonnet en -yx' and whether the subject of 'A la nue accablante tu' might perhaps be a bidet.[5] But not all attempts to make sense of Mallarmé have been senseless. Taking up where Gardner Davies left off in his book *Mallarmé et le drame solaire*,[6] Bertrand Marchal has more recently demonstrated in *La Religion de Mallarmé*[7] a considerable degree of coherence in Mallarmé's thought (and language), especially about 'the Tragedy of Nature' and the status of the divine as a projection of human spirituality. Above all Marchal shows that Mallarmé is to be trusted, that his notorious 'obscurity' is not some pretentious smokescreen concealing triviality, a mere display of linguistic preciousness, but rather a form of writing which repays careful reading. As Marchal rightly asserts in the 'Avant-Propos' to his *Lecture de Mallarmé*: 'Il n'y a pas, en effet, d'écriture plus concertée, plus consciemment maîtrisée que celle de Mallarmé, et de moins directement lisible comme le palimpseste d'un sous-texte inconscient.'[8]

Towards the end of his life, Mallarmé himself maintained that his work was perfectly comprehensible if read in the appropriate manner. He said so to Edmund Gosse in 1893,[9] and he repeated the point in 1896 when Proust launched his attack on Symbolism in the short article entitled 'Contre l'obscurité': 'Je préfère,' replied Mallarmé tartly, 'devant l'agression, rétorquer que des contemporains ne savent pas lire—Sinon dans le journal'.[10] He then goes on to explain how one should read:

Lire—

Cette pratique—

Appuyer, selon la page, au blanc, qui l'inaugure son ingénuité, à soi, oublieuse même du titre qui parlerait trop haut: et, quand s'aligna, dans une brisure, la moindre, disséminée, le hasard vaincu mot par mot, indéfectiblement le blanc revient, tout à

---

[5] Robert Goffin, *Mallarmé vivant* (Paris, 1956), 277–9.
[6] (Paris, 1959).
[7] (Paris, 1988).
[8] Bertrand Marchal, *Lecture de Mallarmé* (Paris, 1985), 9.
[9] *Corr.*, vi. 27, quoted above, p. vi.
[10] *OC*, 386. Proust's article was published in the *Revue blanche* on 15 July 1896 (and republished in his *Chroniques* (Paris, 1927), 137–44). Mallarmé's reply, 'Le Mystère dans les lettres', appeared in the same review on 1 Sept. 1896. For a detailed account of this reply, see Marchal, *La Religion de Mallarmé*, 467–79.

l'heure gratuit, certain maintenant, pour conclure que rien au-delà et authentiquer le silence—.[11]

His advice is to empty one's mind of preconceptions and to read between the lines. Like the empty page itself, we should wait to be 'written' on, ignoring even the possible clues afforded by a title. The text constitutes a break in the silence, a 'dissemination' of signs in the whiteness of the page; and when this text displays 'le hasard vaincu mot par mot', then that silence or whiteness returns (to our attention) 'indéfectiblement'—both inevitably and also purged of 'defect' (i.e. its apparent gratuitousness), a place of certainty (or necessity) which demonstrates symbolically that only language has presented itself to our gaze (i.e. there is no evidence of the 'real', referential world onto which language is conventionally deemed to offer unproblematic access, let alone some transcendental 'au-delà' of a mystical kind).

As a place of certainty this blank space now offers some 'authentication' of silence. Why? Because it is between the lines that 'le hasard' of linguistic contingency has been vanquished. Thus this silence, this space 'between the lines', is a 'Virginité qui solitairement, devant une transparence du regard adéquat, elle-même s'est comme divisée en ses fragments de candeur, l'un et l'autre, preuves nuptiales de l'Idée'.[12] It is as if the whiteness itself has been fragmented by the invisible patterns of significance set up by the visible dissemination of the text. Blankness has been resolved by the prism (or 'solitaire' diamond) of language into separate 'colours', a spectrum of differentiated 'meanings'.[13] A reader who reads 'transparently', without preconception, as 'candid' as the whiteness from which that word derives, will perceive these patterns, will understand the connecting links which bind together and demonstrate the existence of 'l'Idée'. This 'Idée', Mallarmé concludes, is like some underlying, unsung melody, guiding the reader through the text as he or she endeavours to 'divine' its meaning, an invisible display of delicate pattern: 'L'air ou chant sous le texte, conduisant la divination d'ici là, y applique son motif en fleuron et cul-de-lampe invisibles.'[14] Previously, in his remarks to Gosse in 1893, Mallarmé had defined the word 'Musique' as 'au fond signifiant Idée ou rythme entre des rapports'.[15] The reader's task is to 'listen' to the conquest of chance as it is linguistically carried out by the text, to perceive the 'preuves nuptiales' by which apparently unconnected textual elements are married in a union of fertile significance.

[11] OC, 386–7.
[12] OC, 387.
[13] Cf. Mallarmé's comment in his so-called 'preface' to 'Un coup de Dés' (actually entitled 'Observation relative au poème: "Un coup de Dés jamais n'abolira le Hasard"'): 'il ne s'agit pas, ainsi que toujours, de traits sonores réguliers ou vers—plutôt, de subdivisions prismatiques de l'Idée' (OC, 455).
[14] OC, 387.
[15] Corr., vi. 26.

Mallarmé thus requires his reader to be hermeneutic, to seek out the meanings of his texts by 'forgetting' the habits of conventional linguistic communication ('le journal') and by gazing 'transparently' at the page free from all nostalgia for a beyond. But what of the reader's own 'mastery'? Does Mallarmé imply that, given a 'regard adéquat', each text will yield its secret? Vincent Kaufmann has argued strenuously against such a notion. In his view the Mallarméan text encourages its reader to think that there is a 'secret' to be discovered only to reveal that the 'secret' is the free play of language beyond the reader's own ability mentally to control such play: 'Le lecteur trouverait en somme sa place en se découvrant joué, d'avance, par la langue (qui aura en quelque sorte passé un contrat à sa place).'[16] On the one hand, the text 'fait miroiter une position (imaginaire) de maîtrise et de déchiffrement intégral de son propre secret', but this position is contradicted by 'une position de séduction (au sens passif du terme), où la maîtrise s'efface derrière l'écoute de la "signifiance" du texte, que rien ne saurait arrêter'.[17]

In essence Kaufmann transfers the Derridean experience of aporia from the mind of the writer to the mind of the reader, but the implication is still the same: the Mallarméan text is not to be controlled, its 'mysteries' shall remain inviolate in their endless proliferation. Ross Chambers, on the other hand, takes a more positive line. Starting from Mallarmé's famous self-addressed quatrain in *Les Loisirs de la poste*, Chambers constructs a model of reading in which the text 'implies' the proper context in which it is to be read, and the reader—as postman or reading 'facteur/factor'—tries to convey the 'trace' of the letter/text to 'Monsieur Mallarmé': i.e. endeavours by reading to 'deliver' the text back to the man who wrote it. Yet, while the text includes us by addressing itself to us to be read, it also excludes us because our reading will only ever be 'in the mode of textual supplementation, never in the mode of consummation'. Thus, Chambers concludes: 'It is in the shuttle space formed by these two principles, always necessarily included, always necessarily excluded[,] that we critics, the professional letter-carriers of literature, "ply" (or fold) our trade.'[18]

Such a model, however, continues to ply—or imply—a certain Post-structuralist defeatism. 'Never in the mode of consummation'? In seeking union with the text, is the reader of Mallarmé to be condemned to the 'mariage blanc' of an uncomprehending gaze? Shall the 'preuves nuptiales de l'Idée' remain invisible in the virgin spaces of the page? As literary critics, are we 'reading factors' to refuse to purloin the letter because it is ultimately addressed neither to us nor to our fellow-readers? Surely not. And so my

---

[16] Vincent Kaufmann, *Le Livre et ses adresses (Mallarmé, Ponge, Valéry, Blanchot)* (Paris, 1986), 51.

[17] *Le Livre et ses adresses*, 106.

[18] Ross Chambers, 'An Address in the Country: Mallarmé and the Kinds of Literary Context', *French Forum*, 11 (1986), 199–215 (214–15).

ambition in this book is to be a 'postman' of a less proper kind: to steam
some of Mallarmé's 'letters' open before they are returned to sender, un-
received and unread, and, with no little indiscretion, to attempt to unfold
their contents in full public view.

But how? In attacking the obscurity of the Symbolists, Proust claims that
their archaisms and neologisms simply turn poems into theorems or puzzles
awaiting solution: 'la poésie demande un peu plus de mystère.'[19] He argues
instead for a different form of 'obscurity' in literature, the 'obscurité [...]
féconde à approfondir' of *Macbeth*, an obscurity born not of intellectual
design but of 'une sorte de puissance instinctive'.[20] Nature has no need of
neologisms, he writes, for nature already possesses the sufficient means to
express 'les mystères les plus profonds de la vie et de la mort'.[21] The read-
ings of Mallarmé proposed in this book may often seem like solutions to
puzzles (whether or not they are persuasive *as* solutions!), but they will have
done a disservice to Mallarmé if they dispel rather than enhance that sense
of 'mystère' which language inspired in the poet himself.

For Mallarmé, to break the silence with words was to become immedi-
ately implicated in a pre-existing linguistic network:

une langue, loin de livrer au hasard sa formation, est composée à l'égal d'un
merveilleux ouvrage de broderie ou de dentelle: pas un fil de l'idée qui se perde,
celui-ci se cache mais pour reparaître un peu plus loin uni à celui-là; tous s'assemb-
lent en un dessin, complexe ou simple, idéal, et que retient à jamais la mémoire, non!
l'instinct d'harmonie que, grand ou jeune, on a en soi.[22]

Language is a mysterious universe, a strange place in which pre-existing
patterns, dimly perceived, seem to bespeak some original harmony. As we
follow the threads of its labyrinthine lace, the everyday meanings of lan-
guage become obscure. Homophony comes to haunt it with the spectres of
other meanings, and the skeletons of etymology begin to rattle in their
cupboards. Syllables break loose from their verbal context and, like the
sibyls of old, call up the shades from an other, spirit world. In the ensuing
darkness new constellations of meaning begin to glimmer. The former,
seemingly unproblematic representational function of language has sunk
beneath the horizon to be replaced by the non-representational 'Idée', by
Mallarmé's linguistic music of the spheres. For the Poet-Master, the anguish
of language at sunset gives way to the prospect of an alternative navigational
aid as he endeavours to orient himself upon the page: 'RIEN / N'AURA EU
LIEU / QUE LE LIEU / EXCEPTÉ / PEUT-ÊTRE / UNE CONSTELLATION'.[23]

The reader's task (and the critic's) is to listen to this 'music': to follow the
thread—'le fil conducteur latent', as it is called in the preface to 'Un coup de

---

[19] *Chroniques*, 141.   [20] *Chroniques*, 140.   [21] *Chroniques*, 143.
[22] *Les Mots anglais*, OC, 828.   [23] 'Un coup de Dés', OC, 474–7.

Dés'—and, like the poet Mallarmé at his mime-show (in 'Mimique'), to 'translate' the 'authenticated' silence which follows:

Le silence, seul luxe après les rimes, un orchestre ne faisant avec son or, ses frôle-ments de pensée et de soir, qu'en détailler la signification à l'égal d'une ode tue et que c'est au poète, suscité par un défi, de traduire! le silence aux après-midi de musique.[24]

Given the complexity of Mallarmé's music, such a 'translation' must necessarily be a detailed and intricate procedure, the closest of close read-ings, and it is therefore impracticable to discuss all his poems in a single book. In order to display the 'development' of his poetic art, I have singled out the 'Sonnet allégorique de lui-même' (May 1868) as a watershed. In Parts I and II every poem or prose poem which Mallarmé wrote before the onset of his physical and mental 'crisis' in 1866 is examined chronologically in an attempt, on the basis of almost exclusively internal evidence, to show how—and to infer the aesthetic reasons why—the 'self-allegorical' nature of Mallarmé's writing evolved before the crisis (which it may even have caused). Several of his best-known poems fall within this first period, and if I isolate them for detailed attention less manifestly than later works and stress their role in a process of development, this should not be taken to imply any adverse judgement on their poetic quality or their status as 'mature' or 'finished' works of art. But since Mallarmé's whole poetic project seems to have assumed its definitive shape at this point, it may prove instructive to follow him, as it were from the inside, through each stage of the early and rapid process of evolution which turned him from schoolboy versifier into accomplished poet.

Part III contains an analysis of the 'Sonnet en -yx', in both its first and final versions, as well as in relation to the other three sonnets in alexan-drines with which it is grouped in 'Plusieurs Sonnets' ('Quand l'ombre menaça...', 'Le vierge, le vivace...', and 'Victorieusement fui...'); while Part IV focuses on a range of poems in octosyllabic metre which span the greater part of Mallarmé's poetic career from 1868 to 1894. Finally, Part V presents an extensive account of 'Un coup de Dés jamais n'abolira le Hasard' in which this poem is seen as the culmination of Mallarmé's poetic art.

For reasons of length I have held over for a subsequent volume all those poems by Mallarmé where a particular circumstance—a birth, a death, a circumnavigation—is more or less explicitly the starting-point for the poem.[25] This division is somewhat arbitrary since, as will be seen, it is

---

[24] OC, 310.

[25] This category includes all the Shakespearean sonnets (including the first, 'La chevelure vol d'une flamme...', which, as part of 'La Déclaration foraine', is a poem *about* being a 'vers de circonstance') and all the poems in heptasyllabic metre, as well as 'Dans le jardin', 'Toast

essentially the 'circumstances' of language itself which provide the 'starting-point' for Mallarmé's poems. But such a distinction at least has the merit of limiting the focus of the present study to poems which are more or less explicitly concerned with Mallarmé's own pursuit of poetic beauty.

At the same time the readings which follow are far from being exhaustive. Constraints of space have meant that my disagreements with other critical interpretations remain for the most part implicit: in general, reference is made to other readings of Mallarmé only where these supplement my own or where I am indebted for a particular insight. In any case my overall aim is not so much to supplant other approaches as to encourage a willingness to perceive a wide range of meanings simultaneously. I am especially concerned to demonstrate a 'logic' within the Mallarméan text which 'ties' these meanings together in a rich synthesis that belies the themes of vacancy, negativity, and failure customarily seen as the hallmarks of Mallarmé's writings.

In so far as my own readings have originality, this depends partly on the emphasis given to etymology and homophony: those poetic features usually highlighted in more traditional *explications de texte* (rhythmical variation, sound clusters, syntactic disruption, etc.) are less to the fore. For the etymologies I have consulted Paul Robert's *Dictionnaire alphabétique et analogique de la langue française* but relied where possible on those dictionaries which were available to Mallarmé himself, notably Paul-Émile Littré's *Dictionnaire de la langue française* (4 vols, 1863–72; Suppl. 1877), and Pierre Larousse's *Grand Dictionnaire universel du XIXe siècle* (15 vols, 1866–76; 1st Suppl. 1877–8, 2nd Suppl. [1890]). As to homophony, I have consulted these dictionaries where I had reason to believe that late nineteenth-century pronunciation might differ from today's. All instances of homophonic readings are prefaced 'hom.'; occasionally, as the reader will recognize, the homophonies are approximate—and in some particularly tenuous instances this will be explicitly noted—but in every case the context has seemed to me to justify their relevance.

In sum, this book describes an adventure in language. Mallarmé did inhabit a particular country at a particular time, and he responded in many ways to the wider cultural and political context of his day. His correspondence, his 'poèmes de circonstance', and his prose writings of the 1880s and 1890s on music and the theatre, on literature and religion, and on the role of the poet in society bear witness to this fact. Moreover, through the weekly gatherings in his small apartment at 89 rue de Rome, his celebrated 'mardis', he exerted considerable influence over a younger generation of writers, notably Gide and Valéry. But in the poems under inves-

---

funèbre', 'Sur les bois oubliés...', 'Sonnet au public', the 'Éventails' for Mlle Mallarmé and Méry Laurent, the 'Tombeaux', the 'Hommage' to Wagner, 'Sonnet pour elle', 'Dame / Sans trop d'ardeur...', 'Remémoration d'amis belges', 'Billet', and 'Salut'.

tigation in this book he is especially to be seen coming face to face with the blank page and the demands of poetry as a linguistic craft. Why this verse-form and not another? What is the intrinsic nature of a sonnet? What does a word 'mean'? How does a word 'mean'? The term 'septuor' (at the end of 'Sonnet allégorique de lui-même') 'means' septet. But what sort of 'septet': the musical composition itself, or the instruments (human voices or crafted artefacts) by which it is performed? And how do these meanings relate to the other meanings by which 'septuor' is homophonically 'haunted': like 'cep' (the vine, or the sole of a plough cultivating the soil in which the vine grows?), or 'tu', or... 'or'? Perhaps the true meaning of 'septuor' lies in the fact that it contains seven letters. As Mallarmé unfolds, so also does the mystery of language; a 'mystery'—etymologically, that secret upon which our initiated lips shall remain *closed*, but in Mallarmé that secret which can be glimpsed in the silent interstices of his manifold art: 'le rien de mystère, indispensable, qui demeure, exprimé, quelque peu.'[26]

[26] 'L'Action restreinte', OC, 370.

PART I

Gradus ad Parnassum
(1842–1866)

cette cime menaçante d'absolu, devinée dans le départ des nuées là-haut, fulgurante, nue, seule [...]

('Richard Wagner: Rêverie d'un poète français')

De grands esprits ont commencé par le pastiche [...]
('*Les Poésies parisiennes* d'Emmanuel Des Essarts')

The physical and mental crisis which Mallarmé began to undergo in 1866 has often led commentators on his poetic development to emphasize the contrast between his early works and his later manner of writing. Barbara Johnson lends wittiest expression to such a view when she records how 'après un début précoce et prolixe au lycée de Sens, Mallarmé passe par plusieurs Tournon avant de lancer, avec un coup de dés, les Paris de sa maturité'. For her, Mallarmé's *œuvre* consists of 'deux grandes constellations séparées par une lacune de près de vingt ans [...] une première scintillation, antérieure à 1867, et une dernière fulguration, postérieure à 1884'.[1]

Although very little is known for certain about when and in what guise many of Mallarmé's later poems originated, Johnson argues from dates of composition that his total *œuvre* is 'loin de s'élaborer de façon continue'.[2] However, if one looks at the internal, textual evidence, a different picture emerges; and there is every reason to suppose that Mallarmé's career was one long, sustained, and graduated assault upon the summit of poetic perfection. Four main glimpses of his progress are afforded: the poems published in *Le Parnasse contemporain* in May 1866; the photolithographed edition of his manuscript *Poésies* in 1887; the posthumous Deman edition of his *Poésies* (1899); and 'Un coup de Dés', published imperfectly in 1897 and still awaiting a definitive edition.[3] Each successive glimpse reveals that Mallarmé has indeed 'elaborated', and occasionally the clouds part briefly in between to suggest a continuity of experimentation and advance: 'Sonnet allégorique de lui-même' (1868), 'Fragment d'une étude scénique ancienne d'un Poème d'Hérodiade' (1869), 'Toast funèbre' (1873), 'L'Après-midi d'un faune' (1876), 'Quand l'ombre menaça...' (1883), 'Le vierge, le vivace...' (1885), 'La chevelure vol d'une flamme...' (1887),[4] 'Le

---

[1] Barbara Johnson, *Défigurations du langage poétique* (Paris, 1979), 165.

[2] Ibid.

[3] Mitsou Ronat's excellent edition (Paris, Change errant/d'atelier, 1980) lacks the font which Mallarmé had chosen (and which, having been destroyed, would need to be recast for such a definitive edition to be possible).

[4] The first of Mallarmé's sixteen Shakespearean sonnets, this was published not in the *Poésies* of that year but as part of 'La Déclaration foraine' in *L'Art et la mode* (12 Aug.).

Savetier' (1889),[5] 'A la nue accablante tu' (1892). Far from being an *opus duplex*, as Johnson maintains,[6] Mallarmé's poetic work is a complex phenomenon, evolving 'pli selon pli' over time.

[5] His first heptasyllabic sonnet, along with 'La Marchande d'herbes aromatiques' (both published in *Les Types de Paris*, illustrated by Jean-François Raffaëlli).

[6] *Défigurations*, 165.

I

Initiation and Communion

Stéphane Mallarmé
('Ma chère Fanny...')

Mallarmé's early works are notable for the poet's concerted endeavour to learn his craft. Not for him the gush and turpitude of adolescent introspection, nor self-indulgent posturing before the mirror of the muse: there was work to be done. He wanted to be a poet, he would learn what other poets did, and he would see if he could do better. Ultimately he aspired to a rather more eternal peak of perfection, but by the time he was 24 he had at least gained acceptance as a contributor to 'le Parnasse contemporain'. How had he arrived there?

The earliest extant poem by Mallarmé, his first faltering step towards the summit of Mount Parnassus, is addressed to the woman who taught him the rudiments of French versification. Fanny Dubois Davesnes, the daughter of an actor and herself a sculptress, was a neighbour of the Mallarmés at Passy. At her house the young Stéphane would listen as his stepmother, a keen amateur painter, sought advice from the artist; and on at least one occasion he met the populist poet Béranger (1780–1857), long since a national institution, and of whom Fanny was to sculpt a bust in 1854.[1] Some time around 1850 the grateful 'pupil' sent his 25-year-old 'teacher' the following demonstration of his prosodic prowess:

> Ma chère Fanny
> Ma bonne amie
> Je te promets d'être sage
> A tout âge
> Et de toujours t'aimer.
> Stéphane Mallarmé.

---

[1] See Henri Mondor, *Mallarmé lycéen* (Paris, 1954), 112–13; Austin Gill, *The Early Mallarmé* (2 vols, Oxford, 1979 and 1986), i. 22–3; and Gordon Millan, *Mallarmé: A Throw of the Dice: The Life of Stéphane Mallarmé* (London, 1994), 26.

'Rimes plates' indeed, except for the fortuitous appropriateness that Mallarmé's début should be a poem in which the principal 'idée' (gratitude for the lesson on versification) is conveyed less by the superficial meaning of the words than by the manner of the poem's execution. Like so much of his mature work it is, in its way, a poem about poetry; and its playful rhymes anticipate the later *Loisirs de la poste*. By incorporating the poet's name as a signature, the last line of the poem points forward to the first page of 'Un coup de Dés' where 'Stéphane Mallarmé' figures once more, the emblem of a poet rejoicing in a name that is itself a hemistich.

Whereas towards the end of his life Mallarmé was deeply embarrassed to be elected 'Prince des poètes' upon the death of Verlaine,[2] the schoolboy-poet found competition stimulating. At the Lycée de Sens it was customary on the annual day of first communion for chosen pupils to recite a poem of their own creation in celebration of the occasion. What appears to have been Mallarmé's first attempt to secure this honour, his 'Cantate pour la première communion' (1858), displays less the religiosity of an adolescent than the virtuosity of a promising apprentice. Taking a standard theme (angelic children as rivals of the heavenly hosts in praising the Almighty), he turns his hand to the 'cantate', the poetic form perfected by Jean-Baptiste Rousseau and which he had just been studying in class that year. Adjusting this form to his particular needs with considerable skill,[3] he substituted the language and style of Lamartine and Hugo for that of Rousseau, and there it was: the first of his 'hymnes des cœurs spirituels', the forerunner of 'Prose (pour des Esseintes)' and the 'Cantique de saint Jean'. The octosyllabic metre of the traditional 'prose' of Christian liturgy here suggests both the urgent excitement and the simple innocence of the occasion, while the single alexandrine in each refrain ('De vos ailes couvrez ce joyeux sanctuaire') suggests by contrast an awed appeal to overarching angelic protection. A cantata calling for cantatas ('Chantez, célébrez tous en chœur'), the poem extols the Eucharist as an 'hymen mystérieux / De la force et de la faiblesse', a source of 'douce ivresse' equivalent to 'Un prélude au bonheur des cieux'. Similarly, Mallarmé's first cantata is itself a 'prélude' to the 'Jeu suprême' of his mature art, in which the ritual of Christian communion is transposed into the linguistic enactment of death and resurrection, of sunset and constellation.

At his second attempt he won. In this untitled poem divided into three sections ('La Prière d'une mère', 'Le Ciel', 'La Terre'), the handling of poetic form is once more of greater consequence than the theme, which, like the occasion for it, remains essentially the same. Rousseau's cantatas give way to Lamartine's three-part 'Cantate pour les enfants d'une maison de charité' as the chosen model,[4] but the poem still champions the power of terrestrial

---

[2] Millan, *Mallarmé*, 305.   [3] See Gill, *The Early Mallarmé*, i. 103–11.
[4] See Gill, *The Early Mallarmé*, i. 111–21.

choirs to match the 'sainte phalange' (l. 16) in proclaiming the glory of God. Indeed the 'ange d'un jour' who delivers the third part of the poem, and who may be envisaged as the mother's newly communicant son, seems on occasions slightly too terrestrial in the assertion of his cantorial rights: 'Seigneur, merci! [. . .] / N'était-ce assez de ton chœur d'anges' (ll. 75–7). And when this little angel goes on to pray that the Holy Mother spare their earthly mothers from the taste of gall, his hold on metaphor begins to slip:

> Prions notre immortelle mère
> Pour celle qui donna sur terre
> Nos cœurs à son fils éternel!
> Prions qu'elle écarte l'absinthe
> De la coupe où sa lèvre sainte
> Boit la force qui mène au ciel!
>
> (ll. 99–104)

No wonder the local newspaper reported that 'L'élève Mallarmé a récité un petit poème de circonstance, ingénieusement composé, rempli de vers d'une originalité brillante, bien que parfois un peu risquée.'[5] Requesting salvation from 'mother's ruin' was hardly quite the thing.

But 'ingénieusement composé' the poem is, at least compared with Mallarmé's earlier cantata. The first and third (earthly) sections consist of 40 lines each, the second (as heavenly interruption) of 34; of the 114 lines exactly two-thirds are alexandrines, and the other third octosyllabics. The predominating alexandrines lend Hugolian grandeur and promote no less Hugolian antitheses, while the octosyllabics serve variously to evoke angelic song or to suggest a terrestrial falling short. The 'Mystérieux hymen' (l. 62), present once again, of heaven and earth, of 'force' and 'faiblesse', is thus evoked by the metrical combination of the poem itself.

In 'La Prière d'une mère' the humility and simplicity of the mother is conveyed in ten quatrains of alexandrines in 'rimes croisées',[6] except that the last line of stanzas 1, 4, 7, and 10 is octosyllabic. The heavenly hosts express themselves in three stanzas: one of ten octosyllabic lines rhyming ababccdeed, surrounded by two sixains of alexandrines rhyming aabccb with the fifth alexandrine replaced by an octosyllabic line. In the ensuing choral competition this prosodic effort contrasts unfavourably, after a narrative interval of three quatrains of alexandrines in 'rimes croisées', with the terrestrial offering of the 'ange d'un jour'. Of his six stanzas the first and fourth repeat the form of the celestial dizain; the second and fifth repeat the form of the previous sixain, in the former stanza varying it by deferring the octosyllabic line till last; while the third and sixth reassert the

---

[5] Quoted in Gill, *The Early Mallarmé*, i. 113.
[6] With the seemingly unnecessary exception of the second stanza, which is in 'rimes plates'.

quatrain of alexandrines in 'rimes croisées' that had hitherto in the poem
been the exclusive medium of earthbound voices.

Abstruse though such prosodic analysis may appear, the fact remains that
Mallarmé's winning poem is notable for the way in which, once more, the
'Idée' of the poem is conveyed implicitly in the manner of the poem's
execution. The mother prays that her son be the medium whereby her
own worship may reach the Lord:

> Oh! qu'en ce jour, Seigneur,
> Un chant de joie au ciel sur les ailes d'un ange
> S'élève jusqu'à vous, faible écho de mon cœur!
>   (ll. 18–20)

A heavenly angel appears at the altar praising God, only to be interrupted in
turn:

> Chœurs, sont-ce vos chants? Non: de la terrestre cène
> Pur, un ange d'un jour parle à l'hôte éternel!
>   (ll. 73–4)

and, as we have seen, the communicant child proceeds to surpass the
heavenly hosts in poetic skill. Communion with God is presented as a
linguistic drama in which human aspiration triumphs through superior
control of the word; and the poem itself stands as early Mallarméan testi-
mony to that human power.[7]

---

[7] In the other two extant poems from Mallarmé's childhood, language and 'communion' are
also central. In 'Mon cher Papa...', seven artfully versified lines dating from about 1854, the
young poet has forgotten the well-turned compliment he had prepared in celebration of his
father's 'fête', but such are his feelings that 'Je t'aime est le seul mot que j'ai bien retenu'. In
'Dieu bon écoutez-moi...', probably written in 1857, the schoolboy-poet imitates Boileau's
satires as he appeals to God in thirty-four more or less regular alexandrines (in 'rimes plates'
consisting almost entirely of masculine rhymes) to grant him vengeance for the unjust punish-
ment he has received following a classroom incident with an errant shoe. (On both poems see
Gill, The Early Mallarmé, i. 223–4.)

'Les poètes de dix-sept ans':
Entre quatre murs (1859–1860)

Ces vers sont bien mauvais!—mais j'entendais parler
Morale et vérités. . . . moi qui n'en vois aucune [. . .]
('Causerie d'adieu')

Il est difficile de distinguer sous les crins ébouriffés de quel écolier
blanchit l'étoile sibylline.
('Hérésies artistiques: L'Art pour tous')

In *Entre quatre murs* Mallarmé can be seen exploring the power of poetic language by trying on a selection of verse-forms and poetic styles rather as though they were theatrical costumes.[1] Variously, he mourns with the graveside visitor in Hugo's *Les Contemplations*, cavorts with the Hispanophile of Musset's *Contes d'Espagne et d'Italie*, or shadows the repressed sensualist of Leconte de Lisle's *Poèmes antiques*. At 17, like Rimbaud at 15, Mallarmé could be any poet he wished: unlike Rimbaud, he could as yet only seldom better them.

All but three of the poems in this schoolboy collection were written in 1859, during which the aspirant 'bachelier ès lettres' may have moved up from the 'classe de rhétorique' into the 'classe de logique' but the budding poet did not cease to pursue his study of French literature and of French poetry in particular. After the solid grounding of the *baccalauréat* syllabus,[2] he continued to extend his familiarity with Lamartine and Hugo and began to explore the work of other writers, notably Chénier, Musset, Vigny, Gautier, and Leconte de Lisle. By the end of that year he had almost certainly 'discovered' Baudelaire[3]—whereupon, with the exception of three

---

[1] Cf. Mondor, *Mallarmé lycéen*, 228; L. J. Austin, 'Les "Années d'apprentissage" de Stéphane Mallarmé', *Revue d'histoire littéraire de la France*, 56 (1956), 74; and Gill, *The Early Mallarmé*, i. 82.

[2] See Gill, *The Early Mallarmé*, i. 71 n. 50. For a helpful account of Mallarmé's years at the Lycée de Sens, see pp. 50–68.

[3] See Gill, *The Early Mallarmé*, i. 144, ii. 2–4.

poems written in February, March, and April 1860, he temporarily stopped writing his own poems and started copying out other people's. Three such notebooks have survived, his *Glanes*; and in these one can see the apprentice-poet broadening his range beyond the seventeenth century and the Romantics to include not only the sixteenth century (many poems being transcribed from Sainte-Beuve's *Tableau de la poésie française au XVIe siècle*) but, most important of all, *Les Fleurs du mal* and the poems of that other early mentor, Edgar Allan Poe. At the age of 18 Mallarmé was already translating his verse—'from the American'.[4]

The 1850s were rich but daunting years for a poet to grow up in: Hugo's *Les Contemplations* (1856) and Baudelaire's *Les Fleurs du mal* (1st edn 1857) are nineteenth-century monuments, while the Parnassian trend was steadily emerging not only with Leconte de Lisle's *Poèmes antiques* (1852) but also with Gautier's *Émaux et camées* (1852) and Banville's *Odes funambulesques* (1857). Later, in 'Crise de vers', Mallarmé would comment on how Hugo in particular had so shaped readerly expectations that it was as if he had confiscated the right to speak from everyone else.[5] For the moment, like Proust in his pastiches of Balzac and Flaubert, Mallarmé was content to speak Hugo's language (as well as that of Musset, Gautier, and Leconte de Lisle) the better to go beyond it.

Indeed the title of *Entre quatre murs* is itself probably borrowed from Hugo.[6] As Mondor suggests, this is almost certainly 'un titre de circonstance et de rancune',[7] but it would be agreeable to imagine that the future author of 'Un coup de Dés' saw not only the prison-walls of his school but also the four sides of his page as what delimited his poetic enterprise. Be that as it may, the more interesting titles are those of the six sections into which the collection is divided: '1. Fantaisies; 2. Elégies; 3. Rêveries; 4. Odelettes, Stances; 5. Sonnets, Rondeaux, Triolets; 6. Boutades.' For these show clearly where Mallarmé's interest lay: in poetic form. These schoolboy 'vers' are far from being universally 'mauvais', even though the technical virtuosity may be uneven and sometimes unduly ostentatious; but the bored sixth-former who wrote the final stanza of 'Causerie d'adieu' (from which the first of the above epigraphs comes), though simply claiming to be interested solely in wine, women, and song (or, more precisely, rum, brunettes, and verse), is nevertheless also making the telling point that the 'morale' and 'vérités' of his 'classe de logique' leave him cold. For *Entre quatre murs* is almost completely devoid of any first-hand emotional or intellectual content, and it is really only the deaths of Mallarmé's own mother and sister, as well as that of his childhood friend Harriet Smythe, which lend genuine poignancy to the lines in which Hugo's mourning of

---

[4] See Mondor, *Mallarmé lycéen*, 324.   [5] OC, 360–1.
[6] See Gill, *The Early Mallarmé*, i. 79–80.   [7] *Mallarmé lycéen*, 111.

Léopoldine is an evident model ('Sa fosse est creusée', 'Sa tombe est fermée', 'Hier: aujourd'hui: demain').

Austin Gill has given an exhaustive analysis of the poems in *Entre quatre murs*, but his own chapter headings beg the question: 'Devotional poems', 'Confessional poems', 'Poems of dissent', '"Pan": i. The crisis past', etc. Gill rightly disposes once and for all of the old hypothesis about Mallarmé the adolescent mystic,[8] and he concedes that in these poems 'one is never unaware that the schoolboy's verses are the products of a mind and imagination dealing in thoughts and fancies for the most part not their own'.[9] And yet, for all the evidence Gill provides of Mallarmé's debts to other poets, he remains determined to see 'strong personal elements, of thought or of sentiment [...] in several poems'.[10] Thus, in his desire to demonstrate Mallarmé's loss of religious faith about this time (as part of his argument against the 'adolescent mystic'), he takes at face value the title and subtitle of 'Aveu (Réponse improvisée)', imagines the poem 'presumably' to be 'an impromptu reply' to a schoolfriend, and reads it as 'a confession sufficiently intimate and sufficiently forthright to be of real autobiographical interest'.[11] But, as Gill subsequently also suggests,[12] the poem is essentially about a change in Mallarmé's poetic practice and may well be an acknowledgement of the great difference between the 'Cantate pour la première communion' (July 1858) and 'Chant d'ivresse' (dated January 1859).[13] Previously, or so 'Aveu' relates, 'Mon luth ne sut que la prière!'; but now the poet has read Musset, and the poetic potential of 'la grisette' and 'le verre' is evoked in four skilful and not notably penitent quatrains of 'rimes croisées', alternating lines of eight and six syllables, which achieve an effect of improvisation by means of a far from impromptu handling of enjambement and metrical variety. In so far as anything is being 'confessed' here, it is the form of the poem which constitutes an implicit avowal of delight in a new kind of poetry.

Entre quatre murs is a prosodic *tour de force*, and Gill's recategorization of the poems serves only to divert attention from their central function as experiments in versification. Only two of the forty-four surviving texts (or fragments of texts) share the same form.[14] While the alexandrine and the

---

[8] As presented in the works of Adile Ayda (*Le Drame intérieur de Mallarmé* (Istanbul, 1955)), Léon Cellier (*Mallarmé et la morte qui parle* (Paris, 1959)), and Charles Mauron (*Mallarmé l'obscur* (Paris, 1941), *Introduction à la psychanalyse de Mallarmé* (Neuchâtel, 1950)). See Gill, *The Early Mallarmé*, i. 83–5, and *passim*.

[9] *The Early Mallarmé*, i. 82.

[10] i. 83.

[11] i. 127.

[12] i. 130.

[13] The dating of the poems in *Entre quatre murs* is a further imitation of *Les Contemplations* and may, of course, be no less fictitious than Hugo's.

[14] 'Sourire' and 'On donne ce qu'on a' are both in octosyllabic metre arranged in 'rimes croisées', beginning with a feminine rhyme. One minor difference between the two poems is

octosyllable predominate, lines of ten syllables and of every length from
seven to one syllables are also employed, and in a variety of combinations.[15]
The three standard rhyme-schemes ('plates', 'croisées', 'embrassées') are all
in evidence, sometimes also in unusual combination.[16] There are stanzas of
every length from three to eleven lines, with one example of a fourteen-line
stanza. Mallarmé tries his hand at almost every known verse-form, from the
'ballade' and the 'ode' to the 'rondeau' and the 'triolet'. He experiments
with refrains ('Viens') and imitates dance rhythms ('Chanson du fol', 'Chant
d'ivresse'); he flaunts contrived rhyme (e.g. 'De señora' / 'Et caetera' in
'Chanson du fol' (ll. 72/75)) and relishes intricate rhyme-schemes ('Le
Lierre maudit', 'Éclat de rire'). He has four attempts at the sonnet, each
one with a different rhyme pattern in the tercets. It is plainly evident that
experimentation is his motive, and diversity his point of honour: 'morale'
and 'vérités' were the business of mere schoolmasters.

Mallarmé's juvenilia show us the apprentice-versifier—and the very occa-
sional glimpse of the future Master. As many readers have acknowledged,
'Lœda (Idylle antique)' offers an accomplished foretaste of the imagery and
sensuality of 'L'Après-midi d'un faune', and much more so than 'Pan',
masterly pastiche of Hugolian pantheism though this poem is (in its rhetoric
if not in its versification[17]). But only rarely do we hear the poet pushing
language to the verge of 'inanité sonore', as in the penultimate stanza of
'Sourire':

> Si je cueillais aux bords des ondes
> Les myosotis isolés
> Pour étoiler ses tresses blondes,
> Comme les bluets dans les blés!

For the moment, when the poet asks himself in 'On donne ce qu'on a' what
it is that he can provide, the answer is still: 'un écho en son cœur!' (l. 16). He
has learnt to mimic the masters, and he can be merry or mystical, sardonic
or salacious; but he has yet to discover the autonomous power of language.

---

created by the fragmented first line in the final stanza of 'Sourire'. 'La Colère d'Allah' and 'Sa
tombe est fermée' are both written in alexandrines arranged in 'rimes plates', but the former has
'rimes croisées' in ll. 23–6, while in the latter l. 27 has no pair. 'Larme' and 'Réponse (à
Espinas)' are both in alexandrines arranged in 'rimes croisées', but the former begins with
feminine rhyme, the latter with masculine.

[15] 12+8, 12+6, 12+5, 12+4, 12+2; 10+8; 8+6, 8+2; 7+5; 6+4, 6+3; 4+1.
[16] See especially the three-stanza poem 'Donnez!...', in which each is used once.
[17] Cf. Gill, *The Early Mallarmé*, i. 195 ff.

3

'Un faune lascif' (1860–1862)

> Laisse chanter, ô cher bohème,
> Leur chanson à tous ses pervers [...]
> ('A un poète unmoral')
> Il eût fallu, sans doute, au gré de ces Messieurs, s'affranchir des formes
> de nos maîtres, et dédaigner leurs innovations [...]
> ('*Les Poésies parisiénnes* d'Emmanuel Des Essarts')

For Gill the watershed between Mallarmé's juvenilia and his 'early works' is easily located between April 1860 (the latest date appended to a poem in *Entre quatre murs*) and the autumn of 1861. But this 'convenient distinction'[1] owes more to the fact that we have little precise knowledge of the poet's literary activities immediately after he left school in the summer of 1860; and, as with Johnson's 'deux grandes constellations', it serves to present Mallarmé's poetic development as a series of distinct stages rather than as a process of gradual elaboration.

Only three poems in *Entre quatre murs* appear to have been written in 1860: 'Au bois de noisetiers (Chanson)', 'Pénitence (Sonnet)', and 'Réponse à une pièce de vers (où il parlait de ses rêveries enfantines)'.[2] Either Mallarmé had been temporarily silenced by the discovery of Baudelaire and Poe, or else, more prosaically, he had determined to work hard for his *baccalauréat* examinations in August—and even harder when he had to resit them in November! Or perhaps such other poems as he wrote have simply been lost: after all, *Entre quatre murs* only came to light because Henri Mondor, a doctor as well as a 'Mallarmiste', happened to treat one of the poet's descendants.[3] Thus, for example, a letter to Mallarmé from his friend

---

[1] *The Early Mallarmé*, ii. 1.
[2] 'La Chanson de Déborah', contained within his schoolboy prose work which is known by the title of its first part 'Ce que disaient les trois cigognes', probably dates from the same period as *Entre quatre murs* and consists of six octosyllabic sixains rhyming aabccb, which again, as a form not used in *Entre quatre murs* or any other poem by Mallarmé, is a 'one-off' experiment.
[3] See *Mallarmé lycéen*, 112–14.

Eugène Lefébure in April 1862 quotes seven lines of a rather vapid, religiose poem entitled 'L'Enfant à la rose', which may have been written in 1860 or 1861, and also mentions a 'rondeau' entitled 'Six Phillis'—thereby providing clear evidence not only of the poet's early delight in onomastic puns but also of a possible reason why not all of Mallarmé's early works may have come down to us. Did pious heirs destroy the smut?[4]

In the summer and autumn of 1860 and perhaps during the following winter, Mallarmé compiled his *Glanes*, quite possibly under the guidance of the venerable if minor Romantic poet Émile Deschamps, to whom he had been introduced by his grandfather André Desmolins.[5] Part of Mallarmé's purpose was no doubt to possess copies of proscribed works (such as the poems taken from *Châtiments* and *Les Fleurs du mal*) or, as with Poe, to possess poems of which he found it difficult to obtain a printed edition.[6] But clearly also the twin operations of transcription and translation (of Poe) were Mallarmé's way of assimilating and transcending the poetic language of his mentors.

This process continued in the poems which Mallarmé wrote during the next two years before the 20-year-old trainee English teacher departed for London on 8 November 1862 in the company of a German governess, his future wife Marie Gerhard. Some eighteen poems have survived from this period, and they suggest a poet now less concerned with variety of verse-form than with novelty of tone and the delights of wordplay.[7] In his late teens Mallarmé had discovered not only Baudelaire but sex, and several of these poems display what Mondor has elegantly described as 'une habileté d'exécutant vite expert dans l'alliage trouble du mystique et du libertin'.[8] The most obvious example of such an 'alliage' is 'L'Enfant prodigue', in

---

[4] Or even the poet himself? '. . . Mysticis umbraculis (Prose des fous)', two three-line stanzas of alexandrines (aaa bbb) evoking somnolent female masturbation, may have survived its author's subsequent attempts at discretion only because 'Haine du pauvre' was written on the back (see OC (BM), 109). However, it is also possible that he tried to publish it! (See Gill, *The Early Mallarmé*, ii. 231–2 n. 48, where in addition the play on 'cul' in the title is obliquely discussed.)

[5] See Gill, *The Early Mallarmé*, ii. 6–8.

[6] In or before Feb. 1862 he wrote to Lefébure asking to borrow his copy of Poe's poems: see Henri Mondor, *Eugène Lefébure: Sa vie, ses lettres à Mallarmé* (Paris, 1951), 169, and Gill, *The Early Mallarmé*, ii. 246 n. 159.

[7] Apart from the verse-forms of the incomplete 'L'Enfant à la rose' and of '. . . Mysticis umbraculis', Mallarmé uses quatrains of 'rimes croisées' either in alexandrines ('Galanterie macabre', 'L'Enfant prodigue') or in octosyllabics ('A une petite laveuse blonde', 'A un poète immoral', 'Soleil d'hiver'); and alexandrines arranged in terza rima ('Haine du pauvre', 'Le Guignon', 'A un mendiant') or sonnet form ('Placet', 'Le Sonneur', 'Parce que de la viande . . .', 'Vere novo'). 'Le Carrefour des demoiselles', written in collaboration with Emmanuel Des Essarts, is based on the rhythm of a popular song in which one syllable in every other line is twice repeated; it consists of thirty-four couplets of octosyllabics arranged in groups of four lines rhyming abab. 'Apparition' has sixteen alexandrines arranged in 'rimes plates'.

[8] *Vie de Mallarmé* (Paris, 1941), 30.

which the jaded Baudelairean lover[9] seeks to escape his 'gouffre' in the arms—or rather between the legs—of a devout female worshipper. Her piety resembles sexual frustration:

> Ô la mystique, ô la sanglante, ô l'amoureuse
> Folle d'odeurs de cierge et d'encens, qui ne sus
> Quel Démon te tordait le soir, où, douloureuse,
> Tu léchas un tableau du saint-cœur de Jésus,
>
> (ll. 9–12)

while the poet's quasi-spiritual ardour translates without difficulty into a description of the sexual act:

> Tes genoux qu'ont durcis les oraisons rêveuses,
> Je les baise, et tes pieds qui calmeraient la mer;
> Je veux plonger ma tête en tes cuisses nerveuses
> Et pleurer mon erreur sous ton cilice amer.
>
> (ll. 13–16)

A similar 'alliage' is evident in 'Galanterie macabre', in which Mallarmé borrows the vocabulary and allegorical style of Les Fleurs du mal[10] to develop the incongruous analogy of a pipe-smoking undertaker, defeated by the cramped dimensions of a hovel in which a destitute young woman has died, nimbly ascending to the first-floor window like some ardent Romeo and politely removing his pipe as he prepares to defenestrate the lady's corpse: or, as the last two stanzas obscurely have it, within the chamber of the poet's ennui-bound heart stands the coffin of his memory, in which sleeps 'Celle à qui Satan riva mon avenir'; but he will not permit 'le Vice' to remove her body from the prison of hate in which his vengeful eye will watch over her for ever.

[9] For Gill 'Mallarmé's intention [in this poem] is to caricature harshly this Christian poet's eccentric mockery of Christian teaching and practice [...] "L'Enfant prodigue" is his travesty of Baudelaire's own travesty of his own religious beliefs' (The Early Mallarmé, ii. 172). Discussing this and other poems ('... Mysticis umbraculis', 'Le Guignon', 'Haine du pauvre', and 'A un mendiant') Gill argues that Mallarmé's pastiches of Baudelaire are often condemnatory parodies or lampoons (cf. ii. 170). This argument rests heavily on the comments attributed to Mallarmé by Henri de Régnier in the latter's diary (late in 1887), in particular Mallarmé's alleged opinion 'que chez le Baudelaire des dernières années s'était développée une manière factice de fumisterie qui montrait que le fond naturel était épuisé' (this unpublished diary is quoted by Gill, The Early Mallarmé, i. 88 n. 14). It may be that Gill's own sensitivity to obscenity and sacrilege has led him to overstate the degree of Mallarmé's objections. Moreover Mallarmé's speculation to Cazalis in May 1867 about Léon Dierx weaning himself from Leconte de Lisle ('S'en séparera-t-il comme moi de Baudelaire?') has more to do with Mallarmé achieving an independent poetic voice than with any break with Baudelaire on moral or religious grounds (see The Early Mallarmé, ii. 219–20). It is highly improbable that Mallarmé, either in his early twenties or at any other period in his life, 'accused [Baudelaire], more or less darkly, of fundamental errors and grave moral lapses' (ii. 220).

[10] Gill considers this poem 'complimentary in its intention [...] an over-ambitious "à la manière de", not a critical parody' (The Early Mallarmé, ii. 156). But then, of course, it lacks the obscenity, sadism, and blasphemy of the other pastiches.

The sadistic delight expressed at the end of this poem dominates 'Haine du pauvre', in which some of the themes of Baudelaire's 'Tableaux parisiens' are orchestrated with particular venom.[11] Revelling in the elderly beggar's wretchedness, the poet taunts him with a gift of 20 sous, ready to pay for his total abjection:

> Vieux, combien par grimace? et par larme, combien?
>
> Mets à nu ta vieillesse et que la gueuse joue,
> Lèche, et de mes vingt sous chatouille la vertu.
> A bas!...—les deux genoux!...—la barbe dans la boue!
>
>   (ll. 9–12)

and finally suggesting, in the tellingly isolated last line of the terza rima form, that he buy himself a knife and put an end to his own misery. That Mallarmé here is simply trying out a poetic voice is clearly evident from the contrast between this poem and 'A un mendiant', which is also written in terza rima and which, as Gill rightly notes, takes up the last rhyme-word of 'Haine du pauvre' in its first tercet as if it were a sequel.[12] Here a rather more generous ('voici cent sous') yet still distinctly Baudelairean almsgiver is concerned that his beggar should neither save the money nor spend it on something useful. Rather he should dream of sins more 'bizarre' than avarice and savour other 'fleurs du mal': tobacco (with its 'sveltes feuillaisons'), opium ('à vendre en mainte pharmacie'), or an all-night drinking session in the local café (where 'Les plafonds sont fardés de faunesses sans voiles'). Sex is again an option, and no more attractively presented than in 'Haine du pauvre':

> Veux-tu mordre au rabais quelque pâle catin
> Et boire en sa salive un reste d'ambroisie?
>
>   (ll. 11–12)[13]

---

[11] Gill takes this poem together with 'A un mendiant' and elaborates the questionable thesis that 'Haine du pauvre' condemns by parodic exaggeration Baudelaire's 'Don Juan aux enfers' (first published in 1846, so hardly from the poet's 'dernières années') and his recently published prose poem 'Le Mauvais Vitrier' (in La Presse on 26 Aug. 1862) which (by common consent) rather savagely debunks Arsène Houssaye's prose poem 'La Chanson du vitrier' in which worthy sentiments of human fellowship are somewhat ineffectually expressed. According to Gill, Mallarmé 'thereupon devised a plan to turn the tables on Baudelaire the disloyal friend' by reshaping 'the parts played by the protagonists in the two "prose poems"' so that 'Houssaye's part [i.e. as represented by 'A un mendiant'] would sound both nobler and more original than Baudelaire's' (The Early Mallarmé, ii. 214–26, in particular p. 225). Again it may be that Gill's antipathy to Baudelaire's writing has led him to attribute to Mallarmé rather more earnest motives than the poetic 'role-playing' which is being described in the present chapter. The subsequent suppression of 'Haine du pauvre' and the refinement of 'A un mendiant' into 'Aumône' may have more to do with the fact that the second of these is a better poem than it has with avoiding any 'public affront to Baudelaire' (ii. 226).

[12] The Early Mallarmé, ii. 220.

[13] In the version published in Le Parnasse contemporain and entitled 'Un pauvre', the last three passages quoted are amended respectively to: 'Et l'opium puissant brise la pharmacie!',

—but at least now there is a chance of ambrosia (if not nectar). And once again the point of the poem is effectively, and bathetically, conveyed in the isolated last line: 'Et surtout, ne va pas, drôle, acheter du pain!'

The frank view of human sexuality presented in these two terza rima poems and in both '... Mysticis umbraculis' and 'L'Enfant prodigue' finds its most extreme—or at least most ribald[14]—expression in 'Parce que de la viande...' where the sonnet form becomes the vehicle for an account of the 'Cleopatra's nose' theory of history as it might have been expounded in the first pages of *Tristram Shandy*. For how *are* great poets made? A good meal, a nice read of a rape story in the papers, the chance glimpse of a servant's ill-concealed bosom, the dalliance of a sculpted couple on the mantelpiece clock, these are all it takes to stir the old Adam:

> Un niais met sous lui sa femme froide et sèche,
> Contre ce bonnet blanc frotte son casque-à-mèche
> Et travaille en soufflant inexorablement:
>
> Et de ce qu'une nuit, sans rage et sans tempête,
> Ces deux êtres se sont accouplés en dormant,
> Ô Shakspeare et toi, Dante, il peut naître un poète!'
>
> (ll. 9–14)

We have come a long way from cantatas about Holy Communion.[15]

But Baudelaire and bawdy were not Mallarmé's only concerns during these two years, and his taste for the poetry of Gautier and Banville was no doubt reinforced following the arrival of a new teacher at the Lycée de Sens (in October 1861 after he himself had left), the well-connected young poet Emmanuel Des Essarts. This sophisticated Parisian had won a national poetry competition while still at school and was about to publish his *Poésies parisiennes*, which, thanks to Des Essarts, Mallarmé soon reviewed in *Le Papillon* on 10 January 1862 and in *Le Sénonais* on 22 March.[16] Des Essarts was particularly keen on Banville, whose prose tales *Esquisses parisiennes* (1859) were doubtless responsible for the title of his own collection of verse.[17]

'Les plafonds enrichis de nymphes et de voiles', and 'Robes et peau, veux-tu lacérer le satin, / Et boire en la salive heureuse l'inertie?' Further revised, this poem appeared as 'Aumône' in the 1887 *Poésies*.

[14] The most pornographic of Mallarmé's extant poems is possibly 'Image grotesque', written some two years later. Four quatrains of alexandrines in 'rimes croisées' would appear to describe a lesbian paedophile preparing for oral sex.

[15] Gill's thesis of an anti-Baudelairean Mallarmé is at its weakest here when he argues that this poem, albeit humorously, reflects an 'interest in Baudelaire of a somewhat critical kind [...] For the subject [...] is a calm contradiction of the most savagely misogynistic of Baudelaire's poems ['Tu mettrais l'univers entier dans ta ruelle']' to which 'Mallarmé replies by pointing out that nature's mysterious ways of producing a genius involve the other sex too, and indeed the two together' (ii. 185–6).

[16] OC, 249–52, 254–6. See also Millan, *Mallarmé*, 40 ff.

[17] Gill notes that Des Essarts's aesthetic of 'sincerity' was in fact diametrically opposed to Banville's, as Mallarmé's review diplomatically intimates. For discussion of this question see

As Des Essarts later recalled, '[Mallarmé] faisait volontiers à ses débuts des vers coquets, sortes de tableautins à la Wat[t]eau, des stances en octosyllabes gracieuses et mignardes'.[18] And indeed Mallarmé's 'A une petite laveuse blonde' employs the verse-form[19] and refined allusions of *Émaux et camées* to achieve a more delicate form of eroticism than is to be found in poems like 'Parce que de la viande...', one that recalls—in anticipation of Verlaine's *Fêtes galantes* (1869)—the paintings of Watteau and Boucher. Ill-concealed bosoms here assume a more pastoral air:

> Tu ris au soleil du rivage
> Qui d'un traître rayon brunit
> Ta gorge entr'ouvrant son corsage
> Comme un ramier sort de son nid;
>   (ll. 77–80)

while in 'A un poète immoral' the poet prefers fireside reverie in the company of 'ce blond cigare' to being led astray by 'Quelque bonnet blanc inconstant' (l. 6). Again using the verse-form and playful preciosity of Gautier, he encourages Des Essarts[20] to ignore the disapproval of the unimaginative and hypocritical Sénonais who know neither how to love nor how to write verse. For this young writer cares not for bourgeois prose or the Legion of Honour:

> Tu ne rêves pas pour ta prose
> Ce ruban rouge où pend la croix,
> Et préfères la gance rose
> D'un corset délacé, je crois?
>
> Tel le sage. Il fait à la pomme
> Mordre quelque Eve au fond des bois
> Et baise ses cils dorés comme
> Le thé qu'en t'écrivant je bois.
>   (ll. 29–36)

The Early Mallarmé, ii. 82–90. As Mallarmé's 'Symphonie littéraire' written in 1864 makes clear, his allegiance went to Banville (as well as to Gautier and Baudelaire).

[18] Quoted from Emmanuel Des Essarts, '*Souvenirs littéraires*: Stéphane Mallarmé', *Revue de France*, 15 July 1899, in Gill, *The Early Mallarmé*, ii. 49 n. 4.

[19] Quatrains of octosyllabics in 'rimes croisées' with the first rhyme invariably feminine. Gill's suggestion of Banville's 'La Voyageuse' (from *Odes funambulesques*) as a model is less convincing since its quatrains begin with masculine rhymes, and since in any case Gautier's verse-form was celebrated as being the metrical equivalent of the 'bloc résistant' in which the 'rêve flottant' of *Émaux et camées* was to be 'sealed' (see Gautier's 'L'Art'). But, as Gill suggests, Banville's 'A une petite chanteuse des rues' (in *Les Stalactites*) may well have inspired Mallarmé's title (see *The Early Mallarmé*, ii. 152).

[20] Gill disputes the traditional view that Des Essarts is the dedicatee on the grounds that 'Mallarmé regarded his schoolmaster friend as more conventionally respectable than it was proper for so young a poet to be' (*The Early Mallarmé*, ii. 153). He notes that the poem was written on 11 Dec. 1861, four days after the appearance of the first of Mallarmé's three articles on 'Monsieur Besombes et sa troupe' in *Le Sénonais*. This troupe included a 32-year-old actor-

'A un poète immoral' is, of course, an ephemeral piece and, as l. 36 suggests, not wholly accomplished. The incorporation of the date of its composition into the first stanza,[21] the reference to its Watteauesque subject being depicted on a fan (l. 40), and the comparison between the writing of a poem and the smoking of a cigar (ll. 7–10, 48) all point forward to later Mallarméan motifs. But above all perhaps we see once again how the principal 'Idée' is conveyed by the manner of the poem's execution. Here Mallarmé's solidarity with the mannered exuberance of Des Essarts[22] is expressed in no less mannered and exuberant verse, which seeks—like the later 'Tombeau' and 'Hommage' poems—to include multiple references to the 'circonstances' of the tribute. Likewise in 'Le Carrefour des demoiselles', a poem on which the two poets collaborated, the carnivalesque atmosphere of the picnic at Fontainebleau is brilliantly conveyed in a virtuoso song, in which the double couplets in 'rimes croisées' evoke the excited permutations of 'mixed company', while the wordplay, contrived rhyming, and repeated in-jokes suggest the delighted and self-assured intimacy of a group of young people who are masters and mistresses of all they survey—and of all that it occurs to them to say. An 'illustre partie' of 'neuf Parisiens', muses all, is thus transformed into a kind of 'Parnasse sur l'herbe'. Similarly but conversely, when Mallarmé later distances himself from his friend's passion for dancing in 'Contre un poète parisien', he combines within the difficult and time-honoured form of the sonnet stately rhythms, solemn images, and extensive references to the traditional accoutrements of poets (Dante, Anacreon), all the better to disparage (in the final line) 'Un poète qui polke avec un habit noir'. May this demonstration of poetic dignity be a lesson to his friend.

But friend he was, and thanks partly to Des Essarts, Mallarmé's first poem to be published ('Placet') appeared in the Parisian literary magazine

playwright and poet Léon Marc, with whom Mallarmé struck up a friendship. Gill suggests that the dedicatee may be 'one of Léon Marc's younger colleagues' (ii. 153)—and not Léon Marc himself presumably because of the reference in the poem to a 'vieil épithalame / De la folie et des vingt ans' (ll. 17–18). Des Essarts himself was then 22. Gill's further argument in rejecting Des Essarts is based on his erroneous view that the poem is 'vaguely claiming to be a preface to one of his [Marc's younger colleague's] comedies, also anonymous' (ii. 153). But the poem refers only to the poet's resolve to 'te rimer / Une préface où l'on sommeille, / Moi qui songe à les supprimer!' (ll. 10–12); and here Mallarmé may well be making the humorous suggestion that his poem might serve as a preface to Des Essarts's forthcoming *Poésies parisiennes* which was published approximately a fortnight later (for this date see *The Early Mallarmé*, ii. 81 and cf. n. 45 on pp. 56–7). The reference to an 'odelette parfumée' (l. 13) and the poem's celebration of the poetic style of Gautier and Banville serve further to confirm the traditional identification of the 'poète immoral' as Des Essarts.

[21] 'Puisque ce soir, onze décembre / Mil huit cent soixante-un [. . .]'. Gill suggests an echo of Villon's *Testament* ('Escript l'ay l'an soixante et ung [. . .]'): *The Early Mallarmé*, ii. 153.

[22] See Millan, *Mallarmé*, 41, for a contemporary's description of Des Essarts in which these qualities are emphasized and which suggests strongly that it is Des Essarts's 'gaîté' which is referred to in l. 20 of the poem.

Le Papillon on 25 February 1862. Appropriately, given what was to come, it was a self-referential sonnet. Since the editor of *Le Papillon* was Mme Olympe Audouard, it is not surprising that the poet should present himself in this poem as an aspirant Hebe, cup-bearer to the gods on Mount Olympus, nor that his 'galanterie' should take the form of a desire to be depicted upon his editor's Sèvres tea-cup (where the lady's lips might kiss him). But when this wish to be pictorially represented becomes the request to be painted on a fan by Boucher that there, as shepherd and flautist, he may lull the ovine flock of her raspberry smiles... one begins to see a subtler Mallarmé at work.

Of course this is a 'sonnet Louis XV',[23] a rococo example of the 'Jeux mièvres' (l. 6) to which the sonnet alludes; and Austin Gill is right to remark that 'the Trianon component would be less foolish with the traditional crook and a silvery tinkle, untroubled by the munching and bleating of the lambs'.[24] But it is also a poem about being published, a 'Placet': that is to say, a written request to someone in authority for a permission or favour, in this instance that a poem be 'placé'. Exploiting the traditional division of the Petrarchan sonnet, the poet uses the octave to hint at the possibility of amorous congress with his 'duchesse': but the intimacy of the 'tu' form and the prospect of physical contact in the kiss are mitigated by the poet's ambition to be depicted in female guise (Hebe) and by his playful humility ('Mais je suis un poète, un peu moins qu'un abbé'). In the sestet, by contrast, he withdraws to the more respectful 'vous' as his address becomes more insistent (the thrice-uttered 'Nommez-nous'), but now he requests the status not of a female cup-bearer but of the (male) poet he truly is. Pictorial depiction serves as a metaphor for appearing in print, and the poem itself becomes the 'rose éventail' (l. 12) upon which the shepherd plays his flute, lulling the smiles of his Olympe into the repose of aesthetic delight. The poet who might have been 'kissed' by a tea-time duchess now places his lips upon a musical instrument the better to emulate the painting of the (in the context) suggestively named Boucher and, as the newly appointed guardian of his lady's mouth, to erect the barrier of a fan between her sweet and artful smiles ('un troupeau poudré d'agneaux apprivoisés') and the grasslands of the slippery slope upon which they are wont to graze ('Qui vont broutant les cœurs et bêlant aux délires').

'Placé' this poem duly was: or 'Placet futile' as the amended title punningly has it when Mallarmé later considered it worthy of inclusion (in a slightly amended version) in his *Poésies* of 1887.[25] It was followed into

---

[23] *Corr.*, i. 28 (to Cazalis, 24 May 1862). Gill notes the precedent, a century earlier, of Voiture's *Vers burlesques* in which four poems are entitled 'Placet' (*The Early Mallarmé*, ii. 160).

[24] *The Early Mallarmé*, ii. 162.

[25] In which 'futile' is written beneath and slightly to the right of 'Placet', suggesting an afterthought. The amendments are few ('Princesse' for 'duchesse', and 'Amour' for 'Boucher'

print by a second self-referential sonnet, 'Le Sonneur', which was published
in the prestigious *L'Artiste* on 15 March together with the first five stanzas
of 'Le Guignon'; and these two poems introduce the poetic persona of the
doomed artist which was to dominate several of Mallarmé's poems over the
following four years.

As Gill persuasively suggests,[26] 'Le Guignon' was published in truncated
form not because it was too long[27] but because it contains a clear condem-
nation of Baudelaire (an honoured contributor to *L'Artiste*), whose recent
foreword to Léon Cladel's *Les Martyrs ridicules* (published in *La Revue
fantaisiste* in October 1861) ridiculed the younger generation of poets[28] a
betrayal which the author of *Les Fleurs du mal* was thought to have
repeated by his decision to stand for election to the Académie française at
the end of 1861. All poets suffer for their calling as 'mendieurs d'azur', but
some (like Baudelaire) find consolation by turning their suffering into
poetry which brings honour to them and their family ('Le peuple s'agen-
ouille et la mère se lève' (l. 18)). But there, vilified and crawling at their feet,
are their fellow-poets—'Dérisoires martyrs d'un hasard tortueux' (l. 21)—
who are just as capable of giving expression to the misery of the human
condition ('faire aussi sonner comme un tambour / La servile pitié des races
à l'œil terne' (ll. 25–6)), but who are harried by ill-fortune, 'le *Guignon*',[29]
here represented as the toothless and ill-tempered skeleton of a dwarf. The
poem as trumpet fanfare or amorous floral gift is degraded (in a kind of

being the most significant), and the sense of the poem remains unaltered in this later version.
The addition of 'futile' may represent the humorous (or plaintive) reflection of a 45-year-old
that his teenage sexual designs on a beautiful blonde editor came to nought, or more plausibly it
may have been intended to reinforce the theme of a 'princesse lointaine' to whom all pleas are
futile. The homophonic presence of 'fut-il' and a wistful 'fût-il' is no less relevant in either case.

[26] *The Early Mallarmé*, ii. 186–206.

[27] See OC (BM), 116 n. 71.

[28] Baudelaire expresses his disgust at 'la Jeunesse' in general ('Bref, je me sens en mauvaise
compagnie'), and divides them into four categories: those who are stupid and rich, those who
are stupid and would like to be rich, those 'qui aspirent à faire le bonheur du peuple', and 'la
jeunesse littéraire, la jeunesse *réaliste*, se livrant, au sortir de l'enfance, à l'art *réalistique* (à des
choses nouvelles il faut des mots nouveaux!)'. He accuses the latter group of relying on
bohemian posturing and not realizing that so-called 'génie' 'doit, comme le saltimbanque
apprenti, risquer de se rompre mille fois les os en secret avant de danser devant le public'.
Baudelaire is therefore attacking the sort of poet perhaps typified by Des Essarts (rather than
Mallarmé, whose career to date exactly matched Baudelaire's requirements for the apprentice-
acrobat). (See Baudelaire, *Œuvres complètes*, ed. Claude Pichois (Bibliothèque de la Pléiade) (2
vols, Paris, 1975–6), ii. 182–7.) But Mallarmé's poem is a vigorous response on behalf of his
friend and of 'la jeunesse littéraire' in general. When he recalled to Henri de Régnier in 1887
that 'Baudelaire détestait les jeunes gens, avait horreur de ceux qui venaient' (quoted by Gill,
The Early Mallarmé, i. 88 n. 14 and ii. 203), Mallarmé himself at his 'mardis' was displaying a
rather different approach to the young generation.

[29] The title and the central vision of Mallarmé's poem derive from Baudelaire's introduction
to his translation of Poe in 1856, while the verse-form may be modelled on Gautier's 'Ténèbres'
and the concept of 'mendieurs d'azur' may derive from Banville (see Gill, *The Early Mallarmé*,
ii. 190–5).

'alchimie de la douleur' perhaps) into a child's mocking toot or a breeding-ground for slugs (ll. 34–9), and 'le Guignon' itself becomes a verbal travesty of the 'mendieur d'azur':

> Et ce squelette nain, coiffé d'un feutre à plume
> Et botté, dont l'aisselle a pour poils de longs vers,
> Est pour eux l'infini de l'humaine amertume.
>
> (ll. 40–2)

'Plume', 'vers': the poet dressed as Hamlet in plumed felt hat finds his quill become the adornment of a fleshless grotesque and his verse now the worms of an armpit 'chevelure'.

The terza rima form is handled with expertise, and once more the isolated last line is used to powerful effect. In the final tercets the vehement eloquence of Hugo's *Châtiments* is turned on the arrogance of 'poètes savants' like Baudelaire, and the poem builds to a climax as Mallarmé parodies them preaching at these 'dérisoires martyrs' but 'ne voyant leur mal'. Then comes the anticlimax which takes the other word in Cladel's title and applies it to the suicide of Nerval, showing us at the end that 'Le Guignon' is not just a Gothic 'exercice de style' but a poem with a point:

> Quand chacun a sur eux craché tous ses dédains,
> Nus, assoiffés de grand et priant le tonnerre,
> Ces Hamlet abreuvés de malaises badins
>
> Vont ridiculement se pendre au réverbère.

The apprentice-acrobat had turned on his master with a somersault of satire.

But for the writer of 'Le Sonneur' the master's example was still one to follow. Partly reminiscent of 'La Cloche fêlée', one of the Baudelaire poems previously transcribed in *Glanes*, the traditional sonnet structure is again exploited as the octave describes the bell-ringer who can scarcely hear the angelus on high (while he himself groans away in Latin down below) and the sestet 'explains' the analogy with the poet, in whose efforts to 'sonner l'idéal' 'la voix ne me vient que par bribes et creuse!' Perched astride the stone at the end of his bell-rope, he foresees the day when he will have had enough: 'Ô Satan, j'ôterai la pierre et me pendrai!'[30] The dutiful Christian's Latin prayers have been replaced by a suicidal address to Satan, reminiscent now of Baudelaire's 'Les Litanies de Satan'; and the bell-ringer's abandonment of his calling becomes a kind of 'Reniement de [la] Saint[e] Pierre'.

Of particular interest in this sonnet is Mallarmé's play on the word 'sonnet' itself. Already in his first flurry of three sonnets in February–March

---

[30] Quotations are from this 1862 version, which differs only slightly (in the passages quoted) from the version published in *Le Parnasse contemporain*. See OC (BM), 120–1, and Gill, *The Early Mallarmé*, ii. 207.

1859 he had observed that verse-form's tradition of self-reference.[31] In 'Réponse (à Germain)' the sonneteer claims to be celebrating Margot 'la catin' by imitating her dance in his verse: 'Comme elle, en mes sonnets, je danse un fandango' (l. 6). Playing on the expression 'voix de crécelle' he likens his sonnet to the hand-rattle with which she would appear to have replaced the more usual castanets:

> Moi, j'imite en ses jeux la verte demoiselle.
> Je vais de folle en folle, agitant ma crécelle:
> Bohème est ma patrie! à toi le ciel et l'air!
>
> (ll. 12–14)

In 'Sonnet (à R.)' the poet calls on the dedicatee (perhaps Émile Roquier, an older schoolfriend and a poet) to follow his example:

> Mais le Ciel, c'est pour moi comme à mon vieux Shakspeare
> Un sonnet!—où l'esprit jouit d'être au martyre
>
> Comme en son fin corset le sein de Camargo!
> —Quoi! J'ai tant bavardé! plus qu'un vers pour te dire
> Mon vœu: 'Pour moi demande un   à ta lyre.'
>
> (ll. 10–14)

Again the analogy with a dancer (La Camargo, who appears in Musset's 'Les Marrons du feu'), and here also the first case of the sonnet (in this case the word itself) being required to occupy an 'espace blanc'! Both poems thus make explicit the parallel which remains implicit in the first of these three sonnets ('En envoyant un pot de fleurs'), where the poet reproduces the musical rhythms of the carnival:

> —Mille voix du plaisir voltigent à moi: l'une
>
> M'apporte ris, baisers, chants de délire: suit
> Une fanfare où Strauss fait tournoyer la brune
> Au pied leste, au sein nu, que sa jupe importune.
> —Tes masques! carnaval! tes grelots! joyeux bruit!
>
> (ll. 4–8)

From the start, therefore, the Mallarméan sonnet is musical and reflexive; and 'Le Sonneur' exploits the etymology and homophony of 'sonnet' to suggest the paltriness of the poet's attempt to attain 'l'idéal' by ringing church bells. His voice which 'ne me vient que par bribes et creuse!' recalls the wordplay on 'crécelle', and perhaps even the latter's liturgical function as a replacement for church bells on the Thursday, Friday, and Saturday of Holy Week.[32] The poet of 1866 (in the version published in *Le Parnasse*

[31] See David H. T. Scott, *Sonnet Theory and Practice in Nineteenth-Century France: Sonnets on the Sonnet* (Hull, 1977).

[32] Mallarmé's three 1859 sonnets are dated 'Dimanche de Carnaval 1859—Minuit et quart', 'Mars 1859', and 'Mars 1859', and 'Pénitence (Sonnet)' is dated 'Grand'messe. Mars 1860'. Is

contemporain) will embellish this playful self-reference further by having the 'sonneur' 'effleuré par l'oiseau qu'il éclaire' (l. 5)—where 'effleuré' echoes the lavender and thyme in the previous line, and the bird brushing against the bell-ringer is transformed by the 'explanation' of the tercets into 'un plumage féal' of 'froids Péchés' which 's'ébat'—that is, into an image of the impotent poet, burdened with passionless, unproductive sin, and of his trusty quill hopping about the page in the frolic that is this poem. The final words of the poem ('et me pendrai') begin, in *Le Parnasse contemporain*, to look less like a Nervalian hanging and more like the resurrection of a 'sonneur' in the shape of a pen.

The only other poem which Mallarmé published in 1862, 'Soleil d'hiver', appeared in the rather less prestigious *Journal des Baigneurs* published in Dieppe. But where better to find the first traces of the 'drame solaire'? Here, as in 'A une petite laveuse blonde' and 'A un poète immoral', Mallarmé adopts Gautier's octosyllabic quatrains in 'rimes croisées' with the first rhyme feminine, but by limiting the number of stanzas to four achieves an effect of symmetry which anticipates the intricate structure of 'Sainte'. The first two quatrains recall the summer sun which brought on the deep, intoxicated slumber of 'faunes ivres' and swelled the grapes to bursting point, as though they had been slashed by a swashbuckling swordsman in gold brocade; while in the last two stanzas the winter sun now resembles don Guritan, the burlesque duellist of Hugo's *Ruy Blas*, whose innumerable written challenges ('cartels') are torn up in disdain by their recipients. The delight of the poem lies in the precise mirroring between the two halves: a mythological deity in russet wig ('Phébus') becomes a bald theatrical car-icature, and the vermilion 'lames' (sheets, waves, *and* blades) of sunlight that sent drunken fauns to sleep in the moss are transformed into the single rusty sunbeam of a sword wielded by a man who is locked in the chilly heaven of his own obsession. The purple of the grapes is now the mauve of his breeches, the slashes of burst ripeness now the torn paper of his foolish 'cartels', falling like snow. The brocade of finest gold has become some sorry, dangling, tasselless braid, silvery icicles on a frozen fir. And language, too, has sunk low: from the precious eloquence of the opening line ('Phébus à la perruque rousse') and the declamatory apostrophe of the third ('Ô faunes ivres dans la mousse') to the doggerel of l. 11 ('Le long de sa culotte mauve') and the banality of l. 15 ('Et la neige qui tombe est faite').

But from the 'inanité sonore' of l. 13 ('Son aiguillette, sans bouffette') we may perhaps infer that the 'ors fins' of the summer sun's brocade have been transposed into the strands of poetic sound from which this poem is woven. These four, intricately intertwined quatrains represent a sort of 'sound-

---

it coincidental that the association with Easter should later take the form of a poetic transposi-tion of the Crucifixion in 'Sonnet allégorique de lui-même'?

braid', a 'son-aiguillette'; while 'sans bouffette' might homophonically suggest ('sans bout', 'fête') that such textual needlework constitutes a celebration of the power of language in which the threads of meaning and association seem to have no end. As the title intimates, the poem displays both 'soleils divers' (of summer and winter) and a 'soleil, dit "vers"', a sunburst monstrance of 'phones ivres'[33]—or 'phones lascifs'. For sound in this poem appears indeed to be wanton in the promiscuity of its relationships: the drinking in 'Phébus' calls forth (cf. 'Provoquaient' (l. 4)) the drunken fauns, while the source of their drunkenness is revealed not only in 'la pourpre des raisins' (l. 8) but in the 'broc' (wine pitcher) of 'brocart'. Brocade is not just woven text but intoxicating art. At the same time their 'lourd sommeil' ('provoked' by the 'lames de vermeil' linguistically as well as 'in reality' since 'vermeil' demands 'sommeil' as its rhyme) is echoed in the elaborate homophonies of l. 8: 'Dont le brocart [été] [dort] fin[s]'. It is as if the word-grapes had burst, releasing not only their juice but their seed; and this dissemination threatens the poet's role as a 'bretteur aux fières tournures'. His proud turns of phrase are undone by homophony, and what seemed to be 'brocart' may just be 'brocards', gibes or lampoons mocking the mastery with which he imagines himself to be wielding his pen. It is not he who calls out words (the duelling sense of 'provoquer'): words call out other words, rhyme-word summons up rhyme-word, and homophony is master. The poet's written texts are torn asunder by polysemy, and his 'brocart' becomes mere 'cartels déchirés', snowflakes of 'espaces blancs' betokening his death: 'Et la neige qui[,] tombe[,] est faite'. Or (again) 'fête': death from dissemination may be a cause for celebration, a summit ('faîte') of poetic achievement. The 'mousse' upon which the 'faunes/phones ivres' lay sleeping has become the foam generated by linguistic turbulence, a spume of enhanced significance sparkling in the 'soleil, dit "vers"'.

Presuming such wordplay even to be viable, did Mallarmé 'intend' it here? Subsequent analysis of the 'Sonnet en -yx' and the 'Triptych', among many other Mallarméan texts, will suggest that he may. What is more immediately important, however, is that 'Soleil d'hiver' shows the beginnings of an important development in Mallarmé's poetic practice: namely, his attempt now to reproduce the binary structure of the Petrarchan sonnet within verse-forms of no predetermined length and thereby to create a mirror-effect which greatly increases the density and unity of the poem in question. Already here one can see how this binary structure is an extension of the principle of rhyme itself: for all rhyme establishes relationships of similarity and difference, and in this poem it is as if the second half 'rhymes' with the first. This is partly true even at the level of terminal rhyme itself: the first rhyme-words of the poem 'rousse' and 'vermeil' (in ll. 1 and 3),

---

[33] On the meaning and pronunciation of the word 'phone', see below, Part II, Ch. 4 n. 58.

evoking colour and warmth, are ironically echoed in the clever rich rhyme of 'verrouillé' and 'rouillé' (ll. 10 and 12), which suggest the cold and damp of prisons. But, as we have seen, it is true also on a much broader level. The literal 'echo' of 'ivres' from line 3 in the third-last line of the poem ('givrés') is just one example of the kind of verbal intricacy which Mallarmé now evidently recognizes as the proper task of the poet. Six years later, in 'Sonnet allégorique de lui-même', he would develop this intricacy to extraordinary effect, and in a sonnet where, as will be seen, rhyme 'writes' the poem.

The three remaining poems which Mallarmé wrote before his departure for London do not anticipate later developments to quite the same extent. Nevertheless two of them were sonnets and as such the occasion of Mallarmé's comments to Cazalis in June 1862:

Tu riras peut-être de ma manie de sonnets [. . .] mais pour moi c'est un grand poème en petit: les quatrains et les tercets me semblent des chants entiers, et je passe parfois trois jours à en équilibrer d'avance les parties, pour que le tout soit harmonieux et s'approche du Beau.[34]

Individually entitled 'Vere novo' (retitled 'Renouveau' in 1887) and 'Tristesse d'été', Mallarmé grouped then together at first as 'Soleils malsains' and then (in 1864 and 1865) as 'Soleils mauvais' before publishing them as independent texts in Le Parnasse contemporain in 1866. Despite his enthusiasm for the sonnet form, his own description of 'Vere novo' as 'un pauvre sonnet éclos ces jours-ci, triste et laid' is not just modesty, and his account of its 'hatching' appears somewhat disingenuous in its failure to mention the evident Baudelairean influence:

Emmanuel [Des Essarts] t'avait peut-être parlé d'une stérilité curieuse que le printemps avait installée en moi. Après trois mois d'impuissance, j'en suis enfin débarrassé, et mon premier sonnet est consacré à la décrire, c'est-à-dire à la maudire. C'est un genre assez nouveau que cette poésie, où les effets matériels, du sang, des nerfs, sont analysés et mêlés aux effets moraux de l'esprit, de l'âme. Cela pourrait s'appeler Spleen printanier. Quand la combinaison est bien harmonisée et que l'œuvre n'est ni trop physique ni trop spirituelle, elle peut représenter quelque chose.[35]

If 'Soleil d'hiver' was written during the previous winter,[36] it may be that the brilliance of that poem had caused the 'impuissance' to which Mallarmé here refers. How could he follow it? Perhaps by continuing with the solar theme while yet reverting to the ready-made fixity of the sonnet form? The first two lines of 'Vere novo' prompt a biographical reading of this kind:

> Le printemps maladif a chassé tristement
> L'hiver, saison de l'art serein, l'hiver lucide.

---

[34] Corr., i. 32.   [35] Corr., i. 30–1.   [36] See Gill, The Early Mallarmé, ii. 164–5.

Moreover the title 'Vere novo' suggests a continuation of the play on 'vers' present in 'Soleil d'hiver' ('hiver', 'vermeil', 'verrouillé'), but this is not developed in the poem itself. Hence perhaps the later change of title to 'Renouveau', which better highlights the sad paradox of this spring which has put an end to the artistic creativity of winter.[37]

Whatever the biographical 'circonstances', the 'mirror-effects' in the sonnet are much less intricate than in the earlier poem, and they are mainly confined to (extensive) internal rhyming: 'printemps', 'tristement'; 'serein', 'serre ainsi'; 'cercle', 'de fer', 'serre', 'j'erre', 'terre'; 'L'impuissance', 'la sève immense'; 'Par les champs', 'creusant', 'Mordant', 'J'attends', 'en m'abîmant', 'Cependant', 'De tant'. The repetition of sounds and even of certain words ('tristement', 'triste' [added in 1864]; 'Rêve' twice; 'tombeau', 'je tombe') here creates a sense not of wanton dissemination but of impotent spleen and prolonged waiting. The lack of contrast between octave and sestet serves to reinforce this impression of the poem as 'un long baillement' (*sic*, l. 4), the inconsequential oral expression of a poet overwhelmed by the creativity of nature itself and by the exuberance of the birds, his rivals in song:

> —Cependant l'azur rit dans la haie en éveil
> Où des oiseaux en fleur gazouillent du soleil.
>
> (ll. 13–14)

The irony of a spring that turns the poet suicidal ('creusant de ma face une fosse à mon Rêve'[38]) is matched by the irony of a sonnet that proclaims poetic renewal in its title and achieves novelty only by refusing to exploit the potential of its own structure. The 'faune lascif' is here reduced to slumber.[39]

'Tristesse d'été' reads as a sequel to both 'Vere novo' and 'Soleil d'hiver', beginning as it does: 'Le Soleil, sur la mousse où tu t'es endormie' (l. 1). Spring fever has been replaced by hot sun, vernal twittering by 'l'air sans oiseaux' (1.3), and the poet now ventures his own blend of Baudelaire's 'La Chevelure' and 'Obsession'. Here the quatrains and tercets of the Petrarchan sonnet are mobilized in the service of several analogies (hair and

---

[37] Given the wordplay of 'Placet futile' and the double sense of 'été' in 'Tristesse d'été', one wonders if 'Renouveau' may not imply (in the 1887 *Poésies* when the title was first used) a republishing of the poet when he was a 'nouveau'. Less fancifully, it may simply be that he no longer thought it appropriate to purloin Hugo's title from *Les Contemplations* (Book 1, poem 12).

[38] 'ce rêve' in the 1887 version, in which the last two lines read: 'Cependant l'azur rit sur la haie et l'éveil / De tant d'oiseaux en fleur gazouillant au soleil'.

[39] Gill's thesis that this poem displays the 'intention [...] to omit, by way of experiment, the poetic process [as described in the letter to Cazalis]' (*The Early Mallarmé*, ii. 211–12) is perhaps exaggerated. 'Vere novo' does not lack for poetic effect, and 'beauty', far from being 'deliberately withheld' (ii. 212), is achieved by an art no less conscious than that of 'Soleil d'hiver'.

river, make-up and poison, sleep and death). The first quatrain divides
between the woman's hair and her make-up, which division is then mirrored
in the two tercets which take first the hair and then the make-up as their
theme. The sun as bath in the first two lines of the octave is paralleled by the
hair as river in the first two lines of the sestet, while make-up as evaporating
scent at the end of the first quatrain becomes make-up as fatal potion at the
end of the poem. At the same time the quatrains contrast the woman's warm
repose with the poet's abhorrence of white heat (famously, 'De ce blanc
flamboiement l'immuable accalmie') and with his desire for 'un sommeil de
momie'; while in the two tercets the prospect of the woman's hair as a
Lethe-like place of amorous oblivion ('jouir du Néant où l'on ne pense pas')
gives way to the more terminal solution of suicide and a heart granted
'L'insensibilité de l'azur et des pierres!'[40] These effects of analogy and
antithesis dominate the poem, which lacks the insistent sound-patterns
of 'Vere novo'. In later sonnets Mallarmé would combine the virtues of
each.

The remaining poem probably written during this period is 'Apparition'.
While it owes something to sixteenth-century verse as well as to *Les Misér-
ables* (published between April and June that year)[41], this poem marks an
important stage in Mallarmé's poetic development and the partial emer-
gence of an original poetic voice. Consisting of sixteen alexandrines, it is his
only poem composed exclusively in 'rimes plates' between 'La Colère d'Al-
lah' (December 1859) and 'Soupir' and 'Las de l'amer repos...' (1864). It is
notable not only for the richness of its vocabulary but more especially for
the boldness of its enjambement (throughout ll. 1–4, and in ll. 8–9, 11–12,
14–15), and the poet may clearly be seen attempting to 'dislocate' the
alexandrine to striking new effect. In both these respects 'Apparition' an-
ticipates the achievements of 'L'Après-midi d'un faune' (begun in 1865) and
the 'Ouverture' to 'Hérodiade' (1866). Although Mallarmé's love poem
does not yet have the syntactic complexity of these later works, its rhythms
are nevertheless expertly modulated; and from the wistful simplicity of its
first hemistich ('La lune s'attristait'), it builds in a crescendo via the wo-
man's appearance in the street to the climactic comparison with 'la fée au
chapeau de clarté' of the poet's childhood dreams, who:

> Passait, laissant toujours de ses mains mal fermées
> Neiger de blancs bouquets d'étoiles parfumées.

---

[40] This use of the sonnet structure remains essentially the same in the 1866 version of this
poem, which differs substantially in other respects by developing the theme of the lovers'
disharmony and by transforming the poet's desire for 'un sommeil de momie' into his doomed
(and unintentionally comic) realization that this disharmony would persist even in death: 'Nous
ne serons jamais une seule momie' (l. 7).

[41] On the date of composition and the debts to Hugo and Renaissance poetry, see Gill, *The
Early Mallarmé*, ii. 251–61.

As in this closing couplet, the poem's metrical rhythms are powerfully complemented by assonance and alliteration. Thus the symmetry of the last line (2+4, 2+4) is reinforced by the internal, pre-caesural rhyme on /e/ and by the alliteration of 'blancs bouquets' (itself echoing the phrase 'De blancs sanglots' in l. 4). Elsewhere the musicality of the poem is achieved by alliteration on /m/ (l. 6), /k/ (l. 9), /v/ (l. 10) or /v/ and /r/ (l. 3), and by assonance with /ãn/ and /õe/ (l. 7), /œj/ (l. 9), or /e/ (l. 13). The isolation of words as 'rejets' (e.g. 'Vaporeuses', 'Et dans le soir', 'Passait') momentarily disrupts their syntactic and referential function, and their position in the poem seems briefly to owe more to patterns of sound than to the demands of sense. 'Vaporeuses' is thus linked by symmetry with 'violes' as much as if not more than it is with the 'fleurs' it grammatically qualifies; while 'Passait', long separated from 'Qui', belongs closely and phonetically with the 'laissant' which follows it. Moreover its grammatical isolation weakens its function as a verb in the imperfect tense and enhances its homophonic potential as 'passé', thus underlining the dominant idea of the poem that the newly kissed beloved reminds the poet of an idyllic past experience. Such a dialectic of sound and sense is perhaps the defining feature of what is called 'poetry': in his mature verse Mallarmé will take this dialectic to previously unexplored limits.[42]

More immediately, 'Apparition' suggests a desire on the young poet's part to move beyond the whimsy and irreverence which characterize many of the poems written between 1859 and 1862. A new seriousness is evident, as it is also in 'Hérésies artistiques. L'Art pour tous', the infamous article which he published in *L'Artiste* on 15 September 1862 and which has so often provided opponents of an 'élitist' Mallarmé with just the ammunition they seek: 'Toute chose sacrée [he begins] et qui veut demeurer sacrée s'enveloppe de mystère. Les religions se retranchent à l'abri d'arcanes dévoilés au seul prédestiné: l'art a les siens.' Compared with a musical score which, to the average person, offers only 'la vue de ces processions macabres de signes sévères, chastes, inconnus' (whereupon 'nous fermons le missel vierge d'aucune pensée profanatrice'), the poetic text is displayed in the same common-or-garden letters that serve 'une tirade utilitaire'. The beautiful blooms of *Les Fleurs du mal* are compromised by being printed in our everyday alphabet, the linguistic flower-bed of the common 'citoyen'. Just because a man can read, he thinks he can read a poem: worse still – 'idée inouïe et saugrenue'—he thinks poetry should be taught in schools: 'expliquée à tous également, égalitairement.' No: 'L'homme peut être démocrate, l'artiste se dédouble et doit rester aristocrate.'

But Mallarmé's provocative rhetoric has often obscured his central argument. As he is quick to point out, quoting Baudelaire: 'injurier la foule, c'est

---

[42] The binary structure of 'Apparition' is analysed in Marchal, *Lecture de Mallarmé*, 17–20.

s'encanailler soi-même.' He is not concerned to attack humanity at large but to assert that poetry is a linguistic craft. Though most of us can read, few of us write music, paint, or sculpt; and so we think that poetry is just another branch of learning, a 'science', to be acquired like history or physics, whereas the other arts are best left to the 'gens du métier'. Show the average 'citoyen' a Rubens or a Delacroix, and he may give it 'un de ces regards qui sentent la rue': mention Shakespeare or Goethe, and he thinks they are something he ought to know about. Better that he should be as content not to have read a word of Hugo as he is content never to have set eyes on one of Verdi's quavers. That way fewer man-hours would be lost sleeping through Virgil, hours which might otherwise have been spent 'activement et dans un but pratique'. Yes, everyone has heard of Corneille, Molière, Racine, and some may even have read them once upon a time. But who rereads them?—'les artistes seuls'.[43]

'Hérésies artistiques' is plainly a profession of faith in the doctrine of 'art for art's sake' which was then evolving into Parnassianism, and, as many commentators have recognized, it foreshadows the essentials of Mallarmé's later poetic theory. Taking his cue (and title) from Baudelaire's article on Gautier published in L'Artiste three years earlier, the young poet is rejecting the idea that poetry has a moral, didactic function. His particular target is Auguste Vacquerie, whose ideas on 'l'enseignement littéraire' and 'l'utilité de la beauté' owed much to Hugo,[44] but more broadly Mallarmé is taking issue with the assumption that poetry can be interpreted in the same way as any other piece of language. The fact that words and letters serve utilitarian functions (unlike musical notation) serves to blunt readers' awareness of the non-referential, 'aesthetic' effects of poetic language. Mallarmé's desire to restore 'mystère' to poetry derives not from an anti-philistine wish to prevent the common herd from being able to follow what he says, but from the belief that everyday language should be defamiliarized and its greater potentialities thus made manifest in the very act of thwarting a utilitarian, referential reading.

At the age of 20 Mallarmé was thus already keenly aware of 'le double état de la parole, brut ou immédiat ici, là essentiel'[45] and when he writes in this article that 'J'ai souvent demandé pourquoi ce caractère nécessaire [evident in the precision of musical notation] a été refusé à un seul art, au plus grand', he reveals that his lifelong pursuit of mastery over linguistic contingency stems from fundamental schoolboy puzzlement. The 'faune lascif' had pursued the muse of poetry through so many thickets of verse and through so many different poetic styles that he was left with an acute sense of their relativity. Why this verse-form and not another? Why the

[43] OC, 257-60.
[44] On the background to this article see Gill, The Early Mallarmé, ii. 92–117.
[45] 'Crise de vers', OC, 368.

alexandrine and not octosyllabics? Why this word and not that? Did these poets 'really' mean what they said, or were not their poems just as much linguistic games as those he himself had been playing since Fanny Dubois Davesnes taught him the rudiments of French versification?

Such thoughts no doubt breed the poetic 'impuissance' which became the dominant theme in Mallarmé's poetry between 1863 and 1866. On the other hand, intricately devised poems like 'Placet', 'Soleil d'hiver', or 'Apparition' show that he was already able to confer 'ce caractère nécessaire' on words if he chose; and it was this pursuit of 'necessity' which led him to discover, in the prose poems of 1864 and in the poems submitted to *Le Parnasse contemporain* in 1866, that the impotent poet may paradoxically be empowered by letting language speak for itself. The 'langue immaculée' for which he calls in 'Hérésies artistiques' will be a language redeemed of the sins of utilitarian reference.

4

A Mirror for the Muse (1863–1866)

Maintenant qu'écrire?
('Symphonie littéraire')

aucun de ces poèmes n'[a] été en réalité conçu en vue de la Beauté, mais
plutôt comme autant d'intuitives révélations de mon tempérament.
(Letter to Henri Cazalis, May 1866)

The schoolboy who had wanted only to read and write verse now departed
for London in November 1862, bent on becoming a teacher of English[1] yet
apparently quite persuaded that no schoolboy should ever be taught poetry.
On 10 August 1863 he married Marie Gerhard at the Brompton Oratory,
and in November he was appointed to a teaching post in Tournon, where he
remained until transferred to Besançon in October 1866. During this four-
year period Mallarmé's poetic output declined dramatically in quantity but
increased no less dramatically in originality; and the greater difficulty he
was encountering in writing became itself a productive theme. Symptomatic
of this paradox is 'Symphonie littéraire', published in *L'Artiste* on 1 Feb-
ruary 1865, in which Mallarmé lauds his holy trinity of Gautier, Baudelaire,
and Banville in the most fulsome terms. The muse he now frequents is the
'Muse moderne de l'Impuissance, qui m'interdis depuis longtemps le trésor
familier des Rythmes, et me condamnes (aimable supplice) à ne faire que
relire [...] les maîtres inaccessibles dont la beauté me désespère'[2]—and he
writes, therefore, of his inability to write...

Some twelve poems were written during this period, as well as the first
versions of 'Hérodiade' and 'L'Après-midi d'un faune' and the seven prose
poems composed in 1864. What is most interesting about these texts (as
regards Mallarmé's development as a poet) is that they show the poet
beginning to evolve in practice an art of reflexivity which he did not begin
to articulate theoretically until the famous letters to Cazalis and Lefébure
from May 1866 onwards. Whatever the nature of the experience he under-

---

[1] 'Ayant appris l'anglais simplement pour mieux lire Poe' ('Autobiographie', OC, 662).
[2] OC, 261.

went in 1866—and the Easter visit to Lefébure in Cannes does seem to have been crucial[3]—it may well be that his 'crisis' sprang principally from his experience as a writer. The 'drame solaire', the loss of religious faith, exposure to Hegel, all these customarily adduced factors no doubt played a part; but they may only have had a part to play because Mallarmé, in the process of writing, had discovered the void at the heart of language. In many of these poems and prose poems written between 1863 and 1866 one sees that Mallarmé's pursuit of formal symmetry leads to a proliferation of internal linguistic relationships which then threaten to overwhelm the referential, traditionally extra-textual function of language. A Structuralist Mallarmé is born: the creator of texts in which words derive meaning from their relationships with other words rather than from their conventional and arbitrary referents in the world. And a Post-structuralist Mallarmé is conceived: the willing, passive instrument of words which have more to say than he can ever foresee or adequately control, what in 'Brise marine' (as we shall see) he calls the 'chant des matelots'.

Most often Mallarmé's poems from this period have been welcomed for their accessibility and investigated as evidence of the continuing or declining influence of Baudelaire.[4] It is certainly true that spleen and 'ennui' are recurrent themes: a gulf of irony divides the 'Idéal' (or the 'Azur') from the 'ici-bas', and the poet is variously 'triste' or 'las'. In 'Les Fenêtres' 'Ici-bas est maître', and filled with the stench of 'le vomissement impur de la bêtise':[5] and in 'L'Azur'

> Le poète impuissant [...] maudit son génie
> A travers le désert stérile des Douleurs.
>
> (ll. 3–4)

In 'Les Fleurs' he is 'le poète las que la vie étiole', while famously in 'Brise marine' 'La chair est triste, hélas! et j'ai lu tous les livres' (where 'hélas!' reads also as 'et las[se]'). Individual lines proclaim the debt openly: 'Dans un grand nonchaloir chargé de souvenir!' ('Les Fenêtres', l. 20) and 'l'adieu

---

[3] See Marchal, *La Religion de Mallarmé*, 54 ff. Was it significant that this experience took place at Easter, given that the Passion would come to serve as *the* metaphor for the death of representation and the resurrection of significance?

[4] Cf. L. J. Austin's comment in 'Mallarmé disciple de Baudelaire: *Le Parnasse contemporain*', *Revue d'histoire littéraire de la France*, 67 (1967), 437–49: 'les onze [*sic*] poèmes que Mallarmé envoya en 1866 à la première série du *Parnasse contemporain* sont une puissante reformulation de thèmes baudelairiens et une application consciente et systématique de la théorie et de la technique baudelairienne des "correspondances" sous un des ses aspects essentiels' (p. 439). See also Gill, *The Early Mallarmé*, ii, *passim*, and Marchal, *Lecture de Mallarmé*, 21–5, 27–9.

[5] Quotations in this section are from the versions of the poems printed in *Le Parnasse contemporain* or, in the case of 'Le Pitre châtié' and 'L'Assaut' (both rejected by the editors), from the versions transcribed in the 'Carnet de 1864': see OC (BM), 150–1, 170–1.

suprême des mouchoirs!' ('Brise marine', l. 12), for example, evidently recall 'La Chevelure'.[6]

But of greater interest perhaps are the apprentice-poet's continuing endeavours to manipulate poetic form. In 1863 his experimentation with the sonnet continues in 'A celle qui est tranquille' (originally entitled 'A une putain' and later 'Angoisse') and in 'Le Pitre châtié', while the four octosyllabic quatrains of 'Le Château de l'Espérance' recall the structure of 'Soleil d'hiver'. In 'A celle qui est tranquille' the poet, envious of the prostitute's sound sleep untroubled by remorse, visits her bed for no other reason than his 'peur de mourir lorsque je couche seul'; and, as in 'Tristesse d'été', the sonnet structure helps to modulate a series of analogies and antitheses: sleep/death, curtain/shroud, barren womb/poetic impotence, peace/anguish, kiss/pang of remorse, etc. The sound-patterning of 'Vere novo' is evident only in some rather mechanical and inconsequential alliteration ('péchés d'un peuple', 'triste tempête', 'sommeil sans songes', 'rideaux [...] du remords', 'native noblesse'), and the poem depends almost entirely for its effect on the surprise of the central conceit.

More subtle, even in its first version, is 'Le Pitre châtié'[7] which allegorically proclaims the principle, enunciated by Gautier and Poe and espoused by the Parnassians, that poetic 'genius' derives not from 'inspiration' but from carefully wrought artifice. And where better to say so than in a sonnet? An even lowlier figure than the Baudelairean 'saltimbanque' for whom it is the function of a 'pitre' to drum up business, the eponymous clown of Mallarmé's last extant sonnet before 'Sonnet allégorique de lui-même' flees his tent to cast himself into the purifying waters of his beloved's eyes only to realize that by washing off his greasepaint (in the transparency of sincere, unsimulated feelings) he has washed away his artistry: 'cette crasse était tout le génie!'

Anticipating the later, highly self-referential sonnet of the same title, this first version establishes an analogy between the tent and the sonnet itself by playing on the literal meaning of enjambement. Thus the description of the clown's flight:

> J'ai, Muse,—moi, ton pitre,—enjambé la fenêtre
> Et fui notre baraque où fument tes quinquets
>
> (ll. 3–4)

refers both to the imagined narrative and to what has just taken place prosodically in the poem:

---

[6] See Gill, *The Early Mallarmé*, ii. 321 ff. for discussion of the debt to Baudelaire in the 'London poems' of 1863.

[7] For discussion of its transformation into the version published in *Poésies* in 1887, see L. J. Austin, 'Mallarmé's Reshaping of "Le Pitre châtié"', in E. M. Beaumont *et al.* (eds), *Order and Adventure in Post-Romantic French Poetry: Essays Presented to C. A. Hackett* (Oxford, 1973), 56–71; reprinted in *Poetic Principles and Practice: Occasional Papers on Baudelaire, Mallarmé and Valéry* (Cambridge, 1987), 155–69.

> Pour ses yeux,—pour nager dans ces lacs, dont les quais
> Sont plantés de beaux cils qu'un matin bleu pénètre,

where the repetition (of 'pour') and the enjambement suggest a poet be-guiled into self-indulgent metaphor and dreamy expatiation beyond the confines of the alexandrine. The enjambement is wilfully repeated at the beginning of the second quatrain, where the terminal position of 'traître' and the placing of the 'lacs défendus' in the 'rejet' emphasize the clown's 'crime'; and the sense of spacious ease consequent on his escape is conveyed by the broad rhythmic sweep of ll. 7–8 (contrasting with the more fragmen-ted, staccato rhythm of the clown's flight in ll. 3–4), before the ephemeral and ignoble nature of this escape is perhaps signalled by the quatrain's bathetic ending on a rhyme-induced 'hêtre':

> Et d'herbes enivré, j'ai plongé comme un traître
> Dans ces lacs défendus, et, quand tu m'appelais,
> Baigné mes membres nus dans l'onde aux blancs galets,
> Oubliant mon habit de pitre au tronc d'un hêtre.

Where the octave narrated the flight from constraint, the sestet describes the aftermath of this quasi-sexual plunge: in the first tercet, the clown's con-tinuing bravado ('loin de ta tyrannie'), and then—after a deferred 'volta'—his recognition of his error.

Once more the sonnet structure orchestrates manifold analogies and antitheses. The interior world of the tent is evoked in the first quatrain and the final tercet, in both of which the muse is addressed directly as 'Muse'; while the outdoor world of lakes, grass, and sunshine fills the second quatrain and the first tercet, in which the muse's presence is more obliquely evoked by 'tu m'appelais' and 'ta tyrannie'. The artificial light of the tent, the heat and smoke, and the 'crasse' of the clown's make-up contrast with the morning sunlight and blue sky, with the whiteness of the clown's naked limbs, the 'blancs galets' of the lake (the whites of her eyes?), and its 'neige des glaciers' whose melted waters wash him clean. The 'quinquets' in the tent, meaning not only oil lamps but (in slang) also eyes, establish a fitting contrast in register between the hackneyed analogy of lakes and eyes[8] (for which Romantic nonsense the poet is betraying the

---

[8] In the later version, the analogy is made more complex by the possibility (in the opening words 'Yeux, lacs') that 'lacs' means not only 'lakes' but also 'knotted cord', 'snare', or 'love-knot'. Like a figure of eight on its side (thus representing infinity), the 'lacs' of the poem is/are both the eyes of beauty and the white interstices, or 'entrelacs', in the black characters of the printed text. In his pursuit of beauty, perhaps, the poet thus finds himself trapped in a textual tangle (cf. 'pris dans le(s) lacs' = to be caught in the toils). Similarly, the overtly Baudelairean figure of the 'pitre' (cf 'Le Vieux Saltimbanque') is later rendered more 'Mal-larméan' in that the etymology of 'pitre' (from Latin 'pedester'), already foregrounded by 'enjambé' in the first version, is further brought to mind by the new insistence on 'jambe' and 'bras' and the suggestion that the 'pitre', in forsaking the traditional tent of his art (or making a

proper calling of the poet as conscious artificer) and an irreverent descrip-
tion of the muse as a figure with smoking peepers. Thus the sonnet may tell
the story of a poet being 'châtié' for succumbing to the temptations of
freedom and transparency, yet it demonstrates by its own intricacy the
virtues of a poet who has 'châtié son style'. And already implicit is the
idea, developed in the final version, that the whiteness of the page must be
defiled by ink if the mountain of the muse is to be climbed.

Mallarmé abandoned the sonnet form for the next five years and sought
instead to create new 'fixed' forms of his own.[9] It is likely that the binary
structure of the sonnet's octave and sestet inspired his attempt in 'Le
Château de l'Espérance', as in 'Soleil d'hiver', to create a stanzaic poem
with two contrasting halves. In this poem (originally entitled 'L'Assaut' and
which, like 'Le Pitre châtié', was not accepted for publication in Le Parnasse
contemporain), the four octosyllabic quatrains in 'rimes embrassées' turn on
the analogy between the beloved's blond hair and 'ce drapeau d'or fin'
which the ardent lover seeks to plant in triumph upon the Castle of Hope,
where Hope herself, weeping in the starless dark, 'rebrousse et lisse / [...] /
La Nuit noire comme un chat noir'. The poem's account of this doomed,
quixotic 'recherche de l'absolu' divides between the first two stanzas, in
which the poet contemplates the disparity between the beauty of his beloved
(stanza 1) and his present unhappiness (stanza 2), and the last two in which
he experiences the disparity between his own glorious assault and the end-
lessly repeated, pointless gesture ('rebrousse et lisse') by which Hope herself
is characterized. The poem pivots on the dramatic 'Marche', placed at the
beginning of the third stanza just as 'Mais' is often placed at the volta of a
sonnet (at the beginning of the sestet).

The embraced structure of the rhymes is mirrored in the thematic move
from rippling, banner-like hair (stanza 1) via a single act of renunciation and
flag-unfurling (stanza 2) and a single military charge (stanza 3) back to the
incessant caress of nocturnal hopelessness (stanza 4). The sense of inevitable
failure suggested by this circular structure is reinforced by the contrasts
between the warm golden sunshine of the beginning and the black chill (cf.
'nonchaloir') of the ending, and by the stanzaic progression in the connota-
tions of liquid from peace ('ondoie'; echoed by 'ta tresse en flots'), to
unhappiness (the copious tears which rather incongruously stave in the

---

hole in the 'toile' of textuality) is now floundering (like a drowning swimmer) out of his
'pedestrian' element. Together with the pun on 'châtié', the relevance of this etymology
may explain why, most unusually, the later Mallarmé did not in this case abandon the use of
a title.

[9] In May 1866, however, Mallarmé wrote to Cazalis that 'Je me repose à l'aide de trois
courts poèmes, mais qui seront inouïs, tous trois à la glorification de la Beauté' (Corr., i. 216).
These may have been early versions of 'Tout Orgueil fume-t-il', 'Surgi de la croupe et du bond',
and 'Une dentelle s'abolit'. See below, Part IV, Ch. 2.

poet's drum in stanza 2), to violence ('des marais de sang'), to cold indifference ('larmoyant de nonchaloir'). The fair prospect of 'ta pâle chevelure' (l. 1) is replaced at the end by a pallid absence ('Sans qu'un astre pâle jaillisse': 1.15), an absence ('Sans qu'un') in which are echoed the tears and blood ('sanglots', 'sang') of the poet's sorry travail; and the frolicking alliteration and wordplay of the first stanza ('les parfums de ta peau', 'la soie au soleil blondoie') is superseded ultimately by feline hissing ('L'Espérance rebrousse et lisse / Sans qu'un astre pâle jaillisse') and the sombre repetition of a poet who has run out of words ('La Nuit noire comme un chat noir'). And yet, once more, 'salvation' is evident in the poem's own success in expressing this assault on the ideal. In 'Soleil d'hiver' the 'brocart d'ors fins' of summer sun is recovered in the 'son aiguillette' of the poem itself, while here the poet has indeed grabbed 'ce drapeau d'or fin' (i.e. the analogy offered by the woman's golden hair) and replaced his stove drum with a golden textuality which triumphs over despair, a despair as black as night, as black perhaps as ink.

Mallarmé may have intended this poem, like 'Les Fenêtres', as a reply to Baudelaire's regretful description of the human condition (in 'Le Reniement de saint Pierre') as 'un monde où l'action n'est pas la sœur du rêve'.[10] As we have seen, 'Le Château de l'Espérance' explicitly illustrates his stated intentions while implicitly demonstrating that poetic artifice may be a means of palliating the anguish consequent upon the unattainability of the ideal. 'Les Fenêtres' offers a more complex version of the same dual message, and again we find Mallarmé elaborating an intricate binary structure (as he will also in 'Soupir', 'Brise marine', and 'Las de l'amer repos…'). Ten quatrains of alexandrines in 'rimes croisées' pivot on the 'Ainsi' of l. 21, as the poet describes first the dying man in hospital and then himself. Each half begins with a sequence of three stanzas which proceed in like manner: from dissatisfaction ('Las du triste hôpital', 'pris du dégoût') to action ('Se traîne et va', 'Je fuis et je m'accroche') to an encounter with the window ('un long

---

[10] 'Mon Dieu, s'il en était autrement', Mallarmé wrote to Cazalis on 3 June 1863, 'si le Rêve était ainsi défloré et abaissé, où donc nous sauverions-nous, nous autres malheureux que la terre dégoûte et qui n'avons que le Rêve pour refuge. Ô mon Henri, abreuve-toi d'idéal. Le bonheur d'ici-bas est ignoble—il faut avoir les mains bien calleuses pour le ramasser. Dire: "Je suis heureux!" c'est dire: "Je suis un lâche"—et plus souvent: "Je suis un niais." Car il faut ne pas voir au-dessus de ce plafond de bonheur le ciel de l'Idéal, ou fermer les yeux exprès. J'ai fait sur ces idées un petit poème Les Fenêtres […]: et un autre L'Assaut qui est vague et frêle comme une rêverie. D'une chevelure qui a fait naître en mon cerveau l'idée d'un drapeau, mon cœur, pris d'une ardeur militaire, s'élance à travers d'affreux paysages et va assiéger le Château fort de l'Espérance pour y planter cet étendard d'or fin. Mais, l'insensé, après ce court moment de folie, aperçoit l'Espérance qui n'est qu'une sorte de spectre voilé et stérile' (Corr., i. 90–1). For further discussion of these remarks see Gill, The Early Mallarmé, ii. 329–31. Cazalis agreed, observing in his reply that 'Le bonheur terrestre, tu as raison, ressemblera toujours à la Hollande, qui malgré ses tulipes est un pays plat' (DSM, vi. 158, quoted in OC (BM), 146).

baiser amer', 'Je me mire'). In the first half this trio is followed by two stanzas celebrating the dying man's temporary 'resurrection' and glorious vision of the sunset ('Ivre, il vit', 'Voit des galères d'or'); in the second, by contrast, the final two stanzas describe how the poet's epiphanic vision is at once interrupted by renewed, nauseated awareness of the human condition—such that he yearns for a way out of this human condition (in the poem's imagery, out through the windows of the hospital) even at the risk of falling, Icarus-like, 'pendant l'éternité'.

   The poet's plea to God is born of a momentary forsaking of the ideal ('me boucher le nez devant l'azur') brought on by the disparity between his vision of an angelic self in the window and the 'bêtise' of the world about him: but salvation had already been granted him, and by an agent other than God. For each half of the poem relates a process of death and resurrection which explicitly replaces that of Christ. In the first, the dying man turns his back on the 'grand crucifix ennuyé du mur vide' and kisses not the crucifix but the 'tièdes carreaux d'or' through which revivifying sunlight pours; and at once 'les poils blancs et les os de sa maigre figure' of the old man are transformed into a young man's 'bouche, fiévreuse [. . .] / Telle, jeune, elle alla respirer son trésor, / Une peau virginale et de jadis!' Similarly, in the second half, the poet 'tourne le dos à la vie' (the bourgeois life of complacency and materialist self-interest described in the sixth stanza) and dies ('Et je meurs'), whereupon he is seen to 'renaître [. . .] / Au ciel antérieur où fleurit la Beauté!' In the former case sunshine has restored the man's creativity (as sexual desire), in the latter it is reflection which restores the poet to a prelapsarian realm of angelic beauty.

   Reflection in what? The poet claims that it does not matter ('Que la vitre soit l'art, soit la mysticité'), but the poem demonstrates that art itself is the means of his resurrection. For not only has the poet sought poetic beauty in the reflection of an analogy between himself and a hospital patient, he has also framed this reflection within the windows of his own 'rimes croisées'. Where previously the 'pitre' had 'enjambé la fenêtre' of his tented art, here the poet '[s']accroche à toutes les croisées / D'où l'on tourne le dos à la vie'—in other words, he clings to the stanzas of a poetic art which rejects reference in the name of self-reference. Windows are made of 'verre', as surely as 'Les Fenêtres' is made of 'vers': hence, 'béni, / Dans leur verre [. . .] / [. . .] / Je me mire et me vois ange!' 'Je me mire', 'je me rime': the crossed rhymes of the poem have replaced the cross of the Christian story, reflexive art has become the poet's new religion—or, as l. 3 has it with a different surface meaning: 'Vers le grand crucifix'. And even at the very moment when, like St Peter denying Christ, the poet allows the 'vomissement impur' of human fallibility to undermine his newfound faith, the perfect symmetry of reflexive art belies his statement with a phonetic palindrome that asserts the power of poetic language:

'Mais, hélas! Ici-bas est maître: [...]'

/me/ /e/ /a/ /i/ /s/ /i/ /a/ /e/ /me/

The poet's final aspiration to 'enfoncer le cristal' is thus tantamount to his being tempted to artistic suicide, because the 'cristal' of the 'vers' is precisely what allows him access to 'la Beauté'. Which is why he speaks, like a fallen Satan, of fleeing 'avec mes deux ailes sans plume': angelic status and genuine poetic flight, achieved by the two reflexive 'wings' of this binary poem, depend on his retaining his 'plume', with which to pen these window-stanzas and place a poetic crucifix upon the 'mur vide' of the empty page. The plumeless poet would plummet for all eternity, but this poem with its carefully wrought structure can end necessarily as its symmetrical pattern becomes complete. And so, where the 'moribond' saw clouds at sunset as 'des galères d'or, belles comme des cygnes', the 'dead' poet of 'Les Fenêtres' offers us these ten stanzas, these poetic 'carreaux d'or' (l. 12), as it might be, 'beaux comme des signes'. In 'Les Fenêtres' Mallarmé discovered the Sign of the Cross which he was later to inscribe in 'Sonnet allégorique de lui-même'.

The structure of the 'mirror-poem', introduced in 'Soleil d'hiver' and elaborated in 'Les Fenêtres', is deployed in other poems which Mallarmé wrote at this time. In 'Soupir' ten alexandrines in 'rimes plates' pivot on the phrase 'vers l'Azur!', which comes at the end of l. 5 and is repeated at the beginning of l. 6. The pivot itself is typographically present in the dash at the beginning of 1.6, an 'espace blanc' which figures the apogee of the 'blanc jet d'eau'. In the first half of the poem the poet's soul rises like water from a fountain towards the azure heavens, the azure heavens which are reflected down below (in the second half) in the basins of the fountain, each superimposed upon the other like the lines of this fountain-poem. Anticipating Beckett's minimalist drama *Souffle*, the poem enacts the aspiration and expiration of a sigh in the rise and fall of its rhythm, ending on the same vowel sound (repeated) with which it started (in the first, fifth, and sixth syllables of the first hemistich). In the first half of the poem the poet aspires to 'l'Azur' of the ideal via the analogy between the freckled forehead and blue eyes of his 'calme sœur' and a landscape of autumn colours beneath a blue sky; and in the second half this analogy is pursued back down to earth as the October sun reflects its languor in the still waters of a now inactive fountain, over which the russet leaves flutter before settling in a golden furrow, one long, last ray of sunlight to cheer the melancholy scene. Parallels of sound and sense abound within and between the two halves: 'vers ton front', 'vers le ciel'; 'jonché de taches de rousseur', 'la fauve agonie / Des feuilles'; 'le ciel errant', 'erre au vent'; 'calme sœur', 'langueur infinie'; 'Monte', 'laisse [...] / [...] / Se traîner'; 'un [...] jet d'eau', 'jaune', 'un long rayon'; 'fidèle', 'erre', 'se traîner'; etc.

As in 'Le Château de l'Espérance' and 'Les Fenêtres', the sense of loss following a brief moment of contact with the ideal is mitigated by the beauty of poetic organization, and the poem's central repetition of 'vers l'Azur' as 'Vers l'Azur' encourages us to see the ideal as synonymous with the 'vers' itself. 'Mon âme vers ton front', 'Et vers le ciel', 'vers l'Azur', 'Vers l'Azur': the repetition of 'vers' suggests a progression towards the poetic union of soul, heaven, ideal, and poetry, just as the phonetic proximity of 'sœur' and 'Azur' may intimate (anticipating 'Prose (pour des Esseintes)') that the 'vers' attains the ideal through the cultivation of linguistic kinship. Where in 'Les Fenêtres' the dying poet found his 'semblable', his 'frère', in a bedridden invalid, here he finds himself mirrored in a sister, perhaps nature herself, who offers him access to the ideal in the golden modulations of an autumnal sigh, in a 'Soupir' 'Qui mire'. In this fountain-poem the word 'eau' homophonically invests key images in seven of its ten lines ('ô calme sœur', 'automne', 'jet d'eau', 'aux grand bassins', 'l'eau morte', 'la fauve agonie', 'au vent', 'jaune'); and the 'blanc jet d'eau', with its homophonic trace of 'jais', may even suggest the quill, erect, with which the poet aspires to an ideal of poetic writing, 'noir sur blanc'. The plumed angel of 'Les Fenêtres' has here become, it seems, at once a fountain and a pen.

This binary structure is repeated in 'Brise marine' and 'Las de l'amer repos'. In the former, sixteen alexandrines in 'rimes plates' divide into groups of eight: the first half of the poem relates the poet's present dissatisfaction and lists those things which are insufficient to deter him from absconding (sex, books, familiar surroundings, writing, a new-born child); while the second envisages the thrill of a sea-voyage. Strongly echoing Baudelaire's 'Le Voyage', the poem pivots on 'Je partirai!' at the beginning of l. 9. The first half, full of negatives, itemizes what the poet would not miss; while the second extols their converse: the sailor's life away from wife and family, 'une exotique nature' instead of 'les vieux jardins', and an exciting shipwreck to replace his failure to write, the 'naufrage' of his poetic craft. Where once, sitting with a wife breastfeeding her child, he felt lost in the 'clarté déserte de ma lampe / Sur le vide papier que la blancheur défend', now he dreams of being 'Perdus, sans mâts, sans mâts, ni fertiles îlots...': the masts and fertile islands are as absent as the pen and the nourishing breast which they resemble. But...

> Mais, ô mon cœur, entends le chant des matelots!

Is there here a final realization that the desire for escape, as at the end of 'Les Fenêtres', is a temptation to be resisted; that the shipwreck in which such immature escapism would end is much less to be preferred than the painful shipwreck that is his poetic 'impuissance'? Has he been listening not to the call of the sea but to a siren song luring him away from the steady course of poetic art?

As before, the poem itself demonstrates the poet's rescue. Following the rudderless repetition of 'sans mâts, sans mâts' and 'fertiles îlots', he hears the 'chant des matelots'—with the word 'matelots' seeming to spring unbidden from the words 'mâts' and 'îlots'. The very principle of homophony comes to his aid, as these fellow-sailors heave into sight; while the written word itself, thanks to the abundance of circumflexes and upright t's and l's,[11] seems magically to restore his lost 'mâture', the masts needed to hoist the sails that will capture this 'brise marine'. The poet can rejoice linguistically to be all at sea ('ce cœur qui dans la mer se trempe'), and aboard his 'Steamer', which 'miraculously' contains the word 'mer'—and (hom.) 'mère'. The syntactic parallel between 'la jeune femme allaitant son enfant' and 'Steamer balançant ta mâture' on either side of the central pivot suggests a thematic parallel between maternal sustenance and poetic creativity. As she gives suck with white milk, so may the poet draw strength from the whiteness of his page, delight in innovative linguistic play like one of the plumed 'oiseaux' who are 'ivres / D'être parmi l'écume inconnue des cieux', and create the lilting rhythms of his 'chant des matelots' as surely as a mother rocks her babe. The poem is the poet's 'son enfant', sound's issue, a linguistic infant (etymologically 'not speaking') endowed with the power of musical expression, his new-born shanty. 'Lève l'ancre', he bids the 'Steamer': and 'l'encre' is just what he needs to anchor sound upon the 'vide papier que la blancheur défend'. 'J'ai lu tous les livres': but the first strains of 'Le Livre' are already in the wind, borne upon a 'Brise marine'.

In 'Las de l'amer repos', placed at the end of the group of Mallarmé's poems published in Le Parnasse contemporain and there entitled 'Épilogue',[12] the same mirror-structure is evident once more. Twenty-eight alexandrines in 'rimes plates' divide into two groups of seven couplets; while each half itself further divides into two groups of seven lines. The poet writes, in the first half, of his decision to abandon a particular kind of artistic effort, the sterility of which has been revealed by the dawn; and in the second, of his intention to 'Imiter le Chinois', that is, to imitate the minimalist representations of Chinese porcelain art. The first group of seven lines describes the poet's dissatisfaction with his own inactivity and of his even greater dissatisfaction with the painful effort involved in his attempts at originality ('creuser une fosse nouvelle'); while the second records his new decision in the form of a question and answer: 'Que dire à cette Aurore [...]?', 'Je veux délaisser l'Art vorace d'un pays / Cruel'. The third group details the Chinese artist's painting of a flower, while the fourth ('Serein, je

---

[11] In a manner which prefigures the 'naufrage' of 'A la nue accablante tu': see below, Part IV, Ch. 3.

[12] As it is already in his manuscript 'Carnet de 1864': see OC (BM), 173.

vais choisir')[13] offers us the poet's projected painting of 'un jeune paysage', complete with lake, crescent moon, and three green reeds.

It is tempting to see the delicate art of porcelain painting as analogous with Mallarmé's own suggestive art, and to see similarities between the white porcelain and the white page upon which a relatively small number of words create a rich poetic landscape.[14] The poem's original status as an epilogue further implies the abandonment of one style of writing and the espousal of another.[15] But the style of the poem itself is far from exemplifying the minimalist art of the Chinese painter; and the external evidence of 'Les Fenêtres' and 'Brise marine' would suggest that here again we have a despairing poet seeking release from the rigours of a poetic practice which he fears has been fruitless but which the poem itself displays as 'Une gloire' (l. 2).

In 'Las de l'amer repos' this theme receives a novel and informative treatment, for the clear implication now is that the 'impuissance' of the poet derives from his ambition to create non-representational art. The Chinese has an easy time of it: his heart is 'limpide', his life 'Transparente', and he paints a flower on the basis of a lifetime's experience ('la fleur qu'il a sentie, enfant, / Au filigrane bleu de l'âme se greffant'). The poet thinks fondly of how he, too, will be 'Serein', 'distrait': and, thanks to the enjambement, there is a hint of cavalier contingency in the prospect that 'Une ligne d'azur mince et pâle serait / Un lac', with the precise position of the crescent moon seeming also to be a matter of little consequence ('perdu par une blanche nue').

Mallarmé 'distrait'? Such ease was foreign to the poet who had adopted the lesson of Edgar Allan Poe's 'Philosophy of Composition' and believed intricate artifice to be the way to Beauty. How different is the unproblematical daubing of the painter from the writer who carefully (and caligrammatically) places two commas and an apostrophe in the vicinity of the words 'trois grands cils' and whose entire poem is a complex network of repeated sounds and thematic parallels. Whereas the Chinese simply paints what he has always known, the despairing poet of ll. 1–14 has precisely cut himself off from a naïve, childhood perception of the world, from 'l'enfance / Adorable des bois de roses sous l'azur / Naturel!' He is weary of the inactivity to which 'impuissance' has reduced him, but he is seven times as weary of the huge efforts consequent upon his resolve to seek artistic glory

[13] Though marking a syntactic beginning, l. 21 ('Et, la mort telle avec le seul rêve du sage') is still part of the description of the Chinese.

[14] Cf. David Kinloch, 'Mallarmé and the Chinese Artist', *Romance Studies*, 14 (1989), 77–88. For the opposing view that the aesthetic of the Chinese artist represents a temptation to be resisted, see Charles Chadwick, *Mallarmé: Sa pensée dans sa poésie* (Paris, 1962), 10–13.

[15] Cf. Marchal, *Lecture de Mallarmé*, 28: 'De Baudelaire à Mallarmé, tel pourrait être en raccourci le propos du poème.'

not by representing the 'natural' world but rather by mental innovation ('une fosse nouvelle / Dans le terrain avare et froid de ma cervelle'). Such are his cherished 'Rêves' of a new poetic art, but now that dawn breaks (after a night of apparently sterile labour) and that he, the poet, is 'visité' by this visual reminder of 'natural' roses (in the pink hues of the sunrise), how shall he remain faithful to his 'pacte dur'? He fears that the beauty born of his nocturnal cerebration may be simply 'roses livides', non-existent perhaps, or at least so pale as to be indistinguishable from the white page, and that his poetic text therefore resembles but a combination of absences like a cemetery so full of unfilled graves that the holes merge into one. This 'ideal' domain of non-representational art is a 'pays / Cruel', its aesthetic 'vorace' in the demands it places upon him; and he would gladly forsake it despite the reproaches of his friends and despite the betrayal which it would constitute of his past and of 'genius' itself. God knows I have tried, he seems to say, or rather 'my lamp knows I have tried'; and the first half of the poem thus ends with a verbal echo of l. 1: 'Et ma lampe qui sait pourtant mon agonie' (cf. 'Las de l'amer repos où ma paresse offense', in which 'ma lampe' is anagrammatically already present).

Yet this symmetry in the first half of the poem is characteristic of a text in which Mallarmé has clearly racked his poetic brains—and dug deep into language—in order to achieve new poetic effects. Carrying on where he left off in 'Apparition', and anticipating the achievement of the 'Ouverture' to 'Hérodiade', he manipulates rhythm and sound with intricate dexterity, perhaps indeed in imitation of Poe. For so difficult is this style of writing that he is, conceivably, 'las de l'amer re-Poe'. Be that as it may, there is evidence here of a 'faune/phone lascif', a horned poet who has abandoned the rosy thickets of naïve representational art and dipped his 'corne calme' into the icy waters of pure sound, with the result that the roses are replaced by that new symbol of beauty, 'roseaux', on which the poem ends. With these pipes of Pan he can create cornucopian sound pictures of which close analysis serves only to destroy the subtlety: compare for example, nevertheless, the way the vowels and consonants in 'Adorable' at the beginning of l. 3 disseminate in the remainder of the line ('des bois de roses sous l'azur'); or how the enjambement in ll. 2–4 not only stresses 'Adorable' and 'Naturel' but sets up symmetries between these words and 'azur' and 'pacte dur' at the end of their respective lines; or the orchestration of /d/, /r/, /s/, /v/, /i/, /o/, and /ɔ/ in ll. 8–9:

> Que dire à cette Aurore, ô Rêves, visité
> Par les roses, quand, peur des ses roses livides [.]

The repetition of key words throughout the poem ('Las', 'roses', 'azur', 'sept' (as 'cette'), 'fosse' (in 'fossoyeur'), 'tasses', 'fleur', 'enfance' (as 'enfant'), 'Rêves' (as 'rêve'), 'pays' (in 'paysage'), 'peindre' (in 'peindrais')), the presence of six 'rimes riches' and two 'rimes équivoques' (on 'fin' and 'nue'), the insistent alliteration ('pure', 'peindre'; 'filigrane', 'se greffant'; 'clair croissant'; 'corne calme'), assonance ('pour qui jadis j'ai fui', 'émeraude, roseaux'), or combinations of the two ('sans pitié', 'stérilité'; 'Imiter', 'limpide'), all suggest a poet who has laboured hard over language to reconcile sense with a maximum of musical effect.

He proclaims himself 'plus las sept fois du pacte dur', but in this poem he has stuck to his poet's pact and displayed the beauty of language not seven times, but four times seven times in the quadripartite structure of this twenty-eight-line stanza, his own 'symphonie littéraire'. His ambition has been 'Une gloire pour qui jadis j'ai fui l'enfance'; and when we consider that a 'gloire' is not only a musical celebration but also an 'Assemblage de rayons divergents au centre desquels apparaît un triangle, symbole de la Trinité',[16] we may begin to wonder if the 'trois grands cils' that turn out to be 'roseaux' are not a perfect emblem of this poem in which poetic glory has been won by deriving radiant orchestration of sound from quasi-geometrical textual organization. At the very least we begin to see how the poet's despair may be a source of hope: how the text as a vast cemetery of 'dead' referents does indeed unite these 'trous vides' in a glorious new dawn of non-referential art wherein the poet, reborn, comes up sounding of (thrice-mentioned) roses: 'cette Aurore, ô Rêves, visité [visitée] [visités] / Par les roses.' For, thanks to the mystery of language, these roses—of which one is already anagrammatically 'waiting' in the 'repos' of l. 1—do indeed 'visit' 'cette Au*rore*, ô *Rêves*', as does also the gold of reflexive verse ('ô Reves': cf. 'ver-or').

Not all of Mallarmé's poems written during this period demonstrate this binary structure, and 'L'Azur' and 'Les Fleurs' constitute two important exceptions. Yet in each of these poems the principles expounded in Poe's 'Philosophy of Composition' are still operative, and neither poem is any less carefully structured than those which have just been discussed. In the case of 'L'Azur', Mallarmé's long analysis of the poem in a letter to Cazalis[17] mentions Poe's essay on 'The Raven' explicitly and gives an unambiguous account of his own intentions. Recalling Poe's dictum that Beauty is 'not a quality [...] but an effect', Mallarmé describes his labours:

Je te jure qu'il n'y a pas un mot qui ne m'ait coûté plusieurs heures de recherche, et que le premier mot, qui revêt la première idée, outre qu'il tend lui-même à l'*effet* général du poème, sert encore à préparer le dernier.

L'*effet produit*, sans une dissonance, sans une fioriture, même adorable, qui distrait,—voilà ce que je cherche.

He mocks Emmanuel Des Essarts who 'prend une poignée d'étoiles dans la voie lactée pour la semer sur le papier et les laisser se former au hasard en

---

[16] Littré, 'Gloire', 10°.
[17] *Corr.*, i. 103–4 (Jan. 1864). Quoted (from *DSM*, vi. 176–8) in *OC* (BM), 153.

constellations imprévues!', whereas he, Mallarmé, proposes to be 'fidèle à ces sévères idées' which he has derived from Poe. As an experiment in reader-response he then describes the 'effect' he has sought to develop in each stanza of the poem, to see if Cazalis has responded as he had wished. Alas, the experiment miscarried, for Cazalis had flu; Mallarmé's guinea-pig merely gushed: 'Tes vers sont superbes, je les lis à tout le monde.'[18]

'L'Azur' lacks the subtlety of some of Mallarmé's other poems of this period, perhaps because he has sought to achieve a specifically dramatic effect: 'pour ceux qui [...] cherchent dans un poème autre chose que la musique des vers, il y a là un vrai drame.' And he admits that 'ç'a été une terrible difficulté de combiner, dans une juste harmonie, l'élément drama-tique hostile à l'idée de poésie pure et subjective avec la sérénité et le calme de lignes nécessaires à la Beauté'. The attitudinizing of the poet as he seeks refuge from the mocking, ironic presence of the ideal makes the poem much less persuasive than Baudelaire's 'Obsession', of which it is thematically highly reminiscent. The Hugolian apostrophe (for example, 'Brouillards, montez! Versez vos cendres monotones') fails to carry conviction, and the art of repetition displayed in 'Jeter, lambeaux, jeter' and even in the famous last line '*Je suis hanté*. L'Azur! l'Azur! l'Azur! l'Azur') serves the vain cause of grandiloquence rather than a complex art of orchestrated sound.[19] For the poem is reflexive only in its failure: witness the poet's lament that his 'cervelle, vidée / Comme le pot de fard gisant au pied d'un mur, / N'a plus l'art d'attifer la sanglotante idée'. He lacks the wherewithal to be a 'pitre', and can merely echo the mocking angelus in mindless, uninventive repeti-tion: 'L'Azur! l'Azur! l'Azur! l'Azur!'

In 'Les Fleurs' on the other hand, Mallarmé combines Poe's conscious art of composition with a theme and use of language which make this work a clear forerunner of later achievements. Consisting of six quatrains of alex-andrines in 'rimes croisées', the poem divides into two groups of four and two stanzas (an even more 'top-heavy' version of the proportions of the Petrarchan sonnet). Because the first three quatrains comprise one sentence, there is a marked pause at the end of the third, which briefly offers the prospect of a poem falling into two equal parts. But the continuation of the list of flowers into the fourth quatrain leads to the poem dividing more emphatically into proportions of two-thirds and one-third. In the first four quatrains the poet describes how flowers were divinely created out of the primordial light of the sun and stars,[20] while in the last two he gives praise and draws comfort from this lesson in creation, or rather re-creation. In the

[18] *DSM*, vi. 182.

[19] Despite an evident attempt to rival Poe's 'The Bells': see Paul Surer, 'Explication de texte: "L'Azur"', *L'Information littéraire*, 19 (1967), 96.

[20] Created by 'Mon Dieu', 'Notre Père', in the *Parnasse contemporain* version, but by 'Notre dame', 'Ô Mère', in later versions.

first three stanzas there is a predominant rhythm of descent and bestowal, which derives largely from the inversion and enjambement of the first quatrain and is reinforced by the subsequent listing; while the fourth stanza, at the same time as it completes the list of flowers, initiates (in 'Monte rêveusement vers la lune qui pleure!') the counter-rhythm of worship and upward aspiration which characterizes the fifth and sixth stanzas. In this way 'Les Fleurs' presents the same rhythmic symmetry as 'Soupir', but in reverse.

Like 'Les Fenêtres', and in common with many of Mallarmé's later poems, this text turns principally on the theme of death and renewal. Parallels are drawn between the resolution of white light into the colours of flowers, the distillation of floral scent within a phial of perfume, and the revival of a fading poet which may attend the purification of everyday language within the sacred 'hosanna' that is a poem—the implicit parallel with the Christian resurrection being reinforced by the 'calices', framing the poem in stanzas 1 and 6, which suggest not only flowers but the chalice of the Eucharist. In the first stanza, the glory of creation is the glory of re-creation, thanks to the contrast between the 'vieil azur' and 'La terre jeune encore', and between 'la neige éternelle' and 'la terre [...] vierge de désastres': God's new world is somehow the more joyous for being created not *ex nihilo*, but out of monotone, ever-present elements. Similarly, the stimulus of incense (from the burning of an aromatic plant), the redolence of perfume (from decayed flowers), and the power of balsam to preserve a corpse all suggest the heightened value of a beauty born of death. Thanks to their mythological associations, some of the individual flowers mentioned in the poem connote the same theme: thus the Apollonian metamorphoses of Daphne and of Hyacinthus' blood are evoked by 'ce divin laurier' and 'L'hyacinthe', while 'le myrte' (itself used in perfume-making) is sacred to Venus as a symbol of love's renewal (as well as being, like the laurel, an emblem of poetic glory). The 'rose / Cruelle', by implicit reference to its thorns, evokes Christ's Passion, while in conjunction with the reference to Hérodiade, it further evokes the beheading of John the Baptist and his subsequent sanctification. The white lily, implicitly both 'vierge' and 'vivace' in anticipation of the famous later sonnet, is at once purely new and a perennial re-creation, like the swordlike 'glaïeul' with its swanlike flowers. Be they evergreens or perennials, the flowers of this poem share a common capacity, like so many 'aurores foulées' (l. 8), to salvage beauty from a mortal darkness and to offer balm to soothe the weary poet's soul.

The most remarkable feature of 'Les Fleurs' is the way in which it mirrors this process of death and renewal in its own linguistic procedures. For the opening line of the poem ('Des avalanches d'or du vieil azur, au jour') looms like the eternal sky over the new landscape of the poem, as the latter takes up each of the colours evoked in it and repeats them in different guises throughout the first four quatrains. Thus the white of 'avalanches' is echoed in 'neige éternelle des astres', 'vierge', 'cygnes', 'myrte' (and its 'éclair'), 'blancheur [...] des lys', and 'horizons pâlis'; the 'or' of the setting sun in the evening sky ('du vieil azur') recurs in 'fauve', 'laurier [...] Vermeil', 'Que rougit la pudeur des aurores [hom. 'or, or'] foulées', 'chair de la femme', 'rose', and 'sang'; and the 'vieil azur' itself returns in 'L'hyacinthe', 'des mers', and 'l'encens bleu'. The poem tells how the 'désastre' of the first sunset has been overcome by the star-rise and the survival of light in the spectrum of different-coloured flowers, while the poem shows how the 'désastre' of the poet's fading pursuit of the ideal ('le poète las que la vie étiole') is overcome by the careful constellation of words and the renewal of language in a poetic display of polysemic 'word-flowers'. The 'herbiers' of 'Prose (pour des Esseintes)' lie close to hand.

The beginning of the poem evokes the first day of creation and that moment of 'crisis' just as the sun is setting and the stars are becoming visible. The poem adopts this as a metaphor for language, poised on the edge of darkness as the bright light of referentiality fades and other patterns of significance begin to manifest themselves. Language is an 'in-between' place, the 'jardin de nos limbes!'; and in the use of the word 'limbes' we see Mallarmé beginning to cultivate polysemy in exactly the manner character-istic of his later work. For 'limbes' is not only the realm between life and death in which those who have not sinned linger temporarily before their accession to paradise, but also the plural of 'limbe', meaning the outer edge both of a star (or sun) and a calix, or corolla. 'Limbes' is thus a typically Mallarméan 'nexus' word, where the various threads of a text are laced together in one semantic knot (here the themes of death and resurrection, astral bodies, and flowers). Similarly, 'L'hyacinthe' may also be seen as a 'nexus' word, uniting as it does the three principal colours of this poem's spectrum and echoing its religious theme: homophonically anticipating the white 'lys' of l. 13, the name of this traditionally blue flower is also that of a semi-precious, reddish-yellow stone which gives off a blue haze when heated—like 'l'encens blue';[21] and in its homophonic saintliness it further anticipates the holiness of 'Notre dame' (in the final version) and the '*scint*illement des nimbes'.

And how appropriately the poem proclaims itself the 'hosannah du jardin de nos limbes!': for the 'Hosannah', deriving via Greek from the Hebrew words meaning 'Save me, I pray', is a Catholic hymn particularly associated with Palm Sunday, that horticultural foretaste of the Passion. The weary poet has been 'saved' by 'detaching' (cf. l. 3) words from the eternal sky of everyday language and by investing them with a luminiscence of suggestive-

---

[21] Robert, 'Hyacinthe', 2°. But cf. Larousse, 'Hyacinthe', and Littré, 'Hyacinthe', 2°, neither of which mentions a blue haze.

ness, a 'scintillement des nimbes'. By this detachment within a poetic context, these 'flower-words' are permitted to bloom in their full polysemic glory, to assume an aureola of enhanced significance, a halo (like St John's) betokening their sanctification as instruments of 'divine' music. The poem is a sacred 'cistre'[22] which takes the 'or' of l. 1, and provides it with 'l'écho par les mystiques soirs'[23] by repeating the sound 'or' not only in 'aurores' but in the penultimate rhyme of 'fort' and 'Mort'. And there is the moment of linguistic resurrection: the word 'or' at the very heart of 'Mort', beauty in death. This poem is not just a sequence of rather precious and religiose images, but a demonstration of the golden power of language. In 'Les Fleurs' the Sign of the Cross is joined by 'l'absente de tous bouquets'— and from the ashes of conventional 'sens', consumed in its 'encensoir', rises a nimbus of hazy brilliance, the poet's crowning glory.

[22] A stringed instrument like a lute or Apollo's lyre (or the mandora of 'Une dentelle s'abolit'). 'Cistre' also bears the trace of 'sistre', the ancient Egyptian sistrum (or kind of wire rattle) used in the worship of Isis, the mother goddess. Perhaps the 'Mère' addressed in the final version of the poem owes something to this homophony.
[23] In the final version 'l'écho par les célestes soirs'.

PART II

The Pursuit of Beauty
(1864–1874)

En un mot, le sujet de mon œuvre est la Beauté, et le sujet apparent n'est qu'un prétexte pour aller vers Elle. C'est, je crois, le mot de la Poésie.

(Letter to Villiers de L'Isle-Adam, 31 Dec. 1865)

'Mes principes actuels' (1864–1866): 'Don du poème' and 'Sainte'

Mon esprit se meut dans l'Eternel, et en a plusieurs frissons, si l'on peut parler ainsi de l'Immuable.

(Letter to Henri Cazalis, May 1866)

Mallarmé's own moment of crowning glory should have come on 12 May 1866 when ten of his poems were published, together with those of Henri Cazalis, in the eleventh issue of the *Parnasse contemporain*.[1] He had been eager to publish them in one group ever since he had copied them all (except 'Brise marine') into his 'Carnet de 1864' for the perusal of his friends.[2] But so rapid was the development in his poetic art that by the spring of 1866 these poems had come to seem like distant memories; and when revising them for publication he professed himself anxious, as if they had been composed several decades ago, to 'rester dans la manière de ces époques, en ne faisant que corriger ce qui, alors, comme maintenant, eût été fautif'.[3] To his dismay, especially as he had not been sent the proofs which he had requested, the poems were published with several errors (of punctuation and case size), and he promptly bought up as many copies as he could find in the shops of Tournon 'afin de les retirer de l'hostile clarté du grand jour'.[4]

---

[1] In the order 'Les Fenêtres', 'Le Sonneur', 'A celle qui est tranquille', 'Vere novo', 'L'Azur', 'Les Fleurs', 'Soupir', 'Brise marine', 'A un pauvre', and 'Épilogue (Las de l'amer repos...)'. When all eighteen issues of the *Parnasse contemporain* were bound together and published in book form later in the year, a number of additional poems appeared at the end of the volume, including Mallarmé's 'Tristesse d'été'.

[2] See *OC* (BM), 734–7.

[3] *Corr.*, i. 211. In this letter to Catulle Mendès, Mallarmé expresses his wish that the poems be printed with as much space between them as possible since they were not intended to be read 'd'une traite et comme cherchant une suite d'états de l'âme résultant les uns des autres, ce qui n'est pas, et gâterait le plaisir particulier de chacun'. Nevertheless he has arranged them so that 'les premiers servent d'initiateurs aux derniers', although he has placed 'A un pauvre' ['A un mendiant'] as the last but one 'ne sachant pas où le caser'.

[4] As he apologetically confessed to Cazalis himself (*Corr.*, i. 215).

Already he had been worried about publishing these poems since they did not conform to his 'principes actuels':[5] now their shoddy presentation further threatened his nascent reputation.

But what were these 'principes actuels'? Were they so different? He tells Cazalis in the same letter that 'aucun de ces poèmes n'[a] été conçu en vue de la Beauté, mais plutôt comme autant d'intuitives révélations de mon tempérament'; and this comment recalls his letter to Villiers de l'Isle-Adam on the previous New Year's Eve, in which he mentions 'mon poème entier d'"Hérodiade"':

J'ai le plan de mon œuvre, et sa théorie poétique qui sera celle-ci: 'donner les impressions les plus étranges, certes, mais sans que le lecteur n'oublie pour pas une minute la jouissance que lui procurera la beauté du poème'. En un mot, le sujet de mon œuvre est la Beauté, et le sujet apparent n'est qu'un prétexte pour aller vers Elle. C'est, je crois, le mot de la Poésie.[6]

Still conscious of Poe's doctrine that beauty is not a quality but an effect, Mallarmé here seems to be saying that this effect, a 'jouissance', will be achieved not so much by the poem's extra-textual referents as by the beauty of its own procedures.

By way of illustration of this theory, he sent Villiers a copy of 'un petit poème' dating from the beginning of 1865. At first entitled 'Le Jour' and then 'Le Poème nocturne', it was finally published (anonymously) as 'Don du poème' in *Paris Magazine* in December 1866.[7] Here again we see the mirror-structure which characterizes several of the poems published in *Le Parnasse contemporain*. Fourteen alexandrines in 'rimes plates' recall the Petrarchan sonnet by dividing thematically into groups of eight and six lines. In the simulated octave the poet describes his 'enfant d'une nuit d'Idumée!', the sorry poem-child of his nocturnal labours; in the simulated sestet he calls on his wife to suckle it into life as she has their daughter. There are evident parallels here with the image of breastfeeding in 'Brise marine' and the idea of dawn-induced despair in 'Las de l'amer repos...'; but where once the poet was a 'mendieur d'azur' (in 'Le Guignon') and 'hanté' by 'L'Azur! l'Azur' as it sounded in the angelus, now it is the poem itself which is said to have 'des lèvres que l'air du vierge azur affame'.[8] Thus it is in the explicitness of its self-reference that this poem differs from Mallarmé's previous 'mirror-poems', in which, as he tells Cazalis, he had 'intuitivement' revealed his reflexive poetic temperament. With 'Don du

---

[5] Ibid.

[6] *Corr.*, i. 193.

[7] See *Poésies*, ed. Bertrand Marchal (Paris, 1992), 202.

[8] For Marchal and others the poem is not self-referential but a biographical account of the experience of writing 'Hérodiade': see Marchal, *Lecture de Mallarmé*, 31. A. R. Chisholm, on the other hand, interprets it as referring to itself in '"Don du poème"', *Essays in French Literature*, 3 (1966), 33–7.

poème' (soon to be followed by 'Sainte' and the 'Ouverture' to 'Hérodiade') such conscious reflexivity constitutes the new way to beauty, Mallarmé's chosen path beyond *Le Parnasse contemporain* to the timeless summit of Mount Parnassus.

As in other poems of this period, the binary structure of 'Don du poème' supports an elaborate network of parallels and contrasts. In the first section the gradual advent of the dawn is evoked in successive, brief analogies: first, with a black bird and its pale, bleeding, featherless wing; then (implicitly) with a burning phoenix, as it looms through the window ('Par le verre brûlé d'aromates et d'or') whose 'carreaux' are still nevertheless 'glacés' and 'mornes'; and finally with a source of light sufficient to 'se jet[er] sur la lampe angélique', whereupon the conventional rosy-fingered dawn is figured dramatically as 'Palmes', palm-leaves of light holed by darkness (or vice versa), and the completed sunrise brings a 'solitude bleue et stérile' as the father-poet vainly tries to smile upon the relic of his 'nuit d'Idumée'. In the second section, these images are in turn transformed: the dawn into a nursing mother, the cold window-panes into 'vos pieds froids', the 'aile saignante et pâle' into her 'doigt fané', the 'Palmes' of spreading light into the 'blancheur sibylline' of her milk, and the blue, sterile solitude into the 'vierge azur' of which the poem-infant may drink.

The poem-infant's aspiration is figured in terms of a progression from the unwritten to the written, and from the unspoken to the musically expressed. Thus the dawn (which is the dawn of this poem, its birth) is at first 'déplumée', then a series of 'Palmes'; it looms through the 'verre/vers' which is 'brûlé d'aromates et d'or' in that its first two (phoenix-like) rhymes contain a homophone of 'humée' (cf. 'aromates') and then 'or' itself. As in 'Les Fenêtres' rhyme-schemes resemble windows: not the 'croisées' of crossed rhyme now but the straightforward 'carreaux' of 'rimes plates'. The undifferentiated whiteness of the 'lampe angélique' and the white, unmarked paper of the failed poet-father is successfully overcome when the word 'Palmes', denoting quill-like emblems of writing and symbols of glory, incorporates and rewrites the word 'lampe'—and follows it with an exclamation mark which figures the quill itself.[9] By following this line of reading, 'cette relique' comes to appear positive, a holy relic of the heroic, saintly father's nocturnal struggle; and the shudder of 'La solitude bleue' may be the shudder of a defeated enemy. 'Cette relique', or (hom.) 'sept reliques': for the poem is a quatorzain made up of seven couplets wherein rhyme, phoenix-like, is the resurrection of a phonetic relic.

In the second section of the poem, the written text aspires to musical expression: the 'poème-enfant', as etymological 'non-speaker', hungers with

---

[9] Cf. Mallarmé's use of this device in the final version of 'Le Pitre châtié' (l. 7), and his explicit comparison of an exclamation mark to a 'plumet' in the *Vers de circonstance* (CXXI: see OC (BM), 682).

its lips of rhyme for 'l'air du vierge azur'—not just air to breathe but a song to sing, the unsung song of the ideal. The 'poème-enfant' would be its own lullaby ('Ô la berceuse': hom. 'oh, là, berceuse'), an aural text (written by 'le doigt fané') fingering the strings of a 'viole' or the keys of a 'clavecin' as a mother presses her breast to express the whiteness of her milk. The 'blan-cheur sibylline' for which the 'poème-enfant' thirsts is the whiteness of a page that might express some sacred and inscrutable truth, 'le mystère dans les lettres'; but the final, unanswered question of the poem gives on to the white page itself, leaving us with a nursing mother and a lullaby that are each in their way a 'musicienne du silence'. The black ink of writing needs the whiteness of the page for the 'enfant' to find a 'voix' and for 'une nuit d'Idumée' to be replaced by the golden dawn of music, an 'Idée ou rythme entre des rapports'. The artful reflexivity permitted by poetic language is what saves the 'père essayant' from sterility: that is the 'don' which this 'poème' has itself bestowed upon him. For, as we know, in the mythical land of Idumaea the kings themselves give birth.[10]

This conception of poetry in terms of silent musical relationships receives full expression in 'Sainte', written towards the end of 1865. Originally entitled 'Sainte Cécile jouant sur l'aile d'un Chérubin (chanson et image anciennes)', it was first published only in November 1883 (as part of Verlaine's article on Mallarmé in Les Poètes maudits) and in a slightly revised form. But it is remarkable how slight these revisions are, and the 1865 version already displays all the subtle reflexivity of Mallarmé's mature style. Together with 'Le Démon de l'analogie' it demonstrates that the Mallarmé who was later to advocate 'la disparition élocutoire du poète, qui cède l'initiative aux mots'[11] had already ceded this initiative in practice during the mid-1860s.

In its origins 'Sainte' belongs with the 'poèmes de circonstance'. Written for Mme Cécile Brunet, it celebrates her name-day, the feast of St Cecilia, patron saint of music; and Mallarmé accordingly described it as 'un petit poème mélodique et fait surtout en vue de la musique'.[12] Mme Brunet's husband being a glasssmith as well as a poet, the 'croisées' of 'Les Fenêtres' and the 'carreaux' of 'Don du poème' now become the 'vitrage' of a stained-glass window. Four quatrains of octosyllabics in 'rimes croisées' are ar-ranged with perfect symmetry: the first two stanzas enumerate the objects surrounding the Saint in her window, while the second two evoke her specific pose, finger placed on the harp-like wing of a cherubic angel. The intricate symmetries of this poem have often been admired,[13] each line of

---

[10] See Denis Saurat, 'La Nuit d'Idumée', Nouvelle Revue française, 1 Dec. 1952, Chisholm, '"Don du poème"', 34, and Charles Chassé, Les Clefs de Mallarmé (Paris, 1954), 75.

[11] 'Crise de vers', OC, 366.

[12] Corr., i. 181.

[13] See especially Hans Staub, 'Le Mirage interne des mots', Cahiers de l'Association inter-nationale des études françaises, 27 (1975), 275–88. For a résumé of the critical reception of this

stanza 1 being precisely mirrored in the equivalent line of stanza 2, with 'Le santal vieux' and 'Le Livre vieux' of each stanza then being recalled as absences ('sans le vieux santal / Ni le vieux livre') in the final stanza. In anticipation of many of Mallarmé's later poems, words seem to expand and contract, disintegrate and reassemble, before our eyes, as (for example) 'santal' is echoed in 'Sainte, recelant'[14] and 'Viole' is recalled in 'vol du soir'. But above all the binary structure of the poem serves to reinforce a central theme of substitution: the old sandalwood viola and the old score of the Magnificat are explicitly superfluous to the Saint's musical performance at the end; the viola, flute, and mandora have been replaced by a harp-like wing, and vespers and compline by some sacred ritual of silence.[15]

The reflexivity of the poem turns on the fact that the principal referent of 'Sainte' in l. 5 is the poem itself, a device enhanced by the shortened title of the final version and the change from 'une Sainte' to 'la Sainte' in the relevant line. The poem itself is a new St Cecilia ('Cé-cile' being audible in the symmetrically placed penultimate syllables of the first and last lines: 'recélant', 'silence'[16]); and as this poem-saint performs its novel music of silence, it is framed in a 'vitrage d'ostensoir', the window of the poem's stanzaic structure. As 'ostensoir' this structure displays the 'hostie' of a language that is being consecrated in the ritual of a poetic act, words become the Christlike 'victim' of a death (of their conventional, referential function) and a resurrection.

More specifically, this poem-saint rejects one view of sacred art and celebrates another. Two 'old' ideas are dismissed: that music is exclusively a matter of sound, and that sacred texts are sacred (like the Magnificat or the Bible) because of *what* they say. Two 'new' ideas are proposed instead: that the power of music derives from its structure, from the 'rapports' created between notes (and 'present' therefore in the silence between the notes), and that sacred texts are sacred because of *how* they say what they say. This supersession of euphony is suggested by the image of musical instruments losing their former gilt, while the rejection of explicit, 'referential' sacred texts is figured in 'Le livre qui se déplie', unfolding and thereby destroying the 'mystère' of its sacred message (an idea reinforced by 'étalant' in the final version).

---

poem, see Marchal, *Lecture de Mallarmé*, 91–6: Marchal argues for a reflexive reading but without analysing the poem in detail.

[14] In the final version 'santal' is echoed in 'Est la Sainte pâle, étalant', which removes the repetition of 'recelant'.

[15] The substitution of one kind of music for another has been discussed by Jean-Claude Carron, '*Sainte* de Mallarmé: Poétique et musiques', *Kentucky Romance Quarterly*, 26 (1979), 133–41.

[16] In the final version. In the 1865 version similar symmetry is achieved between the ends of the first and last lines by the reversal of the last two syllables in each (from '[re]ce-lant' to '[si]len-ce').

Also superseded is the simplistic 'fenêtre' of representational art, here replaced by a 'vitrage d'ostensoir', the poem itself, in which the 'vers/verre' displays the visual and aural power of reflexive language. The inadequate 'fenêtre' is 'recélant', in that it both contains these emblems of traditional music and liturgy and yet also conceals them by not permitting the full potential of the words ('santal', 'viole', 'flûte', 'mandore') to be made manifest; while the 'vitrage' of reflexive language is able, especially in rhyme, to 'regild' and 'refold' the faded sandalwood and the opened book by exhibiting such potential. Thus the gold is restored via the rhymes of 'dédore' and 'mandore', and the folds by the rhymes of 'déplie' and 'complie'—'or' and 'pli' being made to seem closely parallel by the fact that the other rhymes in stanzas 1 and 2 both repeat '-lant'. The mirror-effect of the poem is such that the echoing of this repeated /lɑ̃/ in the rhymes of stanzas 3 and 4 ('l'ange', 'phalange', 'balance', 'silence') suggests that 'or' is echoed in 'ostensoir' and 'soir' (as it visually is) and 'pli' in 'santal' and 'instrumental' (as it thematically is).

The self-displaying power of the poem is particularly marked in the third stanza with its complex homophonies. The poem's structure is likened to an angel's wing and a harp, the implied feathers and strings being the lines of the poem. That this is a poem in which words must be heard is proclaimed in the phrases 'une harpe par l'ange' (hom. 'une harpe parle, ange') and 'Offerte avec son' (in the final version 'Formée avec son')—that is, a harp-poem offered or made with sound. The 'livre vieux' of literal reading has been replaced by a 'son vol du soir', a sound-volume for evening celebration, a vesperal 'Magnificat' welcoming the sunset of merely functional language and the Annunciation of a new poetic art, the future offspring of this 'Sainte' who is now the Virgin Mary, she who sings the 'Magnificat'. And who or what shall play this new instrument of the harp-like wing?—'la délicate phalange / Du doigt'. A finger, of course, and a finger echoing the 'célestes phalanges', or heavenly hosts, to whom this one angel belongs; but also a phalanx. For phalanxes are formations arranged in squares in multiples of four up to sixteen: the poem, a jointed composition of two eight-line octosyllabic units, is the 'délicate phalange' that plays itself by 'balancing' on its own 'plumage instrumental', on its 'plus mage instrument, mental'. If it turns out to be a 'musicienne du silence', that is because so many of the poem's beauties are implicit, like sacred mysteries enfolded in the white spaces between its words. Like 'Don du poème', 'Sainte' announces the birth of a poem-infant; but this time, by creating an instrument 'par l'ange' for 'la phalange', the poem has, if only by its rhymes, provided the 'langes' in which the infant shall be swaddled.

2

'Anecdotes ou poèmes' (1864–1868)[1]

quelques poèmes en prose [...] anciens et puérils.
(Letter to Henri Cazalis, Oct. 1867)

In both 'Don du poème' and 'Sainte' it is thus possible to see a Mallarmé who has moved beyond 'autant d'intuitives révélations de mon tempérament' and acceded to the manner of writing outlined to Villiers in which 'le sujet de mon œuvre est la Beauté, et le sujet apparent n'est qu'un prétexte pour aller vers Elle'. In the short term the epitome of this new manner of writing will be 'Hérodiade', but before considering this poem it may be instructive to consider some of Mallarmé's prose poems from this period and to examine the emergence within them of his new 'principes'. Such an examination is problematic since he revised them for later publication and in some cases the earliest extant versions of texts known to have been first drafted in 1864 date from at least three years later. Nevertheless they provide substantial evidence that he was already consciously aiming at reflexivity in these texts as in the verse poems of the same period.

In each of the first two prose poems published by Mallarmé one can see that the 'sujet apparent' is closely linked to the question of achieving beauty through poetic art, and that Poe's principle of carefully wrought composition is no less operative here than in the verse poems written during the same period. 'Pauvre Enfant pâle' (originally entitled 'La Tête', later also 'Fusain') and 'Plainte d'automne' (originally entitled 'L'Orgue de Barbarie') were both published in July 1864 and dedicated to Baudelaire. The former consists of eight paragraphs preceded by a title and followed by an exclamation ('Oh! pauvre petite tête') which balances the title and completes the structure of the poem by recalling the opening words of the first and fifth paragraphs. For the poem falls into two halves, each beginning with a direct apostrophe describing the singing urchin: 'Pauvre enfant pâle', 'Petit

---

[1] 'Anecdotes ou poèmes' is the title under which Mallarmé presented his prose poems in *Divagations*.

homme'. In their development of the central subject the two halves imitate the structure of 'rimes embrassées' and 'rimes croisées' respectively. Thus the first and fourth paragraphs mirror each other ('tue-tête' and 'chanson' becoming 'ta tête nue' and 'complainte'), while the second and third also reflect one another ('tu chantes fatalement', 'tu chantes [...] pour manger';[2] 'qui [...] travailles pour soi', 'tu travailles pour toi'; 'l'assurance tenace d'un petit homme', 'vêtements déteints faits comme ceux d'un homme'). In the second half (where the patterning is albeit less marked), the fifth and seventh paragraphs are particularly linked by the idea of the boy's head finally parting company with his body, while the sixth and eighth contrast the failure of people to give alms to the boy with his destiny as the one who will pay for the shortcomings of others.

Thematically, this prose poem belongs with others by Mallarmé which follow the example of Baudelaire's *Le Spleen de Paris* in taking the underprivileged or the decrepit as their subject and drawing a parallel between such inadequacies and the poet's own splenetic inability to attain the poetic ideal. Accordingly, the principal thrust of the text would seem to be the pathos which such a sorry sight evokes, a pathos lent sharper edge by the suggestion that the orphan's deprivation will turn him into a criminal. But the insistent sound-patterning of the poem may begin to suggest a form of word association at work here, as the terms of the opening question 'pourquoi crier à tue-tête' begin to echo at once in 'rue', 'aiguë', and 'tu'; and when in the fifth paragraph (the symmetrical counterpart of the first) we read 'quand, après avoir crié longtemps dans les villes, tu auras fait un crime? car[3] un crime n'est pas bien difficile à faire', it may sound as if 'crime' and 'difficile' have been 'provoked' by the words 'crié' and 'villes' more than by any conscious 'thought' on the poet's part. Indeed language seems to take over at this point, and subsequent published versions enhance this effect by having the paragraph tail away inscrutably,[4] so that the final version comes to read: '[...] à faire, va, il suffit d'avoir du courage après le désir, et tels qui...' In the first version the /i/ and /l/ of 'crié' and 'villes' (introduced previously in 'Petit homme, qui sait si elle [...]' at the beginning of the paragraph) already seem to reverberate of their own accord; while in the final version the possible homophonic presence of 'il suffit d'avoir du cou, rage après le désir' may even be prompted by the image of the boy's neck straining after musical perfection.

---

[2] Unless otherwise stated, all examples are common to the 1864 text and to later versions. Here 'tu chantes avec acharnement pour manger' (1864) later becomes 'tu chantes pour manger, avec acharnement'.

[3] 'Car' is omitted in later versions.

[4] The original end of the fifth paragraph reads: 'il suffit d'avoir une main au bout de son désir'; in the 1867 version, this is amended to 'après son désir, et nous qui désirons...' (see OC, 1558).

Even without this last suggestion, it is difficult not to see in the 1864 version of 'Pauvre Enfant pâle' an anticipation of the 'Cantique de saint Jean', where the severance of head from body becomes a symbol of the purification of language by means of its severance from functional reference. Here, as the boy sings at the top of his voice, it is as though he will undergo an involuntary decapitation; and his predicted tragic end will seem like a proto-Christian sacrifice of self to redeem others ('tu paieras pour moi, pour ceux qui *vaudront* moins que moi'[5]). As in 'Sainte', it begins to look as if the principal referent of 'Pauvre enfant pâle' addressed in the first paragraph is this prose poem itself. Bereft of classical parentage ('As-tu jamais eu un père? Tu n'as pas même une vieille'), it is a new genre ('enfant') and yet without the naïvety or innocence of the new ('Petit homme'); it is a low form of art fit only to keep company (as in Baudelaire) with the world of the fairground and to live among down-and-outs; and it offers a strident, insolent 'chanson' that will go unheard and unrewarded in higher places. 'Nous te verrons alors dans les journaux':[6] which is just where 'Pauvre Enfant pâle' was published, in the obscure pages of *La Semaine de Cusset et de Vichy*. But this poor, pale child of a prose poem offers, as we have seen, the spectacle of sound taking over from sense, of language threatening ('un air qui devient menaçant') to break free and to commit a 'crime' against the conventional referential function of language.[7] 'Et probablement tu vins au monde pour cela, et c'est pour cela que tu chantes dès maintenant': this prose poem came into the world as a display of contingent language, of probability; but 'tu chantes, dés' suggests that thanks to Mallarmé's art, words have become the dice in a new and superior game of chance. There is no knowing what they may say next.[8]

In 'Plainte d'automne', published with 'Pauvre Enfant pâle' the autonomous power of language is once more at issue. The strong narrative and apparently autobiographical elements in this prose poem have diverted attention from its reflexive features and from a textual 'lesson' which plainly anticipates 'Le Démon de l'analogie'. Again Mallarmé creates an elaborate binary structure, consisting here of two paragraphs of almost equal length. In the first the poet describes his happiness in solitude, with only a cat and 'un des derniers auteurs de la décadence latine' for company;[9] in the second, his unexpected delight at hearing a barrel-organ playing in the

---

[5] Later 'valent moins que moi'.

[6] 'Alors' later omitted.

[7] 'Crime' will have this sense in 'Sonnet allégorique de lui-même': see below, Part III, Ch. 2.

[8] 'tu chantes' is replaced by 'tu jeûnes' in 1867, but the final version reads: 'Tu vins probablement au monde vers cela et tu jeûnes dès maintenant'. Contingent language is now said to be consciously arranged as 'vers, cela, et tu'—no longer just prose, but 'vers' and with all the silent, hidden, musical interconnections which the text itself displays.

[9] As with 'Pauvre Enfant pâle', all quotations from 'Plainte d'automne' are common to earlier and later versions unless otherwise stated.

avenue below. Various analogies between the two paragraphs suggest that in some way the second is a repeat of the first: the absent Maria (his late sister, the Virgin, religious faith itself?) figures once and mysteriously in each paragraph before appearing as the last word of the text;[10] 'seul', used four times in the first seven lines, is recalled towards the end,[11] establishing a strong parallel between the solitary poet and the barrel-organ playing (he would like to think) of its own accord; the sunset reflected in his 'carreaux' becomes the 'crépuscule du souvenir' in which he listens to the barrel-organ 'sous ma fenêtre'; and his preference for the 'derniers jours alanguis de l'été' is recalled as the organ 'chanta languissamment'.

More remarkable, however, is the link between the two paragraphs, for it seems to derive from verbal association alone. The poet's literary taste is, as he states at the end of the first paragraph, for 'la poésie agonisante des derniers moments de Rome, tant, cependant, qu'elle ne respire aucunement l'approche rajeunissante des Barbares'; then, as we learn at the beginning of the second, while reading 'un de ces chers poèmes', he hears 'un orgue de Barbarie'. It is as if the organ and the attendant street-scene have been called up by the word 'Barbares' itself; and by its sound alone, since the final words of the first paragraph ('qui ne bégaie point le latin enfantin des premières proses chrétiennes') specifically displays the etymological roots of 'Barbares' as if to destroy in advance any illusion of cognate relationship.[12] And yet the notion of senseless repetition at the root of 'barbare' carries over into the description of the 'orgue de Barbarie'—both explicitly, in the reference to its 'air suranné, banal', and in the very words with which it is described: '*murmur*ait', '*air* [. . .] vulg*aire*' (my emphases). As the poet says in the final version, it is 'L'instrument des tristes, oui, vraiment':[13] where 'oui' also has the force of 'ouï'. When truly heard, the words 'orgue de Barbarie' themselves reveal the source of the instrument's own capacity to inspire sadness (in the poet, but not 'au cœur des faubourgs'): i.e. its mournful repetitiveness. And yet, the poet asks, why does this repetitiveness (now evoked in the etymologically suggestive word 'ritournelle') have the power to enter his soul? His answer may be inferred from his final decision not to toss a coin out of the window 'de peur de me déranger et de m'apercevoir que l'instrument ne chantait pas seul': what he savours is the

---

[10] Early versions end with the phrase 'oh! l'orgue de Barbarie, la veille de l'automne, à cinq heures, sous les peupliers jaunis, Maria!' (see OC, 1556). This was presumably dropped because of its unduly rhetorical tone, but as it stands it provides several reminders of the beginning of the prose poem and so enhances its symmetry.

[11] As the word preceding the 'envoi' quoted in the previous note, it thus became the last word in the final version.

[12] 'Barbare' derives from the apparent stuttering of foreigners speaking an incomprehensible language. An 'orgue de Barbarie', on the other hand, derives from the name of its Italian inventor, Barberi.

[13] Earlier versions have '*oh!* l'instrument des tristes *par excellence!*' (OC, 1556).

sound of an instrument playing itself, this is what makes him (as he has already stated) 'désespérément rêver'.

In this way the 'orgue de Barbarie' becomes a metaphor for the autonomous power of language to repeat sounds in an apparently meaningless and yet potentially significant, 'musical' pattern. The poet is plunged into desperate surmise at the prospect of his own loss of writerly control, and yet he would have it no other way. For, as the first paragraph has already revealed, sensitivity to words and their power is an essential part of him: 'Par *seul*, j'entends sans un être matériel', 'j'ai aimé tout ce qui se résumait en ce mot: chute'. If the 'instrument' of language is playing 'seul', therefore, it may yet have 'un compagnon mystique, un esprit': language is to the poet as he himself is to the cat he caresses. And if he likes the word 'chute', this is doubtless not only because it connotes decadence, the fall of Rome, and even the Fall, but because of the homophonic 'chut!' which it contains: an injunction to the silence in which the 'rapports' concealed within language may finally be heard. His own prose poem, a barbarous thing that repeats itself and speaks in the idiom of a new and foreign genre, may be a superior 'orgue de Barbarie' (its original title): eschewing repetitiveness that might resemble the stammering 'latin enfantin des premières proses chrétiennes', it aspires to the status of a new musical instrument. The piano may 'éga[yer]' and the violin 'ouv[rir] les portes vermeilles où gazouille l'Espérance', but the prose poem as barrel-organ occupies an invisible place beyond the window, the place where 'Maria a passé [...] avec des cierges, une dernière fois'.[14] That lost (linguistic) virginal purity which she perhaps symbolizes is now recovered in the prose poem itself; and the 'chute' of language into prosaic functionality is redeemed, at the emblematic hour of sunset and as summer fades into autumn, by this newly penned 'Plainte d'automne'.

The next three prose poems published by Mallarmé probably date also from 1864, and two of them imply a similar ambition to endow the new genre of the prose poem with the reflexivity of 'mirror-poems' like 'Les Fenêtres' and 'Soupir'.[15] 'Frisson d'hiver' adopts the quasi-stanzaic form attempted in 'Pauvre Enfant pâle',[16] refining it by the addition of an interpolated parenthetical refrain which changes in significance rather like the repeated 'Nevermore' of Poe's 'The Raven'. In 'Pauvre Enfant pâle' and 'Plainte d'automne' the 'mixed' register of the prose poem (caught

---

[14] In the final version, the piano 'scintille' and the violin 'donne aux fibres déchirées la lumière', both thus resembling the stars to which Maria has possibly departed ('Orion, Altaïr, et toi, verte Vénus').

[15] 'Frisson d'hiver' (originally entitled 'Causerie d'hiver') and 'La Pipe' appeared in the *Revue des lettres et des arts* on 20 Oct. 1867 and 12 Jan. 1868 respectively. 'L'Orphelin' first appeared in the *Revue des lettres et des arts* on 24 Nov. 1867, but was later substantially revised and published as 'Réminiscence' in *Pages* (1891) and later *Divagations* (1897).

[16] Suzanne Bernard sees a debt to Aloysius Bertrand's *Gaspard de la nuit*: see *Le Poème en prose de Baudelaire jusqu'à nos jours* (Paris, 1959), 259.

between everyday banality and 'high' poetic art) is symbolized in the singing urchin and the poignant tune of the barrel-organ; here the self-referential 'croisées' of 'Les Fenêtres' now serve as both the scene of a wife's domestic neglect and the very image of the poem's criss-cross structure. 'Frisson d'hiver' turns on the contrast between the old and the new, and the uneasiness of the poet's attempt to lend the novelty of the prose poem an antique air is mirrored in the tense (and one-sided) conjugal conversation which oscillates between frank exchange and poetic reverie. The poet's fanciful thought of the naked female forms once reflected in the 'glace de Venise' provokes wifely protest, which in turn is met by sly reference to undusted corners and the implication that the lady of the house might not have the energy to give new objects the worn look in which they both delight. He, however, is doing just that as he weaves his own thematic cobwebs across the 'vitres' of his reflexive art.

In anticipation of 'Le Phénomène futur', the poet is here a 'Montreur de choses Passées' as he itemizes their belongings and, with playful self-reference, accedes to his wife's desire 'qu'en un de mes poèmes apparussent ces mots "la grâce des choses fanées"'. Not only the words appear[17] but the referent too, as he causes the time-bound, anecdotal colouring of the prose poem to 'fade' into a timeless reverie about time. Opening with 'Cette pendule de Saxe', the poem ends with the poet asking his partner to put down her 'vieil almanach allemand' and listen to him: 'je te parlerai de nos meubles...' Since the poem itself carries out this intention, it comes almost to resemble a miniature *A la recherche du temps perdu*, ending as they both do on how they each came to be begun. In this case the Saxon clock and German almanac (a book of time) are to be replaced by the poet's own book of hours ('je te parlerai pendant des heures'), and the Venetian mirror by the 'vitres usées' of a poem in which verbal cobwebs, long in the making, may linger undisturbed for all eternity. Alas, just as 'ma sœur au regard de jadis' ignored the cobwebs, she ignores the poem ('Tu es distraite?'), and the poet now seems like the 'instrument qui chante seul' of 'Plainte d'automne' as his musing peters out in a silent shiver, a 'Frisson d'hiver' and a 'frisson, dit vers'. A sound-shiver of words rippling across the chilly surface of the page ('profonde comme une froide fontaine'): 'qui s'y est miré?'—'un fantôme nu', he hopes, will have 'baigné dans cette eau le péché de sa beauté'. Once again, 'le sujet de mon œuvre est la Beauté'.

If 'Frisson d'hiver' constitutes an attempt to create a timeless container for time past, so—and even more so—does 'La Pipe'.[18] For a 'madeleine' and a cup of Proustian tea, substitute a pipe not smoked since the poet left the shores of England: 'et tout Londres, Londres tel que je le vécus en entier

---

[17] As they do in 'Symphonie littéraire' (*OC*, 263). Cf. Bernard, *Le Poème en prose*, 256–7, who presumes that 'Frisson d'hiver' was written after the first version of 'Symphonie littéraire'.
[18] Although written in 1864, the earliest extant version of this prose poem dates from 1868.

à moi seul, il y a un an, est apparu'. Strongly autobiographical though this prose poem may be, it shows again Mallarmé's taste for symmetry and extended analogy; and it may not be too fanciful to see a parallel between the pipe and the prose poem itself. While the text consists of one single paragraph, the sentences are carefully constructed so that the poem begins and ends with two short sentences of exactly the same length. Within this frame stand four sentences: the middle two evoke aural and olfactory memories and narrate the central drama of London's 'resurrection', while the second and fifth sentences of the poem, longer and more syntactically complex than the third and fourth, evoke primarily visual memories and establish a parallel between the poet forgetting his work in the joy of rediscovering his pipe and the poet saying goodbye to the woman he loves. Overriding this parallel is the implicit parallel between the pipe and the woman herself: the former is described as 'cette délaissée' and 'la fidèle amie', while the latter is 'ma pauvre bien-aimée errante' wearing one of the straw-hats discarded by 'les riches dames'. The poet should no more have abandoned his pipe than let his beloved go; in recovering the pipe he has recovered their common past.

And the pipe that is this poem, crammed with the tobacco of the past and lit by the flame of involuntary memory, gives the lie to the wistful final sentence: 'Autour de son cou s'enroulait le terrible mouchoir qu'on agite en se disant adieu pour toujours.' The scrolling kerchief resembles the smoke rings rising from this pipe which has reunited the lovers in memory. Throughout the poem specific features of the pipe itself (and the cigarettes it replaces) are responsible for the particular memories evoked. Thus the colour and components of a cigarette may have prompted images of summer and 'le passé qu'illuminent les feuilles bleues de soleil, les mousselines', while the smoke and embers of a pipe call up images of London fog and sooty interiors, of scrawny black cats and maids with red arms. Smoke and ash in turn prompt memories of a steamer and his beloved's 'longue robe terne couleur de la poussière des routes'. Like an urchin singing or a barrel-organ grinding out its tune, the pipe is a quotidian and filthy object revealing beauty within its scrolling, insubstantial vapours, the poetry within the prose.

'L'Orphelin' is much less patterned and reflexive than either 'Frisson d'hiver' or 'La Pipe', which may be why it was so thoroughly revised and condensed. Parallels with 'Pauvre Enfant pâle' suggest that the eponymous orphan wandering round a fairground 'cherchant ma famille sur la terre' may be emblematic of the parentless prose poem mourning its status but discovering that progenitors can be a ridiculous liability. Beauty is still the object of the orphan's quest, but is glimpsed only in a 'tartine de fromage blanc' with its implausible evocation of 'les lys ravis, la neige, la plume des cygnes, les étoiles, et toutes les blancheurs sacrées des poètes'.

More clearly illustrative of Mallarmé's 'principes actuels' are the two remaining prose poems from this period: 'Le Phénomène futur' and 'La Pénultième' (later retitled 'Le Démon de l'analogie'). Although the two paragraphs of 'Le Phénomène futur' are widely divergent in length, a symmetrical structure is achieved by the parallels between the beginning and end of the poem. The first part (preceding the 'boniment') describes a future sunset and the falling darkness, followed by the lighting up of a 'réverbère' which 'ravive' the faces of the crowd; the final paragraph evokes the aftermath of their vision, the dark incomprehension of some, followed by poets 'sentant se rallumer leurs yeux éteints' and hurrying home to their 'lampe'. In the middle of the poem a more subtle contrast is suggested between the 'boniment' of the 'Montreur de choses Passées', describing the beauty on display within his tent, and the 'espace blanc' between the paragraphs during which the vision of beauty is wordlessly enjoyed by the participants.

In this early version of the Mallarméan 'drame solaire',[19] living 'natural' beauty is replaced by the beauty of reflexive artifice. The onset of this future darkness is characterized by dehumanization, sterility, and unease. Human beings are scarcely human, having lost their identity in the crowd, and their only function ('épouses', 'maris') is doomed by sin and sickness to the failure that is the human race's proximate extinction. Nature itself is more human: and its insistent personification reads like the death knell of the pathetic fallacy and a whole tradition of representational art. The sky is leaving, dressed in purple rags, the river is sleeping, the trees are bored, and the sun utters a final cry of despair. The human condition is summarized in the 'silence inquiet de tous les yeux suppliant là-bas le soleil'. Redemption comes in the form of words, the patter of a 'Montreur de choses Passées' that is this prose poem. No painter has been able to represent this 'Femme d'autrefois', and when non-poets see her, they are either uncomprehending or simply 'navrés', weeping 'larmes résignées' in mutual recognition of their impotence. But the wordsmith, be he fairground orator or eager poet, can be the guardian of beauty within the 'maison en toile' that is textuality. Poetic language must abandon the exterior world of nature and cultivate an inner sanctum free from the ravages of time (the 'feuillage blanchi (de la poussière du temps plutôt que celle des chemins)'), a place in which beauty is 'pré-servée à travers les ans par la science souveraine', the sovereign science of poetic art. In the referential penumbra following the sunset of representa-tion, this prose poem constitutes the 'réverbère' itself, an instrument of 'reverberation' or reflection in which (as in the word itself) 'rêve', 'vers', 'verbe', 'ère', and 'air' combine to produce the 'Rythme' (a 'rythme entre des

---

[19] Written in Dec. 1864 but published in *La République des lettres* only on 20 Dec. 1875 (the earliest extant version).

rapports') by which the intoxicated poets are haunted as they return home at the end. 'Maint réverbère attend le crépuscule': like 'Maint rêve vespéral' in 'Ses purs ongles...', the written text is a manual dream, a hand-reflector, in which language shimmers with its original glory ('Quelque folie, originelle et naïve, une extase d'or') and recovers the pristine creative potential symbolized here by the 'Femme d'autrefois'. Her 'seins levés [...] pleins d'un lait éternel' and her 'jambes lisses qui gardent le sel de la mer première' both suggest the timeless, unsullied fertility which is denied to mere 'épouses' and 'maris' but which may be achieved by the poet. As such this 'Femme d'autrefois' is a 'Phénomène futur': for she symbolizes a new poetic art in which the phenomenon that art represents shall be language itself, 'le fait-nomen futur'.

3

'La Pénultième' (c.1865–1874)

La phrase revint, virtuelle [...]

'Le Démon de l'analogie' is commonly assumed to date from 1864 but, as Barbara Johnson has noted, there is no clear evidence that any version existed before Mallarmé sent one to Villiers de l'Isle-Adam in 1867.[1] This text has rightly attracted much critical attention as a prefiguration of Mallarmé's allegedly 'later' aesthetic,[2] but it may by now be evident that its focus on the autonomous power of language is not an isolated or atypical feature of Mallarmé's writing at this period. Nevertheless, borrowing from Poe's 'The Imp of the Perverse' the central idea of a pedestrian pursued by words, it gives a particularly clear account of the way in which Mallarmé now sees language as generating a world of its own. Language is the event, and 'Le Démon de l'analogie' offers an allegorical account of how a poet finds his poetic voice in the face of language's autonomy.

[1] *Défigurations*, 199. See *Corr.*, i. 260 n. 2, for Villiers's comments. In a letter to Cazalis on 7 Oct. 1867 Mallarmé mentions sending Villiers 'quelques poèmes en prose [...] anciens et puérils' for publication in his *Revue des lettres et des arts*: that is (by the titles under which they were published there) 'Causerie d'hiver', 'Pauvre Enfant pâle', 'L'Orgue de Barbarie', 'L'Orphelin', and 'La Pipe' (*Corr.*, i. 262). It is doubtful whether 'La Pénultième' can be classified as 'ancien' and 'puéril'. Although in the spring of 1865 Mallarmé defines the poet as 'un instrument qui résonne sous les doigts des diverses sensations' (*Corr.*, i. 151 (dated '[janvier 1865?]'); *DSM*, vi. 265 (dated '[fin Mars–début Avril 1865]')), the imagery shared with 'Sainte' (Nov. 1865) and the 'Ouverture' to 'Hérodiade' (1866) suggest a date of composition later than 1864, so that perhaps (along with 'L'Orphelin' and 'Le Phénomène futur'?) it was one of the three 'singuliers poèmes en prose' on which Mallarmé was working in the spring of 1866 (see *Corr.*, i. 216). In any case the earliest extant version dates from the first publication of the work in *La Revue du monde nouveau* on 1 Mar. 1874, where (as on several subsequent occasions) it bore the title 'La Pénultième'. 'Le Démon de l'analogie' is the title by which Villiers refers to it in 1867, and this was later adopted by Mallarmé for its appearance in *Pages* (1891) and in *Divagations* (1897).

[2] For a résumé of the critical reception of this work, see Johnson, *Défigurations*, 193–211, especially 195–202. In her excellent account Johnson takes 'Le Démon de l'analogie' as a demonstration of unreadability (of the phrase 'La Pénultième est morte'). To deny this is to deny the penultimate word of the text itself ('inexplicable'): thus 'tout lecteur [...] qui tente de dire *à quoi rime* un texte, ne peut qu'y juxtaposer [...] le vers rompu de sa propre lecture' (211).

This poet leaves his 'appartement' (the 'apartness' of silence perhaps and 'non-insertion' in language) and has the sensation of being an 'instrument', over the strings of which an 'aile' is 'glissant' like the 'délicate phalange / Du doigt' which 'balance / Sur le plumage instrumental' of 'Sainte'. Comparable also with the barrel-organ which the narrator of 'Plainte d'automne' would like to imagine 'singing' of its own accord, the poet is a passive linguistic instrument being played upon by words; and, like the urchin in 'Pauvre Enfant pâle', he will spend much of this prose poem, as it were, singing his head off, straining to hit the right note.[3] Having glided over musical strings, the wing (of words come randomly to mind) becomes a 'voice' uttering the phrase 'La Pénultième est morte'; and yet, for all the contingency of its arrival, this voice's utterance has achieved formal perfection at a stroke. The enjambement severing 'La Pénultième' from 'Est morte' ensures that 'nul' becomes itself the penultimate syllable of the line (since the apparent penultimate syllable 'ti' is suppressed, indeed rendered 'morte', by the prosodic rules governing diaeresis); so that the phrase 'La Pénultième / Est morte' becomes an ambiguous reflexive statement: '[la syllable] "nul" / Est morte', or 'nul[le] est morte'. Similarly, the enjambement ensures that the sense of 'Est morte' is reinforced by its function as a 'rejet', where it hangs 'en le vide de signification': empty of significance (who is dead? is anyone dead?) and yet also signifying the severed 'vide' of death itself.

The poet's response is one of re-cognition: a rediscovery of language's reflexive power as he recognizes 'nul' as the 'corde tendue de l'instrument', because the tautness and 'playability' of the musical instrument that is language is exemplified by the pivotal role of 'nul' in the semantic balancing act just displayed. His return to language is like memory revisiting the past, and this 'visit' has occurred 'certainement' in that linguistic necessity has been achieved at once (and in a 'vers', which contrasts with the apparently contingent prose by which it is surrounded). Accordingly, the poet smiles, 'le doigt sur l'artifice du mystère': he has his finger on this particular piece of linguistic cleverness, just as no doubt he is placing his finger to his smiling lips in a playful gesture of confidentiality. For his lips will soon be the instrument whereby the mystery of language expresses itself. But for the moment he wishes to understand this phrase further ('de vœux intellectuels une spéculation différente'), and back it comes, 'virtuelle', full of possibilities: stripped of former associations with 'plume' and 'rameau' (connoted by the first syllable of 'Pénultième') and now heard as pure (golden) sound ('dorénavant à travers la voix entendue'), the phrase becomes fully auton-

---

[3] Roger Dragonetti compares the first paragraph of 'Le Démon de l'analogie' to a severed head in his cogent Structuralist reading of the text as an allegory of the language-user's doomed quest for origins: see '"Le Démon de l'analogie" di Mallarmé', *Strumenti critici*, 8 (1974), 214–30; revised, translated, and reprinted in Roger Dragonetti, *Études sur Mallarmé*, ed. Wilfried Smekens (Ghent, 1992).

omous: 'elle s'articula seule, vivant de sa personnalité' (again like the barrel-organ). Freed from the constraints of reference the phrase can also be simply looked at, to see how it might appear on the page, perhaps without en-jambement ('la lisant en fin de vers') and thus as the hemistich of an alexandrine; and aurally it can be 'tried on', as pure sound, by a poet temporarily unconcerned by what it might mean ('l'adaptant à mon parler'). The visual gap of the enjambement leads him to try reciting it with a silence after 'Pénultième', but the 'artifice' of 'nul' is lost without the 'Est morte' which follows, and the continuous falling cadence achieved by the original voice ('sur un ton descendant') is interrupted ('la corde de l'instrument, si tendue en l'oubli sur le son *nul*, cassait sans doute et j'ajoutais en manière d'oraison: "Est morte"'): the sound 'nul' ceases to be resonant because it is now 'sans doute', without that artful ambiguity mentioned earlier ('[la syllabe] "nul" est morte', 'nul[le] est morte).[4]

And so the poet tries again, as it were from the other end, from what the phrase might mean (the word 'prédilection' in 'tenter un retour à des pensées de prédilection' suggesting a pre-judged choosing of one referent among several, in contrast to the passive allowing of the phrase to speak for itself and utter all its 'virtualités' at once). Anxious at the 'nul' he is discovering at the heart of language, he wants sense: and so the science of language offers him a possible interpretation, in that 'pénultième' (he here explicitly reveals) is the technical term for the penultimate syllable of a word. But such univocal referentiality is no more than a 'facile affirmation', lacking the richness and indeed truth (cf. 'l'air de mensonge') of a freed signifier. Instead he himself now becomes the 'corde tendue' as, tormented and 'harcelé' (within this display of (hom.) 'art celé'), he lets the words play audibly across his lips with the intonation of condolence and yet while himself secretly trying to 'ensevelir' the phrase, to kill it dead, by adding a plethora of other words. But by this very act of 'tuning in' to the contin-gency of language ('La Pénultième est morte, elle est morte, bien morte, la désespérée Pénultième'), he becomes finally its voice: 'la voix même (la première, qui indubitablement avait été l'unique)'; and, accordingly, his original sensation of a wing sliding across and down him now becomes the sensation of his hand falling in a gesture of caress 'sur quelque chose'. Thanks to the syntax of the sentence, 'la voix même' appears to be in apposition to 'quelque chose' as well as to be the object of 'j'avais': and indeed it comes to the same thing, since the twin images of speaking and writing (having the voice, manually caressing the voice) are two facets of the one activity, the one linguistic act.

The final paragraph describes what results from this attunement of the poet's now subservient voice ('mon esprit naguère seigneur') with language

---

[4] Cf. the lines 'Une dentelle s'abolit / Dans le doute du Jeu suprême', where 'doute' evokes the polysemy from which poetic beauty is resurrected. See below, Part IV, Ch. 2.

itself (in the shape of the insistent phrase); for the referents which his linguistic experience had evoked as analogous ('instrument de musique, qui était oublié', 'aile', 'palme', 'plume', 'rameau') now exist before his eyes. Language as a past revisited by 'le glorieux Souvenir' has become (in the fictive reality of this prose poem) a street full of antique shops where one particular shop (like the one particular phrase that obsesses him) displays 'vieux instruments' ('pendus au mur' like the 'rejet' previously in its 'suspension fatidique plus inutilement en le vide de signification'), as well as 'palmes jaunes' and 'les ailes enfouies en l'ombre'. Instead of the phenomenal world pre-existing language and the linguistic act, words have the power—mysteriously, supernaturally, magically (all terms used in the text) —to create a world of their own. The poet is now filled with 'le commencement de l'angoisse sous laquelle agonise mon esprit naguère seigneur': 'agonise', that is to say still agonizes now in the writing of this very prose poem. This anguish is the language-anguish (literally 'le commencement de l'*ang*oisse') later displayed in the second line of 'Ses purs ongles...', the anguish which results from the realization that the 'virtualité' or polysemy of language 'disempowers' the intellect ('mon esprit naguère seigneur') by overriding discursive intentions with significance unforeseen ('unpredilected') by the language-user. Thus the poet at the end flees this supernatural scene in horror, a strange creature, a nobody ('bizarre, personne'), condemned only to half-understand language: thanks to 'Est morte' he 'knows' he should be in mourning, but the identity of 'la Pénultième' is still unknown. Hence 'probablement': where previously 'le glorieux Souvenir' visited the past 'certainement', and he himself managed to tune his voice with 'la première, qui *indubitablement* avait été l'unique' (my emphasis), now he is in the realm of probability, a deposed master wishing he could be sure. 'Mon esprit naguère seigneur': perhaps he is in mourning for his own intellectual independence, which is therefore but a penultimate staging-post on the slope of truth, on the way to the summit of Parnassus whereon contingent language is mobilized in all its virtuality by a language-user, devoid of 'pensées de prédilection', one who can control and confer necessity upon such virtuality within 'le vers'. '*La Pénultième* / fini[e], le vers e[s]t'...

For the moment, the anguished poet sees only a realm of probability or, as the title has it from at least 1867 onwards, the 'dé-monde, l'analogie'. This title, which derives no doubt from Baudelaire's translation of 'The Imp of the Perverse' as 'Le Démon de la perversité', may superficially seem appropriate to a text in which the poet is pursued by a devil of a phrase and the images of which it puts him in mind, but more fundamentally it points to the demonic power of 'analogie' and the dice-world which 'analogie' creates. For 'analogie' itself is a devil of a word. Conventionally signifying 'ressemblance' or 'correspondance', it refers here to the many comparisons and parallels perceived and indeed created by the poet within the text. But, deriving from 'ana' and 'logos', meaning 'according to' and 'ratio', it can also come to mean 'reverse' or 'rearranged' 'word' (on the model of 'ana-gram').[5] Thus the capacity of the logos to reverse (for example, the priority of world over language) and to produce linguistic similarities (aural or alphabetic) is what makes it a demon, is what creates a dicey realm of linguistic activity.

Such a reading may seem less implausible when one considers that the only revisions which Mallarmé made to his text (after its first publication in 1874) make it begin 'Des paroles [...]' and multiply the homophonic possibilities of the isolated rhetorical question with which the prose poem begins.[6] And these homophonies prefigure the remainder of the poem: 'dés paroles, inconnu chant, air, ailes sûres, vos lèvres, lents beaux mots dits.' Following the assertion that language is a dicey business come repeated assertions that it can achieve the golden harmonies (the matching 'ratios' of an 'analogie') of music itself,[7] that 'discours' can be 'or-[r]aison'. This kind of wordplay is rife within 'Le Démon de l'analogie'; and while Barbara Johnson may question whether this text can or should be 'expliqué', it can at least be 'démon-stré' and thereby perhaps 'dé-monstré'. Its own phrases are only 'absurdes' if, as the etymology of this word suggests,[8] we are deaf to their homophony, to their 'lents beaux mots dits'—which are otherwise just 'badly spoken' ('maudits') shreds of language. After all, is it not when the impatient poet attempts to bury the phrase by which he is obsessed in a 'psalmodie' (hom. 'sales mots dits') that he becomes 'la voix même'? Acts of writing precede acts of speaking in this text (the 'aile glissant sur les cordes' and the 'main [...] faisant le geste d'une caresse' both have priority), but such writing will only transcend 'la facile affirmation' if it attends to homophony and to etymology, that antique shop of language. The same is true of reading, and the point of the wordplay in the opening rhetorical question is that this (and any other Mallarméan) sentence makes no sense if

---

[5] The *Dictionnaire étymologique du français* (ed. Jacqueline Picoche, Paris, 1990) gives four senses of the prefix 'ana-': 'de bas en haut' ('anabase'); 'en arrière' ('anachorète'); 'à rebours' ('anaphylaxie'); and 'de nouveau' ('anabaptiste'). As regards anagrams, Dragonetti notes the near-anagram of 'Pénultième' and 'plus inutilement' ('"Le Démon de l'analogie" di Mallarmé', 220); and one could, as with 'palmes' and 'lampe' in 'Don du poème', point to several other instances in this poem (e.g. 'palmes' and 'psalmodie').

[6] The 1874 version reads: 'Avez-vous jamais eu des paroles inconnues chantant sur vos lèvres les lambeaux maudits d'une phrase absurde?' The final version reads: 'Des paroles inconnues chantèrent-elles sur vos lèvres, lambeaux maudits d'une phrase absurde?'

[7] It is no accident that so many words in the text should connote both linguistic and musical phenomena: 'paroles', 'phrase', 'voix', 'cordes d'un instrument', 'ton', 'chute', 'adaptant', 'psalmodie', etc. Cf. Ursula Franklin, *An Anatomy of Poesis: The Prose Poems of Stéphane Mallarmé* (Chapel Hill, NC 1976), 53–4.

[8] An etymology noted in the context of a different argument by Judd D. Hubert in 'A Post-Mortem on "The Penultimate"', *Substance*, 56 (1988), 80.

it is not vocalized and its etymological origins left unearthed. As readers we are not merely being asked an anodyne question about our psychological experience of language, we are being given a hint as to how to understand what is coming. We must, like the poet,[9] let the words of the text play upon our own lips, murmur them, adapt them, 'remember' their past, try placing unexpected silences between them, and thereby discover 'de vœux intellectuels une spéculation différente', a different (and deferring) way of mirroring intellectual intentions. The poet himself 'implores' such a 'spéculation', and the etymological tears shed by that word ('implorai') anticipate the sobs of his 'noble faculté poétique' when it is interrupted.

There has already been occasion to read some words for possible alternative meanings: namely, 'appartement', 'dorénavant', 'oraison', 'l'angoisse' (and its anagrammatic companion 'agonise'), and just now 'spéculation'. Space does not permit an exhaustive analysis of the 'analogical' play of this text, but it is important to analyse at least some of it in order to make subsequent analyses of such texts as 'Ses purs ongles...', 'Prose (pour des Esseintes)', and 'Un coup de Dés' seem less unexpected. Thus, for example, in the words 'la première, qui indubitablement avait été l'unique', one hears also 'la première qui, indue [...]', recalling the unseasonal, 'irregular' appearance of the obsessing phrase. The 'rue' in which the poet wanders is already present in the 'instrument' he senses, so that the later 'rue des antiquaires' (hom. 'rue des antique[s] airs') in which the poet finds 'de vieux instruments pendus au mur' is a street created by the instruments it contains. And when he relates how 'Je fis des pas dans la rue et reconnus en le son *nul* la corde tendue de l'instrument de musique', one suspects that 'pas' has instigated his recognition of nullity, and that the insistent /n/, /u/, and /l/ sounds have given him this word itself. Indeed if we listen to the latter part of this sentence carefully, it also 'reads' 'et reconnus en le son *nu* la corde tendue ('l'accord de temps dû') de l'instrument de musique': 'naked', non-referential sound is the string of his instrument upon which he will achieve due chords and tempi, a not undue harmony (or 'ana-logic', proportional sound). This linguistic 'birth' of 'nul' ('son apparition') is just what the text goes on to record: 'que le glorieux Souvenir venait de visiter de son, aile', 'de son /l/'.[10]

Igitur, written within five years of this text (and maybe substantially less), has often been examined in relation to 'Un coup de Dés', and Igitur's dice-throw clearly anticipates the later masterpiece. But how about the use of 'dés' in 'Le Démon de l'analogie'? The sound /de/ or the letters 'des' between them occur twelve times (the maximum number thrown by two dice) and in

---

[9] As Jean Dornbush notes, the opening rhetorical question sets up an analogy between poet and reader: see 'The Death of the Penultimate: Paradox in Mallarmé's "Le Démon de l'analogie"', *French Forum*, 5 (1980), 248.

[10] Cf. the homophony of 'un coup d'aile ivre' in 'Le vierge, le vivace...'.

linguistic forms which mark key moments in the text. In each case they connote the contingency which appears to thwart the intentionality of language and yet which offers the possibility of other, more 'poetic' patterns: (i) 'Des paroles inconnues chantèrent-elles [...]'; (ii) 'une voix prononçant les mots sur un ton descendant'; (iii) '*Est morte* / se détacha de la suspension fatidique plus inutilement en le vide de signification'; (iv) 'Je fis des pas dans la rue et reconnus en le son *nul*', etc.; (v) 'La phrase revint, virtuelle, dégagée d'une chute antérieure de plume ou de rameau'; (vi) 'tenter un retour à des pensées de prédilection'; (vii) 'l'avant-dernière syllabe des vocables, et son apparition'; (viii) 'la désespérée Pénultième'; (ix) 'quand, effroi!—d'une magie aisément déductible et nerveuse'; (x) 'une caresse qui descend sur quelque chose'; (xi) 'dans la rue des antiquaires instinctivement suivie'; (xii) 'et, à terre, des palmes jaunes et les ailes enfouies en l'ombre'. Respectively: (i) the unknown words that 'sing' out from under the surface of conventionally perceived language; (ii) the voice pronouncing language in the falling tone of tumbling dice-words; (iii) the 'rejet' is 'ce dé' which 'tacha/tâcha [...] plus inutilement [i.e. less referentially]' in the 'vide de signification'; (iv) the poet walks randomly ('dés pas') in the street at the mercy of language (later he describes his itinerary as 'la rue des antiquaires instinctivement suivie'); (v) the phrase returns 'virtuelle, dégagée', a 'virtuel dé, gage': contingency is a source of potential, and the phrase both a token of, and a challenge to, the poet's power; (vi) the poet trying to start again, to go back to the 'dés' with which the poem began; (vii) 'Pénultième' means not only 'l'avant-dernière syllabe' but also (because this is the particular function of this word within this text) 'dés vocables', 'son apparition'; (viii) the successful recitation of the phrase with other words added brings 'la désespérée Pénultième', or 'là, dés espérés'; (ix) he feels that he has achieved 'la voix même' by means of 'une magie [...] déductible', a form of magic in which the 'dé' itself can be 'led down', a form of conscious control to match the 'ton descendant' of the original voice, and now in the form of (x) 'une caresse qui descend sur quelque chose'; (xi) the poet finds himself in the 'rue Dés' of 'antiques airs', a 'rue' instinctivement suivie' in which (xii) he finds words as 'dés, palmes jaunes', forgotten instruments of writing, lying there silently – 'à terre/à taire'.

In the throes of his language-anguish, the poet of 'Le Démon de l'analogie' gives voice to such silent words, brings them to life by 'revisiting' their potential, and 'amplifies' the 'palmes' alphabetically and metaphorically into a sacred 'psalmodie'. In 'Prose (pour des Esseintes)' he will later summon up a similar linguistic 'amplification': 'Hyperbole! de ma mémoire / [...] ne sais-tu / Te lever'; and in 'Un coup de Dés' the text will turn on the 'vieillard/vieil art' being 'induit' by the 'ultérieur démon immémorial' [of language] towards 'cette conjonction suprême avec la probabilité'. Both poems will, as we shall see, proclaim a triumph over contingency by virtue of their own textual composition; and in each of them legal terminology ('litige', 'insinuation') will serve to suggest that the poet is master in his own domain. In 'Le Démon de l'analogie', as yet, the 'esprit naguère seigneur' is more given to displaying the manner of his dispossession, the loss of his 'appartement'. He flees at the end, a 'personne condamnée', as if the 'voix prononçant les mots sur un ton descendant' at the beginning had pronounced a death sentence on him ('La Pénultième est morte'). Perhaps, even, he has been condemned for the 'labeur de linguistique par lequel quotidiennement sanglote de s'interrompre ma noble faculté poétique': for his passing attempt to deal with the obsessive phrase by the 'facile affirmation' of the Penult's literal meaning is described as 'le reste mal abjuré' of such a labour. He has not quite been able to abjure this quotidian reliance on reference,[11] but the evidence that language can 'supernaturally' create a world of its own is 'irrécusable'.[12]

And yet the manner in which this dispossession is displayed suggests a language-user very much at home in language. As he wanders the streets of this verbal past, words provide the legal 'instrument' that puts an end to his 'apartness', and he achieves unison ('j'avais [...] la voix même') with language through 'l'am*pli*fication de la psalmodie'. 'Le Démon de l'analogie' itself exhibits the generous linguistic 'plis' which are to characterize Mallarmé's work from now on, and 'psalmodie' anticipates the later use of 'grimoire' as an early example of Mallarmé's Janus-words, words which simultaneously reflect the two poles of his poetic experience, 'le néant' and 'la beauté':[13] here, poetic text as a paltry catalogue of woe or poetic text as sacred music, a holy combination of words and sound, of psalms or 'antiques airs' played upon a verbal, vocal 'instrument à corde'.

'Le Démon de l'analogie' reads rather like Mallarmé's equivalent of Poe's 'The Philosophy of Composition', except that it provides a very different and much more subtle account of what it means to be a poet and of the creative tension which exists between a poet's intentions and the constraints (and possibilities) of his chosen medium. At the same time it offers a convenient contrast with Baudelairean 'surnaturalisme', thus demonstrating also the distance Mallarmé had by now established between himself and his mentor. For Baudelaire it was 'l'imagination qui [...] a créé, au commencement du monde, l'analogie et la métaphore'.[14] For Mallarmé, in the

---

[11] Biographically no doubt a reference to his schoolmastering, but here also perhaps an evocation of everyday language-use as a form of unpoetic 'universel reportage', a dull labour as opposed to an act of magic.

[12] Some of this legal terminology is noted by Judd D. Hubert but again as part of a different argument: see 'A Post-Mortem on "The Penultimate"', 85–6.

[13] Cf. the famous remark to Cazalis in July 1866: 'je te dirai que je suis depuis un mois dans les plus purs glaciers de l'Esthétique—qu'après avoir trouvé le Néant, j'ai trouvé le Beau' (*Corr.*, i. 220).

[14] From 'Salon de 1859', in Baudelaire, *Œuvres complètes*, ii. 621.

beginning was the word; language is the 'lieu' 'où s'installe l'irrécusable intervention du surnaturel'.

In a way this prose poem offers its own spectacle of a 'suspension fatidique plus inutilement en le vide de signification': for it constitutes a suspension of literary and linguistic norms[15] that is 'fatidique' (etym. 'foretelling'), prophetic of Mallarmé's future work and his music of the word. The obsessive phrase is 'enseveli[]' in the 'amplification' of the text as a whole, but the folds become a 'sépulcre' no less worthy of the name 'Pulchérie' than that of 'Prose'. What is buried is 'La Pénultième', the poet of old, but he has been saved by a friendly spirit, 'le Démon de l'analogie'. Here finally Mallarmé has his finger, or 'délicate phalange', firmly on the 'artifice du mystère': 'mystère', from the Greek 'mystêrion', deriving originally from 'myein', to close (the mouth). Like an initiate into the 'mystery' about which he is sworn to silence, the future poet will orchestrate the mysteries of language within the silent interstitial whiteness of the page. It shall be the reader's task to listen to that silence. 'La phrase revint, virtuelle, dégagée d'une chute antérieure de plume ou de rameau, dorénavant à travers la voix entendue, elle s'articula seule, vivant de sa personnalité': 'la phrase (etym. 'phrazein'=to speak) revint, virtù elle/aile, dégagée d'une chute antérieure de plume [i.e. returned divested of its previous written form] / dé, gage e[s]t d'une, "chut" hante, et rieur!, deux [reflexive] plumes ou deux rameau[x], mots doré[s]navant, à travers la voix (la voie: la rue des antiquaires?), vers—la voix entendue, ailes, art': 'Phrase [parler/écrire]—rameau—mots dorés—art.' To 'read' Mallarmé like this is to give an affirmative answer to the apparently rhetorical question posed in the first paragraph of 'Le Démon de l'analogie'; and to 'read' the phrase 'La Pénultième / Est morte' like this is to realize that in 'La Pénultième' the /e/ has lost its upward sloping 'accent aigu'[16] ('é morte', we hear) and that we are therefore in the presence of 'la penne ultième' 'qui descend sûr, quelque chose', an experimental *nec plus ultra* of writing.

---

[15] Cf. the vocabulary of 'rupture' noted by Franklin (*An Anatomy of Poesis*, 54): 'lambeaux', 'interrompre', 'détacher', 'casser', 'discontinuer', etc. Cf. also Johnson, *Défigurations*, 206–11.

[16] Cf. Johnson, *Défigurations*, 199, for an alternative account of the accents on 'La Pénultième'.

4

'Couples'

(i) 'Hérodiade' (1864–1869)

'Hérodiade', où je m'étais mis tout entier sans le savoir, d'où mes doutes
et mes malaises, et dont j'ai enfin trouvé le fin mot [...]
(Letter to Henri Cazalis, July 1866)

When Mallarmé began writing 'Hérodiade' during the winter of 1864–5, he
saw himself as putting a new poetic theory into practice: and the celebrated
terms in which he describes this suggest that he was seeking to replace a
Parnassian focus on objects with Poe's concern for 'effect':

J'ai enfin commencé mon 'Hérodiade'. Avec terreur, car j'invente une langue qui doit
nécessairement jaillir d'une poétique très nouvelle, que je pourrais définir en ces
deux mots: *Peindre, non la chose, mais l'effet qu'elle produit.*

Le vers ne doit donc pas se composer de mots; mais d'intentions, et toutes les
paroles s'effacer devant la sensation.[1]

The rejection of 'mots' here seems to fly in the face of his developing
aesthetic, but in reality he is insisting that the 'vers', rather than be explicitly
descriptive, should be implicitly suggestive. To this end he is inventing 'une
langue', and his 'intention' in 'Hérodiade' is to convey to the reader a
'sensation' of beauty, of that reflexive beauty which he had begun to
intimate in the poems written during 1863 and 1864, and which is also
evident in the prose poems of the mid-1860s.

Like 'Don du poème' and 'Sainte' written in 1865, 'Hérodiade' is—in its
various versions[2]—a poem about itself ('le sujet de mon œuvre est la
Beauté'), a poem about the virginal power of poetic language unsullied by
representational functions and about the alluring 'sterility' of a text turned
in upon itself: 'J'aime l'horreur d'être vierge' ('Scène', l. 103). But it is
important to note that the 'poetic theory' underlying the text evolved

---

[1] *Corr.*, i. 137 (Oct. 1864) (Mallarme's emphasis).
[2] See Gardner Davies, *Mallarmé et le rêve d''Hérodiade'* (Paris, 1978), 9–29 for a summary.

significantly between its first manifestation ('Scène') and its second ('Ouverture'). It is not only that the earlier version was intended for the theatre and the second as a 'poème', but also that the way in which beauty is 'reflected' becomes more complex. Briefly put, the former depends predominantly on narrative and image, the latter on the 'voice' of language (as it is 'heard' in 'Le Démon de l'analogie'): so that Mallarmé's account of his poetic theory to Villiers de l'Isle-Adam at the end of 1865 ('donner les impressions les plus étranges, certes, mais sans que le lecteur n'oublie pour pas une minute la jouissance que lui procurera la beauté du poème') constitutes a development of the principle enunciated to Cazalis in October 1864 ('Peindre, non la chose, mais l'effet qu'elle produit'). 'Scène' dramatizes the dilemma of Narcissism, while the 'Ouverture' demonstrates linguistically its effects—and in a manner which Mallarmé's readers have perhaps yet to 'hear'. For he may have been using the word 'inouï' literally (and with characteristic deadpan humour) when he wrote to Cazalis at the end of April 1866:

J'ai écrit l'ouverture musicale, presque encore à l'état d'ébauche, mais je puis dire sans présomption qu'elle sera d'un effet inouï et que la scène dramatique que tu connais n'est auprès de ces vers que ce qu'est une vulgaire image d'Épinal comparée à une toile de Léonard de Vinci.[3]

(a) 'Scène'

> Je me suis mis sérieusement à ma tragédie d''Hérodiade' [...]
> (Letter to Henri Cazalis, Mar. 1865)

The earliest extant version of the 'Scène' which Mallarmé began writing in 1864 is that submitted to Le Parnasse contemporain in 1869 and published (after the Franco-Prussian war) in 1871 under the title 'Fragment d'une étude scénique ancienne d'un poème d'Hérodiade'. As a guide to Mallarmé's poetic practice in 1864–5 it is not, therefore, totally reliable. Nevertheless a dismissive comment to Cazalis in April 1870 ('ces vieux vers. [...] Je suis bien loin de cela')[4] suggests that he had not substantially revised his earlier version, while the internal evidence shows that he has not yet attained the level of linguistic complexity to be found in the 'Ouverture' or 'Le Démon de l'analogie'.

From Mallarmé's remarks to Cazalis in March 1865 it is clear that this first version of 'Hérodiade' was intended to 'peindre [...] l'effet':

J'ai [..] trouvé une façon intime et singulière de peindre et de noter des impressions très fugitives. Ajoute, pour plus de terreur, que toutes ces *impressions* se suivent comme dans une symphonie, et que je suis souvent des journées entières à me

---

[3] Corr., i. 207.   [4] Corr., i. 323.

demander si celle-ci peut accompagner celle-là, quelle est leur parenté et leur effet... Tu juges que je fais peu de vers en une semaine.[5]

As in Mallarmé's shorter poems of the same period, this 'symphonic' effect is achieved by careful patterning. Here 134 alexandrines in 'rimes plates' are divided in a now familiar binary structure, pivoting on a couplet which contains the essential ingredients of the entire 'Scène':

N. Que...
H.   Mais n'allais-tu pas me toucher?
N.   ...J'aimerais
   Être à qui le destin réserve vos secrets.

In the first half, the Nourrice makes three physical approaches to Héro-diade, the untouchable and virginal emblem of beauty whom even the lions (here a symbol of primordial physical power) have left unscathed; in the second half, where the tripartite structure of the first is repeated (with two passages of comparatively rapid dialogue surrounding the longer mono-logue (ll. 86–117)), Hérodiade rejects the prospect of union with a mortal male and directs her aspirations, she a mere terrestrial manifestation of beauty, towards her eternal sister ('Et ta sœur solitaire, ô ma sœur éternelle, / Mon rêve montera vers toi'). It is not death she awaits, but 'une chose inconnue': and only the brief dramatis personae in the manuscript version tells us that 'la Tête de Saint Jean' might be this 'chose inconnue'.[6] The base desire of the involuntarily chaste Nourrice to give herself to Hérodiade's future husband (in order to have a description of her 'charms') contrasts with beauty's dream of eternity in a union with mystery. Implicitly (at this stage) such a union can be achieved only with a severed head, whose gaze may behold her beauty yet whose lips shall never tell.[7]

In each half Hérodiade's dialogue with the Nourrice is interrupted, as though contrapuntally, while she apostrophizes surrounding objects which mirror her aspirations: and the reflexivity which Mallarmé now regards as an intrinsic attribute of beauty is conveyed in these addresses, in the first half to metal and precious stones (ll. 40–1) and the mirror itself (ll. 44–51), and then, in the second half, to metal and precious stones again (ll. 87–94) and to the reflection of her own lips in the mirror (ll. 129–34). As a symbol of reflexive, non-representational poetic art, Hérodiade rejects all that the Nourrice stands for: life itself, the milk of physical creativity (with the homophone 'lait/laid' suggesting that such milk is the opposite of beauty), and the outmoded use of language as the medium of prediction (ll. 95–7). Being a 'nourrice d'hiver' this nursemaid has outlived her function, as

---

[5] *Corr.*, i. 161 (Mallarmé's emphasis).
[6] See *Les Noces d'Hérodiade: Mystère*, ed. Gardner Davies (Paris, 1959), 47.
[7] As suggested by the 'Cantique de saint Jean'.

though—'nourrice, dit[e] vers'—she represented the whole lyric tradition which has nourished 'Hérodiade' itself and from which 'Hérodiade' constitutes such a radical departure. Hérodiade remembers her nurse's breast milk as one remembers paradise (ll. 83–4), but she lives now in anguished solitude (ll. 73–4), a symbol of 'virginal' poetic language exiled (l. 17) from the familiar land of representation and beholding from time to time the 'nudité' of its 'rêve épars' within its own reflection (ll. 50–1).

In the midst of anguish, beauty shall derive her power (as 'princesse' and 'reine') not from describing the world but from this very self-regard: the physical beauty of real flowers (which has inspired former poets to write representational poems) is replaced by 'jardins d'améthyste', verbal antidotes to the easy intoxication of inspirational verse,[8] to that 'ivresse' (l. 34) which Hérodiade fears from the approach of perfume and its heady distillation of material floral beauty. Jewelled words, these 'Ors ignorés' (l. 89) unearthed from the subterranean depths of etymology and a philological past ('enfouis / Sans fin dans de savants abîmes éblouis': ll. 87–8), will adorn her 'corps solitaire' (my emphasis); and their brilliance will be reflected in the 'tresses' of rhyming couplets that are the 'hair' of this poem called 'Hérodiade', the repeatedly invoked 'cheveux' which are the outward manifestation of her immortal light (ll. 5–7).[9] Like words at the poet's fingertips, the jewels are worn as rings, the rings which the Nourrice attempts to kiss and the 'froides pierreries' which eventually 'separate' themselves out (and 'wean' themselves) from the 'rêveries' of non-speaking 'enfance' at the end of the poem. And the 'tresses' of hair that constitute the lines of the poem are an etymological source of the 'horreur' (in the sense of 'hérissement' and 'horripilation'[10]) which characterizes Hérodiade's gleaming, leonine beauty: in poetic terms, the jagged enjambements, the disrupted syntax, and the abrupt collations which constitute the unruly mane of 'Hérodiade'.

From the beginning of the poem poetic beauty is presented as an 'ombre', at once the spectral shade and shadowy 'dark side' of reference, and also a ghostly source of diamantine light, an 'ombre' of non-representation emitting the stellar brilliance of word-stars, a luminous obscurity. Eschewing the 'myrrhe' of distilled reality (l. 29), beauty requires the 'miroir' of the poem, the punningly frozen reaches of a 'glace' in which to observe 'her' own (linguistic) past (ll. 44–51). Before it she stands, uncertain ('Nourrice, suis-je belle?') and anguishedly aware of the 'Néant' inherent in mere reflexivity, the nakedness which appears as she 'effeuille [...] / Les pâles lys qui sont en moi' (ll. 17–19), or searches for 'mes souvenirs qui sont / Comme des feuilles

---

[8] 'Améthyste' etymologically means that which prevents intoxication.

[9] This possible analogy between hair and lines of verse is most evident in the self-referential stichomythia of ll. 52–3.

[10] Cf. the use of 'hérisse' and 'horrifié' in 'Les Noces d'Hérodiade' ('Prélude. III', ll. 30–2).

sous ta glace au trou profond' (ll. 47–8), or envisages the impudence of a
mortal gaze 'devant qui, des calices / De mes robes, arôme aux farouches
délices, / Sortirait le frisson blanc de ma nudité' (ll. 97–9).[11] In her anguish
she fears that all she is left with may be mere fragments (like the 'Fragment'
in the title under which Mallarmé first published this poem), mere 'lan-
guides débris' (l. 20), 'mon rêve épars' (l. 51); and yet she comes momenta-
rily also to believe that pure reflexivity is sufficient, that as a diamantine
'solitaire' she can shine unto herself alone in a 'monotone patrie' of pure
virginal whiteness:

> Et tout, autour de moi, vit dans l'idolâtrie
> D'un miroir qui reflète en son calme dormant
> Hérodiade au clair regard de diamant...
> Ô charme dernier, oui, je le sens, je suis seule!
>
> (ll. 114–17)

But she realizes at the end of the poem that such self-sufficient solitude is
an illusion: 'Vous mentez, ô fleur nue / De mes lèvres.' Her rosebud lips have
deluded her, she cannot survive alone; or rather, irrespective of the ultimate
'mystère' with which she aspires to be united and despite these her protesta-
tions, perhaps the sobbing sounds which have issued from her lips bespeak
at last the emergence of 'ses [hom. 'ces'] froides pierreries' that are the words
of the poem. At last beauty has completed her 'toilette' (hom. 'ce, c'est
[s'est] paré, enfin') and is ready to face the new day which she so much fears
(l. 61). For if she has displayed her jewels, does she not want them to be
seen? If she has spoken, does she not want to be heard? Hérodiade, in
becoming 'Hérodiade', has revealed her expectation, her expectation of a
reader, the perilous but necessary gaze of a beholder's eye if she, beauty, is to
be. As the representative of a new form of poetic language, she exists in a
time out of time, a new morning 'oublié des prophètes / Vers[e]' (ll. 9–10),
not the 'âge ignoré' (l. 3) of the forgotten historical past from which the
Nourrice would recall her, but an unforetold, silent era of mystery. Hers is a
form of death (l. 8), and her 'chair' is 'inutile' (l. 106): she derives her
existence from poetry itself ('Mon sang [,] vers sa source': l. 54) and
flourishes, not as an earthly flower but as a symbolic immortelle (l. 65).
But if she is truly to exist, then the impertinent lips of the Nourrice that seek
to kiss her at the beginning must be replaced by the reverent lip-reading of a
future reader. Only if this reader shares 'son pur regard' with St John shall
the 'blond torrent de [s]es cheveux' remain 'immaculés' (l. 4), unbesmirched
by base desires for predictable unions and the consummation of a well-
known story. 'Ah, conte-moi', she demands angrily of the Nourrice, the
purveyor of childhood tales, as she seeks an explanation of the old woman's

---

[11] In later versions 'selon qui, des calices', etc.

importunity: but 'Hérodiade' herself bids 'Adieu' (l. 129) to narrative and representation in the name of 'la splendeur ignorée / Et le mystère vain' (ll. 74–5) of a new poetic art, an art that bids farewell to time.

(b) 'Ouverture' (1865–1866)

> je commence 'Hérodiade', non plus tragédie, mais poème [...] surtout parce que je gagne ainsi l'attitude, les vêtements, le décor, et l'ameuble-ment, sans parler du mystère.
>
> (Letter to Théodore Aubanel, Oct. 1865)

Thus, like the 'Montreur de choses Passées' in 'Le Phénomène futur', the author of 'Hérodiade' presents beauty in the shape of a 'Femme d'autrefois', a woman without a specific history and who symbolizes a new aesthetic—a 'femme d'autre foi'. For 'Hérodiade', too, is a 'fait-nomen'. As Mallarmé himself stresses, the poem has very little to do with the historical world of Herod and Salome. Rather it is born of a word, the word which he had used earlier in 1864 in the third stanza of 'Les Fleurs':

> Et, pareille à la chair de la femme, la rose
> Cruelle, Hérodiade en fleur du jardin clair,
> Celle qu'un sang farouche et radieux arrose!

In these lines Mallarmé's 'Femme d'autrefois' is associated with female flesh, at once cruel and pink, radiant and fiercely proud; and the image of spilled blood, deriving from the colour and thorns of a rose, inevitably suggests not only a deflowering but the decapitation of John the Baptist, his head suffused in saintly radiance. Here, as we saw in 'Les Fleurs', is God's creation re-created in language, the flesh become word; and these evocations of blood-red flows and blushing post-virginal radiance are sug-gested again by the image of the burst pomegranate when Mallarmé thanks Lefébure in early 1865 for the information he has sent him about the historical Salome:

Merci du détail que vous me donnez au sujet d'"Hérodiade', mais je ne m'en sers pas. La plus belle page de mon œuvre sera celle qui ne contiendra que ce nom divin 'Hérodiade'. Le peu d'inspiration que j'ai eu, je le dois à ce nom, et je crois que si mon héroïne s'était appelée Salomé, j'eusse inventé ce mot sombre, et rouge comme une grenade ouverte, 'Hérodiade'. Du reste, je tiens à en faire un être purement rêvé et absolument indépendant de l'histoire.[12]

In 'Scène' the word 'Hérodiade' figures twice and in each case its phonetic composition is highlighted by juxtaposition with other words containing some of its phonemes:

[12] Corr., i. 154.

Ô tour qu'Hérodiade avec *effroi regarde*!
(l. 61)

Hérodiade *au* clair *regard de dia*mant...
(l. 116)

It would seem that the name 'Hérodiade' 'inspires' Mallarmé here simply because of its rich sonority and its potential for 'orchestration' with similar-sounding words. But at the same time it begins to look as if the sound of the word, by prompting similar words, also gives rise to the poem itself. The insistent link between 'Hérodiade' and 'regard', for example, suggests that the word 'Hérodiade' may be its phonetic character alone have prompted the central theme of the 'regard' (and indeed also, in the letter to Lefébure, the image of the 'grenade'). Is it accidental that 'Hérodiade' is collated with 'effroi', the 'roi' thus echoing 'Hérode', or that 'Héro*dia*de' leads to '*dia*-mant' and so to the theme of beauty as a diamantine solitary, a 'solitaire'? Perhaps it is; and perhaps that is what Mallarmé meant when he spoke of '"Hérodiade", où je m'étais mis tout entier sans le savoir'. For the major difference between 'Scène' and the 'Ouverture' is that the latter poem quite evidently exploits the homophonies of the word 'Hérodiade': one has only to hear the presence of 'héraut' to realize that the entire, apparently ana-chronistic medieval décor of the 'Ouverture' which has so puzzled critics has arisen from the 'virtualités' of the word itself.

As Bertrand Marchal has rightly argued, 'Hérodiade' allegorically repre-sents in its various versions the emergence of a new kind of writing demand-ing to be read in a new kind of way: but his conclusion ('Hérodiade, en somme, n'est plus qu'une œuvre à lire'[13]) should in fact be a starting-point. How may one read this 'heraldic' work? As 'Le Démon de l'analogie' suggests, it is necessary to go beyond a traditional referential reading and instead to listen to and observe the words without 'prédilection'. The 'Ouverture' depicts not only the death of representation ('la chose') but the consequences that this may have for poetic language ('l'effet qu'elle produit').

Before analysing some of the vertiginous polysemy of this text, it is important to note the carefully wrought patterns within which this 'incan-tation' is performed.[14] Ninety-six alexandrines in 'rimes plates' pivot on the single verb 'S'élève' (l. 48) in a manner strongly reminiscent of the structure of 'Soupir'; and a series of concentric circles spread out, like the basins of a fountain, around this central 'jet', from the immediate repetition of 'le vieil éclat voilé' to the images of dawn and abolition with which the poem begins and ends.[15] The whole poem 'folds' at l. 48, so that the rise and fall of 'Une

---

[13] *Lecture de Mallarmé*, 35–66 (66).

[14] For the text of the 'Ouverture', see *Poésies*, ed. Marchal, 77–9 (and cf. 258–60).

[15] Much of this structure has been accurately analysed in Jean-Pierre Chausserie-Laprée, 'L'Architecture secrète de l'"Ouverture ancienne"', *Europe*, 54 (Apr.–May 1976), 74–103. See

voix' in the fourth section of the poem (ll. 38–57) is mirrored in the rhythm of the poem as a whole. Although divided into several sections, with most divisions occuring within a rhyme pair (which thus serves to link them), the poem has a ternary structure, particularly as the first three sections are bound into one unit by beginning and ending with closely parallel phrases (and rhyme-word).

Like several of Mallarmé's poems written in the mid-1860s, this text recounts the failure of poetic art ('impuissance') while displaying its triumph, but it does so in a much more radical and textually detailed way. As the homophone 'héraut' presumably suggested, the poem begins by 'heralding' the dawn of a new kind of poetic language while at the same time sounding the last trump at the sunset of a former, representational mode of writing. The value of the dawning language ('Une Aurore') is audible in its mirrored gold, the 'or nu' thrashing/striping ('fustigeant') the 'espace cramoisi' of a linguistic twilight in imitation of the herald's traditional costume (a crimson tunic decorated with groups of three golden fleurs-de-lis);[16] and the new beginning which this innovative language constitutes ('car j'invente une langue') is evoked by the insistent (and twice capitalized) presence of the letter a in the vocabulary of the opening lines. The first letter of the alphabet and of 'Aurore', it is also the first letter of the poem itself, where it is followed alphabetically by b in 'Abolie' and in the dominant 'bassin' of the second line. The 'bassin' that is this concentric poem here reflects these a's (hom. 'qui mire les a, larmes'), 'a' being thus the lachrymose symbol of the passing of the old language (hom. 'ah!') as well as the alphabetic sign of the advent of the new; and it 'mire les alarmes' which are the alarums of a herald in war, the belabouring of 'l'espace cramoisi' as well as the further struggles evoked later in the poem. Not only is the 'bassin' 'aboli' because it does not actually exist outside the bounds of this poem, it is also reflecting 'a' as 'beau lit' (or 'lys'), the lily-white, virginal bed of beauty from which the Nourrice will later fear that the 'voix' of the 'Froide enfant' is absent.

'Une Aurore a' (l. 4) is thus the 'plumage héraldique' that is this new, heralding form of penmanship; and it is 'choisi', unlike the 'bel oiseau, caprice' which has departed the scene, the sorry emblem of a contingent, unconcerted form of writing.[17] The feathered quill of the new dawn, on the other hand, dips 'son aile affreuse' in the lachrymose waters of this 'bassin' in that by foregrounding the phonetic composition of words and their

---

also Suzanne Bernard, *Mallarmé et la musique* (Paris, 1959), 98–103. Cf. Mallarmé's reference to 'une phrase de vingt-deux vers, tournant sur un seul verbe, et encore très effacé la seule fois qu'il se présente' (*Corr.*, i. 213, to Catulle Mendès, Apr. 1866).

[16] See Larousse, 'héraut'.

[17] This replacement of 'caprice' (deriving etymologically from Latin 'caper' = goat) by 'choice' may be compared with Mallarmé's use of 'Églogue' as the subtitle of 'L'Après-midi d'un faune'. See below, 5, (ii).

homophonic possibilities it creates a horrifying, defamiliarized language.[18] It is also literally true that the 'aile' (hom. 'l') of 'Abolie' is reflected in 'les larmes', and indeed that the 'aile' does belong to 'Abolie', since the letters of 'aile' are already present in 'Abolie'.[19]

While reflected in the 'bassin', the new dawn is heralded from the (concentric) tower[20] of a 'mausolée', the pale ('lourde': etym. 'luridus') tomb of the 'mot-soleil', the referential language that is now 'setting' at dusk to be replaced (it is hoped) by the constellations of a new poetic art. The white page, as yet a ghastly tomb of dead representation, has been deserted by the 'bel oiseau', emblem of a former uncapitalized dawn (or form of writing) that did not proclaim its riches (hom. 'sol: y taire d'or', 'or au vain plumage noir'); and for the moment (before the rise of the voice in the central section) the 'lieu' of poetry resembles a manorial seat fallen from glory,[21] and the promise of new beginnings temporarily gives way to the prospect of a dicey world of letters: 'Ah! des pays déchus et tristes le manoir!' (hom. 'a: dés pays dés', 'a, d, p, i, d'). The 'bassin' of the poem now lacks the upward surge of expressive desire, leaving it 'untextured' ('Pas de clapotement!') as it prepares for a different form of linguistic ascent that may release the 'golden' sound promised by the dawn ('L'eau morne se résigne': 'se ré-signe', 'serait signe'?). Temporarily 'unvisited' by the 'plume' and 'cygne/signe' (and cf. hom. 'la plume nie le signe') which are the 'inoubliable[s]' instruments of writing, the text is a void of reflexivity: hom. 'l'eau reflète l'abandon / De l'eau'. The water-words in the poem's 'bassin' are now no longer even tears, but have become deafening noises conflicting one with another and apparently extinguishing all meaning: hom. 'l'eau tonne, éteignant son [et, teigne, en elle/aile, son], brandon'; sound, the fiery source of light for the dawn of the new language, may be a 'brandon de discorde'.

The still waters of the non-representational text reflect the absence of the departed 'bel oiseau', of the 'cygne/signe', 'la plume' which once 'plongea la tête' and thus rippled the surface into texture. But this was the art of 'caprice', the old style of writing represented by the Nourrice herself whose 'gorge', we later learn, is 'ancienne et tarie' (l. 74), a once milky text of contingent language (cf. hom. 'mots au lait', 'dés au lait') in which the 'cygne/signe'—a 'Solitaire d'aurore au vain plumage noir'—despaired at not being the 'diamant pur de quelque étoile, mais / Antérieure, qui ne scintilla jamais': that is, despaired not to achieve the pure diamantine

---

[18] Cf. Mallarmé's reference to the 'terreur' which his new 'langue' inspires in him.

[19] There is more to this opening, therefore, than the 'facile' impressionism suggested by Suzanne Bernard (*Mallarmé et la musique*, 99).

[20] The intertext of Nerval's 'El Desdichado' ('la tour abolie') is noted in Bernard, *Mallarmé et la musique*, 99. 'Ma seule étoile est morte', from the same poem, is also recalled in the 'Ouverture'.

[21] Cf. 'mon esprit naguère seigneur' in 'Le Démon de l'analogie' and the use of 'manoir' in 'Un coup de Dés'.

brilliance of pristine, 'anterior' language, which has not been blackened by the obscurity and contingency that characterize the language of unthinking 'universel reportage'. Like a phoenix, this 'oiseau' has immolated itself upon the 'tour cinéraire et sacrificatrice' of this heraldic poem, and, like some criminal who has murdered univocity, it burns at the stake, tortured into agonized exclamation:

> Crime! bûcher! aurore ancienne! supplice!

Here, nevertheless, the death of the old 'dawn' ('au vain plumage noir') brings also an 'aurore antienne' (cf. l. 52: 'l'antienne aux versets deman-deurs'), an anthem or, more especially, an antiphon,[22] a piece of sacred music sung by alternating voices. And how better to describe a text which orchestrates the tension between the referential and the reflexive functions of language? 'Son aile affreuse' writhes in agony, as these two warring parties vie for supremacy; and yet this 'supplice' is (in its etymological origins) a supplication (or incantation) uttered at the time of a religious sacrifice, a sacred invocation that is, at its literal heart, a 'pli', a creative antiphony, a complicity:

> Pourpre d'un ciel! Étang de la pourpre complice!

Textual reflexivity (hom. 'Pourpre [...] étant de la pourpre') is accomplice to the crime, and the poem (like 'Sainte') proclaims itself another stained-glass window giving onto these verbal incarnations of a sky incarnadine:

> Et sur les incarnats, grand ouvert, ce vitrail.

As both criss-cross lattice window and the technique of making such win-dows, 'ce vitrail' denotes this intricately structured poem which at once displays a new pattern of writing and describes how, fleetingly, it came into being. Taking the colour of flesh rather than the flesh itself, it uses words, not things, to paint and partition its 'verre', to 'embody' the world by reflecting it in the as yet unrippled waters of its 'bassin'. As such 'ce vitrail' is 'grand, ou Vers': and both 'grand ouvert' because it has opened up the potential of language, and a 'grand "ou", Vers' because it offers a poetic synthesis within the dialectic of the referential and the reflexive. The either/ or of indeterminate meaning has been transmuted into the 'or' of a new dawn, the 'Ouverture d'Hérodiade'.[23]

Following the suggestive 'espaces blancs' surrounding the short second section (the vista of the page replacing 'l'espace cramoisi' of dying refer-ence), the actual 'ouverture' of 'Hérodiade', the homophonic 'héraut', now

---

[22] Cf. the opening line of the third part of the projected 'Prélude' in 'Les Noces d'Hérodiade': 'A quel psaume de nul antique antiphonaire'.

[23] Cf. the possible role of the English 'or' in 'Alternative', (see below, Part IV, Ch. 1), and the possible use of 'and/or' in 'Une dentelle s'abolit' (see below, p. 207).

gives rise in the third section of the poem (ll. 20–37) to the medieval décor
of this 'poème-tour'; and the 'vitrail' opening onto a warring sky is replaced
by a no less intricate and no less self-referential 'tapisserie' from which shall
emerge a new and sibylline voice. As we progress towards the centre of the
poem's own concentric structure, where the voice will be raised as in a vocal
sunrise, so we move from the exterior cosmic scene to the interior 'cham-
bre': at once torture-chamber and courtroom, the bedchamber of beauty
and the chamber in which the music of this 'Ouverture' will be played. This
singular 'chambre', beginning with 'c' (like the second section before it and
following the 'a' and 'b' with which the first section began), has a 'cadre',
the frame of rhyme: in particular, the rhyme on 'armes' with which the
evocation of this concentric 'tour' begins and ends (ll. 1–2; l.37). Hence,
perhaps, the description of this 'cadre' as the 'attirail / De siècle belliqueux':
itself 'attiré' by the 'héraut' in 'Hérodiade', the 'siècle *bell*iqueux' recalls the
'*bel* oiseau', each of them emblems of a former beauty which the 'incanta-
tion' would replace with a lily-white bed ('Ah, beau lit/lys'). This 'attirail'
constitutes an 'orfèvrerie' (like 'vitrail', meaning both the object and the
craft which made it) that is 'éteinte', like the autumnal firebrand (l. 12), and
lacking 'l'or nu' of the new dawn; and within this 'armed' frame, the inner
chamber of the poem points instead to that other 'cadre' beyond rhyme, the
'cadre' of the white page. And this whiteness, again associated with alpha-
betic beginnings ('A le neigeux jadis'), is coloured not incarnadine but in the
snowy blankness of a virginal linguistic past, the yet-to-be-exploited, cen-
turies-old potential of language (recalling the 'étoile [. . .] / Antérieure'):

> A le neigeux jadis pour ancienne teinte
>
> (hom. A: le neigeux jadis pour antienne. Tinte!)

Where once the 'plume' used the 'vain plumage noir' of inky words to
create text, now the 'tapisserie' of this 'antienne' will be created by folding
whiteness, those blank spaces between the words in which the manifold
'rapports' within the text may silently weave their criss-cross patterns: 'au
lustre nacré, plis / Inutiles'. Useless because non-representational, these 'plis'
(like silent beds of lilies?) have a pearly lustre: and in 'au lustre' we hear that
the reflexive water of the 'bassin' has become the water of purification used
in the sacrificial ceremony of a lustrum, a sacred ritual of quinquennial
renewal. Buried in these 'plis' are the sibyls of old, the instruments of their
traditional role as 'seers' ('yeux') now obsolete; and the 'ongle vieil' which
they offer 'aux Mages' is both an emblem of outmoded writing and, by the
sound of it, a 'vieil hommage'.

One of these is different: a winged 'sibyl' (hom. 'Une d'ailes'), reminiscent
(like this poem) of floral pattern, birdsong, and infantile, apparently non-
sensical prattling ('avec un passé de ramages') is figured upon 'ma robe
blanchie en l'ivoire fermé'—upon the white page that is the apparel of this

Nourrice locked in her poetic 'tour d'ivoire', where through 'l'argent noir parsemé' of scattered words may be seen a feather-white sky. And this new sibyl, dispensing with the visual ('les yeux ensevelis'), is less tangible, seeming to take wing (like a 'cygne/signe'), a phantom and a carnival mask:[24] in short, 'Un arôme'. From out of the ghostly, clownish whiteness of the page, the 'ramages' of the text, its word-flowers, have released a 'golden' aroma, as the 'or nu' of the new dawn ('Un a') now swirls back and forth in a kind of olfactory reflexivity:

> Un arôme qui porte, ô roses! un arôme [.]

Rising up from the 'lit vide' of a 'livide' page, invisible in the darkness of the former style of writing (the 'cierge soufflé' recalling the 'ongle vieil' of other sibyls), this insistent 'golden' aroma hovers over the sachet-text (as container of flower-petals); and the word-cluster itself ('Un arôme d'os froids rôdant sur le sachet'),[25] by heralding (hom. 'danse, hurle, sachez!') the dawn of the new poetic art, thus resembles 'Une touffe de fleurs' which denies the existence of the night ('parjures à la lune'). In the absence of the moon and of candlelight ('la cire expirée'), 'A [...] encor s'effeuille [,] l'une' (hom. 'en cor, ces feuilles, l'une'): the new dawn, hailed by a herald's horn, is here upon this one and only sheet of paper.

Thus this different sibyl, with her 'passé de ramages', represents language as a 'past' full of flowers, whose aroma may yet be released by the 'ouverture' of this unique text; and the word-flowers, conscious of their origins and borne up by the stalks of their history, enact their own reflection:

> De qui le long regret et les tiges de qui
> Trempent en un seul verre à l'éclat alangui—

the recurrence of /i/ in the first of these lines and the homophone of 'verre' in the second suggesting a possible reading: 'en un seul ver, à l'éclat, à langue i.' Or should we hear 'gui' as a parasitic white mistletoe come to insert itself unbidden amidst this splintering of language? At any rate the repetition of /l/ in these lines recalls the beginning of the poem, as the poem itself now tells us:

> (hom.) Une Aurore traînait ses /l/s dans les larmes!

From the white page has emerged a sibyl, an 'Ombre magicienne aux symboliques charmes!' (hom. 'eau symbolique, charme'), whose function now is to call up the dead, to 'evoke' this linguistic 'past', to find a voice. Like the poet in 'Le Démon de l'analogie', the Nourrice has been seeking the

---

[24] A reading of 'costumée' prompted by the homophonic presence of 'chienlit' (carnival mask) two lines earlier: 'Sur ma robe, blanc chienlit, voir? fermé / Au ciel.'

[25] A word-cluster (itself echoing the name 'Hérodiade') which Mallarmé partially 'salvaged' for 'Les Noces d'Hérodiade' where it figures in the 'Scène intermédiaire' (ll. 7–8).

proper voice with which to utter her 'incantation'; but still she is beset by the 'old' ways of using language. Where the new dawn trails sounds ('ses /l/ s'), the Nourrice is still trailing thoughts, and the 'folds' of her text are yellow with the antiquatedness of this 'thought-inspired' use of language. For the moment her voice rises, not like 'le diamant pur de quelque étoile, mais / Antérieure, qui ne scintilla jamais', but like 'une toile encensée': a textual fabric of traditional 'sens' and redolent with the incense of stale religious practice rather than the 'arôme' of a new and sacred dawn. It lies draped across a jumbled heap of 'encensoirs refroidis' (in an earlier version 'ostensoirs refroidis'), the censers or monstrances from which the burning convictions of faith have gone: lines of 'vers/verre' which display the linguistic host falsely as the symbol of a resurrection through representation, an unconvincing incarnation.

And yet, as her voice rises to its climax, her 'textuality' changes from the negative to the positive: the 'trous anciens' and 'plis roidis', suggestive perhaps of the regular caesuras and endstopping of traditional metre ('Percés selon le rythme'), are replaced by 'les dentelles pures / Du suaire'. Her text becomes, like the 'tapisserie', a weft and warp of whiteness; and the poetic voice emerges through its 'belles guipures' (with their hint of pure mistletoe), 'désespéré', 'le vieil éclat voilé'. The old potential of language, its 'éclat' (the brilliance, the polysemic splinteredness and hoped-for diceyness ('dés espérés') of this 'new' language), had previously languished in a single vase (or 'vers' (l. 36)), and even now is 'veiled' in a lace shroud of text. But it is visible at last, at this climactic moment of the poem: 'Cette voix, du passé longue évocation / [...] / S'élève'; the sibyl is weaving her 'symbolique charme'. Her 'robe blanchie' has become a shroud, and she, 'dead' like the poet who has ceded the initiative to words, is both the voice calling up the dead and that dead voice of language which has lain unheard for so long:

> ô quel lointain en ces appels celé.

Here at the heart of the poem, qualifying 'S'élève', homophony tells us what has happened:

> eau quel (qu'aile/elle) loin tain ansé s'appelle ce lait.

As nursemaid to beauty, the milk-white page ('ce lait': cf. again 'mots au lait', 'dés au lait') has become one with the voice of speech ('elle') and the 'plume' of writing ('aile'); and the reflexive waters of the 'bassin' offer a distant, ansate mirroring, a symbol of resurrection.[26]

---

[26] A heraldic device, the ansate cross is, as Lefébure (an Egyptologist) may have informed Mallarmé, the Egyptian symbol of resurrection. This detail foreshadows the importance of the phoenix, the Christian cross, and the handled container ('amphore': cf. 'anse') in 'Sonnet allégorique de lui-même'.

The 'vieil éclat voilé' is now described as being 'du vermeil insolite'—that is, the 'vieil éclat' of language has become 'voile et du vers (voilé du vers), mais insolite'. The old, polysemic brilliance of language is both a veil of verse (concealing and suggesting mystery) and a sail of verse (soon to be hoisted)—and thus verse of an 'insolite' kind, being (by a false etymology found elsewhere in Mallarmé's works[27] without the sun (of representation). This voice is 'languissant'—as it might be, 'languaging', a form of pure 'langue', 'nulle'; but it is also a 'langue hissant', hoisting the white 'voile' of the text in a manner which, unlike the censer, has no need of an 'acolyte' to hold it. And what will this voice 'say'? Will it cast its 'golden sound' (instead of golden incense) like a dicey trumpet at dusk ('Jettera-t-il son or par dernières splendeurs, / Elle, encore (hom. 'aile en cor'), l'antienne aux versets (hom. 'l'ancienne eau versée [i.e. du bassin]') demandeurs'?

Implicitly the answer is yes, since language now disseminates before our ears: the 'heures' and 'heurts' in 'demandeurs' 'demanding' the 'heure' and 'luttes' of the following line. As in 'Le Démon de l'analogie' and later in 'Sonnet allégorique de lui-même', the prospect of 'pure' sound is tantamount to a crepuscular agony, as reference dies a death in this war with reflexivity. Explicitly, it seems as if the voice is already fading: that the silence and darkness which such 'languaging' brings is not to be avoided, as the voice is swallowed up in 'l'ancien passé', and the former 'untextured-ness' (cf. 'Pas de clapotement') returns ('également [...] / [...] vaincu, monotone, lassé'), like the water in a fountain submitting to the force of gravity. The voice has once more become 'fatidique', predictable and un-mysteriously predicting, no longer new and exploring the language of the past.

And yet, as the final section[28] records, 'Elle a chanté': the voice/wing did sing, sometimes incoherently but also (hom.) 'par foi incohérente'. Its 'éclat' was intentionally fragmented, an act of faith in the age-old potential of language; and though its performance might have seemed merely 'Lamentable!', this 'signe / Lamentable!' is the sign for whom tears can be shed, the sign of the old writing which now 'se ré-signe' as the 'signe' of lament, the poem as solemn act of mourning for the death of representation. This intentional 'incoherence' is figured visually in the 'espaces blancs' between ll. 57 and 58, and within l. 59: here is the 'beau lit' addressed homophonically at the beginning of the poem, a bed of vellum pages, which (unlike real beds) serves no purpose (like earlier 'plis / Inutiles') and (being 'claustral') is thus the potential site of beauty in her virginal solitariness.

The voice/wing sang of this bed, and yet already it is as if the voice had never been raised; and the paginal bed on which it was recorded seems to

---

[27] See below the analysis of 'Quand l'ombre menaça...', Part III, Ch. 4.

[28] Mallarmé abandoned this text while still revising it, and at the end of the poem a further line (l. 97) beginning 'Et [...]' suggests that the extant final section might have had a sequel.

bear no trace of the 'folded' dreams of poetry, of the magic spell which, for a moment, seemed audible. There seems to be no trace of dicey, textured language (hom. 'Nie le dé sépulcral à la dé-serte moire'), no 'arôme' of 'word-flowers': 'Le parfum des cheveux endormis' is gone. Like the Faune, the Nourrice wonders if what she has just experienced ever actually took place ('L'avait-il?'); but whereas elusive beauty is symbolized by midday nymphs in 'L'Après-midi d'un faune', here the elusive 'voice' of beauty is presented as a 'Froide enfant' (etymologically, frigid and unspeaking), with the gold of language latent in her 'cheveux endormis'. Having briefly sung (or so the Nourrice believed), sonorous beauty seems now to be withholding herself, revelling in intangible sound-pleasure ('son plaisir subtil') as she continues her 'promenades' at dawn, this now chilly dawn of a new style of writing: 'Au matin grelottant de fleurs' (hom. 'eau, mat tain, grelots, tant, de fleurs'). Water as a 'loin tain' has been replaced by a matt reflexivity (as it might be, 'un éclat voilé'); and the word-flowers not only shiver in the cold but also, etymologically, jingle like 'grelots', a mere 'tintement' compared with the golden horn of the herald. And even in the evening that marks the end of sunlight and representation and the beginning of poetic reflexivity (hom. 'le soir mais chant'), when the seed-filled pomegranates have fallen, beauty seems to be keeping herself to herself as she steps among the ripened, disseminating fruits.

Like the 'touffe de fleurs parjures à la lune' (and this ahistorical poem), she, eternal beauty, is oblivious to time: she ignores the advent of the crescent moon,[29] its shadow on the moondial, just as she ignores the advent of Lucifer, the planet Venus as morning star and bringer of light. The clock of which this star is the metaphorical pendulum is no more important than the clepsydra, in which water falls, as in a fountain, from one receptacle to another, each drop a wound reminiscent of the fountain's tears. Time may pass

> Que, délaissée, elle erre, et, sur son ombre, pas
> Un ange accompagnant son indicible pas!

There beauty wanders, timelessly, like an abandoned child: she is a wing of song (hom. 'aile, air'), sure sound (hom. 'sûr son'), an 'ombre' ('magicienne aux symboliques charmes') and not an angel (like Lucifer); and she is the accompaniment of sound itself—which is not unsayable ('indicible pas!').

If beauty is a 'froide enfant' (later to be identified as Hérodiade), by whom has she been abandoned? By 'Son père', or rather by 'son pair' (or 'son' as 'paire'), by homophony itself.[30] For, as this poem amply demon-

---

[29] A 'croissant' is also an instrument for harvesting and pruning fruit-trees.

[30] A marginal note at this point in the manuscript reads 'le héros', which suggests that Mallarmé may have envisaged further play on the 'heraldic' first two syllables of 'Hérodiade'. The herald that is this poem replaces the former 'héros' of traditional verse within this poem written in alexandrines or 'vers héroïques'?

strates, it is homophony which undoes the univocity of traditional ('paternal') discourse, setting up an 'agon', or combat, between reference and apparently meaningless sound. Hérodiade, as emblem of beauty and as this very poem, is the offspring of homophony and has been nourished by the white spaces of the page, in which polysemy silently 'chants' in a new, 'heraldic' fashion. Her father-king, the emblem of traditional verse, has paid the Nourrice in white salt ('salarie') to suckle beauty, but this Nourrice (or white page) is now, as mentioned earlier, a 'gorge ancienne et tarie': 'gorge' here being a characteristic Mallarméan nexus-word which, in its two senses of 'breast' and 'throat', unites two of the principal semantic fields of this poem (suckling and singing). Like the still fountain, the Nourrice (one might say, poetry itself) is a dried-up spring; and yet, as the 'or' in her 'gorge-antienne' suggests and as the fourth section of the poem reveals, her voice has the capacity to well up in song ('Est-ce la mienne prête à l'incantation?'): she has the wherewithal to suckle beauty and place it upon a vellum bed of purest white.

But Hérodiade's is an unconscious, unreflecting progenitor (as the banality of the repeated 'ne sait pas cela' suggests), a father-king of old who participates in the 'agon' equipped with his 'attirail / Du sièce belliqueux' but without realizing its true nature:

> Son père ne sait pas cela, ni le glacier
> Farouche reflétant de ses armes l'acier.

Previously the 'attirail / Du siècle belliqueux' was a periphrasis for rhyme (because of the rhyme on 'armes' which frames the first and third sections): here we see unwitting homophony defined as the unawareness that the analogy between steel blades (of his 'armes') and glaciers is primarily a linguistic rather than an extra-linguistic phenomenon. Try as he and the word 'glacier' may to deny the fact, the reflection of rhyme (hom. 'nie-le, glace y est!') renders 'equivalent' two 'faits-nomina' ('glacier' and 'l'acier') which are referentially thought to be separate. Indeed homophony must abandon the notion of real 'armes' and see them symbolically reinstated as the heraldic 'coat-of-arms' which is this poem.

Thus the warring father stands over a pile of corpses, the remains of words which have lost their referential lives:

> Quand, sur un tas gisant de cadavres sans coffre
> Odorant de résine, énigmatique, il offre
> Ses trompettes d'argent obscur aux vieux sapins!—

but as yet these remains lack the container and the redolence ('odorant': hom. 'ode or [-ant]') which have previously characterized this poem ('tour', 'chambre', 'arôme', 'sachet'). Hence, like the sibyls of old, unwitting homophony is merely 'énigmatique', speaking incomprehensibly rather than knowingly mobilizing the full resources of language to achieve the 'pure' voice of this poem. Instead of being a '*cor*' heralding 'Une Aurore', it merely blows its '*trompettes d'argent obscur*' in the direction of the forests from which a container (the resinous coffin) might be hewn. Homophony needs to be consciously sounded for it to achieve its 'arôme' and become the means of a new and sacred form of discourse that will replace the 'encensoirs/ostensoirs refroidis' and 'toile encensée'...of Rome.

Homophony must, as it were, return from Rome across the Alps if this new 'holy' child is not to wander, 'délaissée' and 'dé laissé', for ever:

> Reviendra-t-il un jour des pays cisalpins!

The mark of exclamation rather than interrogation here suggests that the Nourrice may not be above such wordplay, particularly as the allusion to Hannibal which this line has often been thought to contain may further suggest that homophony will then have the ivory in which to contain its offspring (cf. l. 27: 'en l'ivoire fermé') and perhaps even an elephantine 'trompe' with which to replace its inadequate 'trompettes'. Be that as it may, the 'son père/pair' must cease to be unwitting; for if homophony is no more than perfunctory, automatic terminal rhyme, the result is 'présage et mauvais rêve'. Each rhyme-word sets up the expectation ('présage') of its predictable pair, and by 'silencing' the potential of more pervasive and consciously orchestrated homophonies, this makes for bad verse ('mauvais rêve'). Homophony must mean more than mere 'plis roidis / Percés selon le rythme'; it must become the 'plis / Inutiles' of a rich complexity.

The poem now comes full circle by evoking the inadequacies of the 'old' way of writing in terms of the dawn, except that on this occasion (as befits a poem-courtroom) we have reached the day of judgement ('Lever du jour dernier qui vient tout achever'), the critical moment. That which previously had been missing and by its lack facilitated the emergence of the 'voice/ wing' now returns: for the 'souvenir' of these inadequate silver trumpets brings with it the old 'ongle' of writing (cf. l. 25), 'le vieux/Ciel', and a relit 'cierge envieux' (hom. 'en vieux'). In paltry simulation of the rising voice within 'ce vitrail', the 'ongle [...] parmi le vitrage s'élève'; and the former 'espace cramoisi' of representational verse looms once more in the 'rougeur de ce temps prophétique' (cf. 'fatidique'). As at the beginning, dusk and dawn seem indistinguishable, except that the dawn is no longer 'L'Aurore' but simply the 'Lever du jour'. The 'old' way of writing is thus still seen as having the potential new dawn of 'le ver[s]' literally within it (in 'Lever'); but timelessness ('l'on ne sait plus l'heure') is now not so much that of eternal beauty as of the ambiguity surrounding the fate of poetry, the 'suspended' state of the 'crépuscule' which etymologically betokens a 'doubtful' time of day. Does this new art of the 'fait-nomen' mean the end of creation or a new beginning?

At this moment of crisis, the abandoned, wandering 'enfant' is exiled within this 'rougeur' (hom. 'rouge heure'), just as (thanks to characteristic 'two-way' Mallarméan syntax) the 'rougeur' is exiled within the 'enfant': the new style of poetry waits to be brought home to its bed of vellum, while this very poem (the 'Ouverture d'Hérodiade' being in one sense a periphrasis for the childhood of Hérodiade) contains within it the 'rougeur' of representation exiled from its referents. In the former case, the child is exiled in 'son cœur pré-cieux', the sound of language preceding the visible skies of representation; in the latter, the 'rougeur' is exiled in the 'cœur précieux' of beauty, the 'incarnats' within its 'cor' (the etymological source of 'cœur'), an 'incantation' intoned by its 'chœur'.

This possibility of a double reading, the one suggesting the unwanted return of the former 'ungolden' poetic language, the other looking forward to the future that is this poem, allows the reader to experience directly the 'agon' of this 'crepuscular' moment:[31] 'Si triste se débat [...] / La rougeur de ce temps prophétique.' Where once the 'or nu' was to be observed 'fustigeant l'espace cramoisi', now the 'rougeur' struggles in 'ce débat' and even (hom.) 'ce débâcle' ('se débat, que l'on ne sait plus l'heure'), in the antiphonal 'debate' of reference and reflexivity, or the melting ice of a splintering 'glace'. This duality, evoked in the ambiguous double exile (of 'enfant' and 'rougeur'), is further figured in a double ocular concealment: on the one hand, the 'enfant' (Hérodiade, 'Hérodiade') hides her (representational) eyes in her 'plume', thus achieving a new reflexive and self-consciously homophonic art; on the other, the old 'cygne/signe' 'mit' its eyes 'en sa plume', that is to say, used its pen for visual representation. But the phrase which follows

> allée
> De la plume détresse, en l'éternelle allée
> De ses espoirs

depends grammatically both on 'enfant' and on the 'plume' of the 'vieux cygne'; so that apparent opposition is again reconciled as both the 'vieux cygne/signe' and the 'enfant' ('Hérodiade') simultaneously proceed from a state of 'plume détresse'—etymologically, from the straitened circumstances of former penmanship, and, homophonically, from 'des tresses', the earlier 'cheveux endormis' of the 'Froide enfant' (anticipating the 'cheveux immaculés' in 'Scène')—to the 'éternelle allée / De ses espoirs'. Here the homophonic 'éther' recalls the 'subtil [eté]' of the child's 'son plaisir', while the homophonic 'aile à lait' may suggest the white and nourishing page upon which the 'voice/wing' rises on its flight-path of hope.

The disappointment apparently described in the final couplet

---

[31] On the manuscript ll. 90 to the end are the most substantially revised (see OC (BM), 218).

De ses espoirs, pour voir les diamants élus
D'une étoile, mourante, et qui ne brille plus!

is, nevertheless, only apparent. It may seem that the dawn of a returning 'old' style of writing blots out that to which the 'enfant' aspires; yet the epitome of beauty has already been defined as 'le diamant pur de quelque étoile mais / Antérieure, qui ne scintilla jamais', a 'pre-representational', non-existent star, a verbal constellation of diamantine purity. As the 'real' star dies (as it might be 'Lucifer', Venus as the morning star), so the 'diamants élus' (cf. the 'plumage héraldique, choisi') of word-stars may shine more brightly.[32] Indeed homophony tells us that they 'éludent une étoile mourante', not to mention the moribund 'toile' of former writing that has been superseded by this 'tapisserie, au lustre nacré, plis / Inutiles'. Thus shall the word-stars of this crepuscular 'poème-enfant' prove playfully elusive in what Mallarmé elsewhere calls 'le doute du Jeu suprême'.[33] As the 'aile' of the poem finally falls silent (like the /l/ in 'brille'), the 'Ouverture' gives on to the white page of the future, the future of reading: 'pour voir les diamants, et lus'. The constellation will shine only if we see it; it now depends on us to 'evoke' by our homophonic reading the beautiful child that is 'Hérodiade'.[34] Only if we 'speak' her and leave her beauty unsullied by non-reflexive interpretations shall she herself find a voice and become the interlocutor of a 'Scène'.

(c) 'Héraut-dyade'

No wonder that Mallarmé later commented to François Coppée in April 1868 that he had 'presque perdu la raison et le sens des paroles les plus familières'.[35] This reading of the 'Ouverture' suggests just why Mallarmé began to undergo a crisis from 1866 onwards. Faced with this dissemination of language, how can the poet ever hope to control such polysemy and 'capture' beauty? Mallarmé's letters over the next two years provide eloquent, if sometimes elusively metaphysical, testimony to the crisis precipitated by the writing of the 'Ouverture'; and the language he uses to describe his experiences during its composition points clearly to 'Hérodiade' being (in its several manifestations) an allegory of its own creation. Thus, for

---

[32] The earlier version of these final seven lines brings in 'avant sa fuite antique / Le cygne légendaire et froid', suggesting that the conceit of the cygne/signe becoming the constellation Cygnus (which informs the final line of 'Le vierge, le vivace...') was already in Mallarmé's mind.

[33] In 'Une dentelle s'abolit', which may in fact date from this period. The 'mandore' in 'Une dentelle s'abolit' is already evident as a variant (for l. 40) in the manuscript of the 'Ouverture': see OC (BM), 217.

[34] 'Cantique de saint Jean' also ends with a rhyme on /lu/. See below, 'Conclusion'.

[35] Corr., i. 270.

example, in December 1865 he tells Cazalis of 'une insaisissable ouverture de mon poème qui chante en moi, mais que je ne puis noter': he is determined to finish 'cette œuvre qui me captive'; 'ce poème, je veux qu'il sorte, joyau magnifique, du sanctuaire de ma pensée; ou je mourrai sur ses débris!'[36] And at the end of April 1866 he bids temporary farewell to 'le cher supplice d'Hérodiade' as he returns to his 'Faune'.

From this famous letter (to Cazalis)[37] it is evident that his 'ouverture musicale', even though 'presqu'encore à l'état d'ébauche', is both the source and the linguistic enactment of Mallarmé's new sense of the Absurd.[38] It is 'en creusant le vers à ce point, [que] j'ai rencontré deux abîmes': one, he remarks wryly, is his weak chest, but the other is 'le Néant'. And if we imagine the first-person voice (singular and plural) in the following passage as that of words themselves speaking, we have a precise summary of the poetic argument of the 'Ouverture':

Oui, *je le sais*, nous ne sommes que de vaines formes de la matière,—mais bien sublimes pour avoir inventés Dieu et notre âme. Si sublimes [...] que je veux me donner ce spectacle de la matière, ayant conscience d'être, et, cependant, s'élançant forcenément dans le [?ce] Rêve qu'elle sait n'être pas, chantant l'Ame et toutes les divines impressions pareilles qui se sont amassées en nous depuis les premiers âges, et proclamant, devant le Rien qui est la vérité, ces glorieux mensonges! [...] Je chanterai en désespéré!

Similarly it is plausible to suppose that the 'Secret' which he claims in July to have recently discovered[39] is this new art of writing which allows language to 'speak' for itself; and again one hears echoes of the vocabulary of the 'Ouverture', of its lace shroud and ripening pomegranates, its cloisters and its mausoleum, as well as of its theme of sacrificial death and jewelled purification: 'je vais me cloîtrer en moi' (cf. 'Tel, inutile et claustral'); 'Je suis mort, et ressuscité avec la clef de pierreries de ma dernière cassette spirituelle'; 'Quand un poème sera mur, il se détachera'; 'de merveilleuses dentelles, que je devine, et qui existent déjà dans le sein de la Beauté'.[40] The 'gorge ancienne et tarie' of beauty has been rejuvenated in the voice of a symbolic Nourrice, the 'sein de la Beauté' herself, a new form of poetry to suckle 'Hérodiade'—as if the 'sein' of 'Don du poème' and the title of 'Sainte' had combined in Mallarmé's mind to give birth to a new myth of 'saint Jean'. And the display of language's autonomy within the

---

[36] *Corr.*, i. 180.

[37] *Corr.* i. 206–10, corrected by *DSM*, vi. 307–10.

[38] Cf. the 'lambeaux maudits d'une phrase absurde' in the first paragraph of 'Le Démon de l'analogie'.

[39] *Corr.*, i. 222 (to Aubanel, 16 July 1866).

[40] *Corr.*, i. 222, 225 (to Aubanel, 28 July 1866). Cf. also a letter of 17 May 1867: 'je rejetterai toujours toute compagnie, pour promener mon symbole partout où je vais et, dans une chambre pleine de beaux meubles comme dans la nature, me sentir un diamant qui réfléchit, mais n'est pas par lui-même' (i. 248–9).

'Ouverture' finds its clearest theoretical expression in a letter to Coppée of December 1866, where the 'death' of reference and the overriding importance of reflexivity are categorically stated:

ce à quoi nous devons viser surtout est que, dans le poème, les mots—qui déjà sont assez eux pour ne plus recevoir d'impression du dehors—*se reflètent les uns sur les autres jusqu'à paraître ne plus avoir leur couleur propre, mais n'être que les transitions d'une gamme.*[41]

The consequences of Mallarmé's 'discovery', his so-called 'crise de Tournon', are well known and have been much discussed. Again the famous remarks in his correspondence carry powerful echoes of the 'Ouverture', and one of the most celebrated of these remarks (to Cazalis in May 1867) recalls its 'plumage héraldique'; namely, Mallarmé's reference to his 'lutte terrible avec ce vieux et méchant plumage, terrassé, heureusement, Dieu'.[42] This 'lutte' evokes the 'agonie' described in the 'Ouverture' (l. 53), with its 'vain plumage noir', its 'vieux / Ciel' and 'soir méchant'; and Mallarmé describes his own struggle with the 'vieux et méchant plumage' as being unexpectedly arduous, rather as the 'vieux / Ciel' threatens to reassert itself at the end of the 'Ouverture':

comme cette lutte s'était passée sur son aile osseuse qui, par une agonie plus vigoureuse que je ne l'eusse soupçonné chez lui, m'avait emporté dans des Tenebres [*sic*], je tombai, victorieux, éperdument et infiniment—jusqu'à ce qu'enfin je me sois revu un jour devant ma glace de Venise.

J'avoue du reste [...] que j'ai encore besoin, tant ont été grandes les avanies de mon triomphe, de me regarder dans cette glace pour penser, et que si elle n'était pas devant la table où je t'écris cette lettre, je redeviendrais le Néant.[43]

Here Mallarmé seems to be restating the argument of 'Les Fenêtres' as his own recent experience. From being at one with God, he is now a Lucifer, a fallen satanic hero—and a mirrored double who needs reflexivity to be sure of his own existence; in other words, he is an 'héros-dyade'. For the word 'dyade' is as likely to have been suggested to Mallarmé by the name 'Hérodiade' as the words 'héraut' and 'héros'; and there is every reason to suppose that he understood it in the sense defined four years later in Larousse's *Grand Dictionnaire universel du XIXe siècle*: 'État imparfait dans lequel, selon les pythagoriciens, tombe un être qui se sépare de Dieu.'

In Pythagorean thought, as Mallarmé could have known from his last year at school, from any work of reference, and perhaps also from his discussions with Lefébure, the dyad is an important principle, and the forerunner of the Platonic Idea. Taking the article 'Dyade' in the *Grand*

---

[41] *Corr.*, i. 234 (Mallarmé's emphasis).   [42] *Corr.*, i. 241.
[43] Ibid., corrected by *DSM*, vi. 341.

Larousse as representative of contemporary understanding of the matter, it is possible to see what Mallarmé may have understood by the term: namely, the relationship between the one and the many. Having proclaimed Pythagoras 'le père de l'idéalisme', the article explains the Pythagorean dyad of unity and infinity in the following way:

Au milieu des phénomènes du monde [...] il est un seul caractère qui met l'ordre et l'harmonie en toutes choses, et qui leur donne la faculté de devenir intelligibles: c'est le nombre. Mais le nombre ne suffit pas pour expliquer le monde; donnez au nombre une vertu formative et spécifique, il faut à cette vertu une matière sur quoi elle puisse s'exercer. Aussi, à l'idée du nombre, il faut joindre une autre idée qui lui serve de complément. Cette notion nouvelle est celle de l'infini, indéfinissable, indéterminé, matière qui n'est rien par elle-même, mais que la vertu, l'action du nombre élève à l'existence. De là résulte une dualité qui devient le fondement de la connaissance rationnelle. Ainsi, pour expliquer le monde, il faut poser d'un côté l'unité, principe d'être et de connaissance, et de l'autre la pluralité infinie, qui n'est rien sans la participation de l'unité.

At the linguistic level this gives us the dyad of homophony and polysemy which is manifest in the 'Ouverture', a unity of sound leading to a plurality of meaning. Such a dyad is epitomized in rhyme, where one sound unites two words which are different in sense; but as our reading of the 'Ouverture' suggests, this duality of rhyme operates not only in terminal position but throughout every syllable of the text, turning the 'plis roidis / Percés selon le rythme' of traditional verse into the 'plis / Inutiles' of the 'Ouverture', a 'tapisserie' of proliferating relationships.

After explaining the role of the dyad in Platonic thought, the entry in the *Grand Larousse* ends by referring to the 'théologie de Xénocrate' (warning us with unwitting prescience that 'nous sommes ici en plein symbolisme'!) and relating how for Xenocrates 'les dieux étaient l'*un* d'abord, puis la *dyade*':

L'*un* de nature mâle, était à ses yeux le père et le roi du ciel; il recevait aussi les noms de Zeus, d'intelligence; la *dyade*, de nature femelle, était une divinité subordonnée, mère de la justice divine, âme de l'univers. Au-dessous de la *dyade* étaient une multitude de petits dieux planétaires, identiques en nature à la *dyade*, qui elle-même est intermédiaire entre l'unité, le grand Zeus, et les petits dieux planétaires.

This evocation of gender difference recalls both Hérodiade's father ('son père', 'le roi', 'le vieux / Ciel') and her own divided status (as body and reflected image), as well as the 'divided female' represented by the Nourrice and her 'Froide enfant'. Moreover, as mother of divine justice, this perhaps is the 'dyade' who presides over the 'Lever du jour dernier' described at the end of the 'Ouverture'.

Whether or not Mallarmé knew his Xenocrates, it would seem from 'Hérodiade' as a whole that he has been 'inspired' by the notion of the 'dyade' as a principle of creativity, by the idea of duality marking a positive advance from former, sterile unities (God, univocity) towards difference (dramatic dialogue, 'débat', antiphony, dialectic, the 'grand "Ou"', Vers') and even 'différance'.[44] In terms of the imagery used in the 'Ouverture', the dyad is what creates the 'clapotement', is what produces textuality. The dyad of rhyme itself, the further dyadic relationship between distichs alternating masculine and feminine rhyme, the dyadic or 'binary' structure which underlies so much of Mallarmé's poetry during the 1860s and which will soon lead him back to the sonnet (with its 'fold' of octave and sestet), all are brought to mind by the name of 'Hérodiade'—which has, as Mallarmé wished, very little indeed to do with Salome and a great deal to do with the new poetic art which it 'heralds'. Indeed the title itself proclaims a dyadic relationship between the dyad (of homophony and polysemy) and the 'héros/héraut' that is the poet: the herald, regarded in former times as a 'sacred' person charged with the transmission of messages, and often a 'héraut d'armes' (cf. the use of 'armes' as the first and 'framing' rhyme in the 'Ouverture'). As herald, he was the object of a ceremonial 'baptême', when the king would 'anoint' him with wine and bestow a heraldic name upon him;[45] as herald, he announced and proclaimed, becoming synonymous with 'harbinger', 'forerunner', 'precursor'... Mallarmé's 'héraut' foretells the appearance of St John the Baptist himself, and the dyadic relationship of Hérodiade with his severed head, with a Precursor chopped in two.

And this may explain how Mallarmé could dispense with such a masterpiece as the 'Ouverture' when he came back to 'Hérodiade' in the 1890s and replaced it with the three-part 'Prélude' of which the 'Cantique de saint Jean' was intended as the middle section.[46] In this 'Prélude' (a musical, 'preludic' preparation for the appearance of Hérodiade herself in the crepuscular 'doute du Jeu suprême'), it is St John who fulfils the role of herald, with the sunset of representation now being seen as analogous to the halo surrounding his severed head, and the 'langue roidie' (l. 3) of the decapitated saint (like the 'plis roidis' of the old sibyls) giving way to a disembodied voice (like that of the new sibyl) which sings the 'Cantique', this

[44] The term 'dyade' occurs in Derrida's analysis of 'Mimique' but without reference to 'Hérodiade' (see *La Dissémination*, 234).

[45] See Larousse under 'héraut'. This ceremony is thus akin to the 'sacre' of a new king: cf. Mallarmé's comment to Lefébure in May 1868: 'Décidément, je redescends de l'absolu... mais cette fréquentation de deux années (vous vous rappelez? depuis notre séjour à Cannes) me laissera une marque dont je veux faire un sacre' (*Corr.*, i. 273).

[46] In a short bibliographical note at the end of 'Les Noces d'Hérodiade', he refers to 'une ouverture que je remplace par une autre, en le même sens' (*OC* (BM), 456). Another note suggests why it may not be out of place to discuss later versions of 'Hérodiade' at this juncture in Mallarmé's poetic development: 'Dangereux de compléter mûr un poème de jeunesse—mais il était suffisamment en avance sur moi, quand je le fis, pour qu'aujourd'hui je n'aie pas trop à reculer en arrière' (see *Les Noces d'Hérodiade: Mystère*, ed. Davies, 95–6).

'psaume de nul antique antiphonaire'. The 'dyadic' relationship of homo-
phony and polysemy is suggested in 'Prélude. I' by the terms of the analogy
between the poem and the salver upon which the head rests ('Lourd[47] métal
usuel où l'équivoque range / Avec anxiété [text incomplete] gloire étrange'),
and in 'Prélude. III' by the 'irruption au trou / Grand ouvert par un vol
ébloui de vitrage'. Here, like the new sibyl (or heraldic harbinger) replacing
the old:

> Le Fantôme accoudé du pâle écho latent
> Sous un voile debout ne dissimule tant
> Supérieurement à de noirs plis Prophète
> Toujours que de ne pas perpétuer du faîte
> Divers rapprochements scintillés absolus.
>
> (ll. 7–11)

'Équivoque'; (hom.) 'trou / Grand "ou", Vers'; (hom.) 'un vol. [i.e. un
volume] [...] de vitrage'; 'écho latent'; (hom.) 'du faîte, dit "Vers"': the
'equi-vocal', alternating reflexivity of echoing homophony upon the summit
of poetic endeavour was, in the unfinished 'Les Noces d'Hérodiade', about
to be redisplayed in an even more complex manner than in the 'Ouverture'.
Further homophonies are exploited, with 'sein/saint' replacing the play on
'sein/bassin/symboliques': thus 'le manque du saint' at the beginning of
'Prélude. I' is echoed by the 'seins abolis' at the end of 'Prélude. III'. Thus
also the symbolic 'lait' of the Nourrice returns, contrasted (perhaps as 'laid')
with the more 'creative' 'sang' that is shed by a decapitation and a ruptured
hymen ('Finale', l. 32): hence /sã/ provides the opening rhyme of 'Les Noces
d'Hérodiade', while /le/ marks the end of the 'Prélude' and the beginning of
the 'Finale'. The milk of childhood nurture gives way to the Baptist's gory
'baptême du sang' and to the blood of Hérodiade's nuptial consummation:

> Pour que je m'entr'ouvrisse et reine triomphasse—

the plethora of 's' sounds recalling the 's' with which 'Les Noces' begins, as
well as Mallarmé's famous description of the letter 's' as 'dissolvante et
disséminante'.[48]
    The theme of union and severance which informs the earlier manifesta-
tion of 'Hérodiade' (the 'Scène' and the 'Ouverture') is, of course, taken up
in 'Les Noces d'Hérodiade' by the twin themes of Hérodiade's wedding and
the decapitation of St John. But in both the earlier and the later versions it
seems as though Mallarmé has allowed the idea of the heroic couplet, or
'rimes plates', to 'write' the poem for him, rather as he will allow the idea of
'rimes croisées' to 'write' the 'Sonnet allégorique de lui-même'. From being

---

[47] Recalling the 'lourde tombe' of the 'Ouverture', and again the etymological origin of
'lourd' ('luridus' = pale).
[48] In a note dating from 1895 (OC, 855).

the automatic choice of a poet writing for the theatre in 'Scène', it is maintained in the 'Ouverture', where its 'dyadic' character is foregrounded by the way in which couplets span the separate sections of the poem; and it is further maintained, most unusually, in the quatrains of the 'Cantique de saint Jean'. It is almost as if Mallarmé has transformed the most common verse-form in French poetry into the charger upon which the severed head of St John shall rest, 'rimes plates' into the 'plat d'or' mentioned at the very end of the 'Scène intermédiaire'. 'Jettera-t-il son or par dernières splendeurs', asks the Nourrice in the 'Ouverture' (l. 51): 'son or' will cast its sonorous light not only in the terminal splendours of rhyme, but upon the circular, mirror-like platter of conscious homophonic play.

As the 'Cantique de saint Jean' itself suggests, rhyme is 'un frisson / A l'unisson': a sound-shiver of matching sound, the one and the many. The poetic 'couple' of rhyme-words is at once united and separated—like Hérodiade and her nurse, St John's body and head, Hérodiade and St John's head. Rhyming couplets are the jewelled words which Hérodiade can perceive at the end of 'Scène': 'D'une enfance sentant [...] / Se séparer enfin ses froides pierreries'—homophonies separating, or splitting open, 'en fin de vers', from the 'une' of unsignifying 'infancy'. From the perfect wholeness of homophony as uniform sound, the 'dyade' of difference epitomized by rhyme spawns the multiple folds of poetic language, a milky white page from which the poem rises, anadyomene, like Venus from the waves: Venus, the morning and the evening star (respectively, Lucifer and Hesperus); Venus, the goddess of beauty in cisalpine Rome; Venus, the mother of Eros, that anagrammatic 'rose cruelle' with 'armes' of his own who here presides over 'les di-amants élus / D'une étoile, mourante', Hérodiade and St John chosen by beauty for this strangest and most fecund of unions; Venus, the mother of 'Ero[s]diade'.

May it be that the word 'dyade', accidentally 'discovered' within 'Hérodiade', led Mallarmé to envisage a philosophical basis for the reflexive art which he had been developing since the early 1860s? It is plain from his correspondence in 1866 that his dream of the 'Grand Œuvre' begins here:[49]

---

[49] 'J'ai jeté les fondements d'un œuvre magnifique' (*Corr.*, i. 222 (16 July 1866)); 'J'ai voulu te dire simplement que je venais de jeter le plan de mon œuvre entier'; 'je prévois qu'il me faudra vingt ans pour les cinq livres dont se composera l'œuvre' (*Corr.*, i. 224, 225 (28 July 1866)); 'Ainsi, je viens à l'heure de la Synthèse, de délimiter l'œuvre qui sera l'image de ce développement. Trois poèmes en vers, dont Hérodiade est l'Ouverture, mais d'une pureté que l'homme n'a pas atteint[e] et n'atteindra peut-être jamais [...] Et quatre poèmes en prose, sur la conception spirituelle du Néant'; 'mon œuvre, qui est l'*Œuvre*, le Grand' Œuvre, comme disaient les alchimistes, nos ancêtres (*Corr.*, i. 242, 244 (14 May 1867), corrected by *DSM*, vi. 340–4); 'mon œuvre est si bien préparé et hiérarchisé, représentant comme il peut l'Univers, que je n'aurais su, sans endommager quelqu'une de mes impressions étagées, rien en enlever' (*Corr.*, i. 279 (18 July 1868)). Cf. 'Autobiographie', *OC*, 662–3.

was it the very principle of the 'dyade', of the one and the many, which led him perhaps to envisage a work in several, interlinked parts? Did the original plan to have an 'œuvre' made up of 'cinq livres' spring from his use of the word 'lustre', the five-year ceremony of purification?[50] Did his elaborate project of an 'œuvre [...] si bien préparé et hiérarchisé, représentant comme il peut l'Univers' derive from the philosophical debate concerning the unity and infinity of the universe to which his investigation of the word 'dyade' had led him? Is there not a direct link between the Pythagorean and Platonic 'dyade' and Mallarmé's later description of the 'Livre' as 'l'hymne, harmonie et joie, comme pur ensemble groupé dans quelque circonstance fulgurante, des relations entre tout'?[51] Is it not the 'dyade' which leads to Mallarmé's individual use of the word 'Idée', for example, in 'Prose (pour des Esseintes)' or 'La Musique et les lettres'? Is it not the 'dyade' which led eventually to his apparently idiosyncratic definition of music in January 1893: 'Employez Musique dans le sens grec, au fond signifiant Idée ou rythme entre des rapports.'[52] Or, as he put it in 'Crise de vers':

ce n'est pas de sonorités élémentaires par les cuivres, les cordes, les bois, indéniablement mais de l'intellectuelle parole à son apogée que doit avec plénitude et évidence, résulter, en tant que l'ensemble des rapports existant dans tout, la Musique.[53]

In his pursuit of Beauty, Mallarmé had stumbled upon a conception of 'musical' art which would take him to the summit of Mount Parnassus.

(ii) 'L'Après-midi d'un faune' (1865–1876)

> ce mal d'être deux.

'L'Après-midi d'un faune' began as an interlude in a summer break. In June 1865 Mallarmé informed Cazalis of his new poetic project in the following terms:

J'ai laissé Hérodiade pour les cruels hivers: cette œuvre solitaire m'avait stérilisé, et, dans l'intervalle, je rime un intermède héroïque, dont le héros est un Faune. Ce poème renferme une très haute et très belle idée, mais les vers sont terriblement

---

[50] The 'lustre' recurs in 'Finale' (l. 43), and is also to be found in 'Quant au livre' and in Le 'Livre' de Mallarmé, ed. Jacques Scherer (2nd edn, Paris, 1977), fos 50B, 86B. By May 1867, however, the number of projected parts had grown to seven: 'Trois poèmes en vers [...] Et quatre "poèmes en prose"' (see previous note).

[51] 'Le Livre, instrument spirituel', OC, 378.

[52] Corr., vi. 26.

[53] OC, 367–8.

difficiles à faire, car je le fais absolument scénique, non *possible au théâtre*, mais *exigeant le théâtre*. Et cependant je veux conserver toute la poésie de mes œuvres lyriques, mon vers même, que j'adapte au drame.[54]

Having envisaged 'Hérodiade' originally as a 'tragédie', he had just been working on its 'Scène'; and his idea for an 'intermède héroïque' would appear to spring in the first instance from an ambition, encouraged by Banville, to have his own 'acte en vers' put on at the Théâtre français. As an 'intermède' it would have been performed as an 'entr'acte' within another play, which may explain why Mallarmé speaks of its being not only possible in the theatre (like the 'Scène' of 'Hérodiade') but actually requiring the theatre. For the poem, from its earliest conception to its definitive version,[55] is a poem about interruption; and its performance as the 'interruption' of another play would have been a brilliant and reflexive 'coup de théâtre'. Moreover, like 'Le Démon de l'analogie' and the 'Ouverture' to 'Hérodiade', it requires to be 'heard'; and it is quite possible that the reason Mallarmé now aspired to be performed derived not simply from an ambitious young poet's eagerness to cash in on the fashion for the Banvillian 'acte en vers', but more especially from his growing awareness of the central role of homophony in his poetry.

The written text impoverishes homophony by 'plumping' for one particular spelling and thus obscuring the other words which are simultaneously audible. By means of rich rhyme, and particularly of punning rhyme ('rime équivoque'), and by dint of careful sound-patterning, it is possible to draw attention to these homophonic possibilities; but how much more effective ('peindre, non la chose, mais l'effet qu'elle produit') if the receiver can only hear the words. In the event Banville and Coquelin rejected the 'Intermède' when Mallarmé took it to them the following September (because it lacked 'l'anecdote nécessaire');[56] but Mallarmé never relinquished his ambition to have the poem 'performed', and in 1890 he welcomed Paul Fort's proposal to put it on at the Théâtre d'art and enthusiastically envisaged 'une ré-publication définitive, avec quelques réflexions de moi sur la poésie et le théâtre, la récitation de ce poème et le point de vue exact d'une mise en scène'.[57] As is evident from his theatre criticism and from his private notes (those published by Jacques Scherer

[54] *Corr.*, i. 166; *DSM*, vi. 289 (Mallarmé's emphases).

[55] 'L'Après-midi d'un favne. Éclogve', published by Derenne, with illustrations by Manet, in 1876. The Latin use of 'v' instead of 'u' has been adopted in Bertrand Marchal's edition of the *Poésies* (1992), but it is not clear that Mallarmé wished to retain this in the Deman edition. In the last published version of the poem within his lifetime (on 15 Mar. 1896 in *La Plume*), 'u' replaces 'v'.

[56] *Corr.*, i. 174 (to Aubanel, 16 Oct. 1865).

[57] *Corr.*, iv. 165 (to Edmond Deman, 29 Nov.). This project came to naught, and it was ironic that the poem should eventually achieve public 'performance' only in the non-verbal form of Debussy's prelude (in 1894).

as Le 'Livre'), oral performance remained an abiding interest; and 'Mimique' is of particular importance in this respect because it addresses what happens when there is a soundless 'performance', the 'evocations' of mime being akin to the silent 'evocations' within the white spaces of the poetic text.

There is reason to suppose, therefore, that Mallarmé's perception of the tension between speech and writing begins to become more acute at the time of these early 'dramatic' experiments, 'Hérodiade' and the 'Intermède héroïque'. The images of mouth and hand in the verse and prose poems of this period—'bouche', 'lèvres', 'dent', 'baiser', 'gorge', 'voix', 'tête'; 'doigt', 'main(t)', 'plume', 'aile'—become more insistent and more central within these works, notably 'Plainte d'automne', 'Le Démon de l'analogie', and 'Don du poème'; and the parallel evolution of a concept of 'silent music', most particularly in 'Sainte', suggests that this paradox constitutes a kind of Hegelian 'synthèse' of speech and writing.

As a poem about 'interruption', 'L'Après-midi d'un faune' would seem to spring from the notion of the dyad which Mallarmé had encountered in the word 'Hérodiade'. The plausibility of a 'dyadic' reading of 'Hérodiade' is much enhanced by the clear evidence (to be discussed presently) that the duality of rhyme was the 'source' of a major poem written in seasonal counterpoint with it. Indeed, quite simply, an 'intermède héroïque' is what results from a 'héros-dyade'. In 'Hérodiade', beauty, the object of Mallarmé's pursuit, is portrayed as caught in a dilemma, a dilemma or dialectic that is represented by the drama of rhyme: the 'oneness' of perfection requires duality if it is to exist (cf. the reflection of Narcissus), just as the 'oneness' of homophony requires the duality of rhyme (internal as well as terminal) if the poetic text is to exist and the 'virtualités' of language are to be released—and just as the text must 'reflect' on itself if its beauty is to be recognized. Further, 'Hérodiade' is the voice of language speaking: in the version conceived in the 1860s, the voice of the Nourrice (in the 'Ouverture') which 'separates' into the dual voice, or dialogue, of the Nourrice and Hérodiade; in the later version (in so far as this may be surmised), a 'preludic' voice containing that of St John and calling up the voice of Hérodiade herself, in dialogue (the 'Scène') and then in triumphant monologue (the 'Finale'). In the various versions of 'L'Après-midi d'un faune' the Faune is also the voice of language speaking: he is, after all, 'un phone'.[58] Here, possibly, is Mallarmé's 'très haute et très belle idée': the Faune, or phonetic

---

[58] Now pronounced /fɔn/, the word dates back beyond 1857, when it was a term in linguistics meaning 'Unité sonore servant à l'expression linguistique' (Robert). The word does not appear in either Larousse or Littré, but these dictionaries show that the first syllable of all cognate words (e.g. 'phonique', 'phonétisme', which date back earlier in the century) was then pronounced /fon/. As a newly qualified language-teacher Mallarmé would have been especially alert to the possibilities of these terms.

unit, pursues beauty in the form of two nymphs, the elusive *dyad* of rhyme.[59]

(a) *'Intermède héroïque'*

The 'Intermède héroïque' would have been in three parts, the Faune's waking monologues ('Monologue d'un faune', 'Le Réveil du faune') being interrupted by his dream of the nymphs conversing ('Scène entre Iane et Ianthé'). The 'Monologue d'un faune' alone 'survived' to become, first, the 'Improvisation d'un faune' (the version rejected by the editors of the *Parnasse contemporain* in 1875), and then 'L'Après-midi d'un favne. Églogve'. This final version is discussed below, but it is important to note first how Mallarmé's 1865 version was taking shape before he abandoned it to return to 'Hérodiade' and its 'Ouverture'.

In the case of the 'Monologue', the familiar binary structure is once again in evidence: 106 alexandrines divide into two groups of 58 and 48 lines respectively, the first recounting the Faune's reaction to the nymphs' departure and his search for evidence of their having been there at all, and the second displaying his verbal re-enactment of his remembered encounter. The second part mirrors the first by recalling many of its images in a similar sequence, while the final eighteen lines of the poem constitute a finale to reflect the opening eighteen lines, which end with the Faune calling on the marsh reeds to relate what happened ('contez'). Thus two central sections of thirty lines (ll. 19–58, 59–88) each begin with narrative accounts of the nymphs (what the reeds might say, what his memories recall); while the surrounding 'frame' exhibits the Faune's dual attempts in the present to deal with their absence, each of these attempts ending (respectively, in rapt reminiscence and intoxicated sleep) with references to his reliance on the resource of wine. The poem ends, much as it does in the final version, with the Faune saying 'good riddance' ('Oublions-les!'; later 'Tant pis!') and thinking of multiple further conquests ('Assez d'autres encore'); but the final line of the 'Monologue':

> Adieu, femmes: duo de vierges quand je vins

suggests that there has been a move from virginal duality to deflowered and plural womanhood.

This progression from aspiration to resignation, and from purity (cf. also l. 33: 'Serais-je pur?') to promiscuity, is reflected in the rhymes themselves,

---

[59] The possible equation of the nymphs with rhyme is noted but not further developed by Rosaline Crowley, 'Towards the Poetics of Juxtaposition: "L'Après-midi d'un faune"', *Yale French Studies*, 54 (1977), 34.

as we proceed from the opening rhyme on 'l'air' to the final rhyme on 'vins', from song to wine, from a spiritual to a physical source of 'ivresse'. This rhyme-frame, and the important thematic duality which it summarizes, will remain in the 'Églogue'; but in the 'Monologue' it is further reinforced at the 'pivot' of the poem where the first part ends on the rhyme on 'vers' ('des souvenirs divers'; hom. 'des souvenirs dits "vers"'), and the second begins with a rhyme on /yːr/ in which it may not be too fanciful to hear the shaggy, bearded head ('hure') of a Faune.[60] Thus the dyadic nature of the poem itself reflects the double nature of its eponymous hero: its top half bespeaks a superior (human) aspiration to beauty through the art of music, its bottom half wantonly evokes a baser, more physical pursuit of 'la grande Vénus' (l. 97).

Rhyme is also an important structuring agent in the 'Intermède' as a whole. The 'Scène entre Iane et Ianthé', of which only four short fragments survive, 'dramatizes' the split which has occurred between the two nymphs (of such similar names). Where the Faune wondered what he had seen, Iane now (in the first fragment) herself appears, alone, wondering what she has heard and whether her recent 'soupirs' betokened 'charme ou [...] tristesse'. The 'main du faune' has severed her from Ianthé 'que ma chevelure aime', her sister nymph to whom she had been bound as though in the tresses of rhyme. Accordingly, her first line

> Adieu!
>   S'il entendait!
>   Je vins,

responds to the final rhyme-word of the Faune's monologue.[61] When the two nymphs appear together (in the second fragment), they again share the rhyme ('songe' / 'plonge'); and in the final fragment, after Iane has played the Faune's 'flûte', they continue to share the rhyme in urgent preparation for flight. But Iane refuses to follow Ianthé, and their final shared rhyme transpires to be a poignant pun ('tu me suis' / 'je suis') when Iane's 'suis' turns out to be not a sign of acquiescence but an assertion of individuality:

> je suis
> Celle qui dois errer sous l'épaisse ramure
> Des forêts!

Iane belongs to the Faune and not to her sister nymph; hence 'Le Réveil du faune' begins with the Faune taking up Iane's rhyme:

---

[60] The insistent presence of this syllable in all versions of the poem is noted in Jean-Pierre Chausserie-Laprée, 'Équilibres mallarméens', *Europe*, 54 (Apr.–May 1976), 168.

[61] For this purpose Mallarmé would have had to remove 'duo de vierges quand je vins' from this line, so that the Faune's 'Adieu, femmes' is reduced to the four syllables necessary for the shared alexandrine (as pointed out by Marchal (ed.), *Poésies*, 207).

Doux éclat par quoi cesse un murmure!

—the very rhyme on /yːr/ which began the second, 'wanton' half of the 'Monologue'.

The scene with the nymphs, which mirrors many of the images used in the 'Monologue', also makes explicit what is more veiled in the 'Églogue', namely that the nymphs are analogous with the reeds which the Faune has cut down and turned into his 'flûte' (like Pan's pipes):

> Vois
> Cette flûte ... A l'horreur ténébreuse les voix
> Seules des grands roseaux murmuraient sous la brise.
> L'homme, sa rêverie interdite te brise,
> Les coupa pour verser en eux ses chants sacrés.
> Les femmes sont les sœurs des roseaux massacrés.
>
> (ll. 25–30)

In other words, rhyme comprises the twin pipes of sundered homophony, sounds ripped from the marshy wastes of noise and bound together as the sacred instrument of the poet. And the rhyming couplet resembles two nymphs, with the second rhyme-word ready (like Iane) to go in search of a new partner, and the other (like Ianthé) desperate that they should stick together, two virginal sisters needing to be parted by the lips and fingers of a Faune and so transformed into the instruments of a fertile, poetic beauty. This fertility stems in the first instance from the proliferation of subsequent terminal rhymes which Iane's 'desertion' of her sister permits; and also from the move beyond terminal rhyme to more widespread homophony within the broader ramifications of the text, here figured as the 'épaisse ramure / Des forêts!'

'Le Réveil du faune' begins with a punning reference to the sweet rewards of a splintered alexandrine and a stichomythic rhyme:

Doux éclat par quoi cesse un murmure!

The repetitiveness of rhyme ('mur-mure'), immediately re-evoked in the phrase 'L'eau parlait avec l'eau', is but a murmur compared with the burst of poetic sound (hom. 'douze! éclat') released by this 'prosodic union' within one alexandrine of Iane and the Faune, and of 'ramure' and 'mur-mure'. Now describing what he has just been dreaming, the Faune relates that where previously Cypris (an alternative name for Venus) was absent from his dream, Iane's brief tune on his flute (in the previous 'Scène') has been 'une mélodie à sept notes'. Beauty has played the full gamut of sound, and, newly inspired, the Faune echoes her 'ramure' in his first 'independent' rhyme-word after 'murmure': 'ramiers', which in turn 'provokes' his next new rhyme-word: 'roucoule'. Having recalled early artistic success (ll. 45–7) and subsequent failure (ll. 48–52), he now falls under the spell of Iane's

remembered scale (as the stage direction indicates) and affirms his faith in a
return to the origins of language ('Mélodie, ô ruisseau de jeunesse qui
coule!') and the advent of a new kind of non-representational, homophonic
art:

> L'art, quand il désigna l'un des faunes élus,
> [text incomplete] ne le déserte plus.
> A des sons, dans le vice inutile, il recule.
> Et, l'impuissant fuyant dans un vil crépuscule,
> Le remords sur sa lèvre amènera, fatal
> Les stériles lambeaux du poème natal.
> Et la voix part des joncs unis, que nous n'osâmes
> Briser, pour demander le reste de nos âmes.
>
> (ll. 53–60)

Here, satiated by the vain and mistaken pursuit of physical beauty (cf. ll.
48–9: 'quand notre être s'ennuie / De cheveux lacérés et de robes'), the
Faune/phone reverts to his original nature; and, powerless to possess the
world, this remorseful emblem of language mouths once more the 'sterile'
sounds of non-representational words—and thereby, like the Nourrice,
temporarily finds a voice, the voice of rhyme, at once plural ('joncs') and
united, not a random phonetic break but a controlled, reflexive separation
('que nous n'osâmes / Briser').

While he slept (in ignorance of this art), his fingers were 'appesantis' and
his 'souffle inerte'; but now the waking Faune, the instruments of speech
and writing freshly restored, heralds this return to his origins by evoking the
dawn in terms of ancient Greek mythology. Half-human and half-animal
like the Faune himself, tritons sound their conch-shells to announce the
chariot of the sun ('quadrige effaré'), as it rises like Venus Anadyomene
from a primordial sea, a 'Prélude ruisselant [...] lever' (cf. 'le vers'). The
Faune has renounced physical beauty in favour of a pure and crystalline
reflexivity, an 'Idéal limpide' (l. 79):

> Je veux, dans vos clartés limpides, innover
> Une âme de cristal pur que jette la flûte
>
> (ll. 74–5)

and, like the new 'voice' in the 'Ouverture', he will undergo the watery
ceremony of a lustral rebirth (thus 'resurrecting' the 'transparente pluie'
(l. 47) of his earlier artistic success):

> A la piscine
> Des sources, à l'horreur lustrale qui fascine
> L'azur, je vais déjà tremper l'être furtif
> Qui de leur glace va renaître, primitif!
>
> (ll. 79–82)

The seven notes played by Iane have been transformed into a musical prelude of 'tritons' and 'quadrige'; that is, into an artful combination of bold intervals (a 'triton', or tritone, being also a musical interval of three whole tones, or an augmented fourth) which celebrate the quadriga of a rhyming couplet, the distich and its four potential hemistichs (a 'quadrige' being a two-wheel chariot drawn by four horses abreast).

'Douze! éclat!' indeed, for the horses that are Mallarmé's hemistichs seem also to pull in different directions. As he later told Jules Huret, with reference to the 1875 'Improvisation':

> J'essayais, en effet, de mettre, à côté de l'alexandrin dans toute sa tenue, une sorte de jeu courant pianoté autour, comme qui dirait d'un accompagnement musical fait par le poète lui-même et ne permettant au vers officiel de sortir que dans les grandes occasions.[62]

Already in the 'Intermède héroïque' there is, as subsequently in the 'Ouverture' (to 'Hérodiade') as well as in the 'Improvisation' and the 'Églogue', considerable tension between syntax and metre. Many of the alexandrines are fragmented (both on the page and in intended performance) by the silence of surmise and the dramatic urgency of question and exclamation. The first line of the 'Monologue' sets the tone:

> J'avais des nymphes!
>   Est-ce un songe? Non: le clair

—and this 'interrupted' style is maintained throughout the 'Intermède'. At the same time, even in the absence of such 'espaces blancs', the syntax rarely matches the pattern of the alexandrine; and both the high incidence of enjambement and the constant dislocation of word order by a wide range of grammatical constructions (apostrophe, inversion, imperatives, apposition, etc.) place the metrical 'frame' of the poem under great pressure. Hence terminal rhyme emerges as a vital unifying feature, perhaps the one remaining 'protection' against a collapse into prose: 'des joncs unis, que nous n'osâmes / Briser'. Rhyme, therefore, is both a stimulus to linguistic promiscuity and a last bastion of order, a 'source' of dissemination and the means of its control.

(b) 'Églogue'

Mallarmé returned to his Faune in May 1866, and it is impossible to determine precisely when and how he revised the poem between this time and 1875. However, coming between the 'Intermède héroïque' and the 'Églogue', the 'Improvisation' shows by its title where Mallarmé's emphasis

---

[62] OC, 870.

lay as his earlier project evolved towards a final version. As an 'improvisa-
tion' the poem is to be at once a speech, a dramatic performance, and a
musical display. Language will twist and turn in 'unforeseen' ways within
the confines of the rhyming couplets.

In a manner long recognized as characteristic of Mallarmé's revisions, the
devices and conceits of the first version are compressed and rarefied. Taking
the 'Monologue' as his basis, the appeal to Pan (l. 38) is omitted, and 'le
Faune' becomes both satyr and Faunus, the Roman equivalent of Pan. The
'Scène' is dropped since its mirroring of the 'Monologue' is now subsumed
within the revised version of the latter, which in any case already contained
a complex evocation of the nymphs' duality. And the less accomplished
verse of the 'Réveil' is likewise abandoned, the references to Greek mythol-
ogy being a distraction from the focus on a Sicilian setting, and the final
affirmation of imminent poetic renewal being redundant in a poem which
reveals it in practice. The previously approximate binary structure con-
tinues to be approximate (rather than numerically precise), and the central
division of the poem (between ll. 51 and 52 in both the 'Improvisation' and
the 'Églogue') is now less pronounced within an otherwise more fragmen-
ted, apparently 'improvised' structure.

But the title 'Improvisation', too redolent perhaps of 'le hasard', was
immediately superseded in 1876 by the definitive title ('L'Après-midi d'un
favne. Églogve') in which the symbolic time of the drama and the Latin
background are both emphasized, the latter by the use of the Roman 'v' in
place of 'u'. For the final version of the poem is indeed an 'églogue': 'A
short, conventional poem, usually a pastoral, in the form of a dialogue or
soliloquy', and generally 'without appreciable characterization or action.'[63]
From the Greek 'eklegein' = to choose, it becomes 'églogue' in French after
the spelling popularized by Dante on the basis of a false etymology: 'aix' (=
goat) + 'logos'. Thus supposedly a 'goatherd's tale', the 'églogue' harks back
to the tradition of Virgil's bucolic eclogues, themselves deriving from the
idylls of Theocritus (the eleventh of which mentions the slopes of Mount
Etna).[64] For Mallarmé what better term to apply to a poem which remains,
like the earlier 'Monologue', as divided as the Faune himself between an
upper humanity and a lower animality, a poem half-'logos' and half-goat?
And what more ambivalent term to denote at once the 'chosenness' of
conscious art and the 'capriciousness' (from 'caper=goat') of language
itself?[65]

As the new presence of 'Syrinx' (l. 53) and the swarm of bees (l. 96)
suggests, Mallarmé had decided to complement his basic allegory more

---

[63] *Princeton Encyclopedia of Poetry and Poetics*, ed. Alex Preminger (2nd edn, London,
1975).
[64] Ibid.
[65] Cf. the departed 'bel oiseau, caprice' in the 'Ouverture' to 'Hérodiade' (l. 6).

elaborately with the mythology of Pan. The god of shepherds and flocks, half-human, half-goat, Pan/Faunus is traditionally associated with reed pipes, a shepherd's crook, and a crown of pine leaves. Usually depicted with two horns on his forehead, he is said to spend his time spying on nymphs or sleeping through the midday heat. It is dangerous to disturb him (or there will be panic!), and his sexual energy is generally expended in onanism. In many versions he is indeed akin to a satyr (a Greek god of the woodlands with a tail and long, goat-like ears), and is said to be part of the cortège of Dionysus (identified with Bacchus, the Roman god of wine). Sometimes thought to be the son of Zeus and Callisto, and sometimes the son of Hermes (the messenger god of alchemy), he is also associated with bee-keeping and with Priapus. In Ovid's *Metamorphoses* Pan pursues Syrinx, an Arcadian hamadryad (or wood-nymph), who is 'saved' by being changed into a reed. The wind blowing in the reeds gives Pan the idea of joining reeds of different lengths to make a musical instrument, which he calls Syrinx in her memory. In other versions Pan loves Echo (the Greek word for sound), variously a nymph of the air or of trees and springs, who had loved Narcissus and, on being changed into rock, retained the ability to repeat the final syllables of spoken words. The daughter of Pan and Echo was called Iambe and gave her name to iambic verse, which was used in satire (from 'satyr'), which was originally a mixture of words, music, and dance performed during bacchanalia...

Just as Mallarmé minimized the historical aspects of Hérodiade the better to allow the 'virtualités' of her name to 'provoke' the poem, so here he insists on no one aspect of the mythology of Pan but allows all of it to play a part in his allegory of beauty. Representing 'pan-language', this poem presents a single 'Faune', or 'phonetic unit', in pursuit of beauty. Poetic beauty, symbolized by the nymph-rhymes, is here also represented as both Echo and Syrinx: and the dialectic of sameness and difference to be found in rhyme and which was formerly exemplified by Iane and Ianthé is thus again present in that Echo personifies repeated terminal sound and Syrinx a musical instrument capable of playing different notes. Appropriately, Echo appears in the 'Églogue' in homophonic disguise: 'Et qu'au prélude lent où naissent les pipeaux' (l. 30).[66] Syrinx, for her part (l. 53), is envisaged as consisting (like rhyme) of two pipes ('deux tuyaux': l. 18; 'le jonc vaste et jumeau': l. 43), her dual or dyadic nature thus reflecting the dual nature of the Faune and the poem itself. Nevertheless the role of Echo and Syrinx is limited. The central dialectic of sameness and difference is more elaborately symbolized within Mallarmé's own mythology of the two nymphs who constantly elude the Faune's grasp: the one chaste and faithful to her

---

[66] In 'Improvisation d'un faune' this line reads: 'Et que, dans le prélude où partent les pipeaux'.

sister nymph, the other more receptive to the intervention of an alien 'phone'.

Like the Faune of the Monologue, this Faune, too, is split: not only between man and goat, but between inertia and caper, piping and drinking, dreaming and chasing... He simply is a divide, and his song the (allegedly) unsatisfactory aftermath of that divide: an 'Églogue', or 'goat-logos', following the climactic moment of midday, that priapic temporal moment (cf. 'marquer midi') of daylight division[67] poised between anticipation and recall, desire and memory, the moment of silence which precedes the text, the 'fier silence de midi' (l. 106).

The allegory of the Faune's pursuit of beauty is predominantly sexual, as one would expect of the story of a 'phone lascif'. By one of those happy linguistic chances which Mallarmé would now spend a lifetime exploiting, the word 'nymphes' has two further meanings which are of relevance, the one anatomical and the other entomological, and both deriving from the original Greek signifying 'nubile girl'. In the former sense 'nymphes' means 'les petites lèvres de la vulve, replis membraneux'; in the latter, insects (like bees or butterflies) which have reached the intermediate stage in their metamorphosis from larva into imago.[68] These senses of 'nymphes' are further interconnected by the word 'hymen' (l. 34), since not only does a 'hymen' (from the Greek, meaning 'membrane') unite the 'nubiles plis' of the vulva, it is also synonymous with 'aile': the bee belongs to the 'Hymenoptera' order of insects, which have four transparent wings ('hymen' + 'pteron'=membrane+wing). The four hemistichs of a distich, previously present as the four horses of a 'quadrige' (in 'Le Réveil du faune'), have now become the wings of poetic flight; and the poem itself, as 'l'essaim éternel du désir' (l. 98), a swarm of rhyming couplets buzzing with the expressivity of language. Moreover, by an alternative calculation, the alexandrine itself is a bee since the latter comprises twelve parts (a head and a sting, three pairs of legs, and two pairs of wings): the sting, of course, is in the rhyme. Thus the disseminating pomegranate of the 'Ouverture' to 'Hérodiade' has become another form of 'douze! éclat':

> Chaque grenade éclate et d'abeilles murmure.
>
> (l. 96)

And, as with the insistent 'ab' cluster at the beginning of the 'Ouverture', this apian murmur suggests a plethora of 'ab's, an exploded alphabet of innumerable bees—and an endless chain of rhyming couplets: aabb...(in an approximate homophony 'ab murmure').

---

[67] Comparable with the nocturnal division of midnight, which figures centrally in *Igitur* and the revised version of 'Sonnet allégorique de lui-même'.

[68] A 'nymphéa', on the other hand, is the botanical term for a 'nénuphar blanc', which would later give Mallarmé his title for another allegory of the pursuit of beauty.

The poem begins, therefore, as a self-referential statement of poetic desire:

> Ces nymphes, je les veux perpétuer.
>
> (hom. Ces nymphes, je/jeu les veux/t, perpétuées)

The Faune wants these nymphs, wants them perpetuated, wants to perpetuate them himself: here, in the 'Jeu suprême' of this poem, the 'phone', or single unit of language, desires poetic beauty, and this desire expresses itself as the desire to perpetuate rhyme, these nubile folds, these labia, these half-formed bees. And 'si clair' (hom. 'cycle, air'): as a cycle of sound worthy to constitute a musical air. The demonstrative adjective with which the poem opens, by stating that these nymphs exist, somewhere, somehow, not only tells us what our readerly eye can see but refutes in advance the insistent suggestion that the glimpsed ideal does not exist.

But how shall the Faune perpetuate rhyme? A 'phone' is at once a unit of sound and a potential unit of sense: shall rhyme go forward on the basis of homophonic accident, or shall the meaning of the words determine the sequence of 'perpetuation'? Shall the Faune's desire to be expressive display itself in music or in narrative? Similarly, a 'phone' is at once an oral and a written phenomenon: as a Faune blows and fingers his pipes, or holds up empty grape-skins which he then inflates, so the poetic text is an artful combination of the aural and the visual. Which shall hold sway? In all these cases there is a balance to be struck, a union to be sought.

The poem divides at the end of l. 51. In the first part the Faune attempts to capture beauty by playing on his 'flûte', but the sound of music seems to frighten beauty away. His 'Syrinx', herself created by divine transposition as she fled the Faune's clutches, has put the nymphs maliciously to flight ('instrument des fuites, ô maligne | Syrinx'); and the Faune's continued playing (in an effort to recapture the experience of beauty) leaves him with little more than 'Une sonore, vaine et monotone ligne'. In the second part the Faune attempts to capture beauty by talking; but this talk ends in the escape of the nymphs, and he is left with such an excess of expressive possibilities that beauty herself is blasphemed. Sleep and silence await—and a union in the mysterious, ghostly shadows of the page:

> Couple, adieu; je vais voir l'ombre que tu devins.

Has he failed or has he succeeded? The great subtlety of 'L'Après-midi d'un faune', as of so many of Mallarmé's sonnets from this period onwards, is to create an ambivalence in this respect which is belied by the very success of the poem itself.[69] In each of the two parts of the poem, the Faune's

---

[69] Cf. L. J. Austin '"L'Après-midi d'un faune": Essai d'explication', *Synthèses*, 258–9 (1967–8), 24–35, and Harold J. Smith, 'Mallarmé's Faun: Hero or Anti-Hero?', *Romanic Review*, 64 (1973), 111–24. For Austin the Faune is a hero of poetry who loses the real nymphs

endeavours seem doomed: the tune vanishes into thin air ('Une sonore, vaine et monotone ligne'), the nymphs flee his clumsy embrace. Yet each part in its way can also be read as a success: the musical air transcends the paltry art of representation, and the physical assault climaxes in the momentary possession of the queen bee, symbol of the swarming expressivity of language. In a sense, therefore, the poem has four wings: two flights of fancy, each with a negative and a positive aspect. As will be seen, a traditional representational reading suggests failure, while a reflexive, homophonic reading offers the prospect of a triumph; and the reader must endeavour to reconcile the two rather as the Faune himself tries to seduce two nymphs at once or as the poet tries to combine the virtues of a spoken and a written text. Indeed all three—Faune, reader, poet—experience that 'mal d'être deux' that is rhyme itself: for what is rhyme but the pursuit of a fruitful union, the versifier's attempt to introduce his will between two homophonic units and cause them to take on new meaning from their juxtaposition? Figured in this poem as a blush of pink, this heightened 'phonic' power is an elusive objective; and the fleeing nymphs symbolize the poet's experience of uncooperative rhyme pairs, the one word perhaps just right, the other refusing to play the game. And so for the reader: some words in the poem fit a purely representational reading, others have significance only if 'heard' in the manner advocated by 'Le Démon de l'analogie'.

(c) *'Ce vol de cygnes'*

First, then, the poem read as an account of failure. From the beginning the Faune is troubled by a fleeting glimpse of beauty, a roseate hue. Seeming to hover in the heavy, sleep-laden air of early morning, now the vision is gone, leaving perplexity and a crepuscular moment of doubt. The woods are empty, and what he had seen was all in the mind, an absence of rosy hues ('la faute idéale de roses'), a hollow, onanistic 'triomphe'. It is time to reflect: what if the female forms he is describing ('dont tu gloses') are indeed merely the illusory projection of his desires? It might have seemed that one nymph had chaste blue eyes like the cool waters of a spring (suggested perhaps by the first rhyme-word, 'clair'), and that the other sighed like a warm breeze in his fleece-like hair (suggested by the second rhyme-word, 'air'); but no, the only water was the musical notes pouring from his 'flûte', and the only wind the breath 'inspired' into and exhaled from its two pipes. Like

---

but compensates for their loss by recreating them in the ideal realm of art; for Smith 'The Faun is stricken with creative impotence, while Mallarmé triumphs as creator of the poem' (p. 124).

the still fountain in the 'Ouverture' ('pas de clapotement'), no trace of beauty is left: 'l'horizon pas remué d'une ride'.

Even the source of his 'flûte' refuses to bear witness to his experience; and the marshy shores from which he tore the reeds remain tacit despite his appeal that they relate how a group of white shapes (swans? naiads more like) took flight the moment he began to tune his reeds ('au prélude lent où naissent les pipeaux'). Silence: nothing to indicate that his excessive desire to possess the nymphs and to achieve a harmonious musical sound ('Trop d'hymen souhaité') foundered on his attempts at perfection and achieving the right note ('de qui cherche le *la*'). And so the Faune must wake from his fond dream under the primordial heat of the sun ('la ferveur première'): as upright (not slumbering) and alone (without nymphs), as white and 'untouched' ('l'ingénuité'), as the lilies ('Lys'; previously 'fleurs d'étincelles' (l. 25)) growing in the marsh.

Yet not only was there the sound of his 'flûte' (the kiss of an instrument asserting the presence of perfidious, elusive beauty), his untouched breast also testifies to some mysterious bite; as though some secret, or arcanum, had chosen to confide in his twin pipes, and as though the solo played by this instrument, hiding its blushes from view (the roseate hues of imagined nymphs now no more than the pink cheeks of an embarrassed flautist), constituted the realization that the beauty to be found in the real world laughed to see the Faune and his pipes mistake their credulous song for that beauty. The secret of which the pipes sing is that natural beauty and aesthetic beauty are different; and so instead the pipes dream of attaining the highest realm of desire, in which to distil from the Faune's banal fantasies of naked female forms a pure and meaningless line of sound.

Unconscious of the true significance of the instrument's solo, the Faune now rejects these suspect pipes, casting them back into the lake with the sarcastic suggestion that they try to come back to life. Instead of playing music, the Faune will content himself with speech and paint idolatrous word-pictures of goddesses as though he were undressing them. He will seek solace in wine, feigning that his regret (for the vanished nymphs) no longer exists; and through this transparent, empty medium of physical intoxication he will seek new visions of beauty in the past. Thus he recalls how his eye, like the sting of a bee, darted through the reeds, snatching a glimpse of immortal beauty which promptly vanished, stung and outraged, into the shimmering, jewel-like waters of the pool. Running to the scene, he comes on two nymphs asleep in each other's arms after tasting the languorous 'mal' of being two separate entities; and he abducts them as one to a thicket of rose-bushes (where the beauty of floral scent is drained by the intemperate heat of the sun), there to consummate his lust in broad daylight ('A ce massif, haï par l'ombrage frivole').

His memory of this abduction being now so vivid, the Faune speaks in the present tense of an unambiguous (and unitalicized) climax; and with his kisses he drinks in the 'frayeur secrète de la chair' as once he 'kissed' his pipes in vain only then to imbibe the juice of the grape. Here he comes closest to possessing his nymphs, and so the rhyme ('éclair' / 'chair') recalls the opening, antithetical rhyme of the poem ('clair' / 'l'air'). But it is only half a possession: the chaste nymph remains 'inhumaine' even if 'l'autre tout soupirs' (l. 12) now loses her innocence and exudes the dampness of 'moins tristes vapeurs'. And in half-possessing them he finds that the prize has eluded his grasp: he has divided the 'touffe échevelée', both the entangled pair of sleeping beauties and the pubis of the less resistant nymph. But his oral union with the latter (his laughing, dual lips matching her vulval 'nymphes') is not accompanied by a successful digital excitation of the other ('La petite, naïve'): the roseate hue of the one cannot transfer itself, via the Faune's hand, to the cheeks of the other, and her 'candeur de plume' remains as inviolate as once the lily-white Faune himself was ('Droit et seul (...) / Lys! et l'un de vous tous pour l'ingénuité'). The nymphs escape.

Too bad, there will be others. His passion, having reached a sobbing climax and the moment of ripeness ('pourpre et déjà mûre'), now bursts forth, like the blood-red juice of ripened fruit or a lava flow upon Mount Etna (visible within this Sicilian landscape). It is as though in his volcanic eruption of desire he has momentarily been visited by Venus herself, bride of Vulcan and goddess of beauty, 'la reine'. Yet she appears not at the climax itself but as 'tristesse' begins ('Quand tonne un somme triste ou s'épuise la flamme'); a fleeting presence in the immediate aftermath of his sexual 'midi', as the lava flows from him and his body and soul grow limp ('l'âme / De paroles vacante et ce corps alourdi'). Fear of punishment is unfounded, but the moment fades as surely as the nymphs vanished at the beginning of the poem; and the Faune now falls into a slumber, an 'après-midi' of oblivion in which to banish all thought of blasphemy (or sacrilegious invocation of Venus), and salutes once more the joys of vinous intoxication and perhaps of that other oral pleasure 'sous les replis heureux d'une seule'. In the Pyrrhic triumph of sleep he will 'see' the indistinguishable shapes of the nymphs within the darkness of his stupor. He, like the poem, relapses into the 'fier silence de midi'.

Read in this way, 'L'Après-midi d'un faune' is a poem about surrendering to defeat and about the ephemeral consolations of onanistic pleasure. Like the poet-victim of 'impuissance', the Faune is haunted by a vision of beauty which he seeks vainly to recapture: by means of musical performance and of wine-induced sexual fantasy. He abandons his pipes when he concludes that his tune cannot both represent 'La beauté d'alentour' and achieve aesthetic perfection; and he abandons fantasy when he discovers that his sexual prowess is unequal to a no less dual challenge—the satisfaction of both a sensual and an ethereal nymph.

Thus the Faune seems, like the poem, to be split between two conceptions of artistic endeavour which may be identified respectively with Apollo and Dionysus. During the first part of the poem (ll. 1–51), the Faune looks to Apollo: the sun-god who pursued nymphs and drove a chariot (or quadriga) pulled by swans, and the god of music and poetry who epitomizes an art that derives from divine inspiration and aspires to serenity and calm; Apollo, the begetter of lyric verse to soothe the soul. Hence, like Apollo inventing the lyre (or, in some versions, obtaining its secret from Hermes), the Faune has created his pipes, and within this 'calme marécage' with its 'vol de cygnes', he exhales 'Le visible et serein souffle artificiel / De l'inspiration, qui regagne le ciel'. In the second part of the poem, the Faune looks instead to Dionysus (or Bacchus): brought up by nymphs and in various versions associated with goats, this 'discoverer' of the vine is the god of wine, the object of worship in bacchanalian festivals; Dionysus, begetter of drama and the corporeal ritual of dance. Hence the Faune takes inspiration from the grape and dramatizes his abduction of the nymphs to the point of festive celebration ('Une fête s'exalte'; l. 100). At the end of the poem Apollo and Dionysus are recalled in combination: both 'l'âme' and 'ce corps' are spent, 'l'astre [...] des vins' is extolled. The Faune's 'Églogue', half order, half caper, is complete: a lyric poem that requires a dramatic performance—and never received it.

(d) 'Couple'

But if we restore to the poem its power of oral/aural display, this duality seems more like a fruitful union than the two sides of a failed artistic enterprise. The Faune's 'Églogue' can then be seen to unite the virtues of Apollonian order and Dionysian disruption, the calm control of a written text and the unruly noise of spoken verse. As desired, the rhymes have indeed been perpetuated, and the divisions of the Faune modulated in the synthesis of art. Homophony plays its role, but so does the visual display of typography (roman/italic, upper and lower case); 'musical' relationships bind the poem in a unity, but so too does the 'crude' narrative of the Faune's encounter with the nymphs. It is truly an 'Églogue', a masterful re-combination of the divided self of language in which 'man' and 'goat' each has a vital part to play, in which the sound and the sense of a 'phone' are joined in fertile union.

The poem begins, as we have seen, with the intention to rhyme: 'Ces nymphes, je les veux perpétuer'. The second sentence, being a discrete consecutive clause, thus foregrounds rhyme as a sequence of cause and effect: 'Si clair, / [...] qu[e] l'air', and pipes in the rosy dawn of these ensnaring nymphs: hom. 'leurre/l'heure, incarnat léger'. In this linguistic landscape the 'air' is heavy with somnolent meaning, the 'sommeils touffus' or 'touffe échevelée' which will later be 'divisé[e/s]'; and rhyme—the rising voice of the Faune perhaps intimated in 'léger' (hom. 'les jets')—is already flitting like a bee from word-flower to word-flower ('vol-tige'), its dizzy flight reflected in the sinuous arrangement of the first eight lines of the poem. Where will it land? 'Léger' rhymes with 'perpétuer' in flirtatious union before the mirrored /l/ and /r/ of the hemistich which it closes can call up a matching hemistich to complete the alexandrine and thus establish the metre within which rhyme will be perpetuated (after further flirtation, with octosyllabic metre, in l. 3).

The completion of the first rhyme leaves a void, reminiscent of the mid-day silence which precedes this afternoon of discourse; and the 'espace blanc' following 'touffus' (hom. 'tout fut') is fraught with perplexity (hom. 'et/mais; jeu, un rêve?') as the Faune wonders how to proceed at this crepuscular moment ('Mon doute') under a summer sun—in this (hom.) 'monde août' (anticipating the 'auguste dent') filled with an 'amas de nuit ancienne' (hom. 'antienne'). Here on the glaring white page, caught between sleeping and waking, the Faune inhabits a 'monde ou', in which the alternative sounds of rhyme now find antiphonal completion ('s'achève') in the handwritten ramifications of insubstantial, non-representational verse: 'En maint rameau subtil'—each 'ligne' a lignous bough of 'mots subtils' recalling the 'rameau, dorénavant à travers la voix entendue' of 'Le Démon de l'analogie'. This 'rameau' is (hom.) a 'demeure ailée, vraie': a true, winged 'lieu' for the apian 'Vers'; and through the ramification of rhyme the poem has now become a 'Bois' which proves—at this precise spot (hom. 'et là')—that the Faune was able, on his own (without reference to the world), to offer up to himself (in an act of auto-sacrifice) the absence of real roses (or physical beauty represented) as a triumph. Expressed more simply, rhyme has created its own realm of the 'Idée', its own 'ideal' beauty.

Like some latter-day Emperor Augustus, the Faune parades his triumph in the four-syllabled 'quadrige' of 'Réfléchissons', an imperious imperative (using the royal we) which is as good as its word: hom. 'réfléchis, sons'. Determined to press on with rhyme, his doubt (again suggested by the 'espace blanc') is now simulated and creative: the hesitant, interrupted metre seems no longer anxious but playful, as the four syllables of 'Réflé-chissons' are followed by a self-referential and ambiguous 'ou si' (hom. 'ou six' preceding 'les femmes'). Arriving as the sixth syllable, 'si' 'rescues' the threatened metre and combines hypothesis with affirmation: 'or if the women were to figure, etc.', 'or? but yes, the women do figure, etc.' 'Gloses', a characteristic Mallarméan Janus-word like 'grimoire', connotes both explanatory clarification and useless verbiage: the Faune is at once demon-

strating the rhyming process in action and also revealing its inherent va-
cuity. As 'un souhait de tes sens fabuleux!', the nymph-rhymes 'figurent' the
projected desire of the fabulous or mythological Faune's sensual longing and
also the wished-for expressivity of Mallarmé's non-representational
'phone', the poem as 'fiction' aspiring to a plenitude of potential 'sens'.

Now addressing himself, the Faune contemplates the nature of rhyme.
From the one nymph he learns of rhyme's binocular or dual character ('des
yeux'), and how the illusion of representation (the eyes are like the cold,
blue water of a spring) 'escapes' or is dispelled in polysemy (hom. 'une
source ampleur'), while the secret of the ludic potential of rhyme (etym.
'illudere') is let slip by even the most apparently 'chaste' or 'non-promiscu-
ous' rhyme. The other nymph seems different ('dis-tu qu'elle contraste'), but
really she is no more than a rhyme pair which 'stands opposite' (etym.
'contra' + 'stare'): she, too, is polysemic, a source of multiple 'soupirs' or
homophonies. The real question is not whether rhyme is representational or
polysemic but whether its polysemy is spoken or written (hom. 'soupirs dits,
tus?'). Poetic language offers no illusory representation ('Que non!'); and if it
is to interrupt the spasmic, breathless silence of the page ('pâmoison /
Suffoquant de chaleurs') and bring energy to its weary immobility, it must
speak out (hom. 'Que noms parlent!') and exploit the lily-white spaces of
the written text (hom. 'par lys, mots').

If poetic language does speak out, it must resist the 'silence de midi' that
threatens to block out the fresh sounds of its lute (hom. 'le matin frais si[l]
luth') like the clay (hom. 'lut', also 'sil') used in hermetic sealing. Then there
shall be heard, not a representation of the world, but homophony, that pure
repeated sound ('murmure') which is the 'source ampleur' of rhyme itself:
hom. 'vers sema flûte'. The reeds of rhyme grow from the reflexive waters of
poetic language, and the poem proclaims itself at once a watery and a rosy
ramification of harmonious sound: hom. 'eau, bosquet à roses, et d'ac-
cords'. The valuable sound expressed by rhyme is purified of base reference
(hom. 'or des deux tuyaux') and achieves its musical function before its
'watery' polysemy becomes sterile through sheer excess ('avant / Qu'il
disperse le son dans une pluie aride'). Being non-representational it leaves
no mark upon the real world ('l'horizon pas remué d'une ride'); yet here on
the page it is a visible and serenely elevated sign of artifice, a 'soupir'
become the 'souffle' of conscious poetic 'inspiration' with which to re-
capture a heaven of perfection. Not a 'pluie aride' but a 'pluie à rides'—
and a 'serein', a gentle dew falling at this crepuscular moment, a 'rosée
d'accords'.

The Faune now explores what limits can be set to this potentially ex-
cessive homophony and finds them in the alexandrine: hom. 'eau, bords:
six-six, liens'. Metrical structure produces a calm watery place in which
homophony, prevented from escaping, is able to nourish the musical instru-

ment of reed-like rhyme: hom. 'd'un calme marais, cage'. Herein the Faune can exploit the 'non-sense' of homophony, draining word-flowers of their everyday colour that they may sparkle afresh: the 'emptiness' of homophony ('ma vanité', (hom.) 'allant, vide de soleils') at once ransacks and creates new containers ('sac-cage'), so that the structure of the metre ('bords siciliens') remains present but 'tacit' (like the 'soleils' of the real world) beneath the revalorizing of syllables which such homophonic art entails: hom. 'sous les fleurs d'étincelles comptées'.

At this point the poem itself 'narrates', as so enjoined ('CONTEZ'), how each line is a reed of 'empty' sound cut (by a caesura) and 'tamed' (within its cage) by the 'talent' (etym. 'balance', or pivotal structure) of poetic art. When so weighed in the balance of rhyme, sound is heard (cf. hom. 'parle, talent!') as authenticated gold: hom. 'sûr, l'or'. Glaucous and obscure from afar (though, by etymology, 'gleaming'), this golden sound weaves in vine-like 'verdures' (hom. 'vers durs' and 'vers d'hure') around the source, or origins, of language ('fontaines', from 'fons') in a ceremony of sacred dedication (hom. 'dédiant l'heure', 'dédiant leur vie') by engaging in tricky denials of former meanings: hom. 'dédits en leurres'. Against the background of this sinuous display of language (in italic) the whiteness of the page ripples gently like the whiteness of the recumbent Faune in the shimmering glare of midday ('une blanche heure; animal au repos'), the symbolic 'hour' foregrounded by the internal rhyme on 'eur' in the sixth syllables of ll. 28–9.

Explaining further what happens when the reeds of rhyme are cut, the poem narrates how homophony (hom. 'Écho') is a prelude to the supreme 'ludic' moment when the pipes begin to play and (given the alternative meaning of 'pipeaux') the snares are set to catch birds. With terse ambiguity the poem describes how new signs are both captured and frightened off by this new 'phonic' art: the 'cygnes/signes' (hom. 'noms!') are 'stolen' and 'saved' ('ce vol', 'se sauve') but also take flight and escape, disappearing beneath the surface. Here, perfectly expressed, is that characteristic Mallarméan duality, already summarized in 'gloses', whereby the polysemy released by homophony is at once a source of profound significance and the beginning of inanity. Accordingly, the poem breaks off its narration, the 'espace blanc' here echoing the glaring 'silence de midi'. The sinuous twining of 'vers durs' ceases with the italic, and the text becomes self-professedly 'Inerte'.

The Faune now takes up the story in plainer terms, explaining that the 'blankness' of this silence (at 'midi') leaves no trace of the fact that such silence is caused by an excess of the desire to signify. The ambition to take rhyme (this 'art ensemble') to its logical limit of ubiquitous homophony ('Trop d'hymen souhaité') constitutes a pursuit of musical perfection ('de qui cherche le *la*'), music being understood as the 'ensemble des rapports existant dans tout'.[70] The Faune's glimpse of these 'naïades', his brief encounter with this new 'musical' art of interconnectedness, is momentarily at an end; the 'phone' is thrown back on its own individuality, no longer sinuous and entwined, but 'Droit et seul'. Alone, it resolves to forgo the 'blush' of poetic value and to resume its original function as unconnected sound, free from others ('ingenuité'; etym. 'born free'). Awakened from its dream, lily-white, erect within the blinding light of 'pre-poetic' sound ('la ferveur première', (hom.) 'heure première'; 'un flot antique de lumière'), there it will be, no longer witness to the dyad of the one and the many, but simply one among many ('l'un de vous tous').

But even as the Faune proclaims this independence, the dyadic nature of rhyme is whispering its message to him. The intimate story of rhyme narrated to him in italics ended with the words 'ou plonge': but this 'ou', emblem of rhyme and polysemy, continues to surface in the following lines with curious insistence: fleetingly in 'tout', 'souhaité', 'sous', and then in the 'ou-vers' which ends this section: 'vous tous pour'. This 'doux rien' is (hom.) 'parleur', and even a single lip of rhyme ('par leur lèvre ébruité') can intimate its secret 'tout bas' (thus rhyming the fifth syllables of ll. 38–9) in a kiss. The nymphs of interconnected sound may be elusive and untrustworthy ('perfides'), but the presence of this 'paire fid[èle]' continues to be attested. For even a simple 'phone' like 'ou' cannot stand alone: it is a homonym, meaning 'or', 'where', and 'August'. Surround it with all the white space one may, it remains 'musical', interconnected, a form of rhyme.

Thus the Faune cannot simply dismiss the nymphs or the 'vol de cygnes' and decide to go it alone. As he proceeds to explain, even without the demonstration of interconnectedness provided by rhyme ('vierge de preuve'), his 'sein [...] atteste une morsure'. For his breast is a 'sein', which etymologically derives from 'sinus', meaning 'fold' or 'pli'. Even if rhyme appears only in one line (as pure homophone, without its revealing pair), it is in fact surrounded by a duality of white space, the silent bite of the 'espace blanc', that most 'auguste dent'. And in that white space the potential meanings of a homonym echo in endless 'indecidability'. Since 'mystère' derives etymologically from the closing of lips, this bite (itself homophonically the 'mort sûre' which puts paid to any would-be independent life for the Faune) is inaudible; and being (hom.) 'une morsure, mystère, rieuse', it nevertheless involves an opening of lips (as the white page laughs at the Faune's desire to stand alone).

'Mais, bast!': the Faune will not pursue further his false goal of isolated, non-connected sound ('Droit et seul'). The arcanum, or secret, of this homophonic 'music' 'elected' to communicate itself in the 'choice words' of this 'Églogue' and through the medium of rhyme: rhyme, the faithful pair

---

[70] 'Crise de vers', OC, 368.

('confident'), 'Le jonc vaste et jumeau'. The Faune's musical instrument is a symbol of 'jonc-tion', of interconnection; and it exploits the juicy, intoxicating gifts of polysemy (hom. 'jus-mots', 'don soûl') in the long solo that is this 'Églogue'. Here beneath 'l'Azur' of the ideal, language 'dreams' its fullest dream: diverting the turbulence ('trouble') of polysemy into the silken textuality of this reflexive poem ('détournant à soi[e]'), it ponders the former error of representational verse wherein language fondly thought to capture the beauty of the world itself. Compared with 'la beauté d'alentour', such poetry was a mere 'chant (or 'champs') crédule': not golden sound but (hom.) a 'chant [...] / [...] / de fer'.

Instead language, as expressive desire, now aspires to the highest, purest level of beauty: 'aussi haut que l'amour se module' (hom. 'oh, si haut!')—and to extract from 'real' phenomena ('du songe ordinaire de dos / Ou de flanc') the pure, invisible line of perfect form: 'faire [...] / Évanouir [...] / [...] pur[e...] / Une sonore, vaine et monotone ligne.' This 'line' (at once graphic, prosodic, melodic) is homophony itself: 'sonorous', 'empty', and 'monotone', pure sound as a tenuous but infinitely signifying interruption of blank silence. By containing three sounded /e/s, this particular 'vers' itself foregrounds the potential emptiness and 'inanity' of sound,[71] while at the same time it demonstrates by the polysemy of its vocabulary the richness of language freed from exclusive referents. The emblematic 'ou' (of rhyme and polysemy) lies at the heart of such desire ('am*ou*r') to extract pure form ('faire [...] / Évano*u*ir [...] / *Ou* de flanc pur'); and this desire is further described (homophonically) as the ambition to 'faire, et van(ne), ouïr du son-jeu, or, dit nerf': to make the sonorous potential of language audible by means of 'le Jeu suprême' of poetry, to achieve a new vigour of expression (cf. 'le style a du nerf') by passing language through a winnowing-basket ('van', 'vanner') woven from the 'joncs' of rhyme. Newly 'heard' ('avec mes regards clos'), homophony reveals its alternative aspect of purity (its 'Ou de flanc pur'); and it brings not only sinew to the body of this Faune, a 'nerf de dos / Ou de flanc' as if the right-hand side of the poem were its backbone[72] or one of its two flanks (cf. hom. 'Droite et seul'), but also the blood of life itself: hom. 'Une sonore veine', a channel for the blush of enhanced poetic value.

Whereas the previous division of the poem (between ll. 37 and 38) may have reflected the Faune's ambition to go it alone (unconnectedly), now 'Une [...] ligne' stands (l. 51) as evidence that homophony is an inevitable and powerfully expressive feature of language whose importance extends beyond the traditional duality of terminal rhyme. The eventual rhyme

---

[71] On the 'erosion' of the alexandrine by the use of the sounded e, see Jacques Scherer, *Grammaire de Mallarmé* (Paris, 1977), 221.

[72] Note the rhyme on 'os' here, and cf. the analogy 'vers/vertèbre' in 'Quand l'ombre menaça...'.

('maligne') seems now almost redundant (since rhyme can be everywhere), as if something as obviously homophonic as terminal rhyme were a 'tache', or blemish, compared with the purity of the 'vaine et monotone ligne'. As a musical instrument which foregrounds the dispersal of sense in sound ('instrument des fuites'), rhyme (as Syrinx) must return to its origins in the watery reaches of language there to flower in a new guise amidst the ensnaring textual weavings of the 'amorous' Faune (taking 'lacs' in its senses of knotted cord, noose, and love-knot).

Now the Faune changes direction. Impatient and frustrated by the apparent limitations of such a chaste, ethereal art, he is intent upon a more direct, wanton assault on beauty. The Syrinx of rhyme must take care of herself and wait on his pleasure, for as 'phone' he is now going not to play a tune but to speak. The marshy banks of reeds were encouraged to narrate his quest for beauty, but they seemed unwilling to take over from him, and their simulated discourse ended with the flight of the nymphs. Now he himself will voice the words: 'de ma rumeur fier.' There is defiance in the seditious connotation of 'rumeur' and more than a hint of hubris: how will his 'rumeur' differ from the 'fier silence de midi'? May not excessive verbiage ('parler longtemps') be as 'silent' as silence itself, and indeed considerably more 'silent' than the 'silent music' of Mallarmé's ideal art? The crudity of 'non-musical' language is here evoked in the banality of 'je vais parler [...] / Des déesses', a statement of intent in any case undermined by an ugly repetition ('dé') suggestive of the linguistic contingency which always 'undoes' any brutal desire to speak 'in the face of' language. Disobedient Syrinx, it seems, has refused to wait for him in submissive terminal position; and indeed in 'her' terminal rhymes throughout this pivotal section (ll. 49–64) there are the glimmerings of a warning: 'ô ligne tente hure et vide vers l'hure'.

Dispensing (in vain) with homophony, the Faune asserts a new reliance on the pictorial and becomes a blasphemous adorer of images (hom. 'et pardi!'; 'd'idolâtres peintures'). Word-nymphs as intermediate insects between the larva of sound and the imago of sense are now to form into bees, the bees that have dispersed ('grappe' meaning also a cluster of bees) to drink the nectar of beauty from imagined roses. The Faune is determined, as it were, to 'peindre la chose et non l'effet qu'elle produit', and this ambition will eventually culminate in the 'blasphemous' naming of Venus herself as a rhyme-word. For the moment his lips form, not in a kiss of musical rhyme, but in the rictus of a laughing drunkard, stripping the 'ombre' from mystery, removing the chastity belt (or girdle of Venus) from virginal beauty, sucking the grapes (the words previously intertwined in the 'vers durs/d'hure' of the 'vigne') of their juice (cf. the earlier 'jus-mots') and thereby believing that all has become crystal clear: 'j'ai sucé la clarté'. But homophony mocks him (hom. 'j'ai su, c'est la clarté'), having also reasserted the surviving purity of that which he claims to defile: hom. 'A leur ombre enlevées, encore des saintes, hure!' Where once 'Bois' meant the ramifications of a text in which the beautiful nymphs might or might not be present, now the word provides the implicit imperative to which the wanton Faune responds; and in a parody of the Eucharist he raises the empty grape-skins to the light, thus 'consecrating' the 'unmusical' words of narrative that are to be his rose-coloured spectacles, his illusory instrument of ocular rape. By retelling the past—or using words in the old, univocal way—the 'feinte' of his heedless verbiage may banish the regret he feels at the disappearance of the nymph-words which promised a vision of ideal beauty. Blowing now not into a flute but into the empty 'peaux lumineuses' (with its ribald echo of 'boire un pot'), he is at once 'avide / D'ivresse' and (hom.) 'à vide / D'ivresse', gazing at the world through the 'jus' of reference (cf. hom. 'jus, qu'au soir je regarde, autr[e] verre').

Calling incongruously on the nymphs to help him in the risible task of blowing up deflated memories, the Faune's speech here begins, its italics recalling the imagined narrative of the marshy banks but offering a different version of events. It was the eye, not the music, of the Faune which caused the nymphs to flee: the apertures of the musical pipes have now become the holes pierced in the reeds by his intrusive gaze, and the 'incarnat léger' which once he glimpsed now the 'brûlure' of a bee-sting upon numberless and immortal nymphs ('dardait chaque encolure / Immortelle'). Anticipating the tongue and finger with which he will soon penetrate the two abducted nymphs, the cupid-like dart of his eye pricks their circular neck-line and elicits not beautiful sound but a 'cri de rage' as the tresses of their hair disappear beneath the sparkling, jewel-like ripples of the 'source'. The subtle textures of 'tresses' and 'rides' merge into one, leaving only noise and absence: the means of expressing beauty have vanished.

But there, in sleepy absence, like the Faune before and after this poem, lies rhyme itself, ready to arrest his metrical feet:

> J'accours; quand, à mes pieds, s'entrejoignent (meurtries
> De la langueur goûtée à ce mal d'être deux)
> Des dormeuses parmi leurs seuls bras hasardeux;

or, as the Syrinx of homophony tells us, a dormant junction of fortunately connected contingent sounds (hom. 'De la langue, heur goûté à ce mal d'être deux'), bruised like ripe fruit and bearing oral marks (hom. 'meurtries / De la langue') that betoken their poetic calling rather as the Faune bears his own 'morsure / Mystérieuse'. A happenstance of language, these 'deux / Dés d'or' of a rhyming pair embrace with the arms of chance (visually suggested by the parentheses). The delighted Faune, intent on 'perpetuating' rhyme, carries them off to bed, the crude rosebed of an unsubtle art ('ce massif, haï par l'ombrage frivole [hom. 'par l'ombre, rage frivole'], / De roses tarissant tout parfum au soleil'), there to consume and destroy ('consumé') their complexity in the glaring light of the obvious. Though he claims not to have disturbed their union ('sans les désenlacer'), homophony suggests that in his thieving flight ('et vole') he has left their essence behind ('sans les dés enlacés').

The movement from the imperfect tense to the historic present within the italicized narrative culminates in the return to a 'lyric' present (in roman type) wherein the Faune relives the 'rape' of the nymphs (this section being itself an 'interruption' or break within the Faune's narrative). The idolator now 'adores' these virginal creatures who turn incarnadine with anger (hom. 'cou roux') rather than with the beauty of enhanced poetic value as his fiery lips seek out the secret of their trembling flesh in a base re-enactment of the arcanum 'choosing' the 'jonc vaste et jumeau' as its confidant. As he carries off his burden, homophony once more seems to pour scorn on his naked aggression and impious artistry: 'eau des lys / Farouche du sacré fard d'eau nue'. The redness of the nymphs is transparent white beside the sacred blush of true beauty. The gold of poetic sound has been cast away (hom. 'Jeta d'or'), and the Faune's 'délice' is but a pair of lily-white dice that recall his earlier rejection of the nymphs and his spurious assertion of 'phonic' independence ('Droit et seul, [...] / Lys!').

Reverting to the imperfect tense of italicized narrative as the vision of triumphant possession ('ou de moins tristes vapeurs') recedes, the Faune now speaks of his 'crime', which, as the words suggests,[73] is a crime against rhyme and thus against the poetic beauty for which rhyme stands. He has gaily overcome the timidity of one nymph-rhyme and has covered the other in his feverish kisses; but their 'frayeur secrète' and their 'peurs', their reluctance to yield to his 'unmusical', narrative urge, are not so much 'traîtresses' as (hom.) 'traits, tresses'. Connecting lines and interwoven tresses are the secret of rhyme, and with his oral assault he has severed them: 'divisé la touffe echevelée / De baisers que les dieux gardient si bien mêlée'. Poetic art depends on the successful combination of mouth and fingers (or speech and writing), but in achieving an oral union with words (his 'rire ardent' disappearing into 'les replis heureux d'une seule'), his finger has been too 'simple' (as opposed to 'complex' or 'plié'), and the 'candeur de plume' of written (visually perceptible) art has not taken on the 'blush' of poetic value. His talk has brought this story, but it wants for 'silent music'. Unlike the Sicilian reeds, his own embrace proves insufficient as a 'cage'; and in the unconnected and ill-defined waves and post-climactic shudder of dying ardour ('de vagues trépas': hom. 'de vagues, traits? pas!'), the beautiful prey breaks free, heedless of the Faune's sobbing, vocal climax.

Unrepentant, the Faune now looks forward to further chance encounters with rhyme: 'Tant pis!' he says (to '[le] vers'), 'le bonheur d'autres' (hom. 'le

---

[73] Cf. 'Sonnet allégorique de lui-même': see below, Part III, Ch. 2.

bon heur/heurt d'autres') will lead him forward in his quest for perpetua-
tion. While 'm'entraîneront' suggests both a continuing susceptibility to
enthusiasm and the remote possibility of improvement with practice, the
dominant prospect is of a garrulous Faune for whom rhyme is mere textual
decoration: (hom.) 'm'entraîneront, / Parleur, tresses nouées aux cornes de
mon front'. No longer a sinewy backbone or a flank of pure sound, the
right-hand side of the Faune-poem is now a series of twin horns draped by
knots of sound. This is the Faune as 'goat', whose desire ('ma passion') is to
utter word upon word in promiscuous abundance, not the Faune as 'logos'
who desired the higher perfection ('aussi haut que l'amour se module') of
'Une sonore, vaine et monotone ligne'. For this 'capricious' Faune language
bursts with potential like a ripe pomegranate (or a 'mûre'), buzzing with the
swarm of possible rhymes, and he simply 'belongs' to whichever one hap-
pens to arise in the course of his verbiage. Not for him the serene artifice of
the pipes, but instead a kind of passive promiscuity or banal tautology:
'notre sang, épris de qui le va saisir' (hom. 'et pris de qui le va saisir').

   Yet now, briefly, there is a prospect of triumph. The crepuscular moment
at the beginning of the poem ('Mon doute') is recalled at this uncertain,
post-climactic time (hom. 'A l'heure "ou"'); and, in place of the 'rameau
subtil', 'ce bois d'or et de cendres se teinte'. The ramifications of the text
have recovered the 'incarnat léger' in the golden, blood-red hues (hom. 'd'or
et de sang') accompanying the sunset of representational language (the
Faune's sunlit narrative having 'set', upon a '*sang*lot' (l. 92)). The ashes of
burnt-out reference and the fading light of narrative reveal a 'fête' amidst
the textual foliage ('en la feuillée éteinte')—and a 'faîte': the eruptive
summit of Mount Etna. The previous strategic high points of the poem
('Mon doute', 'Mon sein', 'Mon œil', 'Mon crime') have brought the Faune
to this 'mons veneris', the mount of beauty and desire, the very site of the
vulval nymphs. Like bees upon a pomegranate, Venus, goddess of love and
beauty, has alighted with the heels of rhyme upon the lava of words, the lava
that flows (like blood or juice) from the volcanic source of language. Here at
the last, as the flames of wakeful narrative subside into the slumber of post-
ejaculatory 'tristesse', is a sacred celebration: a peak of polysemy to rival
the heights of homophony glimpsed at the end of the first part of the poem.
A celebration, and a union—of Venus and Vulcan, of the feminine and
the masculine (rhyme), of the Faune and his ideal: 'Je tiens la reine! / Ô
sûr [...]'.

   To embrace beauty is to defy the gods, but no punishment awaits this
Faune. Chastised and even purified he may momentarily be, but the silence
of dream shall be the only sequel. As the poem approaches its end, his soul
empties of words, and his body grows heavy with the absence of desire. He
will succumb to the proud silence of midday after one last gulp of wine. By
its typographical interruption the final couplet simulates his open mouth,

thereby suggesting that the 'espace blanc', not words, is now to be the source of an intoxication. The silent space between a rhyming pair is the space of the half-said ('mi-dit') and, in alexandrines, the space between the twelfth and the twenty-fourth syllables. What comes after 'midday' is the period of the rhyme's completion. At the end of the poem, with the final rhyme complete we are left with a phonic 'après-midi' in which sound and sense, language and metre, may finally combine in creative union (hom. 'tard: suc-con, beau fier silence de midi'). The 'couple' becomes a single unit: 'l'ombre'; and the rhyming couplets give onto that deafening silence which follows any musical performance. As the Faune departs into sleep and dream, there to have revealed the shadowy mystery of the nymphs, so the reader is left with the now 'authenticated', 'soothsaying' silence of the white page, 'l'ombre que tu(e): devin [...]':

indéfectiblement le blanc revient, tout à l'heure gratuit, certain maintenant, pour conclure que rien au delà et authentiquer le silence—[.][74]

(e) 'Ombre'

Envisaged now in retrospect as a single unit, the poem constitutes a display of the many facets of rhyme and, by extension, of the poetic use of language. In its two parts it presents an allegorical account of the two principal ingredients of poetry, sound and sense, each being taken to its furthest limit; while in the poem as a whole each and every 'phone' is caught in a dialectic of pure, meaningless homophony and pure, only too meaningful polysemy. Midday is *ante*rior, the literal opposite of the mirrored Etna to come: the sun of language has passed that zenith of searing, destructive univocity when it casts no shadow of a doubt, leaving this phonic afternoon to celebrate the nymphal beauties of the shade. The nymphs are a 'couple', not a pair[75]: a dyadic accident of language transformed 'par quel art ensemble' at the hands (and mouth) of the godlike Faune (hom. 'Couple a/à Dieu'), a fertile copula.

Within Mallarmé's poetic development, 'L'Après-midi d'un faune' offers the most subtle account to date of the elusiveness of his poetic prey. On the one hand, the homophony of language permits the poet to transcend the banal illusions of descriptive representation and to aspire to the harmonic subtleties of semantic 'music'; on the other, it threatens to collapse these

---

[74] 'Le Mystère dans les lettres', OC, 387.
[75] 'Deux choses de même espèce, prises ou considérées ensemble, accidentellement. [...] ne se dit pas de deux choses semblables qui vont nécessairement ensemble, comme les chaussures, les gants. Paire' (Robert, 'Couple').

complex 'musical' relationships into a uniform horizon of sound. Similarly, the polysemy of the linguistic unit, 'revealed' by the homophony of rhyme, allows the poet to transcend narrative and to celebrate linguistic plenitude with the golden bough of verse; yet even as he triumphs in his possession of the queen, polysemy turns to dust as 'la reine' bespeaks 'l'arène' (etym. 'sand'), the thirsting sand (recalling the 'pluie aride') whereon he lies, the desert wastes of an empty page. But in each case a further triumph redeems the failure: just as the water and air of the flute's music become a 'rosée d'accords' and a 'serein souffle artificiel', so the wine-words of the 'Faune parleur' turn into an 'astre efficace', and the 'sable' of his illusion is at least 'altered'. Unlike the 'horizon pas remué d'une ride', the Faune's environment has changed: the text has made a difference to the silence. For this is a poetic sand, cast across the page to absorb the ink of which the thirsty Faune/phone has drunk—and the sand of an arena (with its opposite sides of 'soleil' and 'ombre') in which the Faune temporarily holds the attention of his audience in the dramatic performance of a monologue.

And a 'monologue' this poem is, in effect, since it is the single word 'faune/phone' which (like the name 'Hérodiade') is responsible for its entire contents. That the word 'phone' should itself be a 'homophone' at once raises the central issues of the poem (the relationships between sound and sense, speech and writing, music and letters), and the splintering of one phonetic unit into two meanings itself 'provokes' the notion of rhyme and recalls the Pythagorean dyad of the one and the many which is central to 'Hérodiade'. The Roman origins of the 'faune' and of Faunus in turn dictate a Latin setting; and his caprine attributes give rise, as we have seen, to 'Églogue' and thereby to the Sicilian setting. Accordingly, beauty must feature as Venus (and not Aphrodite as in 'Mes bouquins refermés...'), whose husband Vulcan provides further reason for the volcanic Sicilian setting. As the title of the first published version indicates ('L'Après-midi d'un favne. Églogve'), Mallarmé was particularly attentive to this Latin setting; and so one wonders if the novel alternation of roman and italic type is not a further 'cisalpin' allusion. Clearly it is the double presence of the letter 'v' in the title which stands out as Latin, and it may therefore be that, by seeming superficially unpronounceable to the unaccustomed French eye, the words 'Favne' and 'Églogve' thus foreground once more the 'split' between speech and writing.

At the same time the insistent presence of the letter 'v' cannot help but suggest some of the virginal, vaginal, vulval, and venereal connotations famously elaborated by Robert Greer Cohn[76] and which are in any case explicitly mobilized by this poem. To the sensitized Mallarméan reader the triangular 'v' offers a typographical 'ombre' of the desired nymphs and the

---

[76] *Toward the Poems of Mallarmé* (Berkeley, 1965), 274–5.

'mons veneris' of beauty, just as the sinuous double 'g' in 'Églogve' may possibly conjure up a pair of wriggling nymphs. Unquestionably, as later in 'Un coup de Dés', the contrast between stable roman characters and curvaceous italic hints at a broader dialectic of order and chaos, musical serenity and intoxicated polysemy. At any rate, the 'visual' features of the text are as important as the aural, and it is one of the ironies of literary history that this supremely self-sufficient text should first have been published with illustrations by Manet and subsequently should have inspired Debussy's musical prelude. For the poem itself foregrounds and synthesizes the dialectic of music and image in a manner which renders both pictorial illustration and musical setting not only redundant but impertinent.

And could the 'v' (already the letter which stands for 'vers') be important in another, numerical way? Given Mallarmé's play on 'phalange' in 'Sainte' and given that 'Sonnet allégorique de lui-même' (written during the gestation period of the 'Faune') turns thematically on the fourteen lines of which a sonnet consists, such speculation may not be inappropriate. Moreover, as will be seen, numerical calculation is central to both 'Prose (pour des Esseintes)' and 'Un coup de Dés'. For 'v' is, of course, a Roman five. Is it accidental that this poem consists of 55 rhyming couplets? Strictly lv would be the Roman equivalent, but might a double 'v' in the title of a poem all about rhyme not be more 'reflexive' (as is the x, or 'reflected' v, of 'Sonnet allégorique de lui-même')? And what of the fact that the poem consists of 'cent dix vers'? As a poem that begins with a quest for 'leur incarnat léger' and symbolizes poetic value in the blush of sexual arousal and in the flow of blood through the veins of a priapic Faune ('Une sonore [veine]', 'notre sang coule', etc.), may it be said to consist of 'sang, dit vers'? For in its 110 lines it most certainly displays all the sensual and semantic richness of multiple 'sens divers'.

At any rate, as we have heard ('Écho prélude'), to write poetry is to play: to play an instrument and to play a game of chance with the contingencies of language. Even when he holds the queen, the Faune cannot be sure to have won. His pursuit of the nymphs is not only a dicey business ('je vais parler (. . .) / Des déesses'), it may even be a game of 'ombre', in which one person plays ('solo') against two. Against two nymphs, yes, but also against 'ce mal d'être deux'. The 'mâle' who wants to belong to this beautiful couple finds union with the nymphs of rhyme in the 'ombre' of poetic mystery, in a beauty without compare. And the dyadic couple of homophony and polysemy become the twin peaks of a poetic achievement, a mirrored Mount Parnassus. Or Mount Etna? Just as the Sicilian volcano rises amidst its famous 'monti rossi', 'L'Après-midi d'un faune' stands like some yawning, semiotic crater, its rhymes the roseate summits of a linguistic eruption. For, according to Larousse's entry (1870) on this, the highest volcano in Europe: 'le cratère est situé entre deux pointes suprêmes qui ont fait donner à la montagne la qualification latine de *bicornis*.' The mountain begins to take on the appearance of Pan himself—or of some bicorn uterus from which beauty has emerged, born of the Faune's penetration of the vulval 'nymphes'.[77] Thus has Mallarmé himself sought to capture the Muses, 'les nymphes du Parnasse',[78] within the poetic landscape of Mount Etna.

And what of Empedocles? Does Mallarmé see himself, in his pursuit of beauty, disappearing into the crater of rhyme like the Greek philosopher? Like Empedocles who appeared in public dressed in purple and wearing 'rameaux sacrés' (cf. ll. 5 and 95), who conceived the theory of the four elements, who considered 'l'harmonie du monde, le merveilleux organisme des êtres, comme l'Œuvre d'un être spécial qu'il définit, le Verbe (*logos*)'[79], who believed that man and woman were once united in some androgynous form, who sought to establish that the human soul circulated in the blood? Is this poem like the sandal that was thrown up by the volcano as evidence of his devotion (he is said to have cast himself into the crater in frustration at not knowing the causes of the volcano's eruptions)? The sandal of Empedocles, or the sandal of Venus with her 'talons ingénus' (l. 102)? In 'L'Après-midi d'un faune' the volcano of language has been visited by poetic beauty, and upon its laval flow the metrical feet of Venus have left the mysterious imprint of two heels, the perpetuated couple of naked, free-born rhyme.

[77] The Larousse entries for 'utérus' and 'nymphes' stress the triangular, or v-shaped, configuration of both the womb and the 'petites lèvres de la vulve', while the description of the 'col de l'utérus' as having 'la forme d'un cône à sommet inférieur percé d'une ouverture' suggests a further link between female genitalia and the volcano.

[78] See Larousse, 'nymphes'.

[79] See the Larousse entry on Empedocles. The two halves of 'L'Après-midi d'un faune' are dominated respectively by air and water and by fire and earth.

PART III

Stations of the Cross: The 'Sonnet en -yx'
  (1868–1887–1898)

Ici, reconnaissez [...] la Passion, [...] ou [...] une assimilation humaine à la tétralogie de l'An.

('Catholicisme')

The 'Sonnet en -yx' is perhaps Mallarmé's most famous work. Certainly it has been among the most discussed, and debate has ranged from the entertaining pursuit of a referent for 'ptyx' to more subtle accounts of the poem's reflexive character.[1] Almost always, however, attention has focused on the 1887 version ('Ses purs ongles...'), while 'Sonnet allégorique de lui-même' (1868) has tended to be passed over as the less accomplished version of a hermetic masterpiece. Critics have seized with understandable relief on Mallarmé's famous comments to Lefébure and Cazalis,[2] but then gone on to use these as keys to 'Ses purs ongles...': only one commentary has been devoted to 'Sonnet allégorique de lui-même'.[3]

It is true that Mallarmé felt that the latter was something of a rushed job, and he fully intended to polish it at the proof stage[4] if it was accepted for

[1] A full bibliography is given by Marchal (*Lecture de Mallarmé*, 165), to which may be added: Scott, *Sonnet Theory and Practice*, 61–6; Catherine Lowe, 'Le Mirage de ptyx, implication à la rime', *Poétique*, 15 (1984), 325–45; Robert Couffignal, 'Une catabase mallarméenne: Approches nouvelles du sonnet en -yx', *Littératures*, 20 (1989), 53–62; Deirdre Reynolds, 'Illustration, Present or Absent: Reflecting Reflexivity in Mallarmé's "Sonnet en yx"', *Journal of European Studies*, 19 (1989), 311–29, and 'Mallarmé et la transformation esthétique du language, à l'exemple de "Ses purs ongles"', *French Forum*, 15 (1990), 203–20.

[2] The frequently quoted passages are here reproduced for the reader's convenience: (i) 'comme il se pourrait toutefois que rythmé par le hamac, et inspiré par le laurier, je fisse un sonnet, et que je n'ai que trois rimes en *ix*, concertez-vous pour m'envoyer le sens réel du mot *ptyx*, ou m'assurer qu'il n'existe dans aucune langue, ce que je préférerais de beaucoup afin de me donner le charme de le créer par la magie de la rime' (*Corr.*, i. 274 (to Lefébure, 3 May 1868), corrected by *DSM*, vi. 369); (ii) 'J'extrais ce sonnet, au quel [*sic*] j'avais une fois songé cet été, d'une étude projetée sur *la Parole*: il est inverse, je veux dire que le sens, s'il en a un, (mais je me consolerais du contraire grâce à la dose de poésie qu'il renferme, ce me semble) est évoqué par un mirage interne des mots mêmes. En se laissant aller à le murmurer plusieurs fois on éprouve une sensation assez cabalistique.

C'est confesser qu'il est peu "plastique", comme tu me le demandes, mais au moins est-il aussi "blanc et noir" que possible, et il me semble se prêter à une eau-forte pleine de Rêve et de Vide.

Par exemple, une fenêtre nocturne ouverte, les deux volets attachés; une chambre avec personne dedans, malgré l'air stable que présentent les volets attachés, et dans une nuit faite d'absence et d'interrogation, sans meubles, sinon l'ébauche plausible de vagues consoles, un cadre, belliqueux et agonisant, de miroir appendu au fond, avec sa réflexion, stellaire et incompréhensible, de la grande Ourse, qui relie au ciel seul ce logis abandonné du monde.

J'ai pris ce sujet d'un sonnet nul et se réfléchissant de toutes les façons, parce que mon œuvre est si bien préparé et hiérarchisé, représentant comme il peut l'Univers, que je n'aurais su, sans endommager quelqu'une de mes impressions étagées, rien en enlever, – et aucun sonnet ne s'y rencontre.

Je te donne seulement ces détails pour que tu ne m'accuses pas d'avoir recherché la bizarrerie et encore cette crainte ne justifie pas leur longueur' (*Corr.*, i. 278–9 (to Cazalis, 18 July 1868), corrected by *DSM*, vi. 375–6).

[3] See Paul Bénichou, *Selon Mallarmé* (Paris, 1995), 137–46.

[4] See *Corr.*, i. 280 (to Cazalis, 21 July 1868).

inclusion in Lemerre and Burty's *Sonnets et eaux-fortes*, the volume for which Cazalis had requested a contribution and which was eventually published without Mallarmé's sonnet in 1869. It is also true that 'Ses purs ongles...' is the more complex and compelling poem and that some of Mallarmé's comments apply as much, and perhaps even more, to the later version. But this critical tradition has substantially distorted our view of Mallarmé's poetic development, and not only during the 1860s. For the exclusive focus on 'Ses purs ongles...' has also led, at the other end of the chronological scale, to a neglect of the context in which Mallarmé ultimately intended the 'Sonnet en -yx' to be read, namely as the fourth of 'Plusieurs Sonnets' in the Deman edition of his *Poésies*. It is as if the difficulty of reading the 'Sonnet en -yx', in its earlier version no less than in its later perfection, had left its readers unwilling to contemplate that its 'mirage interne des mots mêmes'[5] could possibly have assumed three quite different shapes.

Since there are therefore, in a sense, three versions of the 'Sonnet en -yx', it is proposed here: (i) to place 'Sonnet allégorique de lui-même' within the context of Mallarmé's writing during the 1860s; (ii) to analyse it as a discrete literary work; (iii) to consider in what ways 'Ses purs ongles...' differs from 'Sonnet allégorique de lui-même'; and (iv) to suggest some possible readings of 'Ses purs ongles...' within the verbal network of 'Plusieurs Sonnets'. It may be borne in mind that the chronological path to be followed is the one that leads also from *Igitur* (1869) to 'Un coup de Dés' (1897).

[5] See above, n. 2.

1

May '68

J'arrive au sonnet.
(Letter to Henri Cazalis)

Happily, 'Sonnet allégorique de lui-même' may have been Mallarmé's four-teenth sonnet.[1] By May 1868, when he first mentions such a poem in his correspondence, the 26-year-old Mallarmé had written between ninety and hundred poems, of which, therefore, the sonnets counted for scarcely a seventh. In *Entre quatre murs*, as we have seen, the sonnet is but one of several verse-forms at which the apprentice-poet tries his hand. In 1862, on the other hand, the sonnet seems to have become a temporary obsession of his,[2] and six of the thirteen poems written during this year adopt the form. In these, as in his earlier attempts, he exploits the self-reference which is a traditional feature of the form. During the five years between 'Le Pitre châtié' and 'Sonnet allégorique de lui-même', Mallarmé apparently aban-doned the sonnet, preferring in many of the poems and prose poems which he wrote at this time to create a fixity of form *ex nihilo*.

In these, as we have also seen, the repeated use of a binary structure sets up a host of mirroring effects between each half of the text in question and thereby confers on each reflected textual feature an air of necessity. In

---

[1] His previous known sonnets begin with the five included in *Entre quatre murs*: 'Sonnet' ['Quand sous votre corps nu...'] (Mar. 1859); 'En envoyant un pot de fleurs. Sonnet' (Mar. 1859); 'Réponse (à Germain). Sonnet' (Mar. 1859); 'Pénitence. Sonnet' (Mar. 1860); and 'Avenir. Sonnet' (of which only the title survives). They continue with 'Placet' (Feb. 1862); 'Le Sonneur' (Mar. 1862); 'Vere novo' [later 'Renouveau'] (June 1862); 'Contre un poète parisien' (July 1862); 'Tristesse d'été' (1862); 'Parce que de la viande...' (1862); 'A une putain' [later 'A celle qui est tranquille' and 'Angoisse'] (?1863); 'Le Pître châtié' (?1863). It is, of course, possible that other sonnets (and, in particular, some first versions of other later sonnets, notably the so-called 'Triptyque') were written before 'Sonnet allégorique de lui-même', but in the absence of firm evidence this must remain a matter for surmise. In his letter to Verlaine known under the title 'Autobiographie', Mallarmé relates how as a schoolboy 'j'ai longtemps essayé [de remplacer, un jour, Béranger] dans cent petits cahiers de vers qui m'ont toujours été confisqués, si j'ai bonne mémoire' (OC, 662). Perhaps they, also, contained a sonnet or two.

[2] *Corr.*, i. 32 (?June 1862): see above, p. 34.

Mallarméan language, the mirror is here providing the 'preuve', the 'Igitur' (or 'therefore') by which poetic language transcends quotidian babble.[3] Just as many, if not all, of the poems and prose poems written between 1863 and 1866 thus fold upon themselves formally, so also they fold upon themselves thematically. As in the sonnet tradition, several of them allude more or less explicitly to the circumstances of their own existence, and almost all of them lend themselves readily to a reflexive reading. Noteworthy above all, in the context of 'Sonnet allégorique de lui-même', is the clear connection in 'Les Fenêtres' between the crossed rhymes of the poem and the 'croisées' in which the poet finds his own angelic reflection (ll. 25–32). The redundant crucifix on the wall (l. 3) has been superseded by the redemption of reflexive art, and the homophonic self-reference of rhyme has become the new sign of the cross.

It is important to note these textual features before turning to the vexed subject of the crisis which Mallarmé underwent during (approximately) the two years which elapsed between his visit to Lefébure at Cannes (29 March–6 April 1866) and his letter to Lefébure of 3 May 1868 in which he first implies the existence of the 'Sonnet en -yx'. The nature of this crisis, which 'rumbles on' in the correspondence until 1871, has been much discussed, most often in religious and metaphysical terms. Did it principally involve a loss of religious faith ('ma lutte terrible avec ce vieux et méchant plumage, terrassé, heureusement, Dieu'[4])? Did Mallarmé see himself caught up in some Hegelian dialectic of 'l'Absolu' and 'le Néant'? Did he, in Cannes, undergo some mystical revelation whereby he came to see the 'drame solaire' as the cosmic projection at once of man's existential anguish and of his inner 'divinité'?[5] To see the crisis in these terms, however, is in part to be misled by Mallarmé's uncharacteristically pretentious language. For the crisis was unquestionably, above all, a 'crise de vers' – and a 'crise' brought on by the writing of the 'Ouverture' to 'Hérodiade'.

As far as we know, 'Sonnet allégorique de lui-même' is the first poem Mallarmé wrote after this two-year crisis, and the first therefore since the 'Ouverture' which precipitated the crisis: ' "Hérodiade", où je m'étais mis tout entier sans le savoir, d'où mes doutes et mes malaises, et dont j'ai enfin trouvé le fin mot, ce qui me raffermit et me facilitera le labeur.'[6] Given the nature of 'Sonnet allégorique de lui-même', it would seem in retrospect that the central importance of the crisis lay in a radical shift in Mallarmé's attitude to language. Put simply, he no longer sought to express himself through language but now sought to let language express itself through him. In 'Hérodiade' he had attempted an allegory of beauty as both virginal and

---

[3] Cf. the end of the 'Argument' in *Igitur* (OC, 434).
[4] *Corr.*, i. 241 (to Cazalis, 14 May 1867).
[5] See Marchal, *La Religion de Mallarmé*, 54–64 and *passim*.
[6] *Corr.*, i. 221.

sterile, cut off from the nourishment of life (la Nourrice) yet sufficient unto itself: 'le sujet de mon œuvre est la Beauté, et le sujet apparent n'est qu'un prétexte pour aller vers Elle. C'est, je crois, le mot de la Poésie.'[7] As the crisis abated, Mallarmé turned away from the longer form ('Hérodiade', 'L'Après-midi d'un faune'), and began his lifelong pursuit of beauty in the sonnet. Given the extraordinary complexity which his new approach to language entailed, the short, fixed form was to prove an ideal 'grid' upon which to place his lexical lacework. In May 1868 his first 'return' to poetry is a return to the alexandrine ('Sonnet allégorique de lui-même'); his second, very soon after, is to the octosyllabic line ('De l'orient passé des Temps').

[7] *Corr.*, i. 193.

2

The Scene of the (C)rime: 'Sonnet allégorique de lui-même' (1868)

la magie de la rime.

The obvious way to begin reading 'Sonnet allégorique de lui-même' is in terms of Mallarmé's own commentary. Many critics have thought that the scene which the poet describes in his letter to Cazalis is the origin of the suggestive 'décor / De l'absence' mentioned in the poem itself. But Mallarmé says only that his sonnet 'me semble se prêter à une eau-forte [...]': that is, he had already written it before receiving Cazalis's request and has decided to extract it from a projected work on 'la Parole' because it lends itself more or less to a volume requiring poems which might suitably be illustrated by etchings. Mallarmé's description is offered only as an 'exemple' of a possible picture. Instead he is adamant that the poem may have no meaning at all in a conventional, representational sense; it is 'inverse', he remarks, indicating (possibly by an interlingual pun[1]) that here is a poem born of itself. Such meaning as it may contain 'est évoqué par un mirage interne des mots mêmes': it is a 'sonnet nul et se réfléchissant de toutes les façons'.

The most convenient way to demonstrate the relevance of these famous phrases to 'Sonnet allégorique de lui-même' is to imitate Poe's essay 'The Philosophy of Composition' and to offer an account of how Mallarmé's

---

[1] Mallarmé's discussion of interlingual wordplay in Les Mots anglais (OC, 996–7) and the number of French/English puns in his own writing suggests conscious authorial intention. Cf. the rhyming of 'cueille' and 'eye' ('œil') in the Vers de circonstance (OC, 156), and the use of 'grief' in 'Le Tombeau d'Edgar Poe' (l.9) where the English meaning makes more immediate sense than the French (and is hence a fitting tribute to an anglophone poet), even rhyming potentially in English with 'bas-relief' in 1.10. Cf. also the play on 'filial' and 'or' (son/sun) in the sestet of 'Une dentelle s'abolit': see below, Part IV, Ch. 2.

[2] Poe, 'The Philosophy of Composition', in Selected Writings, ed. David Galloway (London, 1967), 482.

work on the poem may have 'proceeded, step by step, to its completion with the precision and rigid consequence of a mathematical problem'.[2] Poe's essay, it will be remembered, turned out to be a fiction, but as Mallarmé himself remarked: 'Ce qui est pensé, l'est: et une idée prodigieuse s'échappe des pages qui, écrites après coup (et sans fondement anecdotique, voilà tout) n'en demeurent pas moins congéniales à Poe, sincères.'[3] What follows, therefore, is an attempt to recuperate as much as possible of Mallarmé's 'Sonnet en -yx' in terms of a precise authorial intention.

If we accept that during the period 1866–8 Mallarmé came to see that the greatest or 'purest' form of poetic statement lay neither in the lyrical expression of the self nor in the 'sorcellerie évocatoire' of a Baudelairean concatenation of imagery but in an articulation of the mysterious and manifold 'virtualités' of language itself ('le mystère dans les lettres'), then where might he have started? If the initiative is now to lie with words, from where in language should the initiative come? His answer: from rhyme, for rhyme is at once perhaps *the* defining feature of traditional (French) verse and an emblem of that reflexivity in which Mallarmé now sees his future as a poet to lie. As the letter to Lefébure suggests, X marks the spot. For X is a symbol of rhyme: like rhyme, it is a reflection, a mirrored V, the v. that stands for 'vers', and for 'versus' (the turning at the end of a furrow from which 'vers' etymologically derives); of 'v' the emblem of adversity and opposition and alternatives, of either/OR. So Mallarmé's poem is born of a rhyme in X: not just words which end in 'x', but words in which the endings reproduce the sound of the letter X; of X, the symbol of the unknown, of an absent number, of the mystery which lies at the heart of language and (graphically) of every 'texte';[4] X, the symbol also of connection and relationship, of lace or a network of sounds, a 'son-net', of 'l'ensemble des rapports existant dans tout, la Musique';[5] X, therefore, at once an emblem of cancellation and absence and yet also a sign of multiplication, of manyfoldedness; a cross, a 'point de rencontre',[6] from which four paths lead away, to the four corners of the world, to the four parts of a Petrarchan sonnet, to infinity. The poet dies as a speaking subject that the dead metaphors and fossilized etymologies of language may be reborn: the crucifix of the Passion has become the cross of linguistic reflexivity that redeems the sins of naïve authorial self-expression.

---

[3] 'Scolies', OC, 230.

[4] Thus contained by the 'tête' which is the severed head of the author who has 'died' and become 'le Texte [...] parlant de lui-même et sans voix d'auteur' (OC, 663)? Cf. the severed head of St John in 'Cantique de saint Jean' which has become 'Son pur regard' (i.e. a 'seer' thanks to the 'son pur' of poetry).

[5] 'Crise de vers', OC, 368.

[6] Cf. Corr., i. 225: 'je tisserai *aux points de rencontre* de merveilleuses dentelles que je devine, et qui existent déjà dans le sein de la Beauté' (to Aubanel, 28 July 1866: Mallarmé's emphasis).

From X flows the rhyme-scheme itself: 'rimes croisées' in the quatrains, cdd ccd in the tercets, and the highly unusual 'resurrection' of the ab rhymes in opposite genders as the cd rhymes (with a consequent reduction of the total number of rhymes from the usual Petrarchan five to a crucial four). As in a cross, two straight lines (/or/ and /iks/) become four separate arms (yx/ ix, ore, or, ixe) after they bisect each other. Just as the rhymes in the tercets mirror (and distort by presenting an 'inverse' image of) those in the quatrains, the rhyme-scheme in the tercets may be seen as a distorted version of 'rimes croisées', being cdcd 'filled out' with two mirror-like couplets.

In 'Sonnet allégorique' X gives rise to seven of the terminal rhymes. What sound would Mallarmé choose for the other seven? The schoolteacher and future author of *Les Mots anglais* may have chosen the English 'or' since this would relate the b and c rhymes to the adversarial 'v' reflected in X and to the binary nature of rhyme.[7] More obviously, rhyme is a refined 'sonorité', a 'son or'.[8] Where Baudelaire turned the base metal of experience into the gold of poetic 'extase', Mallarméan alchemy turns the worn-out currency of language[9] into the gold of 'la poésie pure'. 'Or' had already figured in Mallarmé's poems as a symbol of the poet's ideal;[10] but now, in the new world of self-referential poetic practice, it may continue to serve as the emblem of this ideal since the achievement of value through refinement is linguistically enacted by the extraction of 'son or' from 'sonorité'.[11] That it should gleam, inverted, in the word 'croix' came as a bonus, as indeed did

---

[7] It may be noted in this connection that 'De l'orient passé des Temps', written in the same year as 'Sonnet allégorique de lui-même', was revised and entitled 'Alternative' in 1869 (before eventually becoming 'Quelle soie aux baumes de temps' in 1885). In the first version 'or' is present as the second syllable of the first and last lines (as well as in 'Mortes' at the beginning of l. 11 and reversed in the second syllable ('atroces') of the penultimate line); while in 'Alternative' what Jean-Pierre Richard calls 'le nomadisme textuel de l'*or*' ends with 'or' vanishing from all but the last line, in which 'mon horreur' (= also 'mon or, heure' by way of homophonic reference back to the opening line of the poem ['*orient*' and 'Temps']) has become 'son horreur'. Richard ('Feu rué, feu scintillé: Note sur Mallarmé, le fantasme et l'écriture', *Littérature*, 17 (1975), 84–104 (93)) takes his cue from Derrida's account of 'or' in *La Dissémination*, 295–7. For further analysis of the three versions of 'De l'orient passé des Temps', see below Part IV, Ch. 1.

[8] Cf. the beginning of the first section of *Igitur*: 'Certainement subsiste une présence de Minuit. L'heure n'a pas disparu par un miroir, ne s'est pas enfouie en tentures, évoquant un ameublement par sa vacante *sonorité*. Je me rappelle que *son or* allait feindre en l'absence d'un joyau nul de rêverie, riche et inutile survivance, sinon que sur la complexité marine et stellaire d'une *orfèvrerie* se lisait le hasard infini des conjonctions' (OC, 435; my emphases). 'Minuit', 'miroir', 'sinon que sur' are among the elements in 'Ses purs ongles...' which were not present in 'Sonnet allégorique de lui-même'. This suggests that Mallarmé continued working on the latter after he had sent it to Cazalis and that some of what was to be published as 'Ses purs ongles...' in 1887 was already in place by 1869 (when Mallarmé wrote the unfinished *Igitur*).

[9] Cf. 'Crise de vers': 'Narrer, enseigner, même décrire, cela va et encore qu'à chacun suffirait peut- être pour échanger la pensée humaine, de prendre ou de mettre dans la main d'autrui en silence une pièce de monnaie, l'emploi élémentaire du discours dessert l'universel *reportage* [...]' (OC, 368).

[10] See, for example, 'Les Fenêtres', 'Les Fleurs', and the 1865 version of 'Sainte'.

[11] Note also the several references to alchemy and the 'Grand'Œuvre', or 'magnum opus', in Mallarmé's letters at this period (e.g. *Corr.*, i. 244).

its presence at the heart of the 'mot anglais', the 'word' itself;[12] and 'rimes d'or' was in any case the standard term for particularly rich rhyme.[13]

As Derrida notes, 'or' is also O+R.[14] Thus 'or' contains (in O) both absence and perfection (zero and the circle), and so reflects the ambivalence of X (cancellation and multiplying connections). This ambivalence is reinforced homophonically, as /o/ echoes through the poem, being at once the '/o/ du Styx' (l. 7) and the '/o/ pur, Crime' (l. 2)—that is, the zero of death and the linguistic plenitude which will derive from the (C)rime which the poem is committing. R, at least for the Mallarmé of *Les Mots anglais*, was the supreme consonant, 'l'articulation par excellence', and connoted 'L'élévation, le but atteint même au prix d'un rapt, la plénitude; enfin, par onomatopée, une déchirure et, d'après l'importance même de la lettre, quelque chose de radical.'[15] Admittedly he is describing the English R, not the French, and moreover he is concerned with the effect of consonants as initial, not terminal, letters. Nevertheless for one so alive to the expressive power of each letter of the alphabet (be it spoken or written), R clearly represented the highest value. And, of course, it is the initial letter of 'Rêve' (l. 8), not to mention 'rime'.

Having now decided that 'or' shall provide the other seven rhymes, how shall Mallarmé distribute his fourteen rhymes among the quatrains and tercets of his 'sound-net'? Following the logic of the cross, he must locate a point of intersection; which, in the rhyme-scheme of a Petrarchan sonnet, means the end of l. 9, where a new set of rhymes and the different scheme of the sestet traditionally begin. Having already decided to repeat the rhymes of the octave in the sestet but in opposite genders, the most effective terminal rhyme for l. 9 will be 'or', since poetic value is the result of the poem's bold reversal in the sestet. There is the added advantage that 'or' will thus be seen to have been refined from the 'ore' (in an English sense) of the preceding octave, an ore which can forthwith be deposited in its now necessary locations[16] at the end of ll. 2, 4, 6, and 8.

As a further consequence of this choice he must find four masculine rhymes in /iks/. 'Onyx', 'Phœnix', and 'Styx' are to hand, as his reading of Banville will have shown him.[17] But he needs one more[18]—which, given that the pair 'onyx' and 'Phœnix' produce the richest rhyme from the three

---

[12] See above, n. 1.

[13] In Victor Delaporte, *De la rime française* (Paris, 1898), the term 'rimes d'or' is used twice as though it were a time-honoured expression (see pp. 45, 147).

[14] *La Dissémination*, 295.

[15] OC, 959.

[16] Later, in 'Au seul souci de voyager', Mallarmé will exploit the dual sense of location and mineral deposit in the term 'gisement' (l. 11).

[17] See Scott, *Sonnet Theory and Practice*, 62, and Lawrence Watson, 'Some Further Thoughts on Mallarmé's "Sonnet en -yx"', *French Studies Bulletin*, 27 (Summer 1988), 14.

[18] As Pierre Citron has shown, the word 'oryx' became available to Mallarmé only after 1868, when it subsequently appeared in the Supplément to Littré's dictionary (where its first

available, needs to end in /tiks/. Now, on the principle that 'si "tix" n'existait pas, il faudrait l'inventer', he creates his own rhyme-word, thus allowing himself to be the delighted instrument of the self-generating power of language once released from the requirement to communicate a poet's pre-existing thoughts ('afin de me donner le charme de le créer par la magie de la rime'). 'Tix', however, has an implausible air. 'Tyx' looks more Greek, in keeping with the other three available rhymes in /iks/, but one extra letter would make it symmetrical both with 'Styx', its intended pair, and with 'onyx'. For the symmetry, also, the word must remain monosyllabic. And so, of all the letters of the alphabet, 'p' suggested itself as the most appropriate: partly for the visual reminder of the beginning of 'Phœnix'; partly, no doubt, because 'pt' is to be found as an initial consonant cluster in several French words of Greek origin (like 'Ptolomée'); and possibly because 'p', being a musical notation for subdued sound, might thus suggest the shadowiness of the neologism's presence at the rhyme (as if it were some linguistic phantom of the 'styx').[19]

Hence 'ptyx': and who better than an Egyptologist (with a knowledge of Greek) to consult on whether such a word existed? Given the recurrent use of 'pli' in the 'Ouverture' to 'Hérodiade', where it suggests among other things the enfolded, reflexive nature of the text itself, it is difficult to believe that Mallarmé did not already know the answer to the question which he put to Lefébure. Moreover he may well have met the word in Hugo's 'Le Satyre'.[20] At any rate, Lefébure himself is likely to have known that '*ptyx' means 'pli' in ancient Greek—and to have given Mallarmé the information which he had requested.[21] Thus Mallarmé had the pleasure of being led by the logic of the cross to invent a rhyme-word which, in the French language,

recorded use in print, by George Sand, dates from 1875) and in the fascicule of Larousse's *Grand Dictionnaire universel du XIXe siècle* which contains the entries 'licorne', 'oryx', 'styx': see 'Sur le sonnet en -yx de Mallarmé', *Revue d'histoire littéraire de la France*, 69 (1969), 113–16. The role of 'oryx' in the subsequent revision of 'Sonnet allégorique de lui-même' is discussed further below.

[19] In *Les Mots anglais* Mallarmé describes initial 'p' as having 'l'intention très nette d'entassement, de richesse acquise ou de stagnation [...]' (laquelle s'affine et précise parfois sa signification pour exprimer tel acte ou objet vif et net') (OC, 933). If these remarks, published nine years after 'Sonnet allégorique de lui-même', can be relevant, then they suggest that Mallarmé was lending substance and 'presence' to 'tyx' by preceding it with 'p'.

[20] In 'Le Satyre' in *La Légende des siècles*: '[...] on entendait Chrysis / Sylvain du Ptyx que l'homme appelle Janicule' (ll. 18–19). Hugo's usage derives from the Greek word's possible sense of a fold, or cleft, in a hillside. See Émilie Noulet, *L'Œuvre poétique de Stéphane Mallarmé* (Paris, 1940), 454.

[21] Whether he also told Mallarmé (or whether Mallarmé in 1868 already knew) of the various contexts in which the word figures in ancient Greek literature must remain a matter of conjecture. What Mallarmé might have learnt between 1868 and 1887 will be discussed later. On these contexts see Gretchen Kromer, 'The Redoutable PTYX', *Modern Language Notes*, 86 (1971), 563–72. Ross Arthur points out that 'ptyx' is not to be found in this nominative singular form in any ancient Greek text, and that the word is attested only in the accusative and dative singular and in the nominative and accusative plural. In true Mallarméan spirit he

is mere sound (an 'Insolite vaisseau d'inanité sonore'), but which in its linguistic 'vie antérieure' was once a fold, the very 'objet tu' which Mallarmé sees as best symbolizing the nature of rhyme and of poetic expression in general. The birth of the 'ptyx' is thus also representative of the whole process whereby the poet plays with language in the present in such a way as to call up ('évoquer') the shades of language past which haunt its every 'vocable'.

In this way, too, the lacework of the poem begins to sew itself in another direction. For is not the phoenix also a non-existent object of ancient lineage called up by the demands of poetry (as epitomized in rhyme)? More specifically, as an emblem of self-immolation and resurrection, it must have appealed to this poet who had written one year previously of his own 'death' and his resurrection as 'une aptitude qu'a l'Univers spirituel à se voir et à se développer, à travers ce qui fut moi'.[22] The Christian crucifix is now linked with the palingenesis of a poet who has died (in that he no longer tries to express his thoughts and feelings) and is reborn as the receptive and collaborative instrument of language. In one version of the myth of the phoenix, it is a worm which first emerges from the ashes and then turns into a young phoenix: that is to say, 'un ver'.[23] And out of its homophone 'le vers' there rises eventually the sonnet itself, which, in the perfect form to which Mallarmé aspires, will be what Boileau called 'cet heureux phénix [qui] est encore à trouver'.[24]

Fortuitously 'styx' mirrors 'Phœnix' by evoking myth, death—and resurrection, too, if one thinks of Orpheus or the various myths which involve the *crossing* of the Styx (as when Psyche, a mortal woman beloved of Cupid, is required by jealous Venus to obtain a flask of the water of youth from Persephone) or the drawing of water from the Styx itself with a vessel made of gold or horn.[25] And so to 'onyx' (so called in Greek because of its

---

points out that *ptyx is therefore the correct way to designate the nominative singular form; and that Mallarmé's invented rhyme-word is thus already a star... (see 'When is a Word not a Word: Thoughts on Mallarmé's Sonnet en -yx', *Romance Notes*, 27 (1986–7), 167–73).

[22] *Corr.*, i. 242 (to Cazalis, 14 May 1867).

[23] It is uncertain whether Mallarmé knew of this version of the myth in 1868, but he had clearly read about it in George W. Cox's *Manual of Mythology* (London, 1867) by the time he came to translate and adapt Cox's work in his own *Les Dieux antiques* (1880). Bertrand Marchal notes that Mallarmé's account of the phoenix in *Les Dieux antiques* (OC, 1274) is a considerably truncated version of the relevant paragraph in Cox and, in particular, omits reference to the worm. For Marchal 'cette "traduction" vermifuge' is evidence of Mallarmé seeking to 'préserver le prestige et la résonance imaginaire d'un mythe cher au poète en escamotant une variante infiniment moins poétique' (*La Religion de Mallarmé*, 151). On the contrary, may it not be that Cox's worm/'ver(s)' was *too* poetic, and that Mallarmé may have been covering his traces?

[24] See Graham Robb, 'The Phoenix of Mallarmé's "Sonnet en-yx"', *French Studies Bulletin*, 24 (Autumn 1987), 14. The Larousse article on 'Phœnix' quotes the relevant passage from Boileau.

[25] See Larousse, 'Styx'.

resemblance to the horned matter of finger-nails), a semi-precious stone which is often black in appearance but reveals itself to be translucent, multi-layered, and concentrically patterned (rather like Mallarmé's obscure poem). In turn the tautology of 'les onyx / De ses ongles' serves not only to reveal an etymology and to set up a polarity of Greek v. Roman, but also to remind us of the ten fingers (no doubt a Roman ten, or x) which are lighting up the darkness.

So far a mere four words have been considered in detail, but already it is clear just how many other aspects of the poem may have arisen out of what these four words, so to speak, provoke. Moving on to the feminine rhymes in /iks/, here Mallarmé had more than the minimum required number (three) of rhymes at his disposal. But the logic of the cross (and the four rhyme-words already in place) meant that 'nixe' and 'fixe' must have chosen themselves: the first for being a reflection of 'Phœnix' both homophonically and as a mythological creature, and yet also for directly contrasting as female and as teutonic (as opposed to ancient Egyptian); and 'fixe' since the sonnet is a 'forme fixe'. So fitting was the latter connection, presumably, that Mallarmé chose to end 'Sonnet allégorique' on it (with the 2+4 literal pattern of 'se fixe' completing the frame begun by 'La Nuit' in l. 1). Which leaves 'rixe' (rather than, for example, 'prolixe', with its internal reversed 'or'); and 'rixe' may have suited since (in its sense of quarrel) it evokes the opposedness that is part of the cross. At any rate the initial letters of 'rixe' and 'nixe', together with the 'une' which precedes each, provide a parallel with the morphology and consonants of 'un or'.

The remaining rhymes in the tercets allow one similarly to infer their necessity. 'Encor' speaks of the repetition that is rhyme and reflection; and perhaps the homophonic shadow 'en corps' may connect with the theme of the Christian resurrection (discussed below). Anagrammatically, of course, it repeats the 'corne' implicit in the first rhyme of the poem. 'Décor' may also be heard as 'des corps [/ De l'absence]', perhaps those of the 'dieu' and 'nixe' who have vanished in the mirror's obscuring process. The recurrence of 'cor' in 'décor' and 'encor' may prepare for the musical sense of 'septuor', contributing thus to the poem's final assertion of itself as a musical arrangement.

And what of 'dé—', that all-important Mallarméan word which plays such a key role in 'Le Démon de l'analogie'? From the Latin prefix 'dis', indicating separation, distance, cancellation, 'dé' also derives etymologically from both 'datum' and 'digitus', and so combines the physical act of writing with the notion of language as a series of 'données' with which the poet finds himself fortuitously faced. Not only a die, it is also a thimble, a piece of metal used by sailmakers to protect the palm of their hand, and a 'petit verre' (hom.: 'vers'; syn. the 'verre' of a mirror).[26] Like X, therefore,

---

[26] Cf. the play on 'vers/verre' (and 'coupe') in the first quatrain of 'Salut'. These meanings of 'dé' will be further discussed with reference to 'Un coup de Dés': see below, Part V.

'dé' is an emblem of absence, doubt, and combination. Placed before 'cor' in 'décor' it produces a word which epitomizes Mallarméan poetry: the 'musical' arrangement of aleatory features of language to non-representational ends.[27] Hence 'décor / De l'absence'; since, like 'dé-', the prefix 'ab-' also indicates separation, distance, cancellation—here of the 'sens' (of conventionally descriptive, 'scene-setting' language) which is homophonically present in 'absence'. In apposition to 'glace', a comparatively trite image for the reflexive character of this poem (despite the 'vers/verre' homophone), the periphrasis 'décor / De l'absence' is thus on the contrary a dense statement of Mallarméan poetics.

As to 'un or' itself, it has already been noted that here is the crux of the sonnet's rhyme-scheme, the moment of bold reversal. The principal referent of 'un or' is the second syllable of this phrase itself, which has survived the transition from octave to sestet—and literally so, since in l. 9 we see it first, mirrored, in 'croisée' and then restored to its proper order in 'Nord' and duly preceded by 'un' (in 'au Nord'). Whereas 'nul ptyx' was a self-referential statement of non-existence, here (at the end of a line which mirrors the rhythm of l. 5) is a golden self-assertion of the renewal of language after the death of representation.

Returning finally to the rhymes of the quatrains, it is evident that, in this poem born of rhyme, the /iks/ rhymes (which evoke the *nature* of rhyme) are crossed with /or/ rhymes which evoke the two poles of rhyme's *value*: richness and worthlessness. On the one hand we have 'lampadophore' / 'amphore': both a rich rhyme and a rare one, in which the relationship between rhyme-words is figured as a process of salvage and compression, with 'amphore' 'rescuing' more than half of 'lampadophore' from extinction (in contrast to the process of non-survival narrated in l. 4 itself).[28] On the other hand we have 'sonore' / 's'honore': a punning, tautological sonority displaying rhyme as no more than a trivial repetition, a 'vaisseau d'inanité'. When the poet releases language from the duty to express and represent, the free play of the signifier threatens nullity; and homophony can seem no longer to point to mysterious and profound hidden connections but simply to a void of non-sense, the 'neutralité identique du gouffre'.[29]

'Sonore' / 's'honore' can readily be imagined springing to the aid of a poet already intent on refining 'son or' from 'sonorité'. But whence 'lampadophore' / 'amphore'? Perhaps the world of ancient Greece and the thought of a phoenix's ashes needing to be contained were sufficient to bring them to the poet's mind. And there they would have remained, for 'amphore', as a double-handled container, offers an appropriate image of rhyme itself; as does 'lampadophore' (which stands in potential apposition to 'Crime'), a

[27] Cf. Hugo's play on 'Jérimadeth' (hom. 'J'ai rime à dé') in 'Booz endormi'.
[28] As 'allume' in l. 1 condenses the phrase 'allégorique de lui-même' placed directly above it.
[29] 'Un coup de Dés', OC, 473.

torch bearer relaying the golden light of 'or' from the beginning of the poem (in 'allégorique'), via the rhyme-scheme, to 'septuor' at the end.[30] Since the ancient Greek torchbearer also had a religious as well as a sporting role, so the word combines the two elements of 'jeu' and 'sacre' which, in Mallarmé's view, define poetry itself.

With the fourteen rhyme-words now in place, it remains to be seen how the rest of the poem grows out of the rhymes. One may imagine 'onyx' prompting not only 'De ses ongles' (as already described) but also the opening phrase 'La Nuit', both because 'onyx' is a kind of compressed anagram of the Greek and Latin for 'night' ('nyx' and 'nox') and because of a poetic ambition (deriving from the nature of rhyme) to have mirror-effects within the lines as well as between them. 'Phœnix' adds the idea of sunset, since the myth of the Phoenix is a version of the 'drame solaire'; and the fact that it is also a constellation means that, like 'onyx', it first connotes darkness but then reveals itself to be a place of light and pattern. The very word, as it were, enacts a resurrection. From this stems the basic narrative of the poem, which it is perhaps now best to paraphrase to lend clarity to what follows:

Like a torchbearer, the Night, with approval, lights the black onyx of its nails on the pure Crime constituted by the evening being abolished by the vesperal Phoenix (i.e. the setting sun), the ashes of which have no cinerary amphora (to collect them) upon side-tables in the black drawing-room: no 'ptyx', uncommon vessel of sonorous blankness, because the Master has gone to draw water from the Styx (i.e. to seek renewal on pain of death) with all his objects, in which dream (i.e. poetic aspiration) honours itself. And along/upon the north-facing casement, an ill-fated 'or' provokes as a fine frame for itself a scuffle created by a god whom a nixie believes she is carrying off in the darkening of the mirror, a décor of absence, except that upon the mirror still the septet of scintillas fixes itself.

In effect the logic of the cross has thrown up fourteen rhyme-words which suggest the story of their own genesis. Rhyme 'murders' the priority of reference (this is the 'Crime'); and following the rejection of a representational use of language—in ll. 7–8, the controlling master of language has sought renewal by 'dying' as an autobiographical voice and by dispensing with the traditional use of objects as expressive images and symbols—reference is reborn when words take on a new light in patterns which, like constellations, emerge by chance and yet shine forth with a semblance of

---

[30] Mallarmé could have used the form 'lampadéphore', with its telling 'dice' syllable. Why, then, 'lampadophore'? No doubt because of the visual parallel between '-ophore' and 'onyx' in the previous line, and because 'o', as the fifth syllable of the second hemistich, repeats the fifth syllable of the first hemistich; but perhaps also because the homophonic presence of 'à dos fort' suggests the reliability of rhyme as the 'vertèbre' of the poem (cf. l. 2 of 'Quand l'ombre menaça...'). Might one hear a tantalizing echo of 'eau-forte' (the poem's possible future companion) in '-ophore, / D (u Soir)'?

necessity and significance. The octave, although heavily periphrastic, essentially apes the language of representation to tell this story (in reverse); while the sestet demonstrates it in poetic practice.

This is not to say that the octave lacks reflexive features. The alternating 2+4 and 2+3 of the word lengths at the beginning of each line in the first quatrain (with this repetition of initial two-letter words echoed at the beginning of l. 9 and repeated in the final tercet); the echoing of 'De qui' and 'de ci(néraire)' at the beginning of each hemistich in l. 4; the semantic repetition of 'Soir/vespéral' (l. 3) re-enacted in l. 4 ('cendre/cinéraire'); the 'sol' in 'consoles' and 'insolite' providing the suggestion of a false etymology which is thus unable (unlike 'or' later) to perpetuate the dying rays of the sun (in Latin 'sol'); the rhyming of 'allé' and 'puiser' either side of the caesura in l. 7, and the rhyming of the first hemistichs in ll. 7 and 8; the hints of 'jais' (black onyx) and 'geai' (cf. 'phœnix') in 'objets': all these features demonstrate that the comment 'se réfléchissant de toutes les façons' applies as much to the octave of this sonnet as to its sestet.

But in the sestet the actual prosodic events become the subject of the narrative. The first line (l. 9) 'tells' how, from the gaping crossed rhymes (and especially the vacant or 'inane' crossed rhyme of 'sonore'/ 's'honore') which are above it (i.e. 'au Nord', with 'selon' reminding one of the 'Salon' of l. 5), the 'or' rhyme survives (in 'croisée', 'Nord'). This 'or' is 'Néfaste' because it is the product of a '(C)rime' and perhaps even because it is of doubtful linguistic propriety in its collocation with the indefinite article. Yet it is also 'néfaste', because it is a word born of a ceremonial ostentation of opulent rhyming and hence 'faste' also in the sense of 'lawful' and (etymologically) 'favourable'.[31] This 'or' provokes as a beautiful 'rhyme-frame' (a 'beau son-cadre', as well as 'son beau [,] cadre') the word 'rixe', the feminine rhyme in /iks/ being the new 'site' (cf. 'incite') for the masculine rhyme in 'or'.

That the 'rixe' should be 'Faite d'un dieu que croit emporter une nixe' may have derived from Mallarmé's investigation of the connotations of constellation (initiated by 'Phœnix'[32]). Since these produced the 'septuor' of 'scintillations' on l. 14 (which he identifies as the Great Bear in his letter to Cazalis), then the mythical origin of this constellation (the pursuit of Callisto, her metamorphosis into a she-bear and then into a constellation) may have prompted l. 11. Yet in that case one would expect 'qui' not 'que'. Is this another case of inverse reflection (a teutonic nixie believes herself to be abducting a god, whereas the Greek god attempts to carry off a nymph), or might one see in ll. 11–14 a comparatively lame symbolic representation

---

[31] Thanks to the following 'incite', it is also (homophonically) 'né faste ainsi'.

[32] In the southern hemisphere and consisting of seven stars. See Robb, 'The Phoenix', 14. Further chiasmus is created by having a southern constellation in the 'north' (l. 9) of the poem, and the northern constellation of the Great Bear in the 'south' of the poem.

of the poet's struggle?[33] Beauty believes that she is carrying off the god in the obscuring process of the mirror, except that the constellation is there reflected: i.e. in the poet's godlike[34] attempt to capture beauty, it is beauty herself who believes that she is carrying off the god (because reflexivity, which is his means of pursuing her, is in fact allowing her to prove elusive and causing both him and herself to vanish into obscurity)—except that she *has* been captured, albeit at one remove as a constellation and not as a beddable nymph: i.e. the poet has achieved beauty in the guise of pattern and illuminating linguistic configuration rather than of directly represented beauty in the world.

In these lines the process of reflection continues (even while the possibility of its inadequacy is mooted)[35]—in the mirrored survival of 'or' in 'c*roit*' and 'emp*orter*' (which themselves mirror 'croisée au Nord' in the previous framing line of this tercet); in the echoing of ll. 12–13 ('En *l'obs*-cur-*cisse*-m-*ent*' / 'De *l'abs-en-ce, si* (non)'; and in the repetition of 'glace' itself, the banality of which image is saved by this very repetition which breaks the convention whereby no word of any length or significance should appear twice in the one sonnet.

And so beauty has indeed been captured, for 'septuor' provides a brilliant crowning finish to the poem, a celebratory summit, the 'fête/faîte d'un dieu'. A seven-letter word suggesting (because of 'scintillations', not Mallarmé's letter to Cazalis) a constellation of seven stars: a constellation reflected so that we have not only the fourteen lines of a sonnet, but the structure of the Petrarchan sonnet itself (a repeated four, a repeated three) and the rhyme-scheme (two sevens: /iks/ and /or/; or two fours: 'yx/ix' and 'ore'; and two threes: 'or' and 'ixe'): a constellation which suggests the Pleiades (seven beautiful sisters pursued like rhyme and transformed into stars) and brings to mind the poets of the Pléiade: and a constellation which can just as well be 'la Grande Ourse', otherwise called (as it will be in 'Un coup de Dés') 'le septentrion' (etymologically derived from the Latin for 'seven oxen'). The 'Sonnet allégorique de lui-même' fixes itself on paper as the Plough: and Mallarmé will not have failed to be reminded of the etymology of 'vers' (from the turning at the end of a furrow). For 'septuor' demands also to be heard as 'cep-tu-or': the 'cep' being the sole (also known as the slade) of a plough, and 'tu' because indeed this homophonic presence of a 'cep' within the '*sep*tentrion' has gone unheard.

---

[33] And one remembers that Mallarmé was aware of weaknesses in the version of the poem which he was sending to Cazalis. See above, Part III, Introd. n. 2.

[34] 'Le Maître du monde' being one description of God, and thus linking 'dieu' back to 'Maître' in the second quatrain. This establishes a further parallel between the mirror of self-reference (ll. 12–13) and the deadly waters of the Styx.

[35] Cf. the 'receptive' function of 'amphore' as rhyme- word in contrast to its stated absence in l. 4.

And '-or': through his attention to the hidden 'virtualités' of language (which Mallarmé also likes to denote punningly as the 'vertu' of language) the words 'septentrion' and 'septuor' have been refined, and the gold of manifold linguistic relationships made the precious medium of his 'musical' art, of what he described to Edmund Gosse as 'Musique [...] au fond significant Idée ou rythme entre des rapports'.

For some readers the foregoing account of the 'birth' of 'Sonnet allégorique de lui-même' may seem not only implausible and laborious but also indicative of a dispiritingly mechanical approach on the part of the poet. Is Mallarmé's art nothing but a rather rarefied form of crossword compilation? His letter to Gosse is worth quoting further since it provides a close parallel with the earlier reference to a 'sensation assez cabalistique' in his letter to Cazalis:[36]

Je fais de la Musique, et appelle ainsi non celle qu'on peut tirer du rapprochement euphonique des mots, cette première condition va de soi; mais *l'au-delà magiquement produit par certaines dispositions de la parole*; où celle-ci ne reste qu'à l'état de moyen de communication matérielle avec le lecteur comme les touches du piano.[37]

Already in 'Sonnet allégorique de lui-même' we find Mallarmé seeking to create a sense of that 'au-delà' which is *within* language: not an 'absolu' or an 'idéal' located in the outer space of theological or metaphysical longing, but a profound mystery at the heart of the language we unthinkingly spout from day to day. Some of the interconnections within language are explicable in philological terms, but others not. How is it that 'cep' glimmers within 'septentrion'? Or that the only three rhyme-words in masculine /iks/ in French (at the time of the poem's composition) should each connote death and resurrection? Is this merely 'hasard', or is there some hidden necessity of which linguistic data offer the tantalizingly partial remains? The comparative philology of Max Müller and Cox was revealing that myths have their origin not only in the 'drame solaire' but in language itself.[38] No less than Nerval, therefore, Mallarmé was seeking in his poems to create a new mythology: not a mythology based on narrative and the transformation, through imagery (however hermetic), of 'l'expérience de chacun' into 'le trésor de tous', but myths extracted from the 'données' of language itself: what Mallarmé calls 'fiction' (thus restoring the etymological sense of 'poésie'). This is what Mallarmé had 'discovered' by May 1868; and 'Sonnet allégorique de lui-même' is his first fully conscious demonstration of his new-found 'Secret'. From now on the reflexive 'septuor' of the sonnet will be his favoured verse-form; and the relatively small number of his publica-

[36] See above, Part III, Introd. n. 2.
[37] *Corr.*, vi. 26 (my emphasis).
[38] See Marchal, *La Religion de Mallarmé*, 112–18. The thesis was summarized by Max Müller's description of mythologies as a 'disease of language' (Marchal, 115).

tions between 1868 and 1887 (as compared with his production up to 1866) suggests that he decided to keep quiet until he had explored more fully the revolutionary consequences of moving not from world to language but from language to world.

Language-Anguish:
'Ses purs ongles...' (1887)

se réfléchissant de toutes les façons.

Between 'Sonnet allégorique de lui-même' and the publication of Banville's *Petit Traité de poésie française* in 1872, Mallarmé wrote at least two further sonnets: 'De l'orient passé des Temps' (1868: in octosyllables and the only one before 1886 not in alexandrines) and 'Dans le jardin' (1871). Thus, up to 1872, we know of sixteen sonnets by him (although the text of 'Avenir' has not survived). In addition, two of these sixteen sonnets survive also in revised forms completed within the period (the 1866 version of 'Tristesse d'été'; and 'Alternative', the 1869 version of 'De l'orient passé des Temps'). In these eighteen sonnets Mallarmé experiments with twelve different rhyme-schemes, and the number of rhymes in one sonnet ranges from four (on six occasions) to seven (on three occasions).

In his *Petit Traité de poésie française*, however, Banville stipulates that the rhyme-scheme of a Petrarchan sonnet should be abba abba ccd ede, a scheme which Mallarmé had used in none of his previous sonnets. Between 1872 and his death in 1898 Mallarmé wrote twenty Petrarchan sonnets,[1] and revised two of these ('Toujours plus souriant...' becoming 'Victorieu-

---

[1] Beginning with 'La chevelure vol d'une flamme...' (1887) he also wrote sixteen Shake-spearean sonnets (i.e. with the rhyme-scheme abab cdcd efef gg and corresponding stanzaic division). Following the publication of *Poésies* in 1887 Mallarmé's remaining sonnet production is characterized by considerable formal experiment. Of the twenty-four sonnets belonging to this period, only eight, therefore, are Petrarchan. Eleven are in octosyllabic metre (the period up to and including the 1887 *Poésies* contains five), eight in heptasyllabic metre (which he had not previously employed), and only five in alexandrines. Following the omission of punctuation in 'M'introduire dans ton histoire' (1886), eight of the twenty-four continue the experiment, while 'Le bachot privé d'avirons' has but one dash, and 'Éventail (de Madame Mallarmé)' just one parenthesis. The move towards a shorter line (with a corresponding increase in surrounding 'espaces blancs') and the reduction or abandonment of punctuation are part of an evolution which culminates in the 'spatial prosody' of 'Un coup de Dés'. For further discussion of this evolution, see below, Part IV, Ch. 4. It should be noted in passing that Jean Mazaléyrat's 'Note

sement fui...', and 'Méry / Sans trop d'aurore...' becoming 'Dame / Sans trop d'ardeur'). Every one of these follows the Banvillian prescription. Furthermore, when Mallarmé was preparing some of his earlier poems for inclusion in the 1887 volume of *Poésies*, his revisions imply a clear aware-ness of the Banvillian scheme. Thus 'Le Pître châtié' and 'Quelle soie aux baumes du temps' (previously 'Alternative') are brought fully into line with it, while the 'impropriety' of other sonnets remains, even where (as in 'Placet futile' (previously 'Placet')) the poem has been otherwise revised. In the table of contents for the Deman edition Mallarmé acknowledges this 'impropriety' by labelling 'Placet futile', 'Renouveau', 'Angoisse', and 'Le Sonneur' each as a 'sonnet irrégulier'; and in the case of all four one might argue that the prosodic irregularity is appropriate to the sentiments of poetic impotence and futility expressed in these early poems.

'Tristesse d'été', on the other hand, with the scheme abab abab ccd ede, is not given such a label, indicating possibly that Mallarmé considered the restriction to ccd ede in the tercets more 'required' than 'rimes embrassées' in the quatrains. The other unidentified 'irregular' sonnet in both the 1887 and the Deman editions of *Poésies* is, of course, 'Ses purs ongles...'; and here one can see that the first way in which Mallarmé has revised 'Sonnet allégorique de lui-même' is to bring its rhyme-scheme slightly more into line with Banville's prescription. The logic of the cross (as analysed in the preceding chapter) overrides Banville to the extent that Mallarmé retains 'rimes croisées' in the quatrains and the 'crucial' number of four rhymes (i.e. two rhymes in opposite genders). But he has 'sacrificed' the even distribu-tion of seven rhymes in /iks/ and seven in /ɔr/ by adopting, in the tercets, a scheme (ccd cdc) which he had never used before and which parallels Banville's ccd ede by simply repeating the c rhymes instead of having a fifth rhyme. The consequence for 'Ses purs ongles...' is that /ɔr/ rhymes now predominate over those in /iks/, which (as will be seen) is appropriate to the new relationship created between octave and sestet in 'Ses purs ongles...'.

'Sonnet allégorique de lui-même' tells the same story twice, once (in the octave and in essentially traditional symbolic terms of light and dark) from resurrection to death and once (in the sestet and in language describing and foregrounding its own poetic activity) from death to resurrection. In 'Ses purs ongles...', however, 'Et' is replaced by 'Mais' at the *volta* (the begin-ning of l. 9), and the structure of the Petrarchan sonnet is exploited more fully to display not only a mirroring between octave and sestet (as in 'Sonnet allégorique de lui-même') but also an opposition. The notion of light being salvaged at the beginning of the earlier poem has been attenuated to the ambiguous image of anguish sustaining many a dream as if it were a

technique sur les sonnets de Mallarmé' (*Littératures*, 9–10 (1984), 185–90) contains several inaccuracies in its comments on the development of Mallarmé's sonnet practice, and in particular makes no mention of Banville.

torchbearer. The new octave speaks much more (though still not exclusively) of absence and failure, while the new sestet lays less emphasis (though still a little) on quarrel and obscurity, and proclaims (as will be discussed presently) even more triumphantly and ingeniously the rebirth of 'or' from the ashes of the 'northern' octave.

This is part of the change in focus which it is possible to infer from the ways in which Mallarmé has revised 'Sonnet allégorique de lui-même'. Whereas the 1868 poem centred on the 'criminal' abolition of representation and delighted in the display of a poem rising from the ashes via the worm ('ver/vers') of rhyme, the later version elaborates on the poet's experience of language in the absence of a naïve desire to represent external reality. This experience consists in 'L'Angoisse', not only anguish (as if this were just another poem about ennui or 'spleen') but language-anguish: 'langue-oisse'.[2] 'Ses purs ongles...' shows, in its poetic practice, the writer teetering on the edge of a fold: to one side is language as noise, a meaningless babble; to the other, language as constellation, a mysterious and potentially significant domain of revealing interconnections. Thus 'Ses purs ongles...' may be said to display what Julia Kristeva has described as 'l'expérience dialectique du sujet dans le procès de la significance'.[3]

In the first quatrain the 'drame solaire' has been refined by the omission of 'La Nuit' and 'Du Soir';[4] and the punning use of 'Crime' is forgone in favour of the new pun on 'L'Angoisse', which better epitomizes the purport of 'Ses purs ongles...'. The mirror effect of 'La Nuit [...] les onyx' has been replaced by shifting the tautology of 'les onyx / De ses ongles' to l. 1, thus beginning the poem on a statement of self-dedication. It is self-dedicating not only because nails ('ungula') dedicate their onyx ('ungula'), or because 'dédiant' begins with a digital etymology, but above all because the poem now proclaims homophonically at its very outset that 'c'est pur son' ('Ses purs on[gles...]'). The dice-words evoked in 'décor' in the earlier poem are now elevated to l. 1 (hom. 'très hauts dés'), and the transforma-

---

[2] The homophonic presence of 'langue' is enhanced in the sequence 'L'Angoi*sse, ce* [...]' because the repetition of /se/ separates the end of 'Angoisse' off from 'L'Ang(ue)' by relocating it in what may sound like an onomatopoeic expression of anguish. Appropriately, the suggestion of 'inanité sonore' in 'sse-, ce...' is exactly the cause of the poet's anguish about language. The whole effect is mirrored in 'Agoni*se se*lon', symmetrically placed at the beginning of the second line of the sestet, the reflection being reinforced by the evident anagrammatic link between 'angoisse' and 'agonise'. At the same time the placing of '*L'An*goisse' at the beginning of l. 2 creates a mirroring (with '*lam*padophore') which parallels the etymological mirroring of 'ongles' and 'onyx' in l. 1.

[3] *La Révolution du langage poétique*, 80.

[4] At the expense of the 2+4/2+3 alternation of word lengths at the beginning of the lines in the first quatrain of 'Sonnet allégorique'. On the other hand, 'Ses purs ongles...' is so arranged that the quatrains begin with three-letter words and the tercets with four-letter words (thus creating a further chiastic pattern). Moreover the 3+4 of 'Ses purs' at the beginning 'becomes' the 'united' 7 letters of 'septuor' at the end (this symmetry replacing the 6/6 of 'La Nuit' and 'se fixe' in 'Sonnet allégorique de lui-même').

tion of 'les onyx' into 'leur onyx' creates a further homophony ('l'heure onyx') which periphrastically adumbrates 'ce minuit'. The sunset and 'star-rise' of 'Sonnet allégorique de lui-même' have become the symbolic mid-night hour of *Igitur*:[5] of midnight which is the darkness of twelve (the anguish of language in the twelve syllables of the alexandrine, itself thus a maximum throw of two dice), of midnight which is two clock hands raised up, one hand over the other (like the tautology of 'ongles' and 'onyx' in l. 1), in a manual fold;[6] of midnight, the moment of betweenness and temporal suspension, at once yesterday and today and yet also a time out of time.

Language-anguish is thus both a gesture of upward appeal and a ceremo-nial dedication of the dice of language, the fingers of the poet-writer being part of a 'main(t) rêve'. The old 'main(t) rêve' of representational discourse has been burned by the Phoenix (poetry and the poet immolating their traditional functions of lyrical expression), and there is nothing to contain it... 'Mais', says the sestet, which then proceeds to show how poetry may yet rise from the ashes.

Remaining for the moment with the quatrains, we note the paradox that anguish is in fact positive as well as negative. Just as the later 'Agonise' (l. 10) means that the 'or' is still alive, so 'language-anguish' is potentially productive ('soutient, [...] / Maint rêve') because it is, in its very self-consciousness (l. 1), a staging-post (or torchbearer in a relay) between the silence of abolished lyrical expression and the new 'music' ('septuor') of 'la poésie pure'. This positive element, however, is the one residual trace of the salvaged light in ll. 1–2 of 'Sonnet allégorique', an uncertain foreshadowing of the survival recorded in the sestet. Otherwise the emphasis is heavily on lack and absence. The mirror-effect of 'De qui' / 'de ci (néraire)' ('Sonnet allégorique de lui-même', l. 4) has been dispensed with in favour of 'Que ne recueille pas', in which the vocalic monotony of the first three syllables and the sounded 'e' continues the repetitive effects of 'L'Angoisse, ce' and 'rêve *v*espéral' and prepares for the brilliant jingles of 'Aboli bibelot d'inanité sonore'.

'Au salon vide', revising 'en le noir Salon', preserves the link with 'selon' (noted in 'Sonnet allégorique de lui-même') but establishes a more symmet-rical parallel with 'au Nord vacante' in l. 9. 'Vide' confirms the absence of an amphora (as before) but in effect also abolishes the 'crédences' (pre-viously 'consoles'). The 'salon' is empty, and the room has become the space of the sonnet, the place in which 'RIEN / N'AURA EU LIEU / QUE LE LIEU'. As to the replacement of 'consoles', Mallarmé has ceased playing with the false etymology of 'sol' ('insolite' also vanishing, to be replaced by 'aboli') and

---

[5] This symbolic time may owe something also to 'or', since 'heure' derives from 'hora', the root of the adverb 'or' (see Derrida, *La Dissémination*, 295).

[6] Human hands raised in anguish and the twin positions of 'ongles' and 'onyx' might suggest, on the other hand, the letter Y.

abandoned the 'consoling' connotation of the word in favour of one with much richer associations.[7]

'Crédence', being a side-table on which servants 'assayed' the (cr)edibility of their master's food, and also the table on which the wine and host are placed in readiness for the Eucharist, has a lot to say for itself, particularly as domestic 'crédences' in the nineteenth century were often surmounted by a mirror. The implicit reference to poison will link to 'licornes' (l. 11), while the connection with the Eucharist reinforces the parallel between the Passion and the death of representation which was evident in 'Sonnet allégorique de lui-même'. This in turn raises the riddle of the pyx. A. R. Chisholm[8] has suggested that 'ptyx' owes something to the English word 'pyx' (in French 'pyxide'), which is both the small box in which the host is kept after it has been consecrated (and in which it is transported for use in the last rites) and a small container at the Mint in which sample coins are kept for testing (by weight and assay). The centrality of 'or' in the poem makes the latter association compelling, while the connection between 'pyx', the Eucharist, and this poem is not only compelling but may also be confirmed by a further piece of textual evidence. For, in l. 13, 'l'oubli fermé par le cadre' contains the homophonic presence of 'oublie': from the Latin 'oblatus' (offered up, or 'dédié'), meaning the as yet unconsecrated host. Thus 'l'oubli(e) fermé(e) par le cadre' is a periphrastic restatement of 'pyx' if one allows the equivalence between 'cadre' and a box, an equivalence which the self-referential link with the containing box-like (also cubed, or dice-like) shape of a sonnet duly authorizes. Indeed, if one were to see 'ptyx' as representing a pyx which contains the Christian cross in the shape of the letter 't', then 'l'oubli(e) fermé par le cadre' would be a kind of restatement of 'ptyx' itself. Thus in 'Ses purs ongles...', as in some poetic Eucharist, the moment of the elevation (and consecration) of the host (l. 1) is followed by a ceremony in which a crucified reality is resurrected in a process of transubstantiation, the sonnet-box being the container of consecrated language (that threatens all the while to be mere 'oubli') and rhyme the two-handled amphora containing its homophonic blood.

It can only be a matter of surmise whether Mallarmé was aware of the pyx when he wrote 'Sonnet allégorique de lui-même'. In all probability he was not. At any rate the new presence of 'crédence', 'licorne' (for reasons to be discussed), and 'oubli(e)' create a complex nexus absent from the earlier poem. It is in the nature of lacework that one may not be able easily to tell which stitch preceded which, and so it is here. For 'pyx' is also a mariner's compass ('la boussole du Maître') and the source of the constellation *pyxis*

---

[7] Mallarmé 'saves' 'Console' none the less for 'Tout Orgueil fume-t-il du soir', where it performs a central role in a linguistic network. See below, Part iv, Ch. 2.

[8] 'Mallarmé and the Riddle of the Ptyx', *AUMLA*, 40 (1973), 246–8.

nautica in the southern hemisphere which comprises fourteen stars.[9] This connects in turn with the earlier use of constellations (the Phoenix, the Great Bear), and will in turn link later to 'licorne', itself a constellation.

But before leaving the quatrains behind, some brief comments are required about ll. 7–8. Not only does the new use of parenthesis (itself a 'pli') reinforce the idea of the poet's biographical existence being bracketed during the process of poetic creation, it also allows the poem now to consist of one single sentence, with the result that a new tension is created at the *volta* between forward syntactical momentum and logical reverse. More importantly, where the previous version could be interpreted as meaning that the poet had jettisoned the representational function of language in order to achieve artistic renewal in the quest to give expression to his 'dream', now it is the new style of writing which is the referent of these lines. Since 'pleurs' are an expression of 'angoisse', then the Master has 'died' in order to find a means of expressing his 'language-anguish' (indeed he has gone literally to draw on the word 'Styx' for just such a means of expression); and what better expression (or container) of this language-anguish could there be than 'ptyx', which is both lexicographically non-existent ('dont le Néant s'honore') and yet profoundly significant within the constellation of the poem. So intricately woven into the text has it become that 'ptyx' is now 'ce seul objet': the repeated [se] here echoing 'L'Angoisse, ce' and reminding us of the constant threat of 'inanité sonore', and the blackness of homophonic 'jais' (and 'geai') being ever present, but the double sense of 'objet' also announcing the poet's overriding objective, his 'objet d'art'.

This objective is carried out as in the 'Sonnet allégorique de lui-même' but in an even more ingenious way. First, the phonetic survival of 'or' in l. 9 is enhanced by the addition of the word 'proche', which produces the symmetrical pattern of 'ro' twice ('proche', 'croisée', with the accompanying 'c' changing sides) preceding two instances of 'or' ('au Nord', 'un or'), and indeed again (as in 'Sonnet allégorique de lui-même') of 'un or' in these two phrases. Because of the altered rhyme-scheme the sestet now refers not (as in 'Sonnet allégorique de lui-même') to the 'inciting' of an 'ixe' rhyme as a frame, but to the continuance of 'or': 'selon peut-être le déc*or* / Des li*cor*nes', where the surface meaning suggests by its extraordinary nonchalance that these words have been chosen only because they contain 'or', and where the homophonic subtext speaks of 'ce long peut-être' (in 'selon peut-être'), a fine periphrasis for the 'agonie' which is at present sustaining 'or'. Indeed Mallarmé's use of 'peut-être', here as towards the end of 'Un coup de Dés' sounds almost like an affirmation ('peut être'), the nearest he can ever come to asserting presence!

[9] As Deirdre Reynolds also notes ('Mallarmé et la transformation esthétique du langage', 218).

But 'décor' is no more random a word in this context (as was evident in 'Sonnet allégorique de lui-même') than 'licornes'. Even as 'or' is beginning to stud the sestet like the stars of a constellation, so the word 'dé' also proliferates ('décor', 'Des licornes', 'défunte') as a reminder of the cause of the original language-anguish and yet also as a pointer to the shape of the sonnet which permits this constellation of language. The 'Crime' of 'Sonnet allégorique de lui-même' glimmers on in the homophony 'délit' ('Des li-(cornes)'), appropriately here in apposition to 'décor' which refers (as was seen earlier) to the rhyme-scheme itself and to Mallarmé's criminal aesthetic (his 'dé-cor') wherein representation is murdered in the name of rhyme and the 'musical' containment of chance. 'Licornes' itself relates, through 'cornes', both to '(dé)-cor' and back to 'onyx' (horned matter), and is a supreme 'nodal' word in its meaning of 'unicorn'. A fabulous white beast of medieval legend, it breathed fire like a dragon and could be captured only by a virgin, yet its deadly horn, when pulverized or used as a container, served as an antidote to poison.[10] Standing out white against the blackness of the first quatrain, it nevertheless resembles the phoenix in being non-existent, a purveyor of destructive fire, a source of 'resurrection' – and a constellation in the southern hemisphere.

Like the phoenix, therefore, it suggests the twofold nature of language-anguish, its destructiveness and the possibility of creative renewal. By hurling fire at the 'nixe' (by breathing – or in the sparks of its hooves, thus prefiguring the 'scintillations' of the 'septuor') self-referential poetry is endangering beauty (the 'objet' of its quest), yet as a virgin (like Hérodiade) she will remain intact – naked and revealed by the death that is reflexive, non-representational poetry ('défunte nue en le miroir') and/or like a cloud of linguistic obscurity ('nue' being here the equivalent of the 'obscurcisse-ment' in 'Sonnet allégorique de lui-même') which has been dispelled (it is 'défunte') by reflexivity. This reflexivity is no longer exemplified by the repetitions noted in ll. 12–13 of 'Sonnet allégorique de lui-même' but by the echoing from 'ruant du feu' to 'défunte nue', by the more subtle re-appearance of the mirror in a figurative reflection ('l'oubli fermé par le cadre'), and by the reversed presence of 'or' and 'rime' in 'le miroir' itself. At last, thanks to the logic of the cross, 'la rime se mire, or'.

Thus beauty, like a nymph or water-elf, has eluded the rape of representa-tion by being transformed into a constellation: beauty does not fall victim to the language-anguish (the 'licorne') but tames it in the 'musical' arrange-ment of a stellar 'septuor',[11] of a 'site haut' (as we hear in 'sitôt'). This 'site

---

[10] See Citron, 'Sur le sonnet en -yx', 115. In the Larousse entry for 'licorne', the horn of a 'licorne' is also said to have served as a container in which food was 'assayed' (cf. 'pyx', 'crédence'). The unicorn's traditional association with a virgin also links this poem to 'Le vierge, le vivace...'.

[11] As Cohn notes, we hear the numbers mounting up from four to seven in 'cadre', 'scintilla-tions', 'sitôt', 'septuor' (*Towards the Poems of Mallarmé*, 144). This effect has therefore been

haut' refers symmetrically back to 'très haut dédiant' of l. 1^{12} and shows that what the poem displays in its fourteen lines is already evident in its opening line (its 'dédicace'): language-anguish is a form of writing with 'pure sound' which achieves jewelled brilliance from the blackness of non-representation. It is (homophonically) a 'trait haut': the transverse timber of a cross, a heightened connection, a superior mark, a felicitous expression.[13] It is a game of dice as holy as the Mass. And when we learn that 'oublie' means not only the host but also a small biscuit in the shape of a 'cornet', the sacred wafer and the dice-box are joined in the 'oublie' that is Mallarmé's unique way of using language that it may forget the world the better to speak for itself. As he writes in *Igitur* famously: 'Le Cornet est la Corne de licorne – d'unicorne.'[14] And if the 'corne' is the equivalent of Mallarmé's 'vers', then this unicorn is synonymous with the 'univers', the universe of 'un vers uni'.

For within the narrow confines of this Petrarchan sonnet we are confronted with vertiginous contrasts: between cosmic and domestic space, from the inner sanctum of poetic anguish to the outer reaches of beauty and perfection; between eternity and the moment, from the precise instant of midnight to the endless present of an hour that is between yesterday and tomorrow; between the quick and the dead, the real and the mythical, the trivial and the sacred, light and dark, north and south. We are, as it were, at a point of equilibrium, at a crux. And so comprehensive is the referential power of language when it is released from a prior duty to represent that 'Ses purs ongles...' allows one to see the force of Mallarmé's famous remark: 'le monde est fait pour aboutir à un beau livre.'[15]

There were, of course, fourteen stations of the Cross. Each line of 'Sonnet allégorique de lui-même', as of 'Ses purs ongles...', describes the path which leads to Mallarmé's 'death' and his subsequent resurrection, to the Passion of his language-anguish and his survival as 'le Maître' in this sacred writ. In pagan terms we find him as a phoenix, fanning the flames of his

---

achieved by the rearrangement of 'cadre', 'scintillations', and 'septuor' from 'Sonnet allégorique' and the addition of 'sitôt'. Cf. the reference to 'un compte total en formation' at the end of 'Un coup de Dés'.

[12] Via '*au* nord' and '*au* salon' of ll. 9 and 5. This homophonic recurrence of 'eau' in parallel positions in the poem and the thematic connection of water with the Styx and the nixie suggests that the mirror (of l. 12 and of the poem itself) may be regarded as the 'frozen' container of the revivifying waters of the Styx and as a home for beauty. As the Larousse article on 'Styx' indicates, the gods required the water of the Styx (fetched by their messenger Iris: cf. 'Prose (pour des Esseintes)') for ceremonial use when making sacred pronouncements. Moreover the river Styx was thought to circle the world, an O of 'eau'.

[13] Cf. *Crise de vers*: 'Le vers [...] achève cet isolement de la parole: niant, d'un trait souverain, le hasard demeuré aux termes' (*OC*, 368).

[14] *OC*, 441. 'Cornet' is also the term for the small thimble-like container in an inkstand (Littré, 7°); and as a dice-box it is sometimes shaped like an hour-glass. Hence, in part, the darkness at midnight of *Igitur*.

[15] Replying to Jules Huret (*OC*, 872).

own demise with the wings of rhyme and emerging pristine, a new-born 'vers'. Or as a visitor to the Styx—seeking its water for ceremonial use in his sacred pronouncements, and paying Charon his due of a gold coin: not an 'aboli bibelot', but an 'obole d'or', the refined coinage of a poetic language resurrected from inanity. The poet has become Orpheus by visiting the underworld of non-representation: he is 'or fait'. And the 'bibelot' itself, the trinket of meaningless and contingent[16] sound which is the legacy of Babel, has been turned into a 'bible', into 'le Livre'. In this extraordinary sonnet, sound has become a 'septuor': seven pairs of rhymes in -yx and -or, a golden cross to evoke the music of the spheres.

---

[16] Cf. *Dictionnaire étymologique et explicatif de la langue française et spécialement du langage populaire*, ed. Charles Toubin (Paris, 1886): 'A mon avis, le mot [bibelot] a dû signifier d'abord *jouet d'enfants* gagné à des jeux de hasard dans les boutiques foraines, dont la spécialité était de mettre en lot ces menus objets [...] Dans le v[ieux] fr[ançais] *bibelots* signifiait *jeu de dés*' ('Bibelot').

4

Quartet: 'Plusieurs Sonnets'
(?1868–1898)

> Le langage se réfléchissant.
> ('Note sur la linguistique', 1869)

A fold, or 'ptyx', in a single sheet of paper is sufficient to create a minimalist book of four pages, and this 'pliage' is simulated both by the four stanzas of a single sonnet and by the 'quartet' of sonnets entitled 'Plusieurs Sonnets'. The consequences of this enfolding have seldom been explored, and yet it is clear from the fact that Mallarmé experimented with the order in which he presented these sonnets that he was conscious of their combinatory potential.[1] More especially the texts themselves, though grouped under the deceptively simple title of 'Plusieurs Sonnets', plainly suggest that Mallarmé extended the lacework of 'Sonnet allégorique de lui-même' not only by

---

[1] Brief discussion is to be found in A. R. Chisholm, 'Mallarmé: "Quand l'ombre menaça..."', *French Studies*, 15 (1961), 146–9; François Van Laere, 'Le Hasard éliminé: L'Ordonnance d'un livre de vers', *Synthèses*, 258–9 (1967–8), 107–12; L. J. Austin, 'How Ambiguous Is Mallarmé? Reflections on the Captive Swan', in *Literature and Society: Studies in Nineteenth and Twentieth Century French Literature Presented to R. J. North* (Birmingham, 1980), 102–14 (105–6), and 'The Indubitable Wing: Mallarmé's "Quand l'ombre menaça de la fatale loi..."', in *Mélanges Garnet Rees* (Paris, 1980), 1–14 (both reprinted in *Poetic Principles and Practice*). *Pace* Chisholm, the four sonnets are not numbered in the Deman edition. However, in the photolithographed edition of the *Poésies* published in Oct. 1887, the ninth 'cahier' of 'Derniers Sonnets' contains twelve numbered sonnets, of which the first four are 'Le vierge, le vivace...', 'Quand l'ombre menaça...', 'Victorieusement fui...', and 'Ses purs ongles...'. (For the remainder, see OC (BM), 739.) This represents a different order from that given in the 'Table des fascicules' published earlier in January (see OC (BM), 740), in which 'Ses purs ongles...' is not mentioned, while 'La nuit approbatrice allume les onyx' (i.e. 'Sonnet allégorique de lui-même') is billed as an 'inédit' to be published in the preceding fascicule of 'Autres Poèmes'. (Thus although Mallarmé may have begun to revise the 'Sonnet allégorique de lui-même' soon after sending it to Cazalis on 18 July 1868, it would appear that the main revision may have taken place in 1887.) *Album de vers et de prose* (Nov. 1887) contains 'Quatre sonnets', itemized as Sonnet I. 'Le vierge, le vivace...'; Sonnet II. 'Victorieusement fui...'; Sonnet III. 'Mes bouquins refermés...'; Sonnet IV. 'Quand l'ombre menaça...'. *Vers et prose* (1893) contains a grouping of eleven unnumbered sonnets of which

rewriting it as 'Ses purs ongles...' but by linking it with three other sonnets in a quartet which reflects at once the quadriform nature of the cross, the four parts of a symphony, and the passage of the seasons.[2]

The dates of composition of these other three sonnets are uncertain, but they may all have originated much earlier than their respective dates of first publication. The genesis of 'Quand l'ombre menaça...' has frequently been traced back to the late 1860s because of the insistent parallels to be found in Mallarmé's correspondence at this period, and its original title of 'Cette nuit' suggests a possible connection with 'Sonnet allégorique de lui-même' ('La Nuit approbatrice...').[3] The vocabulary of 'Le vierge, le vivace...' links it closely with the 'Ouverture' to 'Hérodiade' (1866); and 'Toujours plus souriant...' (1885) and its revised version 'Victorieusement fui...' (1887) would both seem to owe as much to Mallarmé's early interest in the 'drame solaire' as 'Sonnet allégorique de lui-même' and 'Quand l'ombre menaça...'.[4] If indeed 'Plusieurs Sonnets' all originated at much the same time, then one is tempted to relate not only 'Ses purs ongles...' but also the other three sonnets to the 'étude projetée sur *la Parole*' from which Mallarmé claimed to have extracted 'Sonnet allégorique de lui-même'.[5] What if they are all born of Mallarmé's crisis in the 1860s, and what if each one of them is 'allégorique de lui-même'?

Before considering each of these sonnets in turn, it may be useful to look first at some of the lacework which unites them. Since 'Sonnet allégorique' and later 'Ses purs ongles...' have shown the benefits of beginning with rhyme, we note first that syllabic symmetry and the techniques of resurrected and symbolic rhyme are not unique to these two sonnets. In 'Quand l'ombre menaça...', which (as will be seen) describes the 'death' of the biographically definable poet and his resurrection as an impersonal 'génie',[6]

---

the third, fourth, fifth, and sixth are 'Le vierge, le vivace...', 'Victorieusement fui...', 'Ses purs ongles...', and 'Mes bouquins refermés...': 'Quand l'ombre menaça...' is not included. 'Mes bouquins refermés...', thus twice juxtaposed with these four sonnets, eventually became the final poem in the Deman edition, where its first line is thereby endowed with added significance. In Dr Edmond Bonniot's 1913 edition 'La chevelure vol d'une flamme...' is added to 'Plusieurs Sonnets' for no good reason.

[2] The four sonnets may be thought to correspond to four movements: allegretto, adagio, scherzo, and perhaps largo; while a progression from autumn to winter, spring, and summer is suggested by the failing light of 'Quand l'ombre menaça...', the icy wastes of 'Le vierge, le vivace...', and the rebirth of 'Victorieusement fui...'.

[3] On this question see Austin's useful summary in 'The Indubitable Wing', 10–11. Austin himself suggests 1868–9.

[4] The last two lines of the poem (the only two to survive unchanged in the revision of 'Toujours plus souriant...' into 'Victorieusement fui...') already existed almost verbatim in the rough draft of the 'Ouverture' to 'Hérodiade': see Davies, *Le Drame solaire*, 74.

[5] In this letter to Cazalis (see above, Part III, Ch. 2 n. 2 Mallarmé notes that his 'œuvre' as planned at the time ('si bien préparé et hiérarchisé, représentant comme il peut l'Univers') contains no sonnet, but that does not mean that the 'étude projetée sur *la Parole*' may not have contained other sonnets.

[6] Cf. 'Le Tombeau d'Edgar Poe'.

the 'moi' of l. 4 lives on in 'moins' and 'témoins' (ll. 11 and 13). Similarly, the rhyme on /ter/ in ll. 9–10 is 'refined' (like 'or' in 'Ses purs ongles...') from 'vertèbres' / 'ténèbres' (ll. 2 and 7); while the /i/ rhyme of ll. 12 and 14 prepares for 'Le vierge, le vivace...' with its exclusive /i/ rhymes. At the same time the careful crossing of monosyllabic and disyllabic terminal words in the octave is echoed in the sestet where in each rhyming pair a monosyllable precedes a disyllable.

'Le vierge, le vivace...' is comparable with 'Sonnet allégorique' in that it, too, seems to have been born of rhyme. The one is a 'sonnet en -yx', the other a 'sonnet en i'; phonetically it is as if the latter (second of the four sonnets) is but halfway to the former,[7] an effect reinforced by the plethora of 'v's in 'Le vierge, le vivace...', which adumbrate the mirrored v's, or x's, of 'Ses purs ongles...'. Whereas Gautier had written a 'Symphonie en blanc majeur' (providing a string of images of whiteness) and Mallarmé himself, in Parnassian vein, had celebrated winter in 'Renouveau' as 'L'hiver, saison de l'art serein, l'hiver lucide' (l. 2), here the poet begins with language, not the world, and chooses to write in 'i-vers' about 'l'hiver' and perhaps the 'un-i-vers'. With a uniformity which evokes the whiteness of a scene in which the feathers of a swan and the frozen surface of a lake are indistinguishable by colour, this poem repeats the /i/ sound throughout its fourteen rhyme-words and breaks down the distinction between terminal and internal rhyme by containing a further twenty-four /i/ sounds throughout its length. This blankness or 'inanité' is alleviated, however, by a crossing of rhyme *quality*: the rich b rhymes are embraced by poor a rhymes, while in the sestet the neutrally 'suffisante' rhyme of the couplet (ll. 9–10) serves as a transition between the octave's oscillation of poor and rich and the assured punning richness of the d and e rhymes ('est pris' / 'mépris'; 'assigne' / 'le Cygne'). Thus, in its rhyme alone, 'Le vierge, le vivace...' homophonically evokes the winter of the writer's sense of impotence, his anguished suspension between prospects of poetic success and failure, and his final stoic assertion of value in the midst of sterility.

Moreover, while the b rhymes end in near-anagrams of 'hiver' (itself present in l. 8) and orchestrate the themes of creativity, inspiration, frozen stasis, and deliverance which are the main substance of the poet's concerns, the a rhymes echo (and in one case repeat) the 'nuit' and 'ennui' of 'Quand l'ombre menaça...' (ll. 9, 13) which were themselves closely proximate to the sound of affirmation in 'ébloui' and 'oui' (ll. 8, 9). As it were, the b rhymes of 'Le vierge, le vivace...' continue the negative theme of 'Quand

---

[7] In *Poésies* (1887) and *Album de vers et de prose* (1887), the only collections in which these sonnets are numbered, 'Le vierge, le vivace...' is placed first and thus fittingly bears, almost as a title, the Roman numeral *I*. Its relocation as the second sonnet in the quartet and the inappropriateness of 'Ses purs ongles...' being numerically 'entitled' *IV* (rather than X!) may partly account for the omission of numbering in the Deman edition.

l'ombre menaça...' (just as the c rhymes 'agonie' / 'nie' recall its final rhymes of 'nie' / 'génie') while yet preparing for the positive conclusion of 'Le vierge, le vivace...' and the triumphant 'Oui' of 'Victorieusement fui...' (l. 10, *bis*).

This third sonnet itself begins by picking up the dominant /i/ and /v/ sounds of 'Le vierge, le vivace...' in its first syllable (and in the remainder of the opening line) and then asserting aesthetic victory in the use of 'beau' as its first rhyme-word. The doubts and incapacities of 'Le vierge, le vivace...' have been set aside, and the 'sonnet en i' gives way to a 'sonnet en -beau' in which mortal insufficiency ('tombeau', 'lambeau': ll. 4, 5) finds itself embraced and contained by beauty and illumination ('beau', 'flambeau': ll. 1, 8). In turn the 'beau' rhymes embrace not only the golden locks of the beloved but (as will be seen) the severed head of the 'dead poet': and 'tête' (l. 7), a literal concentration of the 'tempête' of previous turmoil (l. 2), is accompanied by the preparation for a ceremony ('s'apprête' / 'fête': ll. 3, 6), the sacred ceremony of the poetic Eucharist which is performed by 'Ses purs ongles...'.

Moving beyond the rhymes of the four sonnets it is possible to see in the recurrence of certain key words the glimmerings of a narrative development combined with a repeated account of loss and retrieval. The quartet as a whole might be said to describe what happened to the poet's 'Rêve' (I. 2; IV. 3[8]), that is, to his poetic ambition to capture beauty. Likened to a bird, the 'Rêve' folds its wing within the poet (I. 4); once more it seeks to fly, yet its wings are frozen to the ground (II. 11); until, phoenix-like (IV. 3), it is reborn, and the 'aile' (I. 4; II. 2) becomes 'Elle' (IV. 12), beauty herself, a mirrored reflection, a fold, a 'septuor'.

The original folding (I. 4) occurred in response to the menace of the fatal law of darkness (I. 1). As we have seen from 'Sonnet allégorique de lui-même' this darkness and the 'drame solaire' itself may be read as a metaphor for the poet's abandonment of representation: obscurity descends as language ceases to refer univocally to the external world, but illumination ensues as language, thus liberated, reveals its own dazzling mysteries. The world of objects is a vain funeral chamber (I. 5–7; III. 3–4), an unfurnished drawing-room (IV. 5): real stars are but vainglorious garlands, the light of which is as nothing against the darkness (I. 6–7); they are base and worthless fires (I. 13) compared with the 'éclat' (I. 10; II. 12; III. 5) of the 'mystère' (I. 10) that is to be found in language. The false gold of conventional poetic reference, intertwined like the star-garlands in I. 6–7 ('tordent', 'mort', 'orgueil'), is purified of the deadly alloy ('la fatale [a]loi'?) of reality ('l'horreur du sol': II. 11) and gleams anew, 'victorieusement' (III. 1), in splendid

---

[8] For ease of reference the sonnets will be numbered from I to IV, each number being followed by a line number.

isolation (III. 2; IV. 9). The reverse of vain *royalty* (I. 5; III. 4), it is the gold of laughter (III. 3: 'Ô *rire*') and poetic delight (III. 9), the hyperbolic gold of mental effort (a 'trésor [très or] [...] de tête': III. 7): the reverse of '*roses*' (III. 14), that conventional *figure* (III. 14) of beauty, it runs as a rich vein of rhyme throughout 'Ses purs ongles...'. A single word, not a flower, provides the emblem of beauty (IV. 9); and the true stars are the words which, like constellations (II. 1 [Virgo], 14 ('le Cygne'); IV. 3, 5 [pyx], 11, 14), stand in mysterious, signifying relation to one another against the darkness of abolished representation (IV. 6).

The poet's 'Rêve', a mirrored eternity for the teacher of English (cf. 'ever'), is also poetic in its letters in that it displays homophonically a reflected 'ver[s]'. The poet himself, in whom ('Ma*ll*armé') language has indeed 'ployé son aile (hom. [l])',[9] has died and become the skeletons that are his poems, skeletons that are made of an inverse 'rêv(e)', of '*ver*tèbres'. Poetic ambition is a state of pathological (I. 2) language-anguish (IV. 2), a 'désir' which can be both a 'délice' (III. 9) and a 'décor' (IV. 10) – that is, a lordly jousting with chance and a form of 'musical' expression that dices with the contingent.

His 'Rêve' is also a 'songe' (II. 13): a 'son-je' whereby self-expression becomes a surrender to homophony, and a 'son-jeu' in which poetry is a supreme game with the aleatory possibilities of language. 'Son aile [l]' (I. 4), already 'salvaged' from 'T*el* vieux Rêve', at once reappears as the capital of 'Luxe' and duly 'ployé' in 'salle' (I. 5) before recurring *as a sound* thirty-six times in 'Le vierge, le vivace...', in which the first and last lines each contain four 'coups d'[l]'. The wing of poetic inspiration has become a phoneme on the loose, a unit of intoxicated language 'délivré' from the cold grip of reference in which signifier and signified are conventionally glued in sterile union (hom. II. 9: 'Tout son colle'). Instead it has become part of the explosion (which in 'Le Tombeau d'Edgar Poe' Mallarmé calls a 'désastre'), the poet's linguistic Big Bang following which 'son pur éclata signe' (hom. II. 12) – that is, when the linguistic unit, purified of conventional reference, bursts forth with new powers to signify: like a constellation (the Cygnus: II. 14), or like a virgin in the sky (Virgo: II. 1), come to take its sacred place among the twelve syllables of the alexandrine, the poet's own house of the Zodiac.[10]

The 'Rêve' has now become an erotic embrace of language: in III. 8 we hear 'Vers, ce son caressé'. The 'éclat' (I. 10; II. 12; III. 5) of disseminating language has left behind a brilliance that owes nothing to the heat and flame

---

[9] Cf. Mitsou Ronat's comment (in her introduction to her edition of 'Un coup de Dés') that Mallarmé would occasionally sign his name such that the 'deux ls' appear as 'v' (i.e. 'deux ailes').

[10] Like 'Le vierge', 'amphore' (IV. 4) also suggests the Zodiac since it preceded 'Verseau' as the French term for Aquarius (see Larousse, 'amphore').

of real stars (I. 6) or ignited heavenly bodies (I. 14): hence poetry as
'caressed sound' is 'nonchaloir sans flambeau' (III. 8). Dying to the conven-
tional representational function of language, as in some fine suicide (III. 1),
resembles a glorious abandonment of self in the sexual act, as the virgin
resources of language are deflowered. But the foaming blood and the golden
storm (III. 2) give way to postcoital irony and gloom (III. 5–6); sound as a
phallic firebrand ('tison de gloire': III. 2) has become a cool caress. Yet this
presages a renewal of ecstasy in the prospect of the birth that is to follow:
ejaculation and dissemination lead to the 'puéril triomphe' (III. 11) that is
not only the golden hair of the beloved but the head of a new-born babe.
Coming before the Crucifixion of 'Ses purs ongles...', this poetic Nativity
tells of a triumph (III. 11) that echoes the victory of a suicide left behind (III.
1). From the death of representation emerges a fortunate, treasured head[11]
which is cured ('guéri' / 'guerri(er)': III. 13) of its earlier 'mal' (I. 2) and
ready to do battle in the name of the 'Rêve' and to hold imperial sway: and
the poet, addressing himself as well as the head (since indeed they are
synonymous), is lucidly intoxicated (III. 11–12) by the new poetic force of
language thus reborn. The 'coup d'aile ivre' (II. 2) has become the 'coups
saints' (hom. III. 12) of midnight: no longer the midnight of detumescence
(III. 6)[12] but the sacred, elevated midnight of 'Ses purs ongles...'. The head
has become itself endowed (hom. III. 14: 'dont'; cf. 'Don du poème') as a
source of poetic figures, of 'des roses' (III. 14): language deflowered be-
comes a source of chancy word-flowers in which the gold of pure sound is
mirrored, and the 'absent tombeau' (III. 4) of the resurrected poet comes to
situate itself at the end of 'Victorieusement fui...' in the final verb of
(hypothetical) action: 'tomberait'. The phallic firebrand of sound has be-
come a no less phallic 'casque guerrier' from which, as from a cornucopia,
rose petals are strewn as by a 'héros' (cf. 'M'introduire dans ton histoire')
celebrating victory (cf. III. 1) and the dawn of a new age. The poet who
thought to rule the kingdom of reference and could be seduced by the false
light or 'Lux(e)' of objects in the real world has become an imperial child
who will inherit a new empire of signs. In the former realm of his poetic
desire, the 'dé', not the poet, was 'sir(e)': in 'Plusieurs Sonnets' he accepts
that he is no longer lord of all he linguistically surveys and yet finds himself,
by this very awareness, possessed of still greater power. In both senses, then,
he is 'plus sieur'[13] – and 'plus mage' by becoming 'plumage' (II. 11).

[11] 'Coiffe' being the foetal membrane covering the skull, 'être né coiffé' meaning to be born
lucky, and 'coiffe' deriving from Low Latin 'cofea', itself borrowed from German 'kufia',
meaning a 'casque' (Robert). 'Se coiffer' also means to get drunk, and 'se coiffer de' to be
seduced or infatuated by.

[12] 'Marquer midi', meaning to have an erection, is also central to the symbolic chronology of
'L'Après-midi d'un faune' and 'Prose (pour des Esseintes)'.

[13] The voiced s in 'désir' and 'plusieurs' makes the homophonies approximate but the
polysemy no less rich.

And this new age of poetry is heralded homophonically, as we have seen, in the first three syllables of 'Ses purs ongles...', in which poem the 'songe' becomes 'son or', and the 'Rêve' of 'Quand l'ombre menaça...' becomes the poet's 'main(t) rêve'. Poetic aspiration to transcend reality in a traditional quest for illumination has been replaced by an act of writing in which mystery and 'éclat' are to be found within language itself when the signifier is allowed free play and crosses with other signifiers to create new constellations of significance, new signs in an expanding Zodiac. The aching 'vertèbres' of the Romantic striver have been replaced by the 'lampe à dos fort' (hom. IV. 2): the 'mal' (I. 2) of 'Mal-larmé' has been superseded by the 'deux ls [ailes]' of the reflexive phoenix. The 'larme' of lyric effusion has given way to the 'pleurs' (IV. 7) which, as we saw, are the words which give voice to language-anguish, the words of the sonnets themselves: of 'Plusieurs Sonnets'.

This is just some of the lacework which unites 'Plusieurs sonnets' and it will be necessary to return to them later as a group. But it may now be helpful to consider each of the first three sonnets in isolation in order to elaborate on some of the points already made and to show how each poem may be read as being allegorical of itself.

(a) *Reversal: 'Quand l'ombre menaça...'*

> on n'écrit pas, lumineusement, sur champ obscur, l'alphabet des astres, seul, ainsi s'indique, ébauché ou interrompu; l'homme poursuit noir sur blanc.
>
> ('L'Action restreinte')

For Malcolm Bowie 'Quand l'ombre menaça...' is essentially 'an elaborate account of desire as desirous, of human creativity, in its quintessential form, as a radiance that radiates'. In his view the poem has 'nothing to say about poesis or about the resistant medium upon which the artist's craft is exercised', though he recognizes in passing 'the ostensive definition that is no doubt hidden here somewhere – "being a genius means being able to write like *this*"'.[14] When 'Quand l'ombre menaça...' is read within the context of 'Plusieurs Sonnets', such a view seems less tenable; and even if one takes the sonnet in isolation, it is possible to allow the word 'génie' to prompt a more elaborate account of the poem's reflexivity. Certainly desire is a central theme of the poem, as it is (if less explicitly) of 'Le vierge, le vivace...' and 'Victorieusement fui...'. But it is in essence a poetic desire:

---

[14] 'Genius at Nightfall: Mallarmé's "Quand l'ombre menaça de la fatale loi..."', in Christopher Prendergast (ed.), *Nineteenth-Century French Poetry: Introductions to Close Reading* (Cambridge, 1990), 225–42 (236).

the words 'Rêve' and 'génie' are too laden with Romantic connotations of the 'recherche de l'absolu' for one not to see the narrative of 'Quand l'ombre menaça...' in terms of the poet's quest.[15]

Thus, while Bowie sees the poem as being about death, it could be said to be more particularly concerned with the death of a traditional style of lyric poetry, with the 'death' of representation. For Georges Poulet the poem describes a radical mental abolition of the real world so that the poet's 'rêve' of what he knows to be false (a 'fiction') is asserted, like Cartesian doubt, as the basis of a new certainty ('indubitablement'): the material world is denied that the world of thought may exist.[16] Poulet's reading focuses on the 'cogito', whereas at the heart of Mallarmé's literary enterprise is always language. 'Quand l'ombre menaça...' tells of a reversal that stands the universe on its head, as the poet moves no longer from world to language, but from language to world. The poet of old is desirous of expressing 'Tel vieux Rêve' yet constantly feels in his bones the malaise that comes from the anguished awareness of the inadequacy of language as a medium of expressing unique and complex thought and feeling. The 'fatale loi' is not only the diurnal setting of the sun and, by extension, the fact of human mortality, but also the darkness of non-expression deriving from the fateful law which dictates, as Baudelaire put it, that 'l'action n'est pas la soeur du rêve'.[17] For the writer of old, as Stendhal phrases it at the end of Vie de Henry Brulard, 'le sujet surpasse le disant'. Even for such a poet as Rimbaud, the world of experience and material objects precedes the act of expression: 'trouver une langue' comes after 'le dérèglement de tous les sens'.

For such a poet (here relegated to history by the past historic), poetic aspiration soared only to find itself hitting a ceiling of deadly limitation (l. 3); whereas in Mallarmé the wing of poetic ambition has folded upon itself. It will begin with itself, with its own linguistic substance, in the present implied by the 'passé composé'. Now the poet, alone and dazzled by his new credo (l. 8), can mock the starry night to which an earlier poet's soul might have reached out; its light ('lux') is a luxury, a wanton irrelevance like the beguiling garlands of stars, in the dark, funereal chamber of a world to which the poet has temporarily died. And the poet, not only dazzled but dazzling like a diamond ('solitaire'), radiates his new certainty: gone from the world, he finds the darkness replaced by a world which shines like a star, a world of new poetic genius (and ingenuity) which has lighted itself on the sun of creative expression which, for the poet of old, had died. Seen thus

[15] For other interpretations see the bibliographies given in Austin, 'The Indubitable Wing', 9–10, and Marchal, Lecture de Mallarmé, 145. Austin's sober and reliable reading takes much of the previous secondary literature into account, while Marchal interprets the poem in line with the broader thesis which he develops in La Religion de Mallarmé.

[16] La Distance intérieure (Paris, 1952), 336–9.

[17] On Mallarmé's response to Baudelaire's phrase, see above, Part I, Ch. 4 n. 10.

from the distance of linguistic priority, the world of objects and human experience takes on a new air of mystery; and seen *sub specie aeternatis* (in a way which the atemporal world of language permits), the ugly past of the real world is now less able to obscure this radiant mystery which it is the poet's dream to express (l. 11). Real space may expand to infinity or shrink to nought (according to the perception of the poet of old), but it remains the same: a dull, uniform setting for worthless stars which must now look on to see the celebration of genius and the future creation of new stars and new constellations in the universe of language. Where, for the poet of old, language served to express the world, now 'le mystère de la Terre' has become a near-anagrammatic metaphor for 'le mystère dans les lettres'.

And, no less than in 'Ses purs ongles...', we see poetic language at its reflexive work. The 'Rêve' has become the folded wing of the sonnet itself, in which the darkness and negativity of the octave is set against the bright affirmations of the sestet. The scenario of the quatrains is repeated in the tercets but transposed from the key of failure into the key of success. Thus the mortal inability of the old 'Rêve' to transcend the 'plafonds funèbres' becomes the certain knowledge of what goes on 'au lointain de cette nuit'; its resigned folding-in-upon-itself becomes an emission of mystery and light; and the dark ceilings which inhibited the old dream have become the less opaque, if still not yet beautiful ('hideux'), stuff of human experience through the ages (as present in 'fossilized' form within language). In the quatrains the old poet's world is an ebony room (or theatre) in which stars expend their remaining energy in the display of their writhing death throes for the delectation of a man of worldly power; and yet the eyes of a humble solitary can see that it is the surrounding darkness which causes this false representation of stars as celebrated objects.[18] In the tercets the positions are reversed: the new poet's realm is a universe, not puffed up with self-importance and a semblance of rich excess ('Luxe') but uniform and true to itself (l. 12), which rolls the (now passive) stars along. These stars, no longer viewed mythically (or Romantically) in images of heroism and priceless strings of jewels ('guirlandes'), are seen for what they really are, worthless balls of fire; and they now humbly and passively look on at the birth of a new star, the poet-genius, who will later become (in 'Ses purs ongles...') but one star in a constellation of words (and the weaver of some celebrated garlands of verse). The new, unique, original poet, once dazzled by his faith in reflexive art, now becomes a festive sun ready to radiate an 'insolite mystère': the 'sol(eil)' which lay hidden in 'solitaire' and 'insolite' shines forth as 'astre' and prepares, in its etymological sense of 'gold coin', for the 'or' of 'Ses purs ongles...'.

---

[18] As Austin points out, 'mentir' as a transitive verb is defined in Littré as 'figurer faussement, représenter faussement' ('The Indubitable Wing', 13 n. 19). Cf. also Rosemary Lloyd, *Mallarmé: 'Poésies'* (London, 1984), 46.

Thanks to language, literally, the poet as a 'solitaire' is both sun and (homophonically) 'terre'; he is 'l'univers'. In his midst (and in 'ébloui') is the 'l' which was the former poet's 'aile'; and there is a bed ('so*lit*aire') upon which desire may later (in 'Victorieusement fui...') achieve satisfaction and creativity before placing a new-born offspring upon the cushions of the tercets. And the final 'taire' may alert us to the homophonic potential of l. 9: the object of this poem is to silence 'cette nuit' (and 'cet ennui': l. 13). 'La Terre' ('la taire!') comes to sound like an imperative, as does the following 'Jette', so that the 'éclat' of l. 10 is not only a great light but the great sound-burst of affirmation which is this poem. Indeed the last line, with its much debated syntactic ambiguity,[19] may be even more categoric if 'heard' as well as 'read': 'Que c'est un astre, en fait, allumé, le génie.' The certainty of the sestet (the sonnet's own 'aile indubitable') is thus highlighted in its first and last lines: 'Oui, je sais [...] Que c'est [...] le génie.'

This sonnet enjoins us to listen as well as to see: it is, as its *volta* suggests, a poem to be 'ouï'.[20] Moreover, if we listen again to l. 9, we may hear: 'Ouï, je sais qu'au loin, tain de cette nuit, la Terre.' The world of objects has become the silvering on a mirror which allows the blackness of obscurity (or the non-representational use of language) to become reflexive and thus resplendent with light: the naïve transparency of the 'glacier' has become a 'glace'.[21] Anticipating the 'miroir' of 'Ses purs ongles...', this 'tain' and this 'glace' suggest the linguistic mirrorings which are no less a part of 'Quand l'ombre menaça...' than they are of 'Sonnet allégorique de lui-même' or 'Ses purs ongles...'. In l. 12 the echoing of '-ace à soi' and 's'accroisse ou se nie' prepares for 'L'Angoisse ce...' (IV. 2) and 'Agonise se(lon)' (IV. 10); and 's'accroisse' contains the all-important homophony of 'sa croix'. The process of expansion and contraction noted here is also evident in the language of the poem, where, as previously noted, mono-syllabic and disyllabic words alternate in the rhymes. Moreover certain words recur in their own form in the quatrains and then, in the tercets, in the 'expanded' context of other words. Thus not only does 'moi' recur in 'moins' and 'témoins', but 'loi' reappears in 'lointain', 'roi' in 's'accroisse'. Conversely, '*ébè*ne *où*, p*our* séd*ui*re' contracts to 'ébloui' and then to 'oui', as if certainty had been linguistically refined from gloom (which is then recalled in 'nuit' and 'ennui'). Just as 'Rêve' recurs, reversed, in the longer

[19] Bowie makes the excellent point that this ambiguity, like that in l. 10 (which it mirrors), scarcely affects the sense ('Genius at Nightfall', 230).

[20] 'Plusieurs Sonnets' may be said to command attention to homophony on several occasions. In 'Victorieusement fui...' (l. 11) 'en t'en coiffant' becomes 'entends "quoi"' (the 'Quoi' in l. 5); while in 'Ses purs ongles...' the use of 'par le' ('parle') in ll. 3 and 13 perhaps alerts us to the homophonies, respectively, of 'Phénix' ('fée', 'nixe') and both 'oubli' ('oublie') and 'cadre' (almost 'quatre', preceding the homophonic sequence of 'cinq', 'six', 'sept' in l. 14).

[21] Cf. the roles of 'tain' and 'glacier' in the 'Ouverture' to 'Hérodiade': see above, Part II, Ch. 4 (i).

'vertèbres' (l. 2), so 'soi' recurs, reversed, in 's'accroisse'. Add to these examples the movement from the dark, broad /a/s of l. 1 to the bright /i/s of the tercets, and the various echoes (e.g. 'cette', 'Jette': ll. 9–10) and parallels (e.g. 'en moi', 'ennui': ll. 4, 13; 'qui l'obscurcissent', 'qu'il s'accroisse': ll. 11–12) which shape the poem, and what we have here is the demonstration of language as an 'espace littéraire' in which word-stars expand and contract in ever renewed patterns suggestive of a mystery that is hidden amidst the music of the spheres—hidden, as it might be, 'aux cieux du solitaire' (cf. l. 8).

The lesson of 'Quand l'ombre menaça...' is thus that in the previous experience of the poet, and in the past history of poetry, language had stood in relation to experience as a planet to the sun, rotating in its rays but ever distanced across the blackness of space by the 'fatale loi' of gravity and the deadly, automatic attraction of sign to referent within conventional discourse (whereby, for example, 'fleur' is immediately and only what one finds in a bouquet); whereas language now, turning on its own axis and moving across the vast expanse of 'l'espace littéraire', has become the luminous centre of a new system, holding other worlds within its gravitational pull and illuminating them as it projects its inner light upon them. The Copernican revolution has been reversed in a neo-Ptolemaic relocation of the word ('le Verbe' and 'le Vers') at the centre of the poetic 'univers'. The light has gone from the old universe, but poetic genius rekindles itself in language, like a torchbearer lighting his brand from the flame of another and racing towards the future, 'lampadophore', in his hand a 'rêve'.

(b) *Exile: 'Le vierge, le vivace...'*

> le vers, système agencé comme spirituel zodiaque.
> ('*La Littérature*. Doctrine', 1893)

And so, having reversed the priority of world and language, poetic genius goes into exile. 'Il', the poet, is no longer. An 'ex-il', he has become the bird, the 'vieux Rêve' which 'a ployé son aile indubitable en moi', an impersonal 'soi' folded upon the water in 'l'*ois-eau*' (l. 10), an 'il' located in '*aile*' and dispersed throughout the poem with insistence: 'Va-t-*il*', 'stér*il*e', 'resplend*i* l'ennui', 'qu*i* le nie', '*Il* s'immob*i*lise', 'parm*i* l'ex*il*', 'inut*il*e'.[22] He is no longer a person nor a real 'cygne d'*eau*-trefois' (hom. l. 5), but a function of language, part of the sign, even the 'cygne/signe' itself. Is his new poetic 'univers' ultimately and homophonically a form of 'hiver': a cold sterile wasteland, in which the poet-sign discovers that he cannot even take off, let alone die against the funereal ceiling of non-transcendence? Where the

---

[22] See Daniel Bougnoux, 'L'Éclat du signe', *Littérature*, 14 (1974), 83–93 (87).

darkness of frustrated desire had become the illumination of black garlands of words, now the 'impuissance' returns to haunt him as the *uni*form whiteness of a page, the monotony of 'un i-vers' in which 'l'espace littéraire' seems to be nothing but insignificant, unsignifying sound, an endless repetition of the bright /i/ which dominated the sestet of 'Quand l'ombre menaça...'.

For repetition of sound is the hallmark of 'Le vierge, le vivace...'. Exiled from the world in his newly chosen non-representational use of language, the poet is aware of a new beginning (l. 1) and yet conscious that he finds himself in a frozen landscape of blank sound ('cette blanche agonie'; cf. 'inanité sonore'): the situation promises new flights of the wing, yet the sign is beset by a sense of abandonment and ghostliness, of having forsworn 'expression' and yet being still grounded. 'Le vierge, le vivace...' tells of a 'crise de vers': of a crisis of confidence, wherein the non-representational function of language is perceived first as sterility and then as a superior process of signifying, a process exhibited by the poem itself.

In the conventional lyrical terms which have already been suggested by 'Quand l'ombre menaça...', the poet's sense of impotence is figured as a wing which cannot rise above the darkness of a world from which the sun has departed. In the purified language of 'Le vierge, le vivace...' this situation has become that of an 'aile' (both the letter l and the letter v, the one for its homophonic, the other for its visual aspect) beset by a wintry 'i-vers'. Thus not only does the sound /i/ recur on thirty-eight occasions (accounting for almost a quarter of the poem's vowel sounds) including in every rhyme,[23] but the letter v occurs on fifteen occasions: numbering eight in the first quatrain and six in the second (thus mirroring the division of a Petrarchan sonnet), the fourteen v's in the octave evoke the visual image of a bird striving to escape the icy lake, while the final v in l. 14 both recalls the earlier struggle and suggests the bird's final folding of its wings in a willing acceptance of exile (of the reflexivity of non-representational language). The sound /l/ figures on thirty-six occasions (distributed 12, 10, 6, 8 across the stanzas): the four in the first line being mirrored by the four in the last line, where the 'coup d'aile ivre' (l. 2) of the struggling bird finally becomes a purely phonetic activity. V and l combine, not only in 'Va-t-il' but, as is only fitting, in 'vol' (a word subsequently echoed by the two key words 'col' and 'sol': 'col' being the part of the 'cygne' which can move, and the 'sol' being that which prevents 'vol').

In this blank landscape of sound, other vowels echo in tantalizing symmetries across the sonnet. Thus 'ou' comes in 'nous' and 'coup' (l. 2), 'oublié' and 'sous' (l. 3; leading to 'souvient' in l. 5), and 'Tout' and

---

[23] Did the teacher of English think of English 'rime' (hoar-frost) as well as 'hiver' when he composed this sonnet 'en -i vers'?

'secouera' (l. 9); so that the 'coup' of the wing is repeated as implicit 'cou' in 'col' and in 'secouera' (hom. 'ce cou ras'). 'Ant/ent' links 'sans' and 'chanté' (ll. 6, 7) with 'hante' (l. 3); while the double /an/ sound in 'transparent' (l. 4) is echoed in 'Quand', 'resplendi', and 'ennui' (l. 8). /ace/ establishes a parallel between 'vivace' and 'glacier' (ll. 1, 4), which is briefly echoed in 'secouera *cette*' (l. 9) and then repeated in 'espace' and 'assigne' (ll. 10, 12). Present here also are five of the twenty-six unvoiced /s/ sounds in the poem (14 in the octave, 12 in the sestet), and four of the thirty-four s's, that letter which resembles the curved neck of a swan and of which Mallarmé later wrote in a fragment of 1895:

S, dis-je, est la lettre analytique; dissolvante et disséminante, par excellence [...] j'y trouve l'occasion d'affirmer l'existence, en dehors de la valeur verbale autant que celle purement hiéroglyphique, de la parole ou du grimoire, d'une secrète direction confusément indiquée par l'orthographie et qui concourt mystérieusement au *signe* pur général qui doit marquer le vers.[24]

Against this background of haunting sounds which hover between banal repetition and significant combination, the ghost of a poetic argument is to be discerned. In the first stanza, the poet of today wonders whether his new approach to poetry will free the many poetic 'flights' contained and forgotten about within language, having been hitherto frozen there (as by a 'fatale loi') by the rigid conventionality of reference. The exclamation mark at the end of l. 4, replacing the question mark which the interrogative (and the shape of a swan's neck) might have required, at once conveys the excitement of anticipation and some bitter irony ('as if it could do this!') as the poet recognizes his lapse back into old ways of looking at the expressivity of language. As the resemblance of an exclamation mark to a plume suggests, the winged flight of poetry is an act of writing, an 'action restreinte': 'Ton acte toujours s'applique à du papier.'[25]

In the second quatrain, the poet-sign 'd'autrefois'—of other days, and of another 'foi', the Romantic faith in lyrical expression which preceded the new 'dazzling' faith proclaimed in 'Quand l'ombre menaça...'—remembers the truth of his situation. He is a rare bird,[26] etymologically magnificent in doing great things, who has two stories to tell. First, a negative tale: that, as an old-style poet, he surrenders ('se délivre':[27] cf. 'ployé son aile') without hope (of transcending language) since he has not been able to sing of the region of salvation (as it were, beyond the 'plafonds funèbres' of 'Quand l'ombre menaça...') to which swan-poets can migrate when the

---

[24] OC, 855 (the second emphasis is mine).
[25] 'L'Action restreinte', OC, 369.
[26] A 'magnifique' is a bird of paradise. One of the definitions given for 'Phénix' by Larousse is: 'syn. de paradisier ou oiseau de paradis.'
[27] Accepting Chadwick's suggestion of an Anglicism: see *Colloque Mallarmé (Glasgow, novembre 1973) en l'honneur de Austin Gill* (Paris, 1975), 79–80.

triumphant winter of 'ennui' (spleen, impotence, a loss of faith) descends. Second, a positive tale: that without hope (of transcendence or personal salvation) he gains release (from impotence) precisely because he did not sing of some other region beyond the resplendent winter landscape in which he finds himself. The negativity of 'ennui' (the inability to move successfully from world to language in an act of expression) is transformed, like the nocturnal world of 'Quand l'ombre menaça...', into a source of light and splendour.

The tercets repeat this twice-told tale. In the first, the poet of old will try as he may to shake off the cold death of non-transcendence which the universe inflicts upon him; but the law of spiritual gravity is such that, however much he may seek to defy it, he will never achieve the 'élévation' for which he yearns (and which only the sacred poetic mass of 'Ses purs ongles...' will 'secure' in a symbolic act of manual dedication). He will never escape the horror that comes from experiencing the iron grip of the world of reference upon the feathers of his aspiration and the quills of his art. Instead, in the second tercet, the new poet, a ghost of his former self, makes a virtue of this 'fatale loi': unable to move from world to language, he settles (in the eternal present of the poem's fixed and finished state) into an exile from representation, disdaining the world of objects and achieving 'élévation' by becoming a constellation (Cygnus) of words in the heavens of 'l'espace littéraire'.

His swan-song is different from the others (as it might be, Baudelaire's 'Le Cygne'); it is 'Tout son', as the *volta* proclaims in a reversal no less striking than the 'Oui' of 'Quand l'ombre menaça...' and the 'Mais' of 'Ses purs ongles...'. The wintery landscape of non-representational language is a 'blanche agonie', a place of language-anguish: the whiteness of a blank page upon which the sign struggles to 'vivre' (l. 7) in the aftermath of the poet's willing death (his 'suicide beau') as a place of autobiographical take-off for poetic expression, and the whiteness of the white noise that language threatens inanely to be if the sign is set free from its referent. Sounds seem to attach themselves to each other of their own accord (hom. 'Tout son colle'); the intoxication of the 'coup d'aile' has bred only flatness (hom. 'ce coup ras'). Yet for all that the new poet may have to strive to deny the deadly undifferentiatedness of 'l'espace littéraire' in its pure state by giving it poetic shape, he will at least not have to contend with the imprisonment of reference, in which even 'le plus mage' can be caught.

Because of his own new approach to language, 'horreur' and 'sol' may be suggestive of 'or' and 'soleil', the symbols of his poetic quest. Cycnus, we may learn or remember, was a friend of Phaeton, who mourned the latter's death so bitterly that Zeus transformed him into a swan with a beautiful voice, the swan which is at the origin of the legend that swans sing on the point of death. And Phaeton, of course, the son of Helios, drove his father's chariot across the sky: frightened at first to find himself among the animals of the Zodiac, he dropped so low that he endangered the Earth with his fire, and then rose so high that the stars complained to Zeus, who struck him down with a thunderbolt.[28] Is it not as if, in this poem, language itself were Phaeton, first proceeding through the houses of the Zodiac ('Le vierge'), then descending to the level of the Earth ('sol') before rising once more to the level of the stars ('le Cygne')? And who is the friend but Cycnus, the poet-sign, a friend of language, mourning the death of representation following its drunken, magnificent drive across the heavens of lyric poetry and now transformed into a bright constellation of words upon the page, motionless and disdainful in its new-found significance.[29]

In reading the poem in this way it is evident how many words and phrases within the poem can be interpreted in both a positive and a negative manner. The problem lies not so much in what the symbols 'stand for' as in the value to be attributed to them. Is it 'good' that 'un coup d'aile' should be 'ivre' (inspired or simply misguided?); that it should 'déchirer' (open up or destroy?); that the 'glacier' should be frozen (sterile or full of potential movement?) and 'transparent' (pure, or unreflexive and thus lacking in mystery?); that the 'cygne d'autrefois' should be 'sans espoir' (doomed or open-eyed?). We have here, therefore, a fine example of 'symbolism' in action, with Mallarmé carrying out his intention to 'peindre, non la chose, mais l'effet qu'elle produit'. 'Language-anguish', the sense that words may be no more than shimmering, ever-shifting indicators of some obscure but never fully graspable mystery, is conveyed rather than explicitly described. Indeed the sonnet itself is like some transparent glacier in which, clearly visible if dimly understood, are the 'vols qui n'ont pas fui': the meanings that did not take off, yet at the same time the meanings that have not fled. They are incomplete but not absent.

Thus the famous opening line springs a syntactic trap for the reader, as what might appear at first to be two nouns turn out to be adjectives, with the 'coup d'aile (1)' of 'bel' providing precisely the morphological 'coup' that breaks the ice of predictable syntax and opens the way to multiple meanings. Do 'vierge', 'vivace', and 'bel' all qualify 'aujourd'hui' (itself an adverb unexpectedly become a noun[30]), or is 'Le vierge' in proleptic apposition to 'Ce lac dur oublié'? Is the latter in apposition to 'Le vierge [...] aujourd'hui'? 'Nous' appears first to be a direct, then an indirect, object. Is the 'cygne' a 'cygne d'autrefois' or does he remember 'autrefois'? Or does he

---

[28] See Larousse, 'Phaéton'.

[29] Under 'cygne', Larousse records the version of the myth which has Orpheus being transformed into the constellation of 'le Cygne' (next to the constellation of 'la Lyre').

[30] *Pace* Benoît de Cornulier's unconvincing thesis that 'aujourd'hui' is an adverb in this context: see 'Remarques sur le sonnet "Le vierge, le vivace et le bel aujourd'hui" de Stéphane Mallarmé', *Studi francesi*, 22 (1978), 59–75.

remember that he is the one? That he is the one who is magnificent? Does the temporal clause (l. 8) qualify 'chanté' or 'vivre'? In each case it is as if the sense of the poem is about to take off but then aborts its take-off and tries once more as new words add themselves and change the direction of the anticipated flight.

This syntactic ambiguity, frequently commented upon, offers an excellent example of what Derrida calls 'différance', with the linguistic differences upon which the process of signifying depends being blurred in a phonetic landscape of insistent, repetitive sound, while meaning itself is endlessly deferred by a syntax which constantly adjusts itself and causes a rereading of what has gone before. Such 'différance' is figured not only in the syntax of the poem but also in its temporal perspective, as the fixed meanings of former poetry give way to the new today of Mallarmé's sign,[31] which will continue in an open-ended future to shake the white anguish of language. The first quatrain asks whether this new poem will break through the hard surface of language's forgotten reservoir of potential to the frozen block of meanings that have yet to be released; and the tercet answers that the new swan-sign will repeatedly (hom. 'Tout son *col*, ce *cou*') strive to disturb the white uniformity of blank sound and white paper in an 'agon', or 'son-jeu'. 'Fantôme casse lieu', we hear in l. 12: the ghostly swan-sign has broken through: with the result that 'son pur éclata signe'. Sound, purified of conventional referents ('horreur du sol'), bursts forth like 'l'insolite mystère' of 'Quand l'ombre menaça...' and has become significant like a constellation.

Thus 'Le vierge, le vivace...' acknowledges and displays the poet's ambivalence about his new 'foi'. On the one hand, he welcomes non-representational language as virginal: as a new opportunity for the 'aile' to take wing on pure sound in a language undefiled by reference and full of disseminating potential should its 'lac dur' be 'déchiré' by his own 'plume'. At the same time, such language is 'vivace': like a perennial plant it can survive winter and be *ver*nally resurrected in the new blossom of the spring, the poetic 'ver(o) novo' that is latent in the 'hi*ver*' of a wintry exile from the world of objects. This prospect of resurrection (itself evoked in the repeated homophone of 'vie' at the beginning of 'vierge' and 'vivace') suggests a world outside time (the 'siècles hideux' of 'Quand l'ombre menaça...'), an eternal world of beauty ('le bel aujourd'hui') in which time is the tempo of rhythm ('vivace') and musical arrangement (the 'septuor' of 'Ses purs ongles...').

On the other hand, the poet fears non-representational language: the virgin, for all her potential fertility, can only remain a virgin at the cost of sterility, just as 'perennial' may be a synonym for monotonous and repeti-

---

[31] Cf. 'Étalages': 'Suggestion et même leçon de quelque beauté: qu'aujourd'hui n'est seulement le remplaçant d'hier, présageant demain, mais sort du temps, comme général, avec une intégrité lavée ou neuve' (*OC*, 376).

tive. But this is the 'blanche agonie' with which he must contend, and which indeed is his only 'modus vivendi'. As the final tercet homophonically reveals, the new poet-sign 'casse lieu' and 'son pur éclata signe': and the word 'son' literally 's'immobilise' in '*songe*', just as the poet-sign (the reversed 'soi' folded upon the 'eau' in 'oiseau') now settles upon the water ('au songe / eau songe') of the 'son-jeu' which is this poem. And as we hear also, the sound settles 'si mot', if it becomes a word, a 'six-mot', one of the 'dice-words' tumbling in the twelve-syllable alexandrines which make up 'ce dé-livre' (hom. l. 6) that is the poet's new 'Rêve'. A 'dé-livre', or a 'fantôme': a volume (among the 'vols qui n'ont pas fui') which takes flight upon the wing (or fan/ 'éventail') of a poet-sign who is the phantom of his own 'opus', his 'Grand'Œuvre'. Thus does 'Le vierge, le vivace...' tell of 'Un coup d'aile ivre' that is 'un coup d'aujourd'hui': 'un coup "today"', 'un coup de dés'—which looks forward to the morrow and to 'Ses purs ongles...' with its masterly 'coup de "Main[t,] rêve"'.

(c) Caress: 'Victorieusement fui...'

Verse son caressé [...]

But first comes that other 'coup de main', the caress. This poem is generally considered one of the more accomplished accounts of the 'drame solaire' in Mallarmé's work. According to the established view, the golden rays of the setting sun are salvaged from the tempest of sunset in the blond locks of the beloved as she lays them, like the gleaming helmet of a warrior, upon the cushions of a bed at midnight. However, if we continue to see the 'drame solaire' as a metaphor for the poet's 'suicide beau' following which language, not the poet, speaks for itself, then it is possible to see reflexive possibilities in this sonnet.

In 'Le vierge, le vivace...' this 'suicide' was reflected as a form of disdainful exile from the world of objects, a stoic and brilliantly demonstrated acceptance of language as non-representational and potentially 'inane'. Where 'Quand l'ombre menaça...', originally entitled 'Cette nuit', illuminated the darkness of poetic anguish by asserting the diamantine brilliance of the word-star, 'Le vierge, le vivace...' presented the new day of the poet-sign as a metaphorical 'nuit blanche' in which language-anguish manifests itself in the 'unanime' whiteness of non-reference which bursts forth as a constellation, a new sign of the Zodiac.

In 'Victorieusement fui...' the anguish and intimations of defeat caused by this 'suicide' have been left behind: the impotence implicit in 'Le transparent glacier des vols qui n'ont pas fui' has become the glorious flight into the future of a new poetic enterprise. Instead of frozen stasis, we have a victorious linguistic explosion (in l. 2) as noun after noun accumulates in an affirmation of new naming in the wake of the suspension of conventional reference. As suggested earlier, sound has become a 'tison', the firebrand of the 'lampadophore', a smouldering remnant of the linguistic conflagration (the 'suicide beau') and ready to be stirred into new life. The 'or' of 'Victorieusement', together with the latter's meaning, 'sparks off' the associations of 'gloire' (in which the 'fatale *loi*' of previous linguistic inadequacy is mixed with the 'or' of refined, poetic sound in a new 'aloi'); while the English 'gore'[32] which victory may connote, and which 'gloire' literally contains, prompts 'sang'. The alchemical process hinted at here, whereby 'or' is refined from 'Victorieusement' and 'gloire', in turn suggests 'écume',[33] which leads to a renaming of the 'suicide beau' and the implicit conflagration of language as a 'tempête'. Now delighting in the free play of 'or', the poem proceeds with 'Ô *r*ire si là-bas', in which the 'si' is suggestive of an affirmation which will brook no gainsaying. Where later in 'Ses purs ongles...' 'un or' provokes 'peut-être le décor / Des licornes' (IV. 10–11), here 'or' gives rise to '*pour*pre' and '*ro*yal', and to the consequent 'idée' of golden sound becoming a regal decoration of the very fact that the poet has not truly died (just as the negative aspects of his fine suicide have been left behind). Like Christ he is risen; his tomb is empty (as well as absent, or non-existent); the death of his 'suicide' has been replaced (as in the poems which celebrate the real deaths of Poe, Baudelaire, and Verlaine) by his 'ton beau'.

The astonishing release of language in the first quatrain is followed by the lull between stanzas, which may be suggested in the homophony of 'coi' in 'Quoi!' (l. 5). A moment of doubt follows this linguistic orgasm ('tout cet éclat'), and the doubt of language-anguish is now figured by the dark 'hora' of 'minuit'. In the silence there seems not even to be a vestige of the risen poet (unlike in the Christian story), no 'lambeau'; there is further delay (hom. l. 6: 'ça tarde'); and 'or' is now obscured in 'l'ombre' which alone remains to celebrate his victory. Except that...As in 'Un coup de Dés', where 'excepté' presages the final possibility of salvation in a constellation, here the moment of doubt is soon superseded by a triumphant return of 'or' in the hyperbolic guise of 'trésor' ('très or'). What treasure? Let us 'presume' an inner mental treasure (as opposed to the vainglory 'là-bas' of royal tombs: cf. I. 5–7), a 'pré-somptueux', a field of text of gold, which pours out its brilliance without the heat or flame of a real conflagration. The 'sang' of bloody battle disappears in 'sans', and the 'tison' is a 'flambeau' no longer as the 'trésor [...] de tête' takes over the role of 'lampadophore', the bearer of the gold of poetic sound.

As also suggested earlier, we now hear: 'Vers, ce son caressé'. Thanks to the carefully polished language[34] of the victorious poet, the 'éclat' of the

---

[32] Cf. *Les Mots anglais*: 'GORE, *sang coagulé*, Lat. cruor' (*OC*, 938).

[33] See Littré, 'écume', 4°: 'Scorie des métaux en fusion'.

[34] Cf. the phrase 'caresser un ouvrage'.

new 'sign' can be actively caressed into existence. And the caress, together
with the 'trésor [...] de tête' which might be a periphrasis for hair as well as
the poetic 'Idée', gives birth to the erotic scene of the sestet. But first the poet
declares his delight in recovering the 'éclat' of linguistic brilliance. Beauty is
his: it is 'ton beau', he tells himself; the 'tête' of treasured gold is his: 'la
tienne'. 'Si': despite his doubts. And it is his forever ('toujours') in the
eternity of the timeless world of beauty which transcends the 'siècles hideux'
(I. 11) and the divided blessings of 'aujourd'hui' (II. 1). Once more the
associative power of language proves creative, and 'si' (hom. 'six') prompts
the prefix 'dé' (die) and an expression of 'délice' (cf. 'Ô rire si' in l. 3). This
'dé-lice', anticipating the 'décor' of 'Ses purs ongles...', summarizes the
poet's aesthetic (his means of capturing the 'beau'), for in 'lice' we have the
sense of medieval jousting: a courtly dicing with death beneath the eyes of
the beloved princess (or empress) of beauty, a sport or game (anticipating
the 'agon' of 'Ses purs ongles...') from which in this poem the royal poet
has emerged victorious and unscathed, laughingly dismissing the need for a
real tomb. And in 'lice', too, we have the sense of weaving:[35] the golden
thread of sound can be woven into a text to replace the absent 'lambeau', a
purple patch of verse to deck the absent tomb.

If we will but listen to the homophonic criss-cross of this sound-net: 'Oui
seule qui du ciel évanoui.' The sky has gone dark (just as the darkness
inevitably fell in 'Quand l'ombre menaça...' and stayed the aspirant wing
of the 'Rêve' in its flight); but from this absence of sun and light ('évanoui'),
affirmation ('oui') is linguistically wrung, and the poet reasserts his capture
of beauty (suggested by 're-tienne', as if the rhyme-word were in fact
repeating not only the sound but the sense of its pair). The potential 'inanité'
of such word-jousting is never far from the poet's mind; and yet his poem
represents some kind of victory, however infantile the babblings of this
newly reborn user of language may sound. 'Un peu de puéril triomphe en
t'en coiffant': the jingle of the first four words, with the literal reflection of
'peu/pué', the echoing laughter ('ri' twice), the reminder of the original
'victoire', all suggest the continuing euphoria of the 'solitaire ébloui de sa
foi' (I. 8). Once more we are enjoined to listen (hom. 'entends! coi!'); and
finally the 'trésor [...] de tête' delivers itself of the image of hair, the
crowning glory of the poem: 'en t'en coiffant'.

The poet is intoxicated[36] with poetic delight, like a new-born child lately
emerged from the womb. Beauty and victory are his, as he lays down his
helmet upon ceremonial cushions at the end of his joust. The 'casque',
which is etymologically implicated in the birth of 'coiffe', is itself derived
from 'casser': as it might be, the tearing and breaking up of language (cf. II.

---

[35] See Littré, 'lice', sub-sections 1 and 2.
[36] For this and the other senses of 'se coiffer' and 'coiffe', see above, n. 11.

2, and 12: hom. 'Fantôme casse lieu'). The helmet thus becomes an emblem of the poetic process: the poet dices with language in the 'agon' or 'lice' and, by splintering the sign into new 'éclats', produces a container for beauty: rather as the victorious hero strews roses from his helmet as a symbol of peace.

Only the feminine gender of 'impératrice enfant' tells us now finally that the 'nous' of l. 6 might be more than a royal we; and it would be possible to reread the poem such that (as is usually supposed) the 'tête' (which is 'la tienne' in l. 9) belongs to a woman. But it is important, as always in Mallarmé, to see that she has been called up ('évoquée') by a linguistic process, by the logic of the cross which was seen to operate in 'Sonnet allégorique de lui-même' and in the remainder of 'Plusieurs Sonnets'. The poet has sought beauty through language. The victory brought about by his new poetic technique has combined with the delight which it causes to produce the word 'délice'; and this in turn suggests the chivalric hero risking death for his beloved 'princesse lointaine'. Beauty thus becomes the imperial figure to whom he dedicates the helmet, the instrument of his poetic victory ('casser') and that which has protected his own 'trésor [...] de tête'. The helmet (and the sonnet) is also now a container of beauty (the celebratory roses), so that it becomes beauty itself: as a 'casque d'or',[37] a helmet of golden hair adorning his beloved beauty in the darkness of non-representation. This is a new kind of poetic beauty, like a young girl with a rosy complexion (l. 14) but who is born to rule.

Thus the poet and his beauty are united throughout the poem. They are the 'nous' whom 'l'ombre [...] fête' in l. 6 (just as the worthless fires of real stars had to witness the triumph of the birth of genius at the end of 'Quand l'ombre menaça...'). Where the poet and the sign were synonymous in 'Le vierge, le vivace...', here the poet has joined with beauty in an eternal caress: 'vers, ce son caressé'. As already suggested, the phallic imagery of the first quatrain (preceded by the theme of virginity and sundering in 'Le vierge, le vivace...'), the turbulence of the syntax, the sense of 'coiffe' as a foetal membrane over the skull, and the final 'puerile' triumph of a child laid down upon cushions, all combine to suggest an interpretation of the poem in terms of the sexual act.[38] Mallarmé would not be the first poet to see poetic creativity in erotic terms, but here we have also what might be called 'un sonnet puerpéral' (cf. 'une pourpre s'apprête', 'puérile'). The poet joins with language in a moment of orgasmic oblivion, forgetting the world

[37] A 'casque' being a hair-style. Cf. Mallarmé's similar play with 'diadème' and 'le front couronné' in 'La chevelure vol d'une flamme...' (ll. 3–4).

[38] Albert Sonnenfeld, comparing this poem with its first version 'Toujours plus souriant...', sees the latter as an account of male masturbation and 'Victorieusement fui...' as eliminating the allegedly more explicit narrative of 'Toujours plus souriant' in favour of a greater measure of 'Rêve' and obscurity: see his 'Élaboration secondaire du grimoire: Mallarmé et le poète-critique', *Romanic Review*, 69 (1978), 72–89.

of objects; and this surrender of the self to the 'écume' of the sign is followed
by a silent pause, of doubt and anticipation (the etymology of 'présomp-
tueux'), before in the ninth line of the sonnet's gestation an exclamation of
delight greets the emergence of the 'puéril triomphe' (l. 11). A child is born
and laid upon the 'lit' which stood waiting in the 'solitaire' and the 'insolite
mystère' of 'Quand l'ombre menaça...' and (homophonically) in the 'dé-
lice' of l. 9 itself. Where we had a star and a constellation, now we have a
child, as feminine as the new beauty she symbolizes. In 'Ses purs ongles...',
we shall have a Crucifixion.[39]

(d) *Elevation: 'Ses purs ongles...'*

                                                              très haut dédiant [...]

Returning now to 'Ses purs ongles...', one can see that this revised version
of 'Sonnet allégorique de lui-même' is further enriched by its relationship
with the other sonnets in 'Plusieurs Sonnets'. In 'Quand l'ombre me-
naça...', poetic ambition ('Tel vieux Rêve') has ceased from futile attempts
to transcend the boundaries of language and has folded itself within the poet
and his craft. And there, in 'Le vierge, le vivace...', it remains, despite a
hankering after further attempts at flight, in a willing and fruitful accept-
ance of 'immobility' (the non-representational function of language). In
'Victorieusement fui...' any negative thoughts about this new poetic des-
tiny are all but banished in a joyous celebration of the creative potential of
language thus set free: following the poet's coupling with beauty a golden
sonnet scatters its 'dice-flowers' in a cascade of naïve delight.

  'L'aile se ploie'; 'l'aile s'immobilise'; 'elle renaît'; and in 'Ses purs on-
gles...' the 'aile' becomes simply 'Elle': the personification of beauty in a
nymph who is also black night ('nixe'), an elusive mythical creature who has
vanished into and yet also been captured by the mirroring of reflexive
language. Where once the 'Rêve' 'a ployé son aile [...] en moi', now it is
folded in the 'scintil*la*tions' of the 'septuor', emitting 'd'un grand éclat
l'insolite mystère' which language contains. The poet himself gradually
fades from the scene as we move from sonnet to sonnet. In the first, he is
a refuge for the wing, and so becomes a genius, a 'solitaire ébloui de sa foi'.
In the second, this solitary undergoes wintry exile with the 'aile': the poet
has become indistinguishable from the sign. In the third he appears expli-
citly again ('mon absent tombeau'), but the focus of attention has passed to

---

[39] The crucifixion is, as already suggested, perhaps foreshadowed in ll. 4–5 of 'Victorieuse-
ment fui...'. It may also be that the Nativity is foreshadowed in the 'Magnifique' (cf. the
Magnificat) of 'Le vierge, le vivace...' and in the reference to virginity: see Robert Champigny,
'The *Swan* and the Question of Pure Poetry', *L'Esprit créateur*, 1 (1961), 150.

the second person singular, to beauty herself. And in 'Ses purs ongles...' he has gone: 'le Maître est allé puiser des pleurs au Styx.' The central protagonist is no longer a poet who lives alone in the world or who caresses his beloved's hair: it is a personification, 'L'Angoisse'. The poet has become language-anguish; and the 'désir et mal de mes vertèbres' is now satisfied and cured by the self-generating power of his new poetic technique, his logic of the cross.

At the same time the poetic style itself evolves: from the Hugolian monumentality (and dramatic opposition of light and dark) of 'Quand l'ombre menaça...' to the impersonal Parnassian landscape of 'Le vierge, le vivace...' with its symbolic focus on a non-human creature (cf. Leconte de Lisle's animals) to the Baudelairean eroticism (and love of simile) to be found amidst the 'chevelure' of 'Victorieusement fui...'. In 'Ses purs ongles...', therefore, Mallarmé is to be seen finding his own poetic voice (as he had done 'sans le savoir' in the 'Ouverture' to 'Hérodiade' and self-consciously in 'Sonnet allégorique de lui-même').[40]

Language-anguish is Mallarmé's secular equivalent of the Passion. The poet has died to the world of objects that language may be redeemed and a pristine beauty regained. 'Ses purs ongles...', like the Mass, performs the ritual of the Eucharist, raising the host (the 'oubli(e)' that is the oblivion into which purified language consigns the world of objects) and dedicating it in a manual ceremony of sacred writing which re-enacts the story of a resurrection: 'en ptychais biblōn',[41] in the folds of 'le Livre', in a 'vespéral' (IV. 3).[42] At the same time this sonnet is one of four, the last quarter of a cruciform structure resembling the four-part structure of the Petrarchan sonnet itself.[43] At the centre of the quatrains and tercets of 'Ses purs ongles...' lies the 'croisée': the point where nave and transept cross, as if our progress through 'Plusieurs Sonnets' had led from under the dark vaulted ceilings of a 'salle d'ébène' ('Quand l'ombre menaça...') past the north and south transepts of glacial beauty and rosy caress (or 'rosace') to the high altar (and the 'crédences'), the 'site haut' of Mallarmé's poetic cathedral. And at the centre lies, metaphorically, the 'croisée': as Littré defines it, an 'entrelacement de fils bien serrés ensemble'.[44] 'Plusieurs Sonnets' is a text: a 'main(t) rêve' woven from the golden thread of homophony by fingers

[40] This display of an evolution in poetic style is itself reminiscent of Hugo's *Les Contemplations* in which Hugo's own development from a naïve Romantic lyricism to the visionary style of Book VI of *Les Contemplations* is consciously exemplified in the successive poetic styles of the six books of the collection. Similarly, the 'Spleen et idéal' section of Baudelaire's *Les Fleurs du mal* traces a move away from a Lamartinian form of Christian verse towards Baudelaire's own 'Satanic' quest for beauty.

[41] See Kromer, 'The Redoubtable PTYX', 571.

[42] 'Livre d'église qui contient tout ce qui se chante à l'office du soir' (Larousse).

[43] Cf. the 'hyperbolic' sonnet represented by the fourteen quatrains of 'Prose (pour des Esseintes)'.

[44] 'Croisée', 5°.

capped with 'dés', a 'délice' of sound, a supreme 'son-jeu' in place of 'Tel vieux Rêve', of the '[signe] d'autrefois'. A 'songe froid' (II. 13), perhaps, but also a 'nonchaloir sans flambeau' (III. 8): a caress of sound which dispenses with real fire in the capture of a golden beauty. Not a sterile 'lac', but a process of organic growth as the linguistic sign, be it 'pyxide', 'amphore', or 'coiffe',[45] releases its seed on to the fertile 'sol' of 'l'espace littéraire' before blossoming in the beauty of a rose.

And a text woven by a Phoenix: not only the bird whose wing has folded in the poet and taken flight on the double wing of rhyme and the hemistichs of 'le Vers', but Phénix, the Phoenician described in the Larousse entry of 1874: 'fils d'Agénor et d'Argiope: [...] Ce fut lui, dit-on, qui inventa les lettres et l'écriture et trouva le moyen de peindre en pourpre avec la cochenille.' We have already encountered this 'pourpre' in l. 3 of 'Victorieusement fui...': as the etymological origin of both 'Phoenicia(n)' and 'Phoenix', there the word lies in linguistic wait ('s'apprête') to spread its rich hue over the absent tomb of 'Ses purs ongles...'. In 'Quand l'ombre menaça...' we learnt that the old wing of poetic ambition was denied by the fatal law of darkness: in 'Ses purs ongles...' this dream at eventide has been burnt by the Phoenix. In the conflagration celebrated at the beginning of 'Victorieusement fui...' the poet/phoenix has burned the leaves of the old hymn-book ('vespéral') and, like a latter-day Phénix, invented a new form of writing, the reflexive sign. The vesperal hour (the sixth of the seven canonical hours and thus the last but one) is past: 'la Pénultième est morte'. But these seven hours become the fourteen lines of a sonnet, and the sixth hour is now mirrored in the midnight that is the new 'holy' time of Mallarméan verse. Romantic evensong has become 'L'Angoisse, ce minuit'; and the evening star, Venus or Hesperus, has given birth to a 'septuor'—that is, the Hesperides, the nymphs of the setting sun, or, in another version of the myth, the seven daughters of Atlas.[46]

[45] 'Pyxide': 'Terme de botanique. Fruit qui s'ouvre par le milieu, comme une boîte à savonnette' (Littré); 'Capsule à déhiscence transversale dont la partie supérieure se soulève comme un couvercle' (Robert); 'amphore': 'Valve inférieure de certains fruits qui se fendent en travers à l'époque de la maturité' (Larousse); 'coiffe': 'Enveloppe de la capsule (des mousses)' (Robert). Cf. Derrida's brief reference to dehiscence, *La Dissémination*, 243 n. 21.

[46] As well as the Pleiades or the Great Bear, or even the seven planets beyond the Earth in the solar system as then known. The Hesperides were nymphs of the setting sun (in Hesiod, the daughters of the night; in other versions, the daughters of Zeus or Atlas). As the seven daughters of Atlas and Hesperia, Atlas's niece, the Hesperides are an alternative name for the Pleiades. In the traditional version, they lived in the far west and guarded the golden apples, the fruits of immortality sought by Heracles (see Larousse, 'Hespéride' and 'Hespérides'). Thus 'vespéral' is a nodal word, joining the numerical characteristics of the sonnet to the themes of death and resurrection, sunset and victory over the night, constellations, religious ceremony, and the erotic pursuit of beauty (the planet Venus being an evening 'star' rather as, in 'Quand l'ombre menaça...', the Earth also becomes a radiant star). The 'lacework' in evidence here may account for Mallarmé's inclusion of 'Mes bouquins refermés...' with some of these sonnets in *Album de vers et de prose* (1887) and *Vers et prose* (1893) since that poem focuses on the

If 'le Phénix' is an inventor of writing, then the links between 'Plusieurs Sonnets' and Mallarmé's thoughts about language in the 1860s seem all the more compelling. Already we have seen how the experience of writing for the theatre (the original versions of 'Hérodiade' and 'L'Après-midi d'un faune') brought Mallarmé face to face with the disparity between spoken and written language and how he sought to achieve a poetic language (notably in 'Le Démon de l'analogie' and the 'Ouverture' to 'Hérodiade') which would mobilize and combine the resources of the spoken and the written word. We have seen how he 'teaches' us to 'hear' as well as to see his poems and prose poems—and seen also, it is hoped, how such 'aural' readings enrich and illuminate his texts. In his notes on language of 1869, which clearly relate closely to the 'étude projetée sur *la Parole*' mentioned to Cazalis the previous year, Mallarmé sketches out the plan for a study of language which is centrally concerned with the relation between the spoken and the written word. In essence what he wishes to 'demonstrate' is a form of writing which would record the full potential of language as it is performed (spoken and written).

'Ses purs ongles...' brings to an end a cycle of four sonnets which may be said to display 'les deux manifestations du Langage' as Mallarmé defined them in these notes of 1869:

la Parole et l'Écriture, destinées (en nous arrêtant à la donnée du Langage) à se réunir toutes deux en l'Idée du Verbe: la Parole, en créant les analogies des choses par les analogies des sons—l'Écriture en marquant les gestes de l'Idée se manifestant par la parole, et leur offrant leur réflexion, de façon à les parfaire, dans le présent (par la lecture) et à les conserver à l'avenir comme annales de l'effort successif de la parole et de sa filiation: et à en donner la parenté de façon à ce qu'un jour, leurs analogies constatées, le Verbe apparaisse derrière son moyen du langage, rendu à la physique et à la physiologie, comme un principe, dégagé, adéquat au Temps et à l'Idée.[47]

Fascinated by the fact that linguistics is the only science in which the object and medium of analysis are one and the same, Mallarmé adopts the term 'conversation' to denote this very fusion. On the one hand, 'conversation' is language in action, with language-users 'intending' and speaking words in non-univocal ways: 'Sens des mots diffère, d'abord, puis le *ton*: on trouve du nouveau dans le ton dont une personne dit telle ou telle chose.'[48] On the

---

birth of Aphrodite (at Paphos) and evokes the apple of discord in the reference to absent 'fruits' in l. 9, which may recall the golden apples of the Hesperides. In 'La chevelure vol d'une flamme...', the phrase 'l'extrême / Occident de désirs' (ll. 1–2) may also suggest the mythical Island of the Blest in which this garden was situated.

[47] *OC*, 854.

[48] *OC*, 851. Meaning and understanding different things by the same word is also a historical as well as an interpersonal phenomenon, and one which Mallarmé determines to exploit: 'Enfin—les mots ont plusieurs sens, sinon on s'entendrait toujours—nous en profiterons—et pour leur sens principal, nous chercherons quel effet ils nous produiraient prononcés

other hand, 'conversation' is an appropriate term for linguistic study itself, since this takes the form of a kind of dialogue between phenomenon and analyst:

C'est donc puisque la Conversation nous permet une abstraction de notre objet, le Langage, en même temps que, site du Langage, elle nous permet d'offrir son moment à la Science, dans la conversation que nous étudierons le Langage.[49]

In short, 'conversation' is Mallarmé's term for 'le langage se réfléchissant'.[50] Abandoning his projected thesis on language, he would appear to have found in poetry itself the best means of 'conversing' with language.[51]

par la voix intérieure de notre esprit, déposée par la fréquentation des livres du passé (Science, Pascal), si cet effet s'éloigne de celui qu'il nous fait de nos jours' (OC, 852).

[49] OC, 853.

[50] OC, 851.

[51] For further discussion of these notes, see Marchal, La Religion de Mallarmé, 83–91. On their relevance to the 'Sonnet en -yx' see also Reynolds, 'Mallarmé et la transformation esthétique du langage, â l'exemple de "Ses purs ongles"'.

PART IV

Pieces of Eight
(1868–1885–1887–1894)

or, à quelle hauteur qu'exultent des cordes et des cuivres, un vers [...] y atteint.

('Plaisir sacré')

The Stuff of Dreams: Three Versions of 'Quelle soie aux baumes de temps' (1868–1887)

un or / Agonise [...]
('Ses purs ongles...')

Mallarmé's apparent 'return' to poetry in the summer of 1868 after two years of crisis was marked not only by 'Sonnet allégorique de lui-même' (first mentioned in May and then sent to Cazalis on 18 July) but also by 'De l'orient passé des Temps', an octosyllabic sonnet which he sent to Bonaparte Wyse sixteen days earlier. Just as his expressed dissatisfaction with certain parts of 'Sonnet allégorique de lui-même' may have led him immediately to revise it, so too he rewrote 'De l'orient passé des Temps' almost at once and, in the draft which survives (possibly from 1869), entitles it 'Alternative'. The poem was revised again and appeared untitled as 'Quelle soie aux baumes de temps' in 1885.

Mallarmé had already written in octosyllabic metre in 'Le Château de l'Espérance' (originally entitled 'L'Assaut') in 1863 and in the first version of 'Sainte' in 1865. But 'De l'orient passé des Temps' is his first octosyllabic sonnet. It is as if, having returned to poetry with the firm conviction that the sonnet should be his preferred form, he then promptly experimented in each of the two principal line lengths of French poetry. Accordingly, whereas 'Sonnet allégorique de lui-même' ushers in the sequence of great Petrarchan sonnets in alexandrines ('Plusieurs Sonnets', 'Mes bouquins refermés...', the 'Tombeaux', and 'Hommage' [to Wagner]), his first octosyllabic sonnet prepares for the Petrarchan masterpieces of the so-called 'Triptyque' ('Tout Orgueil fume-t-il du soir', 'Surgi de la croupe et du bond', 'Une dentelle s'abolit'), as well as for 'M'introduire dans ton histoire', 'A la nue accablante tu', and 'Salut'.

All three versions of 'Quelle soie aux baumes de temps' are difficult of access, and they have received rather less critical attention than many of Mallarmé's poems. If one considers that the first was written at approximately the same time as 'Sonnet allégorique de lui-même', then it may be that this poem also concerns the poet's new-found poetic faith. Much less complex and ingenious than 'Sonnet allégorique de lui-même', 'De l'orient passé des Temps' may in fact be its direct counterpart. Essentially, it would seem, the poet is describing the temptation presented by his beloved's hair as a source of solace in the world of objects. Whereas 'Sonnet allégorique de lui-même' describes the poet's rejection of mimetic art and displays poetic beauty rising from the ashes in a stellar pattern of self-reference, 'De l'orient passé des Temps' shows him desiring temporarily to shut his eyes to the 'Néant' which the abolition of reference at first entails. Having 'died' to the world of objects (hence his need of a shroud: l. 7), his eyes are tired of the sepulchral drapery of the void: instead he would rather bury his perception in the beauty of this golden hair ('ces beaux cheveux / Lumineux')—a beauty that is natural (because quite separate from the artificial beauty of her jewels: l. 4) and which surpasses that of any material known to history. While the phrase 'De l'orient passé des Temps' is a periphrasis for the past, with time seen as the sun moving from east to west,[1] the implication of the syntax is, of course, that even the richest fabric of the Orient cannot rival these golden locks.

But—and this first version offers a strong reversal at the *volta*, which is repeated as 'Non' in the subsequent versions—the poet then inverts the sequence of the octave. The first tercet tells how the shadowy curtains of a non-referential linguistic world in fact conceal the 'death' of the waves (of real hair); while in the second we learn that the very luminosity of the hair sharpens his mental horror (as a poet) at the world of objects,[2] a world he has disavowed. Here too, therefore, as in 'Sonnet allégorique de lui-même', the structure of the sonnet is chiastic; and a whole range of mirror-effects are established within and between octave and sestet. The values of light and dark are exchanged, so that the conventional illumination of mimetic imagery is replaced by the welcome obscurity of non-representational poetry. The golden gleam of hair and the sparkle of jewels have become the sparks of some excruciating torture, the anguished awareness of the inevitable gap between language and material reality; while the potentially funereal 'tentures' are now 'les rideaux vagues', with their connotations of refuge and domestic comfort. The dark folds (or 'plis') of self-referential poetry furnish the poem; while the real referent, hair, 'studs' the poem (in

---

[1] In 'La chevelure vol d'une flamme...' the future into which desire projects itself is by contrast described as 'l'extrême / Occident des désirs'—i.e. the furthest reach of time before the sun/today must die and the whole cycle begin again.

[2] Cf. 'Le vierge, le vivace...', l. 11: 'l'horreur du sol où le plumage est pris'.

ll. 3, 7, 11) with 'étincelles' which are the antithesis of the 'scintillations' in 'Sonnet allégorique de lui-même'.

As in the latter poem, 'or' once again provides a golden thread with which the poet weaves an 'étoffe' that bids to surpass the poetic fabrics of the past. While the hair is disavowed as a referent, its goldenness survives linguistically. Rising initially in '*orient*', like the golden sun itself, and latent in the darkness of self-referential language (in 'les vagues / M*or*tes' concealed by the curtains), it appears reversed (and, as it were, denied) in 'at*ro*ces': the golden sparks of the real hair are the wrong sort of gold. Finally it recurs as the second syllable of the last line (thus recalling the second syllable of the first line): in the midst of the poet's horrified renunciation of the world of objects lie, as the poem itself narrates, the golden consequences of reflexive art—for all the linguistic contingencies with which he must contend, for all the 'dés' attendant upon his 'désaveux'. The past of real time (l. 1) has become, homophonically, 'mon or: heure aimée, dés à vœux'; the gold of poetry offers a beloved, timeless profusion of desiring word-dice. Indeed 'mon horreur émet dés-aveux': the poet's expression of disgust at the world of objects is an emission of contingent language that 'confesses' its own contingency.

The 'étoffe' of the poem is intricately patterned in other ways. The almost exclusively rich rhymes (the final 'cheveux' / 'désaveux' providing a possibly appropriate exception); the reinforcement of the a and c rhymes with preceding /ɛ/ and the a rhyme itself with /dɛ/; the symmetry of 'passé des', 'las de ces', 'hélas! ces' (ll. 1, 8, 11), partially completed by 'et mes' in the last line; the balance of 'Moi' and 'Mes' at the beginning of ll. 5 and 8, again partially repeated in 'Mais' and 'Mortes' in ll. 9 and 11, and in 'Mon' and 'mes' in the last line; the unadornedness of the hair (l. 3) thrown into relief by its position between 'étoffe' and 'bijoux'; the ambiguity of 'vis' ('I live' or 'I saw'), the less probable sense ('I saw') being made possible by the quatrain's preoccupation with sight; and the ambiguous syntactic position of 'en l'esprit' (does the hair exist only in his mind, or is it rather that it brings painful sparks of being to mind?): all these ingredients combine in a texture which is at once tantalizingly insubstantial and yet rich with suggestion and interconnection. The beauty of the hair has been replaced by the luminosity of a sonnet which is as bereft of reference as the hair is unadorned but which sparkles with stellar pattern.

Nevertheless 'De l'orient passé des Temps' soon dims when compared with its subsequent versions. The second is entitled 'Alternative', thus foregrounding the choice with which the poet is faced between the world of objects and the world of his poetic 'fiction'. At the same time the poem (in all its versions) is concerned with the contrast between poetic artifice and the 'native' or natural, unadulterated beauty of the golden hair. 'Natif' is also a metallurgical term,[3] and so the title suggests the natural gold of the 'other' ('alter', or a 'terre native') to which the poem itself provides the poetic alternative of gold refined from the ore of contingent language.[4] Apparently paradoxically, the 'or' of 'orient' and 'mortes' has disappeared in the process of revision, and we are left only with the final 'horreur'; but this is now 'son horreur', which provides a more economic and climactic account of the way in which the poet has refined golden sound from his aversion to mimetic art.

The 'narrative' of 'Alternative' is essentially the same as that of 'De l'orient passé des Temps', with various 'trouvailles' being added to create a more subtle text. The idea of alternatives is reinforced by the substitution of 'rimes croisées' for 'rimes embrassées' in the quatrains (and the rhymes are now 'redoublées' as they 'should' be in a Petrarchan sonnet). Where previously the hair was more valuable than all the fabrics of the past, now the point of comparison is more complex: 'De l'oubli magique venue.' Even a material (magically) risen from the oblivion into which objects are magically conjured away, even one which was 'musique et temps', could not compare with this unjewelled hair. If the poet, alone with his poetic activity ('mon rêve')—itself an avenue along which things come to him past dark tapestries—should hear the void, then he can bury his eyes in this welcome cloud (of 'naked' hair). To the insistence on vision in 'De l'orient passé des Temps' is added the sense of hearing, which prepares for the change to 'son horreur' in the last line. The poet is now explicitly a listener, one who experiences the sonorous void of non-referential language; and he is ready to take refuge from this void in the real world (of love, of referentiality). The 'chère nue' is potentially, the sounded 'e' apart, 'cette chair nue': the naked flesh of love-making will provide a blessed alternative to the agony of poetic creation.

But no, declares the dramatic volta (made more dramatic in the final version by the addition of an exclamation mark); and the poem proceeds to reverse the argument and images of the octave in a manner similar to that of 'De l'orient passé des Temps'. The potentially funereal 'tentures' of his aural poetic activity (his 'antique avenue') have become the more reassuringly domestic (and interior) curtains of empty sound waves breaking over each other (in the folds of verse);[5] while for the 'dead' poet, a 'fantôme', the

---

[3] Cf. Littré, 'Natif', 2°: 'Se dit des métaux qu'on trouve dans le sein de la terre à l'état de pureté, ou à peu près. Or natif, fer natif.'

[4] 'Étoffe' can mean not only 'fabric' or 'material', but base metal, in particular the alloy of tin and lead used in the making of organ pipes (Littré, 3°). One wonders, therefore, whether the homophone of 'étain' in 'D'atroces étincelles d'Être' ('De l'orient passé des Temps', l. 13) may not evoke this sense of 'étoffe' and thus represent the inadequacy of reality when compared with the refined gold of the poetic text.

[5] Cf. 'Une dentelle s'abolit', ll. 5–6: 'Cet unanime blanc conflit / D'une guirlande avec la même'.

hair brings about 'luxueusement' the rebirth of the perjurious gleam of being. By its rich golden radiance ('lux' and 'luxe') it falsely declares that something is: while the poet can only achieve beauty in language if everything is not (i.e. is non-mimetic). The hair's assertion of being is, as in 'De l'orient passé des Temps', what the poet abhors and disavows. But now the horror and disavowals are those of the world of objects too; and we may be reminded of the 'fatale loi' of 'Quand l'ombre menaça...', the 'luxe' and the 'orgueil menti par les ténèbres'. The world of objects, here represented by the hair, sheds a false light, offers a gleam of beauty but soon withdraws it (mimetic art can 'mime' some of the beauty of the real world, but the 'fatal' gap between language and world soon brings the 'mime' to an end).

Yet the homophonies of 'son horreur' and 'ses désaveux' remind us that the poet's avenue brings also golden sonority and the dice-like avowals of his new reflexive art. In a manner characteristic of Mallarmé's revisions, the poem now shows (if it has not already) that some of its strands may be read in two ways: for not only are the horror and disavowal those of reality and of the poet, the original 'étoffe' which could not stand comparison with the hair turns out to be the poem itself: 'musique et temps'. Poetry is not a redundant drapery that would take away from the naked beauty of real hair, nor an alloy of base metals providing the organ-pipes[6] for the poet's inadequate diapasons: it is a musical text that organizes sound into the octaves, or octosyllabics, of a sonnet—which, as 'Tout Orgueil fume-t-il du soir' will reveal, is the poet's 'orgue'. And, of course, 'Non': real hair, however lustrous, is no match for this 'étoffe' which has derived from the magical conjuring away of the world of objects. Thus does 'l'oubli magique' become a periphrasis for language itself;[7] and the poet's task is to listen down the ancient avenue of homophony and etymology[8] for the music of the void and to enfold himself not in the flesh of the real but in the woven cloth of his poetic curtains—not to bury his complacent eyes (l. 8) but to dig for aural gold.

'Quelle soie aux baumes de temps' seems almost not a revision of 'De l'orient passé des Temps' and 'Alternative' but a completely different poem. While 'temps', 'bijoux' (as 'diamant'), and 'tentures' (as 'drapeaux'?) recur, only 'Vaut', 'nue', 'Que [...] tu (dé)tends', and 'mes yeux' persist in the same line of each version. It is true that the sestet in any case required some revision, given Mallarmé's desire at this period to make his sonnets conform with the Banvillian prescription; but the revision is almost total, and verbally the sestet of 'Quelle soie aux baumes de temps' owes only 'diamant' to the earlier poems (i.e. to 'bijoux'). But their poetic argument survives, albeit in extenuated (cf. l. 2) form and much complicated and

---

[6] See above, n. 3.
[7] Cf. 'Ses purs ongles...', l. 13: 'l'oubli fermé par le cadre'.
[8] Cf. the 'rue des antiquaires' in 'Le Démon de l'analogie'.

condensed by the additional ingredients of the Chimera, the flags, and the lover's bite and stifled cry.

A comparatively straightforward reading of this poem does, of course, suggest itself. 'What ancient piece of silk with its faded pattern of a Chimera can rival the natural waves of your hair as you comb it in front of the mirror? The flags in the avenue may wave in triumph, but I have your hair in which to bury my eyes in equal happiness and exaltation. No! Your princely lover also needs to be reassured by closer loving contact—not just seeing the hair but burying his face (and mouth) in it, there to stifle his cry of triumphant possession.' One could easily adjust this reading to arrive at a more explicitly sexual interpretation, with the 'touffe' becoming pubic and 'Le cri des Gloires' a moment of orgasm: and '*s'exténue*', '*trous*', '*s'exaltent*', 'avenue', 'enfouir', and even 'contents' and 'considérable' might be pressed into service for the purpose. Suffice it to say, for the moment, that the poem is erotic, and thus one of several Mallarméan poems, most notably 'L'Après-midi d'un faune', in which the 'alternative' of sexual and poetic creativity is presented and the physical possession of the nymphs of beauty is rejected in favour of their phantasmal evocation in art.

Whereas in the earlier versions beauty in the real world (the hair) was desired in the octave and rejected in the sestet, here on the other hand it is desired throughout. But, by a masterly use of ambiguity, it is also rejected throughout—in favour of poetic beauty. The mouth (of the 'oral' poet attentive to the spoken sound of words) will only savour his 'morsure'—at once his contact with language and his certain 'death' to reference[9]—if he should stifle his triumphant cry at possessing the world (i.e. 'avow' that he does not 'possess' the world of objects through language). Instead the hair will absorb his diamantine silence, which means that the hair has now become synonymous with the poem itself—not 'la torse et native nue' of real hair, but the 'soie torse' of hair as an analogy for poetry. The 'étoffe' of the earlier poems has been replaced by the silk of sounds smoothly woven, of prosodic accents (the 'temps' present in all three versions) applied like balm to the painful 'morsure' which symbolizes the new relationship in which the poet stands to the world of objects. Upon this silk[10] such a world has been reduced to a non-existent, imagined shape that is almost not alive, a chimera, a mythical symbol of the imagination and a beast (in some accounts) with the upper body of a lion and the tail of a serpent. The chimera is thus the sonnet itself, with its octave and sestet, its 'torse' and 'queue' (homophonically present at the beginning of l. 4 in all three versions), the twisted strands of a 'queue' of golden hair and sound.

[9] Cf. 'L'Après-midi d'un faune', ll. 40–1: 'une morsure / Mystérieuse, due à quelque auguste dent'.

[10] Which, like the resurrected Phoenix of 'Ses purs ongles...', owes its origins to a 'ver', or 'vers'.

For, while the 'horreur' of the earlier versions has vanished, the golden thread of 'or' is still present—and absent. Not only does the hair suggest the picture of a flag unfurling in the street, but Littré gives as the second sense of 'drapeau': 'Petit morceau de drap que le batteur d'or tient entre ses doigts.'[11] When one learns from Littré also (3°) that 'exalter' is an 'Ancien terme de chimie' meaning to 'Redoubler la vertu d'une substance en la purifiant', then it is clear that the poet of 'Quelle soie aux baumes de temps' is as much of an alchemist as the author of 'Sonnet allégorique de lui-même'. As long as the hair or the 'drapeau' hang limply, as if 'méditants', then they are deficient: respectively, either merely 'native' or principally characterized by the 'holes' which are the gaps in the flag's folds. But when this 'meditation' becomes reflexion (thanks to the advent, or 'avenue', of the poet), then the hair is 'torse' and the flags 's'exaltent': both hair and flag display their linguistic value ('torse', and the gold associated with the less common senses of 'drapeau' and 'exalter' just mentioned). Gold is thus reflected in the 'trous', as the golden hair—originally outside the mirror (in the real world of its female owner)—is now reflected by the linguistic play of the poem. For not only is it reflected in 'miroir', it is plurally present in 'hors'. It provides the desired linguistic savour of the poet's 'morsure', while it would be central to 'gloire' if the sharp, diamantine /i/ (stressed by repetition in 'considérable', 'expirer', 'diamant', 'cri', and 'il') were to be stifled.

Be that as it may, real hair has become a 'considérable touffe': the sonnet itself as a linguistic tuft of twisted or reflected hair-like threads, in which the cry attendant upon the glorious possession of beauty has become the authentic silence of Mallarméan verse, a pure, diamantine, and potentially stellar ('con-*sidérable*')[12] source of radiance to rival silk. The 'tone mirror' of the poem, held up by the tone-loving poet (l. 11), offers him the certainty he craves: and, with the power of a linguistic prince (l. 11), he asserts in the first three syllables the presence of this 'rien', of this 'morsure' (and 'mort sûre') of language (l. 10): 'Qu'elle soit'.[13] Now that he possesses the hair, stripped of its 'real' existence and transmuted in poetry, he (and we) can feast our eyes on the glories of the page: 'Moi, j'ai ta chevelure nue / Pour enfouir des yeux contents'. The contented 'eyes' of rhyme pairs are enveloped in the poetic 'chevelure', just as they peer forth from 'Les trous de drapeaux': for each stanza of the poem flaps across the page like a flag—firmly pinned to the flag-pole of its left-hand margin, but reaching out, as it might be 'à l'extrême orient', in lines of metrically similar but typographically different length, into the blankness of the silent page.

---

[11] Littré adds to this definition: 'Terme de relieur. Drapeau à l'or, linge avec lequel le doreur, après avoir tout terminé, enlève l'or superflu en frottant toutes les places, et qu'il conserve à part jusqu'à ce qu'il soit suffisamment chargé de métal.'

[12] Cf. the rich use of 'sidéralement' at the end of 'Un coup de Dés'.

[13] The fourth and fifth syllables of l. 1 further exclaim homophonically: 'Oh, beau!'

2

Organ, Rose, Mandora: 'Tout Orgueil fume-t-il du soir', 'Surgi de la croupe et du bond', and 'Une dentelle s'abolit' (?1866–1887)

> Ce qu'on nomme du *jeu*, il en faut, dans une mesure raisonnable, pour réussir quelque chose comme ce travail complexe et simple: trop de rigueur aboutissant à transgresser, plutôt que des lois, mille intentions certaines et mystérieuses du langage.
>
> (*Les Mots anglais*)

The three octosyllabic sonnets which have come to be known as the 'Triptyque' first appeared in the *Revue indépendante* in January 1887 before being included in the *Poésies* published later that year. On these and all subsequent occasions Mallarmé grouped the poems in the same order and numbered them, which suggests that while each may be read as a discrete work, nevertheless together they form a composite whole, a trio to place beside the quartet of 'Plusieurs Sonnets'.

Like the four sonnets in alexandrines which make up this quartet, the 'Triptyque' may also date back to the mid-1860s. In the famous letter to Cazalis in May 1866 where Mallarmé talks of laying the foundations of 'un livre sur le *Beau*', he notes that, as it were for light relief, 'Je me repose à l'aide de trois courts poèmes, mais qui seront inouïs, tous trois à la glorification de la Beauté'.[1] Several commentators have been tempted to identify these 'trois courts poèmes' as the 'Triptyque',[2] while many have pointed also to the extensive lexical similarities between these three sonnets and other poems written by Mallarmé at approximately this time, especially

---

[1] *Corr.*, i. 216.
[2] Notably Guy Michaud in his *Mallarmé* (2nd edn, Paris, 1971), 68. See also Davies, *Mallarmé et le rêve d''Hérodiade'*, 17, 49–50.

'Don du poème', 'Sainte', and the 'Ouverture' to 'Hérodiade'.[3] The word 'mandore', for example, which plays such a key role in the 'Triptyque', occupies an important position in 'Sainte' and was also considered by Mallarmé as a variant possibility in l. 40 of the 'Ouverture'. One might also note the clear echoes of 'De l'orient passé des temps' and 'Alternative': for example, the use of 'désaveu' and the image of curtains serving as a shroud.[4] But above all the repeated use of 'or' as a lexical unit betokening the value of 'purified' poetic sound suggests a close connection not only with 'De l'orient passé des temps' but also with 'Sonnet allégorique de lui-même'. The 'resurrection' of 'or' from the rhymes of the octave in the 'Sonnet en -yx' is here matched, in 'Une dentelle s'abolit', by the homophonic 'birth' of 'mandore' from the phrase 'Tristement dort' (l. 10). The 'creux néant musicien' (l. 11) is the womb of homophony and linguistic potential from which the 'musical' intricacy of this 'child-poem' issues no less surely than the 'worm' ('ver/vers') emerges from the ashes of the immolated Phoenix.

Further internal evidence suggests that the 'Tripytque' may have developed in parallel with the quartet of 'Plusieurs Sonnets'. The plural 'consoles' which figure in 'Sonnet allégorique de lui-même' were replaced by 'crédences' in 'Ses purs ongles...' but recur (in the singular) as the key element in 'Tout Orgueil fume-t-il du soir'. The 'fatale loi' of sunset in 'Quand l'ombre menaça...' is evoked in the opening stanza of 'Tout Orgueil...', while the terms of the second quatrain of 'Quand l'ombre menaça...'—

> Luxe, ô salle d'ébène, pour séduire un roi
> Se tordent dans leur mort des guirlandes célèbres,
> Vous n'êtes qu'un orgueil menti par les ténèbres—

are recalled in the opening line of 'Tout Orgueil...', in the 'froid plafond' of 'Surgi de la croupe...', and in the 'guirlande' of 'Une dentelle...'. 'Se tordent', with its 'golden' thread, provides a further link with 'Tout Orgueil...' where 'Torche' (l. 2) derives etymologically from 'torquere' (=to twist). Add to these examples the roseate child-birth of 'Victorieusement fui...', and the 'col' of the swan in 'Le vierge, le vivace...' straining upwards no less vainly than the the 'col ignoré' of the vase in 'Surgi de la croupe...', and one begins to sense even more strongly that the 'Triptyque' is born of the same thematic preoccupations and lexical predilections as 'Plusieurs Sonnets'.[5]

---

[3] See especially Émilie Noulet, *Vingt poèmes de Stéphane Mallarmé* (Paris, 1967), 156, and Davies, *Le Drame solaire*, 237–8, 247–8.

[4] Other elements such as the 'couloir' and the 'Chimère' recall 'Toast funèbre', as does 'rose' itself.

[5] A similar unity of 'lexical predilection' will later, in the 1890s, link 'A la nue accablante tu', 'Salut', 'Un coup de Dés', and 'Au seul souci de voyager'.

Accordingly it may be legitimate to approach these three sonnets as no less 'self-allegorical'. For the 'Triptyque', like the single 'ptyx' of the 'Sonnet en -yx', displays the 'music' of poetic language against a backdrop of absence and 'language-anguish'. As an alternative to the movement from sunset to constellation, we find here a 'three-fold' progression from sunset, through a 'veillée amère', to dawn (cf. 'la vitre blême' in 'Une dentelle...'). In 'Tout Orgueil...', the human's hubristic faith in the power of language goes up in smoke as the sun sets on conventional discourse. Poetic aspiration (the 'immortelle bouffée': cf. the phrases 'bouffée d'éloquence', 'bouffée d'orgueil') cannot, it seems, postpone or survive the moment of demise—like the 'vieux Rêve' in 'Quand l'ombre menaça...' perishing beneath the funereal ceiling that symbolizes the restrictions of mimetic language. The poet is heir to the rich but now fallen trophies of humanity's proud but false victory over silence and inarticulacy; but the textual space in which, as poet, he used to operate has become a cold, deathly place in which his own reappearance (as living, self-expressive lyric poet) would make no difference. The Master is absent from the room.

Poetic space is thus a 'sépulcre de désaveu', in which language (and the poet) has 'died' to the world, has 'disowned' it by avowing its own status as arbitrary sign, as 'dés'. Yet language thereby does not become simply blank (the 'inanité sonore' of 'Ses purs ongles...') but retains, in its homophonies and its etymological roots, a residual referential power; meanings cling on like tenacious claws, non-arbitrary, 'necessary' remnants of that prior process of 'language-anguish' which must be undergone before pure, 'golden' sound can be achieved ('Affres du passé nécessaires': cf. hom. 'Affres du "pas", et nécessaires [c'est nécessaire']'). Beneath its marble lid, which it 'isolates' by foregrounding and displaying the 'death of representation', the poem-sepulchre is nevertheless lit and warmed by 'la fulgurante console'.

The word 'console' itself provides a dazzling display of this new power of language. At once verb and noun, it gleams with the dying rays of the sun (Latin 'sol') and suggests that here, in the last resort, 'la fulgurante Beauté' consoles the 'feu poète'. More plainly it is at once the plaster moulding in the form of a scroll or an S which supports a mantelpiece; a table set against a wall with legs of this shape; the upper part of a stringed instrument, particularly a harp, where the tension pegs are situated; and the keyboard of an organ. As such the word 'console' knots together a series of analogies previously adumbrated throughout the poem and prepares for the two sonnets which follow. Thus the poem comes to resemble a fireplace, surmounted (and surrounded) by the white marble suggested in l. 12 ('lourd': from 'luridus'='blême'), its black text the 'fireless', ashen void framed by a 'chambranle' (connoted by 'branle' in l. 2). Or is the poem a console table, set against the 'wall' of its justified left-hand margin while the rhymes of 'golden' homophony scroll down the right-hand side like the single S-shaped leg of such a table seen in profile? And just as homophony is not restricted to terminal rhyme, so the sinuosity of 'S' is displayed on no less than twenty-eight occasions in the course of this brief, octosyllabic sonnet—and displayed with considerable 'fulgurance': e.g. 'Sans', 'puisse', 'surseoir', 'S'il survenait', 'passé nécessaires', 'serres', 'Sous', etc.[6]

While the connotation of 'stringed instrument' prepares for the 'mandore' at the end of the 'Triptyque', the sense of 'organ keyboard' links 'console' with the beginning. For if indeed the 'il' of 'Orgueil' were to disappear in a puff of poetic smoke, then the poem would become an 'Orgue'—and would remain such even if 'il' were to 'surven[ir] par le couloir' (hom. 'par le coup, l'hoir'). Remove the 'il' from 'l'[h]oir', and the gold of poetic sound is delivered from the dross of vainglorious personal self-expression to become the 'or' of this poem's organ music. Did Mallarmé perhaps mentally turn his poem on its (left-hand) side and see each (now vertical) line of verse as an organ-pipe and his whole sonnet therefore as a fourteen-piped 'buffet d'orgue', an 'immortel buffet'? Given that the line-endings of 'Quelle soie aux baumes de temps' are like fluttering flags and that the rhymes of 'Une dentelle s'abolit' will resemble swirling curtains of white lace, such an analogy may not be altogether fanciful.

And what music is this organ playing? No fugue or toccata but 'un branle': that is, a tune or 'air' to accompany a dance of the same name in which one or two dancers take the lead, rather perhaps as rhyme in a Mallarméan octosyllabic sonnet sets the words in motion (cf. 'mettre en branle') and leads them through the 'Affres du pas' of an eightsome reel. Thus while the poem opens by apparently proclaiming an absence, as sunset is compared to a torch being snuffed out by too rapid an oscillation (the primary sense of 'branle'), it simultaneously announces (as it were, 'dans les ténèbres' of non-representational discourse) the presence of a muted ('étouf-fée') dance-tune in which words are twisted (cf. 'Torche', from 'torquere') into refulgent strands of golden light amidst the oscillating rhythms of poetic metre. 'La chambre ancienne' of conventional verse has thus become, as in the 'Ouverture' to 'Hérodiade', the 'lieu' of a new form of 'chamber music', of a quasi-sacred 'antienne'; or, as the homophonic subtext of the second quatrain suggests: 'La chambre-antienne de l'hoir, demain riche! m'échut, trophée'.

Where 'Tout Orgueil...' tempers the bleak vacancy of non-representation with the blazing solace of word-music, 'Surgi de la croupe...' sweetens the bitter consciousness of the discontinuous and non-consummated relationship between language and world with a silent evocation of 'l'absente de tous bouquets' and a discreet suggestion of union and connection. From

---

[6] The effect is prolonged into 'Surgi de la croupe...' which not only begins with a capital s but also contains twenty-one s's.

being an empty, sepulchral room the sonnet form has now become a piece of ephemeral 'verrerie': that is, at once a place where glass (and the 'vers') is made, the process of making that glass, and the finished glass itself. The poem is simultaneously 'lieu', 'action', and 'acte', all apparently void. The form is there, but it displays no flower, no beauteous creation: as if the sonnet were an empty vase (its rim 'ignored' by all blooms), or a goblet or chalice from which no love potion was ever drunk. For lack of a father and mother who together might have supped poetic inspiration ('à la même Chimère'), the poem is a mere non-existent 'sylphe', a mythical offspring inhabiting the cold ceiling of failed poetic flight. As the container of inexhaustible 'veuvage' (etym.='vide'), the sonnet simply manifests the 'death of representation' ('Agonise') but cannot consent, within this referential darkness, to 'speak' of the real presence of a rose. Such an oral act would be 'naïve', a kiss of death to end all hope of poetic conquest.

For, as in 'Ses purs ongles...', the 'agon' of the poetic act can yet promise a victorious outcome, a 'trophée' to be won in the 'Jeu suprême', as the poet jousts and duels with his words. Just as the emptiness of a sepulchre (as implied in 'Tout Orgueil...') may paradoxically testify to the glory of a resurrection, so the silence of this 'vase' may be the most eloquent of annunciations. Eros gave Harpocrates, the god of silence, a rose to bribe him not to betray the amours of Venus, which is why this flower is sculpted as an emblem of silence on the ceilings of confessionals and banquet-halls to remind those engaged in penitent avowal or vineous indiscretion that they are speaking in confidence, 'sub rosa'. Thus the 'vase' of this poem, empty of all real 'presence', nevertheless strives upwards towards an emblematic ceiling rose which might give the lie to the 'sylphe's' own disavowal. Perhaps this 'génie de l'air' is concealing a secret, perhaps the goddess of beauty has indeed entered into a union. David Scott has noted how Mallarmé's syntax and the brevity of the octosyllabic line combine to suggest in l. 14 that there is 'Une rose dans les ténèbres'.[7] Given that the word 'rose' is an anagram of Eros, that Eros hovers (unanagrammatically) in the phrase 'Une rose', and that 'rose' concludes the series of mirrored or's which characterize this particular sonnet ('croupe', 'interrompt', 'crois', 'froid'), it does seem as though the sonnet is evoking a poetic 'rose', 'l'absente de tous bouquets'. It will not 'breathe' the name of the rose, and yet speaks it all the same.[8]

For the beauty lies in the 'verrerie' itself, not in what this might display as a 'real' object. This poem is no mere 'ephemeral' container, but a 'pur vase' (cf. 'Ses purs ongles; (hom.) C'est pur son [...]'), and perhaps by implication the chalice or 'vase sacré' of another poetic Eucharist. Where 'Ses purs

---

[7] David H. T. Scott, 'Mallarmé and the Octosyllabic Sonnet', *French Studies*, 31 (1977), 155.

[8] On the rose as an ancient symbol of the poetic word, see Hugo Friedrich, *Die Struktur der modernen Lyrik* (Hamburg, 1956), 106–7.

ongles...' celebrates primarily the body of Christ ('cor/corps', 'oubli(e)'),
'Surgi de la croupe...' is filled with his blood: the 'sang' which is connoted
by the rose, and which is twice homophonically united with it ('Sans
fleur(ir)', 'annonçant / Une rose'). Like the two-handled 'amphore' of 'Ses
purs ongles...', this vase-poem is made of rhyme pairs; and each partner in
the pair rises up, like the side of a curvaceous vase, and joins its semicircle to
the following rhyme in a circular 'col' of embraced rhyme, in a rosebud kiss
of union—a 'pur vase d'O' (cf. 'Le pur vase d'au (cun breuvage)'). Through-
out the octave 'on' and 'mère' are intertwined, and the interruption lament-
ed at the end of the first quatrain is belied by the required 'rimes
redoublées' of the Petrarchan sonnet, where the two 'mouths' of rhyme
are joined once more in the second quatrain. The kiss thus proffered by the
'mouth' of this poem-vase is 'naïf' in the sense of 'natif': the kiss of poetic
union which is fatal to 'representation' but of which poetic beauty may be
the issue.

For the moment, however, the silence of 'Surgi de la croupe...' is merely
pregnant; the uterine 'col' has yet to offer passage (cf. 'couloir' in 'Tout
Orgueil...') to the fruit of the 'ventre' described in 'Une dentelle s'abolit'.
As yet the surest annunciation of the rose is offered not by words but by
insubstantial scent: hom. 'Le pur vase [...] ne consent [...] A rien expirer
—ah non! sens / Une rose'. Only when we have met the 'mandore' shall we
realize that the 'rose', being the aperture in a lute or other stringed instru-
ment,[9] is also the poem itself: the O-shaped orifice from which the sound of
beauty issues from the 'creux néant musicien', the O in 'or' and 'rose'—a
poetic 'rose' in the darkness of non-representation, or conversely the black
hole of text in the midst of the silent, marmoreal whiteness of the page.

Further connotations of 'rose' are laced together in the verbal network of
'Une dentelle s'abolit'[10]—where the associations with 'lit de roses', 'teint
de lis et de roses', and 'l'Aurore aux doigts de rose' seem to have combined
to bring forth these lily-white curtains and an absent bed at dawn. But this
'lit'—adumbrated in repeated mirror-image in the first line of 'Tout Orgueil
fume-t-il du soir'—is only absent as a real bed: in the poetic context its
homophonic status makes it the lily-white bed of the page upon which the
poem shall indeed be 'brought to bed' at the moment of its birth. The poetic
act—the 'Jeu suprême' which is at once an 'agon' and the ultimate 'musical'
performance—is characterized by doubt, a mental oscillation (cf. 'branle')
between the opposite poles ('doute' being cognate with 'duo', 'duality') of
presence and absence, the real and the verbal, success and failure. The

[9] See Littré, 'rose', 13°.
[10] Bertrand Marchal proposes a self-referential reading of this poem (but not of 'Tout
Orgueil...' or 'Surgi de la croupe...') by equating lace and words, but he argues that the
poet has failed by preferring to continue his idle dreaming rather than take up the musical
instrument which lies within his reach (*Lecture de Mallarmé*, 242–6).

lacework of the poetic text vanishes into nothing (cf. the 'aboli bibelot') if its sole effect is to reveal that the word is not the thing ('A n'entr'ouvrir [...] / Qu'absence éternelle de lit'): then it will have failed, 'spoken badly' (etym. 'blasphème'), sinned against the sacredness of beauty.

Rather the lacework of the poetic text is a combination of silent spaces between homophonies, those 'unanimous' yet 'conflictual' units of sound which are twisted in triumphant (and nuptial) garlands and knotted in terminal rhymes. At once black garlands of 'vers' and white, fugitive wisps of 'espace blanc' which threaten to vanish into the pale background of the white page, the poetic text is (once more) a 'fenêtre' in which the 'vitres' of interstitial spaces (visually evoked by the 'interrupted' word 'n'entr'ouvrir') are organized by the frame (or 'chambranle') of the sonnet form, itself a 'jeu-croix' (cf. 'Surgi de la croupe...', l. 5) of seven rhyme pairs (hom. 'sept unanimes blancs conflits'). Such text does not so much abolish or shroud the 'world', but rather (like net curtains) 'floats'—that is, oscillates and wafts ('doubtfully') in the breeze of polysemy.

But the 'unanimous conflict' of homophony can do more than just 'float' tantalizingly, leaving everything up in the air; the 'indécidable' can also be a source of new shapes, new forms, new meanings. For him who gilds his everyday experience of language with the 'rêve' of poetic imagination, there is a 'musical' instrument waiting 'sadly' (because abandoned and ignored) within the apparent 'inanité' of homophony (the 'creux néant musicien')—an instrument such as the 'vers' itself ('Telle que vers') and the 'fenêtre' of the sonnet form. Indeed, by homophony alone, this 'fenêtre' allows the 'feu' that had been snuffed out in 'Tout Orgueil...' to 'naître'—to be born from no real womb, but in an immaculate birth from the linguistic womb of the poem itself.

The last line of the poem would apparently suggest that such a birth is no more than hypothetical, a missed opportunity, and commentators accordingly have read the poem as a further account of supposed Mallarméan 'failure'. But homophony itself (once again) provides a more positive sub-text. A 'mandore' lies dormant within language (in 'Tristement dort' itself): 'Telle que [le] vers—quelque fenêtre—selon nul ventre que le sien—filial, honoré, put naître.'[11] The 'vers', we hear, has been born of the *ventre*, of language itself, a 'vers' that is both worthy to be honoured (unlike the mimetic discourse which was once humanity's great 'Orgueil') and 'filial': a filial offspring, but a product also of the linguistic 'fils' of a poetic, 'musical' text, the golden threads of sound and polysemic richness which have led from 'Orgueil', through 'rose', to 'mandore' and 'aurait'.

The 'Triptyque' thus presents another supremely 'oral' performance in which the gold at the heart of language—'l'immortelle bouffée'—is

---

[11] 'on aurait' and 'honoré' being only an approximate homophony.

mouthed by the 'deux bouches' of rhyme, and in which from a 'col ign*oré*' the golden rose of Mallarméan verse rises to become the aperture of a four-stringed mandora (or a Petrarchan sonnet in four stanzas). Having resembled curling smoke (in 'Tout Orgueil...') and then two mouths that fail to meet, the S—Mallarmé's emblem of sinuosity and the serpent-tailed Chimera—comes to resemble, at the beginning of the first and last words of l. 13, a 'ventre' bulging above a 'croupe' which ends in a 'queue': 'Selon nul ventre que[ue] le sien'. The 'flanc enfant d'une sirène' of 'A la nue accablante tu' is not far away. For the moment—and can Mallarmé, the author of *Les Mots anglais* (and adept of 'les mots anglés'?), not have been aware of this?—it would seem that an air is born, a poetic son and heir to replace the sun that has set. The 'il' of the personal lyric has been burned, only to be 'mirrored' in the 'lit' that is the 'lieu' of the poem; and the 'moi' of such lyricism, the mythical sylph of failed, outmoded poetic endeavour, has become a 'me' filled with the 'alternative' that is the 'doute du Jeu suprême': a 'm- and/or-e'.[12] And homophonically this 'mandore' is also 'Telle que[ue]', vers [...] / Filial[,] on—or—ait pu naître'. The 'or' which has been 'born' is the 'on': the 'Soi' which Mallarmé took to be that part of universal humanity which projects its spiritual need for pattern and order into the cosmos and calls it the divine.[13] And all thanks to the sonnet, that favourite verse-form of Mallarmé's in which, to be sure, 'le son naît'—a sound-net owing 'filial' loyalty to the 'son amant' ('Surgi de la croupe...', l. 6), the rhyming 'paire/père' which fathered it upon the pristine bed of silence.

[12] Mallarmé's play with the word 'plume' suggests that this reading is not altogether fanciful: see Derrida, *La Dissémination*, 307–8.

[13] See Marchal, *La Religion de Mallarmé*, *passim*, and Peter Dayan, *Mallarmé's 'Divine Transposition': Real and Apparent Sources of Value* (Oxford, 1986), 20–2.

3

With the Eyes of Rhyme:
'Prose (pour des Esseintes)'
(?1871–1885)

(Nous fûmes deux, je le maintiens.)

Lequel des deux faut-il croire, Mesdames, le témoignage de ses yeux ou celui de ses oreilles? (*La Dernière Mode*)

First published in the *Revue indépendante* in January 1885, 'Prose (pour des Esseintes)' may date back to the early 1870s,[1] but the appearance of Huysmans's *A rebours* in May 1884 was probably the catalyst which caused Mallarmé to polish an already well-advanced version into definitive, publishable form. As is well known, the hero of Huysman's novel, Jean de Floressas des Esseintes, is endowed by his creator with a profound admiration for the work of Mallarmé, in particular his prose poems. Returning the compliment, Mallarmé dedicates a poem called 'Prose'[2] to this fictional character (rather than to the 'real' Huysmans), a poem which already contained various features which might have appealed to Huysmans's decadent aesthete. This aristocrat with a floral and saintly name delights in flowers (especially, after too much benedictine, in white lilies) and in the sacred beauty of plainsong and Gregorian chant; while Mallarmé's poem, of course, celebrates 'La famille des iridées' in 'L'hymne des cœurs [hom. 'chœurs'] spirituels'. The further presence of 'dés' and 'Sainte' in this name make it sufficiently 'Mallarméan' to figure as part of a Mallarméan text;[3] and whether or not the English teacher was playfully expressing

---

[1] See *DSM*, i. 9–39, OC (BM), 249–50, and Marchal, *Lecture de Mallarmé*, 106. Cf. L. J. Austin, 'Mallarmé and the *Prose pour des Esseintes*', *Forum for Modern Language Studies*, 2 (1966), 197–213, where Austin argues against such an early date (p. 200).

[2] Whereas in 'Un coup de Dés' he would confer the title 'Poème' on a text which, though far from prosaic, nevertheless appears to dispense with all the traditional attributes of a poem.

[3] Although for *Vers et prose* (1893) he envisaged its removal. See OC, 1397, and Gardner Davies, *Mallarmé et la 'couche suffisante d'intelligibilité'* (Paris, 1988), 208.

compassion ('pour des Esseintes'), the 'scrambling' of the word 'Prose' within the phrase 'pour des Esseintes' must have been sufficient justification for the inclusion of a dedication which is otherwise of only incidental relevance to the poem as a whole. For one of the major features of this text is the manner in which words expand and shrink, collapse and reassemble, before our eyes and ears as we proceed from beginning to end.

Sometimes considered Mallarmé's most enigmatic poem,[4] 'Prose' quickly loses some of its apparent impenetrability when compared with a number of his other works. The much debated relationship between 'je' and the 'sœur' recalls the 'dyadic' character of both 'Hérodiade' and 'L'Après-midi d'un faune', and duality is evidently a central preoccupation of the poem. Prose/poetry, seeing/hearing, speaking/writing, music/letters, sound/silence, handwriting/typography are but some of the more reflexive oppositions: this poem 'pour des Esseintes' is also a 'synthèse'. Moreover, like 'L'Après-midi d'un faune', 'Prose' constitutes a poetic act in the afternoon; following a midday moment of silence ('ce midi', 'cette heure où nous nous taisons'), an attempt is made to recapture an ecstatic moment in which beauty is glimpsed. As by the Faune, memory is invoked, narrative essayed, and 'music' created in a timeless textuality ('pour d'éternels parchemins'); and once more, in his continuing pursuit of 'les nymphes du Parnasse', the poet presents us with a subtle dialectic of sight and sound.[5]

Like many of Mallarmé's earlier poems, 'Prose' evinces a complex binary structure. Dividing into two groups of seven quatrains, the division being appropriately preceded by the word 'sépara', the poem is a subtle combination of sequence and circularity. Framed by two pairs of quatrains, in which the present tense refers to the actuality of the poem's creation, the narrative sequence divides by sense and syntax into symmetrical groups of three, two, two, and three quatrains (these last three providing an explanation of the silence in which the protagonists of the narrative have been left).[6] In this sequence, imperfects and past historics are conjugated with further verbs in the present to evoke a previous sighting of beauty which is now being/has now been 'installed' within this text. Beginning with 'aujourd'hui', the poem ends on a present statement ('Elle dit le mot: Anastase'[7]) but anticipates a possible future (the laughter of the sepulchre): 'Prose' is a poetic moment caught between the silence of 'midi' and a potential aftermath of failure, between the unsayable and the unsaid.

The framing pairs of quatrains are carefully calculated; for not only do the eight-line groupings mirror the octosyllabic metre, each reflects the

---

[4] See *Poésies*, ed. Marchal, 225.

[5] Further parallels with 'L'Après-midi d'un faune' are noted by Carl Barbier in *DSM*, i. 32–3.

[6] As suggested by Austin, 'Mallarmé and the *Prose pour des Esseintes*', 202–3, and reaffirmed by Marchal, *Lecture de Mallarmé*, 108.

[7] Although 'dit' bears the trace of a past historic.

content of the other: 'Hyperbole' / 'trop grand glaïeul', 'livre de fer vêtu' / 'sépulchre', 'grimoire' / 'parchemins', 'j'installe [...] / L'hymne' / 'Elle dit le mot', 'Te lever' / 'Anastase'. Thus, we are twice told, excess finds expression and resurrection in a rectangular block of ancient text—which, as we shall see, is as good an account of the poem as any. This arrangement has been described as 'une structure en V',[8] but it might be more appropriate to the symbols of the poem (as we shall also see) were we to envisage this structure for the moment as a triumphal arch or 'arc-en-ciel', of which the apogee comes between 'sépara' and 'Gloire'. More importantly, the element of repetition in the reflected beginning and end of the poem is reminiscent of the repetition that is rhyme itself, a sound at once similar and different. Indeed one might say that by its combination of sequence and circularity, or of narrative and 'music', 'Prose' figures that 'dyadic' aspect of rhyme which is 'dramatized' in 'L'Après-midi d'un faune': the rhyme-word which moves forward and 'sighs' after new couplings, and its rhyme pair which harks back and repeats with chaste fidelity. This dual nature of rhyme is itself perhaps evoked in the double sense of the word 'Prose': at once (etymologically) 'prorsa oratio', or 'discours qui va en droite ligne, sans inversion' (Robert), and a Latin hymn sung during Mass between the Epistle and the Gospel.

After the heraldic dyad of 'Hérodiade', the nymphs of 'L'Après-midi d'un faune', and the rhyming cross of 'Plusieurs Sonnets', it comes as no surprise that 'Prose' is a poem about rhyme. Once more, as we shall see, the central issues of homophony and polysemy are to the fore, but this time also the history of rhyme is evoked. For when did rhyme begin? Not in ancient Greek or Latin verse, where it is an occasional and optional feature, but in 'proses': those medieval Latin hymns almost always composed (like 'Prose' itself) in octosyllabic quatrains arranged in 'rimes croisées'.[9] Following this precedent, rhyme became a defining feature of French verse, and one wonders if Mallarmé's poem may not have sprung originally (like the versification of his mature sonnets) from a reading of Banville's *Petit Traité de poésie française* (1872). This work is a eulogy of rhyme, and indeed Banville extols it in floral terms: 'Dans la versification française, quand la Rime est ce qu'elle doit être, tout fleurit et prospère.'[10] For Banville, as for theorists before and after him, rhyme is the indispensable element in verse: 'la Rime est l'outil, le moyen universel du vers.'[11]

---

[8] Marchal, *Lecture de Mallarmé*, 108.

[9] Larousse, 'prose'.

[10] *Petit Traité de poésie française* (Paris, 1872), 88.

[11] *Petit Traité*, 69. See also pp. 47, 48: '*l'imagination de la rime* est, entre toutes, la qualité qui constitue le poète'; '*on n'entend dans un vers que le mot qui est à la rime*, et ce mot est le seul qui travaille à produire l'effet voulu par le poète'. Cf. Wilhem Tenint, *Prosodie de l'école moderne* (Paris, 1844), 101: 'La rime est le seul générateur du vers français, et cela est si vrai que les poètes du seizième siècle faisaient consister dans la rime toute la beauté du vers.' For Tenint, rhyme is not a mnemonic device but derives from an innate 'sentiment musical' (p. 85):

Here, on the eve of the advent of *vers libre* (in 1886), Mallarmé publishes a poem which foregrounds rhyme more than any other poem he ever wrote.[12] With its heavy preponderance of 'rimes riches' and wilful cultivation of 'rimes léonines' and 'rimes équivoques', 'Prose' is a celebration of rhyme; and with the insistent homophones woven into every quatrain, it may more generally be called a hymn to sound. The 'lieu' of this poetic display is a 'son site', in which 'son regard' produces 'son extase'. Malcolm Bowie speaks of 'a self-generating verbal universe',[13] and indeed the 'île' upon which the flowers are located seems to spring from language itself (from the line 'Ils savent s'il a bien été'). By such means the poem demonstrates how homophony 'creates' an alternative world of multiple meanings, the polysemic excess that is symbolized by 'La famille des iridées'.

Where once, in his pursuit of beauty, Mallarmé had chosen Venus as his prey (in 'Hérodiade' and 'L'Après-midi d'un faune'), here it is Iris, the Greek divinity and messenger of the gods, the female equivalent of Hermes, god of alchemy. Already celebrated as the ideal of female beauty in seventeenth-century verse,[14] she connotes by her name many of the principal 'threads' of this text. Traditionally adorned with the seven colours of the rainbow, she here manifests herself in the mirrored prism of this divided, fourteen-stanza poem—in which each half reaches 'up' to the climax of 'Gloire' not only as the right- or left-hand curve of a rainbow or triumphal arch but in the mirrored shape of a hyperbola: 'a plane curve consisting of two separate, equal and similar, infinite branches, formed by the intersection of a plane with both branches of a double cone' (*OED*). Through its ocular meaning, 'iris' also suggests the bifocal gaze of poet and sister ('Nous promenions notre visage'[15]), a kind of 'double sight' ('de vue et non de visions') to match the dyadic character of rhyme and the 'hyperbolic' structure of this poem. And, of course, there are irises: tall thin flags, flowering under a summer sun and rising like this visually long and slender poem against the white, sun-drenched background of a 'page' or 'paysage'.[16] Tallest of all is the gladio-

cf. Banville, *Petit Traité*, 4–5, 115; also Louis Becq de Fouquières, who argues in his *Traité général de versification française* (Paris, 1879) that rhyme satisfies an aural need to note a pattern of recurrence: 'Pour obtenir cet effet, il est indispensable que la fin de chaque vers détermine une vibration identique du tympan ou une suite de vibrations se reformant suivant une même combinaison' (pp. 19–20). At the end of the century, Victor Delaporte's *De la rime française* provides a witty, if conservative, defence of rhyme, which he dates back to the 'proses' of the 11th cent. (p. 44) and not the 12th cent. as suggested by Littré in the preface (of June 1877) to his *Dictionnaire de la langue française* (see *De la rime française*, 62–3).

[12] Malcolm Bowie's reading of the poem in *Mallarmé and the Art of Being Difficult* (Cambridge, 1978) includes an analysis of the poem's rhyming wordplay: see especially pp. 53–78. The importance of rhyme in the poem has also been stressed by Paul Bénichou, 'La "Prose pour des Esseintes"', *Saggi e ricerche di letteratura francese*, 27 (1988), 27–58 (40–1).

[13] *The Art of Being Difficult*, 62.

[14] See Littré, 'iris'.

[15] 'Visage' itself derives etymologically from the Latin 'videre' (= to see).

[16] Both words derive from Latin 'pango'.

lus, its name deriving from its sword-like leaves (from Latin 'gladius').[17] Thus the floral beauty implicit in a '*Prose*' has here been conferred upon 'La famille des iridées', and the poem becomes the abundant display of proliferating beauty, a quasi-heraldic 'sol des cent iris'.[18]

As always in Mallarmé, beauty is linguistic; and so the climactic moment of the poem is reached in the clinching, four-syllable rhyme of 'désir, Idées' / 'des iridées'. This contingent feature of the French language rises to meet the challenge (or 'devoir') of the poetic attempt to figure beauty in language. Announced as a 'Gloire', which takes up the first rhyme of the poem and proclaims the coming rhyme as a piece of sacred music (or Gloria), this extended homonym encompasses Mallarmé's poetic art in its entirety. For what is his ambition (or 'désir') but to create 'Idées', the 'rythme entre des rapports' which is his definition of music. And these very words themselves demonstrate such 'music': does not each pole of his endeavour contain the word 'dé', that contingency which is both his enemy and his friend? do not the aural and literal symmetries of the homonymic phrase (/ɛ/ /i/ /i/ /ɛ/: d, s, r, d, s) suggest the mirror-structure of his 'hyperbola' and of rhyme itself? and does not the capital 'I' aurally recall the first syllable of the poem while visually reproducing the iris-like shape of the poem on the page? Because of the elaborate rhyme, the principal referent of 'La famille des iridées' is the verbal kinship between 'désir' and 'idées', and the hundred irises of beauty are first and foremost the potential 'family' relationships which exist within and between words. Indeed, as we shall see, it is just such a family relationship—of 'je' and a 'sister'—which creates the poem.

'Désir' derives from the Latin 'desirare', meaning to regret the absence of, and 'idée' comes from the Greek verb for 'to see' ('idein'). Thus the two words 'désir' and 'Idées' are combined not only within this rhyme but within the poem as a whole, since 'Prose' represents the filling of an empty space with 'visual sound', the written record of a speech act. For the 'je' in the poem is the poet as the voice of poetic language itself, the poet as the desire for expression.[19] In that the 'Idées' are said to satisfy his 'long désir', then the initial address to hyperbole may be understood as the desire that from the memory-bank of language an abundance of linguistic possibilities should in triumph (a)rise, like the sun in the sky or the waters of a flood:

[17] Noted by Austin, 'Mallarmé and the *Prose pour des Esseintes*', 208 n. 18. Seeking to account for the presence of lilies in 'Prose', Austin also notes that the 'fleur de lis', a corruption of 'fleur de Louis', is an 'Iris pseudacorus'. He observes also that the largest gladiolus is a 'gladiolus byzantinus', which for him connects the flowers with the Byzantine elements in *A rebours* and the Byzantine names 'Anastase' and 'Pulchérie' (see p. 212).

[18] In heraldic terms 'sol' is the 'ground' of the shield. Cf. also the use of 'vêtu' (l. 4), which perhaps connotes the structure of the quatrain (see Littré, 'vêtu', 5°: 'Se dit d'un écu rempli d'un carré posé en losange, dont les quatre pointes touchent les bords de l'écu').

[19] Notwithstanding Marshall C. Olds, *Desire Seeking Expression: Mallarmé's 'Prose pour des Esseintes'* (Lexington, Ky., 1983).

hom. 'Te lever, eau.'[20] This rising shall occur in the here and now of octosyllabic verse (hom. 'au jour d'huit'), in which hyperbolic language can take the form of a sacred book of spells, a 'grimoire'. Potentially gibberish (one sense of 'grimoire'), language can be grey (or non-iridescent) and made of goat-hair. Meaning 'mohair' (the white hair of Angora goats) and serving as the first rhyme of the poem, 'moire' recalls the 'caprice' of the 'Ouverture' and the 'goat-logos' of 'L'Après-midi d'un faune' and thus symbolizes the capricious contingency of language (the 'mémoire', or linguistic resources, of the poet). But in the sense of a shimmering, watered textile, 'moire' also symbolizes the way in which the 'white hair' of the 'espaces blancs' are woven into rippling textuality by the grey moire of the printed words and of the typeface by which both page and text combine to leave their mark: 'un livre de fer vêtu.'[21]

At the heart of the word 'grimoire' are both (hom.) 'rime' and 'moi', the agent and instrument of the poem's creation. In the present this 'moi', or 'je/jeu', is installing—with knowledge and patience—this hymn (or 'Prose') of non-physical (and witty) hearts (and choirs). The 'lieu' in which he is installing it is 'l'œuvre de ma patience, / Atlas, herbiers et rituels': like an alchemist engaged upon a search for the philosopher's stone,[22] the poet is engaged upon the transmutation of language into some permanent record or celebration of (golden) beauty. How he came by the 'science' required to undertake such a transmutation is now related. 'Nous'—i.e. 'je' and the 'sœur'—were, as separate entities, sequentially presenting ('promenions') their visual appearance ('visage': i.e. as a poem) and comparing the 'maints charmes' of the 'sœur'. Anticipating the eventual 'vue' of the 'Idées' (themselves 'sights' or 'visual forms', the flickering images on the wall of Plato's cave), the third quatrain of 'Prose' suggests that 'je' and the 'sœur' were surveying the (poetic) scene or 'circonstances' in which beauty might be glimpsed.

Given that the 'sœur' has 'charmes' (perhaps the 'spells' to be found in a 'grimoire' of linguistic magic), and given that Littré defines 'sœur', *inter alia*, as a word which 'se dit de choses (du genre féminin) qui se répètent',[23] one begins to suspect that this 'sœur' may be rhyme itself. Only implicitly is she actually the sister of 'je', his companion in the discovery of beauty; more

---

[20] Cf. the rising rhythm of the fountain in 'Soupir' and the 'Ouverture' to 'Hérodiade'.

[21] On the use of 'moire' to mean also 'not the living sound of music but [...] its dead and silent "shape", that is [...] the wave form by which musical sound is transmitted', see Heath Lees, 'Mallarmé's *Moire*', *French Bulletin*, 51 (Summer 1994), 15. The relevance of this sense of 'moire', both here and in 'Hommage' (to Wagner), is unconvincingly disputed by Eileen Souffrin-Le Breton, 'Mallarmé and *la moire antique*' and Charles Chadwick, 'More on *Moire*', in *French Studies Bulletin*, 53 (Winter 1994), 16–18, and 55 (Summer 1995), 17–19 respectively.

[22] A meaning for 'ouvrage de patience' given by Littré (under 'patience', 4°). The rich associations with alchemy contained within 'Prose' are detailed by D. J. Mossop, *Pure Poetry: Studies in French Poetic Theory and Practice 1746 to 1945* (Oxford, 1971), 158–66.

[23] 'Sœur', 8°.

evidently she is *a* sister, like the sisterly nymphs to be found in the first version of 'L'Après-midi d'un faune', counterparts of the musical reeds. The additional connotation of 'religious sister' or 'nun', in any case appropriate in this sacred hymn, complements this dual notion of rhyme with the unitary connotation of virginal homophony (as in 'Hérodiade'), resplendent with reflexive beauty but severed from contact with the 'real' world, or 'paysage', of reference. As the symbol of rhyme, this is the 'sœur i' (cf. 'Ô sœur, y comparant les tiens'), one half of the 'i: paire' (cf. 'Hyperbole') which will play such a capital role in the 'glory' of 'désir, Idées' / 'des iridées'. It is important to remember that her charms are simply being compared, not necessarily *with* those of the landscape but rather perhaps with each other *within* the 'pa[ysa]ge'. She is the reflected [i] of 'Iris' herself, saved from 'inane' repetition only by the 'r' ('d'autorité') which splits the double 'i'.

The poetic process thus begins with the poet as writer (note the repetition of 'main' in ll. 10–11) being as yet unaware that rhyme, not he, will 'write' the poem: he and his 'instrument' are separate ('Nous fûmes deux, je le maintiens'). However, upon noting the 'comparable' 'charms' of rhyme, the project of writing, of 'authoring', at once becomes problematic: 'L'ère [hom. 'air', or song] d'autorité se trouble.' It becomes apparent (from a consideration of rhyme) that language can speak for itself and at random: 'Lorsque, sans nul motif, on dit.' The very word 'dit' 'provokes' 'midi' (and the 'half-said'), which 'spontaneous' process is continued in 'approfondit' as both 'je' and the sisterly rhyme unconsciously sink deeper into homophony. The 'terra firma' of a familiar 'paysage' is now replaced by a 'sound-site', the poem as a place of proliferating homophony and polysemy. Already hyperbole can be seen rising from the 'memory' of language' as univocity ('on dit') gives way to the 'cent iris' (later increased as 'La fa*mille* des iridées'). The 'or' in 'Lorsque' and the word 'sans' seem to lead on, respectively, to the golden sun of 'sol' (meaning 'ground' but connoting the Latin 'sun') and the 'cent' of 'cent iris'; while 'sans nul motif, on dit' sounds almost as though, in this curious 'sound-site', 'cent nuls mot[s] y font dits.' The poet and the unwitting sister that is rhyme are both without authority, but the 'cent iris' (precursors of the coming 'famille: désir/Idées') are certain that such a linguistic 'lieu' exists: 'Ils savent s'il a bien été.' This place has no name, at least no name that is to be found in the 'real' world of 'Été' (of summer sunshine, of the 'has been'), just as the golden trumpeting of real sunshine has no relevance to the symbolic 'midi' of this poem, or the transmuted gold of its language. Indeed 'trompette' even suggests a degree of trumpery compared with the authentic 'music' of this 'Prose'.

The era of univocity and 'authorial' control is past, and the etymological origin of 'autorité' in the Latin 'augere'='to augment'[24] now displays itself.

---

[24] Also noted by Olds, *Desire Seeking Expression*, 28.

Increase, or hyperbole, is the source, or author, of this poem. If language is positively heard ('Oui': cf. 'Ouï'), then an apparently clumsy, 'unpoetic' sentence like 'Ils savent s'il a bien été' can be the location for a heightened, poetic perception of linguistic possibilities. Here is an 'île' which the 'air', or song of this 'Prose', 'charge / De vue et non de visions': an isolated, defamiliarized linguistic unit which, far from offering a stimulus to any extravagant Romantic 'visions' of a referential or conventionally symbolic kind, simply presents itself to our 'ouïe' and our 'vue'. The letters a, l, and s whirl before our eyes, while the word 'syllabe' (in 's'il a bien') can be heard in this line of 'huit syllabes' or 'ouïe(s), syllabe(s)'.

As we have seen, the word 'iris' means more than, say, a yellow flower that blooms in summer ('L'or de la trompette d'Été'); it is the emblem of proliferating language, and 'we' (the poet as 'je / jeu' and his rhyme) can but observe its spreading display ('Toute fleur s'étalait').[25] The word-flower grows in magnitude independently of the linguistic agency of 'je' or the 'sœur': 'Sans que nous en devisions'—without their speaking and without their orderly devising.[26] Indeed it begins to assume the inscrutable air of some heraldic device (the 'devise' concealed within the punning rhyme 'de visions'/'devisions'), as though the page had been 'fleurdelisée' with cryptic inscriptions. As such these word-flowers are without dimension ('immenses'), stretching to infinity, their only boundaries or contour being a halo of light ('lucide'), the 'lacuna' (or lack of finitude) which sets them apart from the flowers in real gardens, or makes each 'fleur' 'l'absente de tous bouquets'. Yet, without the agency of 'nous', each word-flower adorned itself ('se para') in its own orderly fashion (etym. > 'ordinarius', 'ordo') and in a manner which, as the word itself suggests, is deceptively straightforward and far from ordinary ('ordinaire-ment').

This halo, or 'gloire', of boundless signifying is a paradoxical phenomenon, like rhyme itself that sets terminal limits to what is in fact an ubiquitous feature of language. The glorious climactic rhyme of 'désir, Idées'/'des iridées' displays rhyme spreading backwards over half the line, threatening to engulf the entire text in a flood of homophony. The 'je' is carried aloft in the rhythm of exaltation, as though 'Prose' here were celebrating the 'Exaltation de la Sainte Croix', the elevation of its sacred crossed rhymes upon which language shall be crucified and rise again at the last ('Anastase'). 'Je', the voice of the poem itself, delights to see this polysemic family rise to the challenge constituted by its duty to 'install' a hymn; while the 'sœur' of rhyme remains unmoved. Still sensibly restricted

[25] Cognate with 's'installer', 's'étale' suggests that the word-flowers are setting out their own stall of meanings, or singing from their own choir-stalls. The etymological link is noted by Olds, *Desire Seeking Expression*, 31.

[26] Deriving from 'dividere' and cognate with 'devise', 'deviser' originally meant to display in an organized manner (Robert). Cf. 's'étalait'.

to the tender embrace of line-endings ('sensée et tendre'), this form of homophony, though reputedly an agent of proliferating linguistic display (hom. 'censée étendre') carries its 'sound-sight' ('son regard') no further than a smile, the enigmatic, scarcely parted lips of terminal rhyme. The poem, on the other hand, now pursues its ancient purpose by listening to *and* understanding ('entendre') the smiling 'son regard' of this still unwitting sister.

The poem has reached the point of 'self-knowledge' where it can begin to assert its own validity. Its objective is to 'install' 'L'hymne des cœurs spirituels', a sacred musical poem which will satisfy heart, mind, and spirit. The inherent playfulness of rhyme and its proximity to that maligned form of wordplay, the pun, should not obscure the potentially profound message which rhyme offers to any language-user, namely the naïvety of 'intentional' expression and the overwhelming, perhaps uncontrollable polysemy spawned by homophony. Rhyme points to sound and sense being in conflict, as though the meanings in 'désir, Idées' / 'des iridées' were not a family but parties to a lawsuit. But 'Prose' now asserts, in the face of this wit and litigious spirit displayed by rhyme, that the poem's 'midday' silence, like that of the sister, is caused by an excess of sense, not a vacuum of pointless punning or the collapse of language into mere sound. It is not the 'litige' of rhyme, but the interconnectedness of word-flowers which temporarily defeats the controlling powers of both the poem and rhyme. Being 'multiples', the 'many-folded' product of arithmetical and 'hyperbolic' increase, these 'lis' (and 'plis') of polysemy are joined by and grow from a 'tige' which is so long (like desire itself) that it defies all sense of proportion, all geometric ratios ('raisons') by which it might be brought under 'rational' control. Deriving from 'tibia', meaning flute before it meant a bone in the leg, this 'tige' represents the 'musical' 'rythme entre des rapports' that is the 'Idée' itself.

This 'midday' silence that precedes the 'birth' of a poem is, then, due to the daunting prospect of linguistic richness and not to any belief that the 'lieu' of such word-flowers, the 'île', did not exist. The 'pa[ysa]ge' exists, and the text is an island within/upon it, surrounded by 'espaces blancs'. As the ambiguous syntax of ll. 41–8 demonstrates, the 'flowers' of language to be found there may grow so profusely from the stalk of syntax (or grammatical interconnection) that their multiplicity defies reason. Given the duality of rhyme, and given the textual island and the 'flood' of hyperbole invoked homophonically at the beginning of the poem ('Te lever, eau') and again in the tenth stanza ('Eau! sache l'Esprit de litige'), 'la rive' may be read as a further symbol of rhyme: for, like a bank, rhyme marks the boundary (like 'un lucide contour') between textual land and paginal water, between the island of signifying connections (the 'Idées') and the swirling currents of empty homophony. What is rhyme but a 'son jeu monotone'? And where once it smiled (l. 35) and soon shall laugh (l. 53), rhyme might weep at the prospect that homophony is simply a lie, a forced pursuit of amplified sense ('A vouloir que l'ampleur arrive'). For example, if we hear 'attestés' as 'attester', as Mallarmé's 'floating', unpunctuated syntax here encourages us to do, then heaven and the map affirm indeed that no such land of word-flowers existed.

But no, rhyme is not a lament 'Que ce pays n'exista pas': instead the newly conscious poet/poem experiences 'étonnement' (etymologically, a cracking open, a fissuring, particularly of vaults or arches) to hear Heaven and the boundless map ('la carte / Sans fin') endlessly attested wherever his metrical feet (and insistent rejection of representation) happen to take him ('sur mes pas'). As the poet crosses from one bank of rhyme to the other, like Moses traversing the Red Sea, the uniform waters of homophony are parted, the resultant polysemy bearing witness at every step to an infinity of signification. Like Atlas (l. 8) bestriding the straits of Gibraltar, rhyme bears the heavens on its shoulders and looks out beyond the known world to the mysterious outer reaches of 'la carte / Sans fin'; and there, perhaps, the eyes of rhyme behold the lost continent of Atlantis,[27] an island resurrected from its oceanic grave. For, like Atlas, this poem is the son of Oceanus and Iris: fathered by the circular river (of silence and the blank page) that surrounds the known world (as figured on any ancient 'mappa mundi'), and born of Iris, the rainbow that appears when the flood abates ('s'écarte') and herself the bearer of 'hermetic' messages. Here the poem stands, gigantically, a long 'tige' of interconnected word-flowers stretching from 'sol' to 'Ciel' and from head to foot ('attestées', 'pas'),[28] separating the 'espace blanc' preceding it from the 'espace blanc' that follows, and thus saving the 'univers' of silence from collapsing into an 'inauthentic' oneness— '(Nous fûmes deux, je le maintiens)'.

The final two quatrains now describe the 'birth' of the poem's voice. The etymologically 'non-speaking' 'enfant' 'abdicates' or speaks itself down from its 'son extase', that ecstatic 'sound-sight' of linguistic plenitude (the word-flowers on the island) previously beheld in silence by 'je' and the rhyme-sister. As we approach the end of the poem, we learn how finally this poem came into existence. Having proceeded through the 'pa[ysa]ge' of the poem, rhyme has acquired the 'science' necessary for speech. It is 'docte', and now, like the 'je' who 'installe, par la science', 'Elle dit le mot: Anastase!' Meaning 'resurrection', 'Anastase' sounds at once like a command and an 'exalted' observation that language should be salvaged from silence and 'born' to endure for ever in written form. Yet so tenuous is

---

[27] Cf. Olivier Dumas, 'Mallarmé, Platon et "La Prose pour des Esseintes"', *Revue des sciences humaines*, 126 (1967), 255.

[28] Since the 'atlas' is the top bone of the spine, these lines of verse may again be envisaged as 'vertèbres' (as in 'Quand l'ombre menaça...').

the possibility of verbal beauty that even this 'speech act' (of 'Anastase!' and 'Prose' itself) seems like a pre-emptive move before the sepulchre, or tomb of dead representation (and which is 'Prose' also), should laugh (with the gaping lips of rhyme) to bear the name Beauty, or 'Pulchérie'. Being phonetically 'indécidable',[29] this inscription upon the poetic tomb is unsayable and in any case obscured by the largest 'iridée' of all, the 'trop grand glaïeul'. Perhaps polysemy (symbolized by the spreading word-flowers, of which the 'glaïeul' is the largest) is so 'hyperbolic' that the very purpose of the poet's invocation has been defeated. Has beauty been obscured by an excess of signification?

Yet if we read the poem again as a kind of 'Discours de la méthode' (the etymology of 'méthode' being 'meta hodos', or 'par chemins', and the whole poem being a demonstration of 'hyperbolic doubt'[30]), that is to say, if we read 'Prose' in the light of the poem's own account of its genesis, it is plain that every effort has been made to 'order' this polysemy into patterns of significance. Four things have 'happened': a place has been discovered, flowers have been seen, a resurrection is proclaimed, and something has been said. How shall these events be satisfactorily recorded? By 'Atlas, herbiers et rituels', and a 'grimoire / Dans un livre de fer vêtu'.

First, and most evidently, 'Prose' is a 'rituel': at once a 'sacred' linguistic ceremony (like the 'élévation' of 'Ses purs ongles...') and the written record of how such a ceremony is performed, both a 'memorial' service, celebrating and bringing once more to mind the dead powers of language, and a book of liturgy, recalling the detailed procedures of the sacraments. Further, like some piece of ecclesiastical architecture, the poem offers words a 'stalle', each with its own misericord (one meaning of 'patience'); and from these octosyllabic choir-stalls is sung a 'hymne', a Gloria, and, if not a 'Dies irae', then certainly a triumphant 'désir / Idées'. The hymn itself, in fourteen quatrains of 'rimes croisées', is like a 'hyperbolic' sonnet recording the fourteen stations of the Cross leading to crucifixion and a glorious resurrection ('Anastase').

Similarly, this poem is comparable with a 'herbier': as both a herbarium and a herbal, a collection of plants and a book containing descriptions of plants, 'Prose' is at once a collection of 'word-flowers' and a written record of their linguistic properties—an (hom.) 'air biais' indeed. As for 'Atlas', not only is the poem 'born' of Iris, it also seeks to chart the alternative world of poetic expression, calculating the 'co-ordonnés' of this linguistic Island of the Blest. Concealed within this 'œuvre de ma patience' is a homophonic 'mappe', a 'mappemonde' by which the 'lieu' of the poem may be situated by the 'travelling' eye of the reader. The 'île' to which it leads is a place of

---

[29] [pylkeRi] or [pylʃeRi]? See Bowie, *Mallarmé and the Art of Being Difficult*, 69.

[30] The doubt of 'des cartes'/Descartes? Of Descartes whose analytic geometry refined the measurement of conic sections (and their hyperbolas)? Whose study of optics dealt particularly with the prism and the spectrum (or rainbow)?

'ecstase', of standing outside the 'normal' realms of earth and sky, a place of plenitude which is difficult to 'install' on the printed page. Writing thus becomes a form of cartography, whereby the three-dimensional is inscribed (with inevitable distortion) within a two-dimensional medium. For 'Prose' was published exactly 300 years after the first volume of *Atlas*, the collection of maps by Gerardus Mercator (1512–94) in which the globe is represented according to Mercator's so-called Projection. On these maps a line of constant bearing crosses all meridians at the same angle, and thus they enabled seamen to plot their course more easily. In 'Prose' Mallarmé's quatrains are like the quadrants, or 'quarts de cercle' (cf. hom. 'quart, j'installe, par la science'), by which a mariner takes his bearings, and his octosyllabic lines like 'octants', measuring angles of incidence of forty-five degrees between heavenly bodies. Such are the 'biais' in this 'air biais' (of 448 'syllabes'), which thereby anticipates the geometrical and arithmetical play of 'Un coup de Dés'.

Central to the cartography of both Gerardus Mercator and his (unrelated) successor Nicolaus Mercator (*c.*1619–87) was the geometry of the hyperbola. An expert in the theory of Mercator's Projection, the second Mercator published a *Cosmographia* and an *Astronomia* (both in 1651). In 1666 he claimed to be able to prove the identity of 'the Logarithmical Tangent-line beginning at 45 deg.' with the 'true Meridian-line of the Sea-Charte [i.e. Gerard Mercator's map)',[31] and in 1668 he published his *Logarithmotechnia* in which he took 'the St. Vincent-Sarasa hyperbola-area model to establish, independently of Hudde and Newton, the series expansion'.[32] Or, as Littré has it under 'Hyperbole': 'il donnait, par une suite ou série infinie, la quadrature de l'hyperbole'. What better description of Mallarmé's handling of polysemy within this 'cartographic' poem? By 'quadrature' is meant the expression of an area bounded by a curve, especially a circle, by means of an equivalent square. Thanks to the 'quartered' shield of his poetic page, the composer of these quatrains has managed, in combining circularity and sequence, to square not only the hyperbole but the circle. In 'L'hymne d'équerres spirituels' perhaps?

This binary poem thus figures both two hemispheres and a union of heaven and earth ('tout le Ciel et la carte / Sans fin attestés'): and the parenthesis around 'Nous fûmes deux, je le maintiens' begins to look like a sundered globe. Yet thanks to the etymology of 'climat' (= angle of incidence to the sun) we are reminded in the final quatrain that this 'sepulcre' of language is situated beyond the solar system ('Sous aucun climat') in the alternative 'univers' of poetry. 'Prose' is the offspring not of the 'real' but of sound itself ('son' is its 'aïeul'). A 'son site' seeming to combine the mascu-

---

[31] Quoted in the article on Nicolaus Mercator in *Dictionary of Scientific Biography*, ed. C. G. Gillispie (16 vols, New York, 1970).
[32] Ibid.

line and feminine (hom. 'une "il"') of alternating rhyme and of human procreation, it is ploughed into furrowed 'vers' by a 'ritte tue, Elle'—the 'Elle [qui] dit le mot'.[33]

Finally 'Prose' is a 'grimoire / Dans un livre de fer vêtu'. The surface upon which this poem is displayed is the white 'page' or 'paysage' of the printed book, and the white, 'watery' expanses lapping the shores of the island of word-flowers are themselves bound on both sides by a 'rive' (the technical term for the edge of a piece of paper). The text itself consists of 'tiges', or the shanks of printed characters, which connect the multiple, 'lily-white' configurations of 'espace blanc' and lend them significance. The reference to 'parchemins' suggests the poetic texture of 'Prose' itself, since parchment, sometimes made from goat-skin, is the 'fleur' (meaning 'hair-side' of any animal skin) that lies beneath the mohair of interwoven sound in this 'grimoire'. One might even imagine the 'ideal' 'Prose' printed on 'papier-parchemin' in 'format atlantique': a single folio sheet folded in two. One can just imagine the fourteen stanzas rising and falling across its double-sheet like a rainbow or some triumphal arch, or like the sun rising from the sea and then setting (as it might be, in 'l'extrême Occident') after pausing briefly at its zenith (between stanzas 7 and 8) over this island of linguistic beauty.

Like a magic spell found in a 'grimoire', 'Prose' summons up the hyperbolic potential of language from the grave of oblivious usage. So manifold is the subsequent 'sound-sight' of linguistic plenitude that the agent and instrument of verse are stunned into silence, but at the end the 'unspoken' finds a voice and proclaims a resurrection of 'writable' words (the 'enfant' utters a 'mot' and not a 'parole'). The 'grimoire' thus becomes a 'grammar' (etym. 'art de lire et d'écrire les lettres'),[34] at once a guide to how the poem was written and to how it might be read.

In these ways 'Prose' ceases to be enigmatic and offers up its meanings in a resurrection of significance from the empty sepulchre of homophony. It proclaims 'Anastase' in the face of the laughing lips of rhyme; and the 'son site' is finally endowed with a name, 'Pulchérie'. The legitimacy of this name has been in doubt: the authoredness of univocal language has been disrupted by the turbulence ('se trouble') of homophony and polysemy, by language that seems to speak without motive or motif in a nameless 'son site'. But the litigious dispute is at an end, and the moment of hyperbolic doubt as to the existence of such a place has given way to an assertive naming: the sepulchre bears the name of beauty, not because beauty is departed but because this poem is a rectangular, quasi-three-dimensional container[35] of dead reference from which Beauty has risen like the 'fleur' or

---

[33] 'Ritte: charrue à soc recourbé' (Robert); cf. 'versoir'.
[34] Robert, 'grammaire'.
[35] Analogous with a tomb or with the recess (also called 'sépulcre') within a church wall in which the sacrament and the crucifix are placed from Maundy Thursday till Easter Sunday.

sublimate that results from (al)chemical purification, or like an 'exaltation', this being the term used for the increased activity in a substance which has been purified.[36] Language has been turned into the gold of heightened significance,[37] and the flowers of a new rhetoric decorate the tomb wherein it lies. At the heart of the '*Gloire*', the halo of illumination created by the poetic 'vers', resides a 'loi': the mysterious law of rhyme,[38] and a logic of interconnection by which the apparently disparate images of this poem are joined in two reflexive clusters of seven quatrains like a mirrored Pleiades, the seven daughters of Atlas.

'Only connect': 'Pulchérie' is the name of the 'Prose', and in the last quatrain it becomes the seal of authority and approval (hom. 'Pulchérie! Cachet') placed upon the parchment scroll of this sacred text. Let polysemy 'speak' out in the proliferating word-flowers: hom. 'Parle, trop grand glaïeul!', for the 'plume' (with its 'tige') shall be mightier than the gladiolus. And thanks to rhyme Pulchérie herself shall have the last, syllabic laugh: 'la Beauté y rit', 'la Beauté, Iri[s]'. The penultimate rhyme of the poem is dead, but its meaning shall be resurrected in the anastatic glory of this 'Prose'— 'par ouï-dire', in 'L'hymne des [chœurs] sp*ir*ituels'. At the outset 'Hyperbole' is invoked, etymologically a 'throwing over', a 'throwing to extremes': and literally, at the apogee of the poem, an 'i-paire' has been tossed up in an arching curve of rhyme, the 'rainbow' rhyme on 'désir, Idées'. Here is the moment of linguistic triumph, the centre of this 'mappemonde' as Omphale (cf. 'Triomphalement') was once the centre of the Delphic world, the conic (philosopher's) stone and 'hyperbola-containing' 'site' of the Pythian oracle.

Thus, as desired by the poet, (hom.) 'Hyperbole [...] / [...] ne s'est tue': the word itself has 'thrown up' this poem in an apparent 'cast' of contingency, and yet the 'i-paire' governs all, from 'iris' to 'sœur y' to (hom.) 'la femme i: iridées'. At the same time the poem provides almost a literal exemplification of the dictionary definition of 'hyperbole': 'Figure de style qui consiste à mettre en relief une idée "au moyen d'une expression qui la dépasse"' (Robert)—except that this 'dépassement' is here woven into 'Idées' by an act of supreme artistic control.

---

[36] Cf. 'Quelle soie aux baumes de temps': see above, Part IV, Ch. 1.

[37] Littré gives as one meaning of 'iris' the sparks which fly during the assaying of metal.

[38] Cf. 'Solennité': 'Voilà, constatation à quoi je glisse, comment, dans notre langue, les vers ne vont que par deux ou à plusieurs, en raison de leur accord final, soit *la loi mystérieuse de la Rime*, qui se révèle avec la fonction de gardienne et d'empêcher qu'entre tous, un usurpe, ou ne demeure péremptoirement: en quelle pensée fabriqué celui-là! peu m'importe, attendu que sa matière discutable aussitôt, gratuite, ne produirait de preuve à se tenir dans un équilibre momentané et double à la façon du vol, identité de deux fragments constitutifs remémorée extérieurement par une parité dans la consonance. [Note de Mallarmé: Là est la suprématie de modernes vers sur ceux antiques formant un tout et ne rimant pas; qu'emplissait une bonne fois le métal employé à les faire, au lieu qu'ils le prennent, le rejettent, deviennent, procèdent musicalement: en tant que stance, ou le Distique.]' (OC, 333–4; my emphasis).

Later Mallarmé will go even further with such verbal ballistics, and that other 'throw' of language', 'Un coup de Dés', will demonstrate the extraordinary potential of his 'musical' art to give substance to his quip: 'tout, au monde, existe pour aboutir à un livre.'[39] For the moment we can say that 'Prose' offers the very clearest illustration of that other famous comment: 'Je dis: une fleur! et, hors de l'oubli où ma voix relègue aucun contour, en tant que quelque chose d'autre que les calices sus, musicalement se lève, idée même et suave, l'absente de tous bouquets.'[40] Here his flower-poem rises, resplendent with many a visual and audible 'charme' (etym. 'carmen'= song), its tall 'tige' (or bole) supporting a ramification of 'Idées' like some genealogical tree of linguistic kinship. It rises 'musically': that is to say, like the muse herself—'une enfant' born of memory and suckled by 'la Gloire' on the teats of rhyme, a 'docte sœur'.[41] And it rises (iris-like) as the 'Idée': a 'rythme entre des rapports', the visual form which poetic text lends to sound, and the aural and visual coherence which poetic art brings to the chaotic profusion of linguistic 'virtualités', in short a piece of Mallarméan 'music': 'l'hymne, harmonie et joie, comme pur ensemble groupé dans quelque circonstance fulgurante, des relations entre tout.'[42]

Like all his poems, 'Prose' celebrates the 'mystère'[43] of language: and here the celebration is specifically likened to a hymn heard during the Gradual, that part of the Mass sung from the steps leading to the altar (a gradual being also the book which contains such hymns). 'Prose' is thus Mallarmé's own 'Gradus ad Parnassum',[44] a handbook of poetic craft which both enacts and records how the contingent features of language may be so wrought that even the diaeresis which crowns the poem's final homophony—'aïeul', 'glaïeul'—may come to seem like the eyes of rhyme herself.

[39] 'Le Livre, instrument spirituel', OC, 378.
[40] 'Crise de vers', OC, 368.
[41] See Larousse under 'Muse', where the word is said to derive either from Greek 'mnaô' (to remember) or 'mainô' (='penser, s'exalter, désirer': my emphases), and where it is recounted that in one version of the Greek myth the Muses, as daughter of Mnemosyne (or memory), were suckled by 'Euphêmé ou la Gloire'. Meaning 'celle qui dit des paroles de bon augure', 'Euphêmé' (and thus the 'Gloire' in 'Prose') is the opposite of the 'blasphème' mentioned in 'Une dentelle s'abolit'.
[42] 'Le Livre, instrument spirituel', OC, 378.
[43] Cf. Larousse, where the alternative (but inaccurate) etymology of 'myein' (> 'mystère') is proposed for 'muse'.
[44] The title of a dictionary of Latin prosody published in 1702, which then became, as simply 'gradus', the term used for any poetic dictionary or manual.

4

The Song of the Siren:
'A la nue accablante tu' (1892–1894)

DU FOND D'UN NAUFRAGE.
('Un coup de Dés')

By a curious coincidence Mallarmé wrote sixteen sonnets in octosyllabic metre, eight in the Petrarchan form and eight in the Shakespearean form. By a further curious coincidence he wrote sixteen Shakespearean sonnets, comprising one (his first) in alexandrines ('La chevelure vol d'une flamme...'), seven in heptasyllabics and—as stated—eight in octosyllabics. Had death not intervened in 1898, would he have written further sonnets or might he have sought to preserve this apt numerical distribution? One wonders. What emerges clearly is that he used the Shakespearean form and the heptasyllabic line exclusively when writing in or for particular 'circonstances': as a contribution to a private album, to celebrate a baptism, upon a fan, etc. As such they represent a lower poetic register than the alexandrine, the octosyllabic, and the Petrarchan form of the sonnet.

As well as the 'non-sonnets' in octosyllabic metre ('Le Château de l'espérance', 'Sainte', and 'Prose (pour des Esseintes)'), we have already analysed Mallarmé's first published octosyllabic sonnet ('Quelle soie aux baumes de temps') and the so-called 'Triptyque'. Before proceeding to examine how Mallarmé sought to go beyond traditional versification in 'Un coup de Dés', it may now be appropriate to consider 'A la nue accablante tu'—the last octosyllabic sonnet to be written by Mallarmé which was not (like the last of all, 'Au seul souci de voyager') composed for a particular occasion or 'circumstance'. In particular it will illustrate how the very form of the octosyllabic sonnet serves to make punctuation superfluous and how, within it, spatial organization provides a powerful complement to syntactic relationships. As such, 'A la nue accablante tu' (with its solitary parenthesis) marks the culmination of an experiment with the octosyllabic sonnet which began with the unpunctuated 'M'introduire dans ton histoire'

(1886) and which was to prove an important source of the revolutionary prosody of 'Un coup de Dés'.

In his article on 'Mallarmé and the Octosyllabic Sonnet', David Scott has analysed the particular features of this form which are foregrounded by Mallarmé's poetic practice. He shows how the shortness of the line (and the poem) creates an effect of intense concentration; how the fragmentation of syntax consequent upon the brevity of the line produces 'cet isolement de la parole' described at the end of 'Crise de vers' and which—as, for example, in the penultimate line of 'A la nue accablante tu' ('Avarement aura noyé')— allows individual words to stand out new and strange, and how in parti- cular the pressure to use enjambement leads to words repeatedly giving onto gaps, onto the 'abîme' of silence; how the shortness of the line entails the swifter recurrence of rhyme and hence its greater dominance, which (as in 'Prose (pour des Esseintes)') may be part of a generalized insistence on the quasi-musical patterning of homophonies; and, lastly, how this pre-emi- nence of rhyme reinforces the 'vertical' axis in the poem in counterpoint with the more traditional horizontal or lateral movement of the verse (and the reader's eye). Indeed, as several other commentators have also noted, the rhymes in Mallarmé's poems in octosyllabic and heptasyllabic metre some- times seem to offer a lapidary summary of the poem in question: thus, in 'Une dentelle s'abolit', the rhymes tell us that 'lit—aime—dort/dore—sien— naître/être'.

For Scott, language in the octosyllabic sonnet thus assumes a cryptic quality, even reading on occasions like some mysterious inscription (e.g. 'Solitude, récif, étoile' in 'Salut', or 'Nuit, désespoir et pierrerie' in 'Au seul souci de voyager'); and a tension arises between this static inscrutability of the text and the dynamism of the reader's anxious search for meaning as this meaning is repeatedly deferred. The very appearance of the octosyllabic sonnet on the page—a slim block of text assailed on every side by the whiteness of the page—enhances this impression of a linguistic entity threa- tened with extinction, of meaning about to be submerged in the 'unanime blanc conflit' of swirling 'espaces blancs'. And the removal of punctuation further adds to this naked 'vulnerability' of language.

Mallarmé was evidently aware of both the visual and musical properties of the octosyllabic poem. In the preceding analyses we have seen the importance of the 'phalanx' in 'Sainte' as well as the poem's resemblance to a stained-glass window; and it has been possible to discern parallels with the organ and its 'buffet' and 'console' in 'Tout Orgueil...', with a vase stretching upwards to the ceiling in 'Surgi de la croupe...', and with a window and lace curtains in 'Une dentelle s'abolit'. Similarly, the four- teen stanzas of 'Prose (pour des Esseintes)' can be envisaged as a tall, slender iris rising 'triomphalement' from soil to sun, from 'solum' to 'sol'. The shadowy calligrams of 'Un coup de Dés' are already adumbrated.

While musical parallels are ubiquitous in Mallarmé's poetry, he does seem to envisage the octosyllabic line as especially 'lyric'. Where the twelve syllables of the alexandrine put him in mind, *inter alia*, of dice and the Zodiac, octosyllables suggest the octave; and musical instruments occur in almost all his octosyllabic poems. Already 'Le Château de l'espérance' features 'L'air d'un tambour', and of course 'Sainte'—inspired by a baptism on the day of St Cecilia, the patron saint of music—contains a plethora of instruments: 'viole', 'flûte', 'mandore', 'harpe'. 'Prose' is a hymn, in which a trumpet is heard (l. 20): while the 'Triptyque' echoes to the sound of the organ and the mandora.[1] At the same time, the sounds of the human 'instrument' seem to be particularly emphasized in his octosyllabic verse, be it the sob ('Le Château de l'espérance'), the laugh ('M'introduire dans ton histoire', 'Autre Éventail', 'Éventail (de Méry Laurent)', 'Pour un baptême'), or the orgasmic cry ('Quelle soie aux baumes de temps').

In all these ways, Mallarmé's octosyllabic poems thus provide us with what Elizabeth Barrett Browning in her sonnet 'The Soul's Expression' called

> [. . .] octaves of a mystic depth and height
> Which step out grandly to the infinite
> From the dark edges of the sensual ground!

—of which there is no better illustration than 'A la nue accablante tu'.

There exists a manuscript version of 'A la nue accablante tu' dating from the beginning of 1892, but the poem was not published until 1894 when it appeared in *Obole littéraire*. In 1895 it appeared again in *Pan*, a Berlin periodical, where it was accompanied by a drawing by the Belgian artist F. Khnopff.[2] This was the version seen by Tolstoy, who, in *What is Art?*, alludes to the poem as the epitome of the unintelligible in art.

Just as Mallarmé had insisted to Catulle Mendès some thirty years earlier on the need for his poems to be generously spaced in *Le Parnasse contemporain*,[3] so now he insisted on the visual impression to be created by his latest sonnet: 'Tout dépend de l'art avec lequel il est placé, bien dans son blanc le sonnet.' Moreover there is to be no question of printing it in manuscript (as earlier poems had been so reproduced in the *Poésies* of 1887): 'le vers gagne toujours à être imprimé—en caractères un peu forts ou d'aspect définitif.'[4] The words, it seems, shall stand as dark mounds of

---

[1] Cf. also the 'flûtes' in 'Feuillet d'album' and the ballet music implied in 'Billet'.

[2] See *DSM*, ii. 29–41.

[3] 'Je voudrais un *caractère assez serré*, qui s'adaptât à la condensation des vers, mais de *l'air entre les vers, de l'espace*, afin qu'ils se détachent bien les uns des autres, ce qui est nécessaire encore avec leur condensation. [. . .] je voudrais, aussi, un grand blanc après chacun, un repos' (*Corr.*, i. 212, Apr. 1866).

[4] Quoted in *OC* (BM), 396.

rock against the spume—or as flotsam from a shipwreck upon the raging foam.

For, in 'A la nue accablante tu', 'naufrage' is no mere analogy for the process whereby the 'vessel' of language ceases to 'convey' when stripped of its traditional representational function: the word itself, like so many other nodal words in Mallarmé's poetry, contains homophonically the very causes of this 'naufrage': namely, 'eau' and 'rage'. Deriving etymologically from 'navis' (ship) and 'frangere' (to break), the word 'naufrage' is an allegory of itself. And the poem appears to ask (with a silent and invisible question mark) whether the swirl of text and empty page betokens that some ship/vessel/linguistic container has been wrecked, or whether some siren has suddenly vanished beneath the waves. Or both? Perhaps a ship has foundered because its Master listened to the song of a siren, an elusive creature now slipping like a young mermaid beneath the waves.

Indeed do we not twice catch a fleeting glimpse of this 'infant flank' in the curves of the parenthesis in ll. 5–6, the only punctuation marks in this otherwise unpunctuated sonnet? Just as also, within this particular context, the diacritic mark of the circumflex evokes the masthead of the foundering ship—the circumflex which crowns the word 'mât' itself, which turns the letter 'i' into a calligrammatic mast (in 'abîme' and 'traîne') and which in 'même', 'suprême', and 'dévêtu' may even suggest the top of a mast disappearing beneath the waves. In such circumstances each acute and grave accent comes to resemble half a masthead, momentarily appearing above the raging sea, while 'n', 'u', and 't'—foregrounded by repetition in l. 1—seem to evoke respectively a ship capsized, a ship unmasted or the trough of a wave,[5] and a ship whose 'flank' has vanished beneath the water.

The sounds of the poem are similarly endowed with temporary necessity by their context: the simple vowel /o/ comes, by homophony, to connote water in 'échos', 'faute', and 'haute', while the planks ('les ais') of the broken ship—visually present in 'tu / Le sais, écume'—are repeatedly heard (e.g. in 'A même les échos', 'Suprême une entre les épaves', 'Tout l'abîme vain éployé').[6] The extraordinary aural and visual insistence on the letters 'a' and 'b' throughout the poem, especially in a single cluster ('ab' and 'ba'), comes to suggest the infantile babble ('baves' and 'babil' being also cognate) of an 'enfant' learning its abc,[7] while the sinuous 's' snakes its way through the poem like the eddying hair-like shreds of intratextual 'espaces blancs' before the 'sirène'—which it visually suggests—finally appears.

[5] See Bernard, *Mallarmé et la musique*, 123.

[6] Cf. the play on 'aux durs os entre les ais' in 'Un coup de Dés': see below, Part V, Ch. 2 (b).

[7] Claude Abastado notes also the frequency with which given consonants are repeated within the same line and how certain vowel sequences are repeated and/or modulated throughout the poem (both of which factors enhance this 'babble' effect): see his 'Stéphane Mallarmé: "A la nue accablante tu"', in Hartmut Stenzel and Heinz Thoma (eds), *Die französische Lyrik des 19. Jahrhunderts* (Munich, 1987), 221–2.

In this linguistic 'naufrage', therefore, words are seen and heard as 'rage': a rabid fury in which the white spaces are both spume ('écume') and the slobber (or drivel) of a poem foaming at the mouth like this watery abyss that is 'furibond' (with its waves rising in 'furious bounds'). Yet in the midst of this 'rage' (or 'folie' as 'Un coup de Dés' will call its own crazed discourse), perhaps it is possible to discern some meaning by clinging to the life-raft of syntax[8] and remembering to 'listen' to the special 'music' of Mallarmé. Thus a laboured paraphrase of the poem might run as follows:

what sepuchral shipwreck—which an ineffectual fog-horn kept silent from the over-whelming dark storm-clouds above (which resemble a sunken reef of basalt and lava) because its bass voice simply echoed slavishly and impotently around the dangerous rocks themselves—and you, spume, know the answer to this question but simply slobber over it—abolished/abolishes the mast which has been stripped of its sails, the single mast which looks like the number 1 and is the longest piece of wreckage tossing about in the waves: or concealed/conceals the fact that [or was it that] the whole empty, gaping abyss of the waves may—having failed to achieve destruction in the fury of its upward surge—greedily have drowned, amidst the white hair-like streaks of foam upon the dark water of the sea, the child-like flank of a siren (which might have been taken for an upturned hull).

In other words, does the shipwreck of language simply mean the death of the 'real', or may it perhaps afford the tantalizing glimpse of something beyond the real? Did the Faune see those nymphs? Can Hérodiade be observed by mortal eye? Yes, if beauty be seen and heard with the 'eyes' of rhyme. Conventional language, we may perhaps infer, is a 'trompe sans vertu': by connotation, a deceitful trumpet lacking the 'vers tu' which is Mallarmé's implicit 'music'. Messages proclaimed 'à son de trompe' are likely to deafen or to go unheard by the more discerning ear: language then will be a 'trombe',[9] and the poet one who merely spouts or expels hot air. Whereas this poem offers us the song of the 'siren': no less deceitful perhaps, being (as already suggested) a beguiling and mellifluous orchestration of linguistic sounds, but offering us beauty—and a warning! For a 'sirène', too, is a means of signalling danger by sound;[10] and this poem, by its own unique sign system, is signalling the dangers of univocal reading. Is not 'la nue' both a cloud and the naked siren herself? Is the siren not sliding into a sea that is measured in 'câbles' (cf. hom. 'câble: hantes-tu?'); and do we not hear the poet 'câblant': twisting the strands of language (like the hair of the siren, or the streaks of spume) into the measured cable-lengths of octosyllabic verse? By its ambiguous syntactic position, 'basalte' is both the rock

[8] Cf. 'Quel pivot [. . .] à l'intelligibilité? il faut une garantie—La Syntaxe' ('Le Mystère dans les lettres', OC, 385).

[9] For which Littré offers the Italian 'tromba' (= trumpet) as an etymological origin: cf. Bernard, Mallarmé et la musique, 123 n. 98.

[10] Robert dates this usage to 1888.

and the dark clouds above, both 'base' and 'alte' (cf 'haute' in l. 10), just as
the waves themselves effect at once a furious upward leap and an abysmal
engulfing down below.

And what of 'laves'? Do not the waves indeed *wash* over this lava, the
lava that is the solid residue of a former eruption? Is not the poem a verbal
residue after language has spewed forth?[11] If we look more closely at the
word 'aura', so boldly isolated in l. 13, we may note that as a noun it is the
Greek and Latin word for 'breeze' or 'breath of air' and that in ancient
physiology it meant a material but invisible emanation from a physical
object, the spark of life itself (*aura vitalis*), and (as *aura seminalis*) the
very seed from which all living beings spring. The shipwreck of language
has become a quasi-volcanic ejaculation of seminal fluid, and the 'aura' that
is drowned or submerged in the indistinguishable whiteness of the page
contains the embryo of a siren-child: 'faute / De quelque père', as we hear in
ll. 9–10, the sign itself is father to the song. 'La mer/mère', of course, is all
around; and the (Fallopian) 'trompe' along which the egg will travel to meet
the seed is now a 'trompe avec vertu'.

As so often in Mallarmé, if we begin to listen to the lesson of homophony,
to the reverberations of these 'échos esclaves',[12] it becomes possible to see
assertions of mastery and control, of salvation from the 'perdition' of end-
less dissemination. For is not this 'aura' itself an emission of the word
'avarement'? Are not the letters of 'aura' (allowing a Latin substitution of
v for u) submerged within it? As with the 'mandore' which 'sleeps' within
'Tristement dort', has not an emblem of the poet's means of 'salvation'
(hom. 'or a') risen from the depths of language itself, ready to be given
the poetic kiss of life? Language 'ment', is deceitful, only if we cannot hear it
properly, only if we lack the (Eustachian) 'trompe' of a more discerning ear
(another 'trompe avec vertu');[13] and in the midst of a wild tempest of wind,
this 'aura', this 'breath of life', is what will animate the mute ('enfant': etym.
non-speaking) flank of a siren. The rhymes that are the flank of this poem
shall sing their siren song.

In this way the poem apparently displays a foldless or unfolded waste
('vain éployé'); but at the same time its linguistic folds replace that which is
apparently lost. Instead of being mere pieces of random flotsam, these
linguistic 'épaves' are brought together by the poem: a fractured 'navis' is
reassembled and becomes a vessel once more, and the poem rises up on
the page like the mast itself, but with the sails of white page hanging

---

[11] Cf. the volcano of rhyme and the eruption of language in 'L'Après-midi d'un faune'.

[12] Cf. Boileau's famous comment in his 'Art poétique' that 'La rime est une esclave et ne doit
qu'obéir' (Chant premier, l. 30).

[13] Cf. the role of 'tympans' ('ear-drums' being one of this word's meanings) in the hearing
or understanding of 'La chevelure vol d'une flamme...' in 'La Déclaration foraine'
(OC, 283).

purposefully from its (implicit) 'vergue' and hoisted on the rigging of its versification.[14] Perhaps, like Ulysses, we must lash ourselves to its mast with the ropes (or cables) of this poetic text if we are not to be destroyed by the song of the siren and left floundering in the watery wastes of the unintelligible. For the poem is also the siren herself: a Petrarchan sonnet with the two breasts of its octave surmounting the forked tail of its sestet (the double 'que[ue]' being 'echoed' in the first tercet). The spume knows this secret—and reveals it: 'y baves', the 'y' that displays the very shape of the siren.

Like the 'licorne' in 'Ses purs ongles...', the 'sirène' is at once an agent of death and a means of renewal and salvation; and the poem as siren song both destroys everyday language and offers the prospect of poetic beauty. But such renewal is possible, such beauty manifest, only if we read between the lines—and the sides: like the 'ventre' of 'Une dentelle s'abolit', this poem seems to 'porter un enfant dans ses flancs', the fruit of dissemination. In this case it is not a 'mandore' which issues from the 'ventre' (though 'Avare*ment* *aura*' provides an echo of this[15]) but again a 'trompe avec vertu': for there, momentarily glimpsed and heard in the 'abîme' between the first and second lines of the poem, lie the 'drowning' vestiges of a 'tube' and a 'tuba' (originally, 'basse tube', or 'basse tuba', from the Latin 'tuba'= trumpet).[16] As a slim sonnet upon the page, this quasi-cylindrical 'tube de verre/vers' or 'tube acoustique' becomes a means of turning the 'breath of life' into music, an 'aura' into the instrumental 'enfant' of the 'tuba'. 'Tu', or gently whispered (cf. 'Tout bas'), this latest addition to the Mallarméan orchestra thus quietly proclaims its presence amidst the insistent clamour of the terminal rhymes, the 'échos esclaves', and enables 'A la nue accablante tu' to add its bass octaves to the high treble of the 'Triptyque'.

And finally—after the quadratic endeavour of 'Prose (pour des Esseintes)'—Mallarmé has once more squared the circle. For a 'trompe' is also that architectural feature—a pendentive—which allows the builder to reconcile the vertical surge of his pillars with the curved ribs of his vault.[17] The natural rock of language—with its own geological 'plis' and 'flancs'— has been fashioned by human artifice into the solid, basalt-black construct of a sonnet in which the curves of overarching rhyme spring from the four stanzaic 'bases' of which traditionally it is built. Thus does the 'naufrage' become 'sépulcral': fractured language reassembles to form a dark sepulchre

---

[14] Cf. 'Un coup de Dés': see below, Part V, Ch. 2 (*b*).

[15] Just as 'Basse de basalte' may connote a double-bass, or 'contrebasse', so that here again the four stanzas of the Petrarchan sonnet may (as in 'Une dentelle s'abolit') be analogous with the four strings of a musical instrument.

[16] Cf. also '*tu* / [...] *baves*' spanning the 'abîme' at the beginning of the second quatrain.

[17] Cf. 'Crise de vers': 'Tout devient suspens, disposition fragmentaire avec alternance et vis-à-vis, concourant au rythme total, lequel serait le poème tu, aux blancs; seulement traduit, en une manière, par chaque pendentif' (OC, 367).

haunted by hoary shapes (hom. 'hante, tu'; 'le si blanc cheveu'),[18] a solid block of black print wreathed in livid white, and a place where words shall rise again at the last to the sound of a trump—or, in this case, to the golden sound of a tuba.

[18] Cf. the 'maniaque chenu', or drowning Master, in 'Un coup de Dés'.

PART V

At Sixes and Sevens

'*Un coup de Dés jamais n'abolira le Hasard*' (1897)

selon un thyrse plus complexe [. . .]
('La Musique et les lettres')

In his letter to Verlaine on 16 November 1885, the so-called 'Autobiographie', Mallarmé maintains that he has spent the last twenty years trying to write 'un livre, tout bonnement, en maints tomes, un livre qui soit un livre, architectural et prémédité'. 'J'irai plus loin', he continues, 'je dirai: le Livre'. This book will provide 'L'explication orphique de la Terre, qui est le seul devoir du poète et le jeu littéraire par excellence: car le rythme même du livre, alors impersonnel et vivant, jusque dans sa pagination, se juxtapose aux équations de ce rêve, ou Ode.' 'Voilà', he continues, 'l'aveu de mon vice, mis à nu'; 'cela me possède'. And he hopes to succeed, not in finally producing 'cet ouvrage dans son ensemble (il faudrait être je ne sais qui pour cela!), mais à en montrer un fragment d'exécuté'.[1]

'Un coup de Dés jamais n'abolira le Hasard' is such a fragment, and it represents both the culmination of Mallarmé's work and his most innovative piece of writing. Like almost all of Mallarmé's poems after *Entre quatre murs*, it is essentially an allegory of its own creation, as its author makes explicit in his letter to Gide on 14 May 1897 where he describes what he has tried to achieve in this poem: 'car, et c'est là tout le point de vue [...] le rythme d'une phrase au sujet d'un acte ou même d'un objet n'a de sens que s'il les imite et, figuré sur le papier, repris par les Lettres à l'estampe originelle, en doit rendre, malgré tout quelque chose.'[2]

One can take this allegory at three different levels: versification, language, and human action. First, the poem 'displays' an attempt, following the advent of *vers libre* in the mid-1880s, to create order out of the prosodic chaos caused by the abandonment of traditional versification. Second, we see Mallarmé once more endeavouring to overcome linguistic contingency by creating a 'musical' structure. Third, and more generally, here is an account of human action which owes something to *Hamlet*; to be or not to be, to write or not to write, to throw or not to throw. The whole (hypothetical) event of 'Un coup de Dés' can be seen as an allegory of human enterprise, what the text calls 'le fantôme d'un geste'.

In order to elaborate these claims it will be necessary first to discuss the circumstances in which the text was composed and how it has since been received; then to describe some of the mathematical calculations upon which the poem is based, its radically new 'versification'; and finally to discuss some of the ways in which Mallarmé wrestles with linguistic con-

[1] OC, 662–3.   [2] Corr., ix. 172

tingency and tries to achieve 'authority'. This he does by an art of 'insinua-
tion', for when the text refers to itself at its centre as 'une insinuation simple
au silence', Mallarmé means more than one thing by the term 'insinuation'.
Most obviously he means what Robert defines as an 'Action ou manière
adroite, subtile de faire entendre une chose qu'on n'affirme pas positive-
ment': i.e. oblique discourse. From 'sinus'—meaning a 'fold-like cavity'—to
insinuate is to introduce by windings and turnings; and this sense has
obvious relevance to the obliquity of Mallarmé's own language, the appear-
ance of the words on the page, and the indirectness of the allegories which
may be traced through the poem.[3]

Less obviously, 'insinuation' is the legal term for an act of registration:
Littré, for example, defines this as the 'Inscription d'un acte sur un registre
faisant autorité, afin de donner authenticité à l'écriture'.[4] The term is
particularly applied to the registration of wills; and of course the text refers
also to a 'legs en la disparition'—the legacy that is the vanishing prosody of
rhyme and the alexandrine, or the legacy that is language itself, vanishing in
a whirl of 'dissémination'. The following analysis will show in what sense
'Un coup de Dés' is an insinuation of *text* into the *con*text of silence, and
also how it represents the inscription of a linguistic act in such a way as to
confer upon it some kind of authenticity, some kind of authority (or autho-
redness). The Mallarméan text is a testament (following the so-called
'death' of Mallarmé, the demise of the speaking subject and of the repre-
sentational function of poetic language): and in what the poem describes as
its 'conjonction suprême avec la probabilité' one can observe its endeavours
to be granted probate—or the 'preuve' referred to in *Igitur.*

---

[3] Cf. Larousse: 'Figure qui consiste à se concilier la faveur des auditeurs par des paroles à la
fois douces et habiles'.
[4] Cf. Robert: 'Notification ou inscription (d'un acte) sur un registre qui lui donne authenti-
cité'. Cf. also English 'insinuate': 'To enter (a deed or document) in an official register; to
register; to deliver or lodge for registration'; and 'insinuation': 'The production or delivery of a
will for official registration, as a step towards procuring probate' (*OED*).

'Circonstances'

QUAND BIEN MÊME LANCÉ DANS DES CIRCONSTANCES /
ÉTERNELLES.

(a) 'La Mémorable Crise': Vers libre and the Prose Poem (1886–1897)

> reconnaissons aisément que la tentative participe, avec imprévu, de
> poursuites particulières et chères à notre temps, le vers libre et le poème
> en prose.
>
> ('Observation relative au poème')

As the obvious parallels with *Igitur* indicate, the central analogy between
the poetic act and a throw of the dice dates back to the 1860s; and the
desperate final hope that the poem may at least offer some semblance of
order and necessity in the manner of a 'constellation', notably the Plough,
recalls the argument and imagery of 'Sonnet allégorique de lui-même'
(1868). Certain formal features, on the other hand, develop out of Mal-
larmé's more recent experiments during the period since 1887. The move
from the Petrarchan to the Shakespearean sonnet in which the lines of verse
are increasingly permutable by the reader;[1] the growing preference for the
shorter octosyllabic and heptasyllabic lines because of the heightened sense
of the precariousness of language amidst the whiteness of the (silent) page;
the replacement of conventional punctuation with spatial disposition as a
complement to syntactic ambiguity; all of these features come to brilliant
fruition in 'Un coup de Dés'.

Yet here for the first time Mallarmé abandons traditional versification.
'On a touché au vers', he had famously proclaimed to his Oxford audience
on 1 March 1894 at the beginning of his lecture on 'La Musique et
les lettres'. While Mallarmé himself had been 'fingering' French prosody
with considerable subtlety and originality for some thirty years, it was of

---

[1] This aspect of Mallarmé's sonnet technique will be examined in a subsequent volume.

course the advent of *vers libre* in 1886[2] which had provoked the 'exquise crise, fondamentale'[3] of which he informed his British audiences and which he had already discussed with the journalist Jules Huret in 1891.[4]

One might have expected Mallarmé to reject *vers libre* out of hand. After all, as we have seen, fixity of verse-form (be it the sonnet or his earlier use of a binary structure) and experimentation *within* standard metres are the hallmarks of his *Poésies*. How could this man who had spent a lifetime struggling with the contingencies of his poetic medium now accept arbitrary line lengths and the absence of rhyme? But from the start he writes warmly to Gustave Kahn (in June 1887), praising him for the 'délicieux affranchissement' of *Les Palais nomades* (1887), and in January 1888 he compliments Émile Verhaeren on *Les Soirs*, not only for the exquisite beauty of its book-production but also for the poet's 'traitement du vers [...] Vous le sortez de la vieille forge [...] et c'est toujours le vers'.[5] One might discount these remarks as examples of Mallarmé's famous 'politesse', but both in his interview with Huret and in 'Crise de vers'[6] he recognizes that the time is perhaps ripe (especially in view of Hugo's death in 1885) to give traditional metre a rest, particularly the alexandrine—or at least, like the national flag, to bring it out only on special occasions—and that in any case the individualism of the younger generation of poets and their desire to be free of constraint is to be expected given the instability of contemporary society itself. Fifteen years earlier, he confesses, he would have been 'exaspéré' by *vers libre*, 'comme devant quelque sacrilège ignare!',[7] but now he finds pleasure in the way 'des infractions volontaires ou de savantes dissonances en appellent à notre délicatesse'.[8] One should remember, he says, that traditional prosody is simply a means to writing good verse, not a set of precepts to be obeyed for the sake of it. At present its principal benefit, as with the prose poem, is to provide an implicit foil to *vers libre*: 'Je dirai que la réminiscence du vers strict hante ces jeux à côté et leur confère un profit.'[9] Poetic delight is what counts: 'envisageons la dissolution maintenant du nombre officiel, en ce qu'on veut, à l'infini, pourvu qu'un plaisir s'y réitère.'[10] Far from there being any schism between Parnassian rigour and the new aesthetic, *vers libre* brings a welcome breath of fresh air, such that the alexandrine, 'au lieu de demeurer maniaque et sédentaire comme à présent, sera désormais plus libre, plus imprévu, plus aéré'.[11]

---

[2] See Clive Scott, *Vers libre: The Emergence of Free Verse in France 1886–1914* (Oxford, 1990), 54–5, 63–74.
[3] 'Crise de vers', OC, 360.   [4] OC, 866–8.   [5] *Corr.*, iii. 120, 166–7.
[6] See respectively OC, 866–8 and 360–3 (the latter containing the sections of 'Crise de vers' taken from his article 'Vers et musique en France' in the *National Observer*, 26 Mar. 1892).
[7] OC, 362.   [8] Ibid.   [9] Ibid.   [10] OC, 363.   [11] OC, 868.

Nevertheless Mallarmé's tolerance went only so far, and by the time of his 1894 lecture in Oxford and Cambridge he was beginning to distance himself more evidently from *vers libre*. As in his interview with Huret, he accepts that poetry does not necessarily have to obey traditional prosodic rules to be called such:

en raison que le vers est tout, dès qu'on écrit. Style, versification, s'il y a cadence et c'est pourquoi toute prose d'écrivain fastueux, soustraite à ce laisser-aller en usage, ornementale, vaut en tant qu'un vers rompu, jouant avec ses timbres et encore les rimes dissimulées: selon un thyrse plus complexe. Bien l'épanouissement de ce qui naguères obtint le titre de *poème en prose*.[12]

But at once he adds the rider: 'Très strict, numérique, direct, à jeux conjoints, le mètre, antérieur, subsiste; auprès.' Prose poetry depends for its effects on the pre-existing conventions of prosody 'against' which it is written. As for *vers libre* itself, Mallarmé continues to see a certain value in the diversity of practice among its exponents and in its consequent ability to offer a 'modulation (dis-je, souvent) individuelle, parce que toute âme est un nœud rythmique'. As such, *vers libre* marks the culmination of the metrical innovations of the Romantics and should not be regarded as a waste of time since French poetry has been enriched by it: 'de vraies œuvres' have been written in *vers libre*, and even if these are not recognized as such, the absence of traditional metre has in itself been a blessing ('la qualité du silence [...] à l'entour d'un instrument surmené, est précieuse'). But to those 'initiateurs [...] partis loins' who imagine themselves to have finished once and for all with traditional versification ('un canon (que je nomme, pour sa garantie) officiel'), Mallarmé says simply: 'il restera, aux grandes cérémonies'; and he believes that the time for the 'repos balbutiants' which *vers libre* has permitted from the 'canon officiel' is now at an end: 'voici que de nouveau peut s'élever, d'après une intonation parfaite, le vers de toujours, fluide, restauré, avec des compléments peut-être suprêmes.'[13]

By the following year[14] the note of resistance has grown stronger still. Again he welcomes the successes of *vers libre*, arguing that poets should indeed go beyond 'le legs prosodique' which they have inherited and should stray from the beaten track to gather new specimens 'dans l'infinité des fleurettes'. But he stresses once more the dependence of the non-prosodic on the prosodic: 'un jeu, séduisant, se mène avec les fragments de l'ancien vers reconnaissables, à l'éluder ou le découvrir, plutôt qu'une subite trouvaille, du tout au tout, étrangère.' Such play is welcome:

[12] OC, 644. Cf. his remarks to Huret in 1891 as recalled in the rather plainer language of the journalist (OC, 867).
[13] OC, 644.
[14] In the sections of 'Crise de vers' taken from his eighth 'Variation sur un sujet', 'Averses ou critique', published in the *Revue blanche* on 1 Sept. 1895.

mais, de cette libération à supputer davantage ou, pour de bon, que tout individu apporte une prosodie, neuve, participant de son souffle—aussi, certes, quelque orthographe—la plaisanterie rit haut ou inspire le tréteau des préfaciers.[15]

Already in praising Kahn he had reminded him that *vers libre* did not necessarily mean the end of traditional versification:

car notez bien que je ne vous considère pas comme ayant mis le doigt sur une forme nouvelle devant quoi s'effacera l'ancienne: cette dernière restera, impersonnelle, à tous et quiconque voudra s'isoler différemment, libre à lui;[16]

and now he reasserts the desirability of rhyme and metrical regularity:

Similitude entre les vers, et vieilles proportions, une régularité durera parce que l'acte poétique consiste à voir soudain qu'une idée se fractionne en un nombre de motifs égaux par valeur et à les grouper; ils riment: pour sceau extérieur, leur commune mesure qu'apparente le coup final.

Why? Because the real crisis facing poetry derives not so much from the efforts of the *verslibristes* as from its new rivalry with music:

Au traitement, si intéressant, par la versification subi, de repos et d'interrègne, gît, moins que dans nos circonstances mentales vierges, la crise.[17]

(b) *Music and Letters (1885–1894)*

> Leur réunion s'accomplit sous une influence, je sais, étrangère, celle de
> la Musique entendue au concert; on en retrouve plusieurs moyens
> m'ayant semblé appartenir aux Lettres, je les reprends.
>
> ('Observation relative au poème')

Mallarme's reference in 'Crise de vers' to 'nos circonstances mentales vierges' leads on to a discussion of Wagner and the nature of the relationship between poetry and music, a subject which he had already addressed in his Oxford and Cambridge lecture and still earlier in 'Richard Wagner. Rêverie d'un poète français'.[18] Before considering these texts and the ways in which they may help us to understand 'Un coup de Dés' as the response to

---

[15] *OC*, 364.

[16] *Corr.*, iii. 120. In his newspaper articles of 1887 (reproduced in 'Solennité') he is more categoric: 'Que tout poème composé autrement qu'en vue d'obéir au vieux génie du vers, n'en est pas un' (*OC*, 332).

[17] *OC*, 364–5. For further evidence of Mallarmé's attitude towards *vers libre* in 1895, cf. his response to Austin de Croze's 'enquête' for *Le Figaro* (which response ends with 'Toute l'âme résumée'), and in particular his comments that 'Le vers officiel doit demeurer' and (of *vers libre* itself) 'En résumé, peu mais bon' (see *OC* (BM), 432–3).

[18] First published in Édouard Dujardin's *Revue wagnérienne* on 8 Aug. 1885 and described by Mallarmé as being 'moitié article, moitié poème en prose' (*Corr.*, ii. 290, to Dujardin, 5 July 1885).

a 'mémorable crise', it may first be useful to look again at Mallarmé's letter to Edmund Gosse in January 1893, where he sets out plainly what he understands by the terms 'Musique' and 'Idée'.

Thanking Gosse for his article on him in the *Academy*, Mallarmé quotes one sentence in particular, in which, he says, 'vous écartez tous voiles et désignez la chose avec une clairvoyance de diamant':

His [Mallarmé's] aim [...] is to use words in such harmonious combination as will suggest to the reader a mood or a condition *which is not mentioned in the text*, but is nevertheless paramount in the poet's mind at the moment of composition. (Gosse's emphasis)

'Tout est là', observes Mallarmé, and it is clearly the question of 'harmonious combination' which preoccupies him since he then goes on to give his own definition of 'Musique':

Je fais de la Musique, et appelle ainsi non celle qu'on peut tirer du rapprochement euphonique des mots, cette première condition va de soi; mais l'au-delà magiquement produit par certaines dispositions de la parole; où celle-ci ne reste qu'à l'état de moyen de communication matérielle avec le lecteur comme les touches du piano. Vraiment entre les lignes et au-dessus du regard cela se passe en toute pureté, sans l'entremise des cordes à boyaux et des pistons comme à l'orchestre, qui est déjà industriel; mais c'est la même chose que l'orchestre, sauf que littérairement ou silencieusement. Les poètes de tous les temps n'ont jamais fait autrement et il est aujourd'hui, voilà tout, amusant d'en avoir conscience. Employez Musique dans le sens grec, au fond signifiant Idée ou rythme entre des rapports; là, plus divine que dans l'expression publique ou symphonique.[19]

Music, then, for Mallarmé is not so much a question of sound as of structure, of 'orchestration', and for a poem to be 'musical' is for it to be not only mellifluous or 'euphonique', but a system of relations, of combinations, a rhythm. This is what he means by 'Idée'. Hence his famous declaration in 'La Musique et les lettres': 'la Musique et les Lettres sont la face alternative ici élargie vers l'obscur; scintillante là, avec certitude, d'un phénomène, le seul, je l'appelai, l'Idée.'[20] But what is the status of this 'Idée'? Is it merely a suggestive configuration of relationships (as it might be, phonetic, etymological, semantic, or typographical relationships), or does it have some more solid, recoverable intellectual content? Is it the same as a 'Pensée' or something superior? 'Un coup de Dés' offers answers to these questions, but for the moment it is important to examine how Mallarmé develops these notions in his other writings.

In his 'Rêverie d'un poète français'[21] Mallarmé responds to the challenge of Wagner's concept of the *Gesamtkunstwerk*, this 'Singulier défi [...] aux poètes dont il usurpe le devoir',[22] and gives vent to his 'malaise que tout soit

---

[19] *Corr.*, vi. 26.   [20] *OC*, 649.   [21] *OC*, 541–6.   [22] *OC*, 541.

fait, autrement qu'en irradiant, par un jeu direct, du principe littéraire même'.[23] He praises Wagner for rescuing drama from sterile mimeticism by the addition of music, for this 'simple adjonction orchestrale change du tout au tout, annulant son principe même, l'ancien théâtre'.[24] From being crudely representational and a form of 'intellectuel despotisme' in its naïve and authoritarian demand to be believed as an event really happening, the 'acte scénique' at once becomes 'strictement allégorique', 'vide et abstrait en soi, impersonnel'.[25] Thanks to the musical accompaniment, the observer—a sceptical 'Moderne' who 'dédaigne d'imaginer'[26] that he is actually present at a real event—becomes emotionally implicated in the allegory. The spectacle before him comes alive: without the music, 'le mime resterait, aussitôt, statue'.[27] And yet, for all that Wagner has effected 'l'hymen' between 'le drame personnel' and 'la musique idéale', between 'la scène et [...] la symphonie',[28] there has been no true union. All music has done is to 'se juxtaposer', and 'son principe même, à la Musique, échappe'.[29] Wagner's operas, like Greek tragedies, transcend the particular by offering a mythical and even symbolic account of a nation's origins, but they are still 'legends', particular stories bound by place and time: 'Tout se retrempe au ruisseau primitif: pas jusqu'à la source.'[30]

Mallarmé aspires to something higher, prior. Bayreuth, Wagner's 'temple', stands only halfway up the slope of the 'montagne sainte', 'cette cime menaçante d'absolu'.[31] It offers merely a 'conviviale fontaine', whereas Mallarmé—as he states at the end of the preface to 'Un coup de Dés'—believes poetry to be the 'unique source'. In that poem, he says in the preface also, 'on évite le récit', and here in the essay on Wagner he rejects Germanic narrative in the name of 'l'esprit français, strictement imaginatif et abstrait' which 'répugne [...] à la Légende'.[32] Being, as he sees it, more creative and 'en cela d'accord avec l'Art dans son intégrité, qui est inventeur', the poet has as his goal not legend but 'la Fable, vierge de tout, lieu, temps et personne sus [qui] se dévoile empruntée au sens latent en le concours de tous, celle inscrite sur la page des Cieux et dont l'Histoire même n'est que l'interprétation, vaine, c'est-à-dire, un Poème, l'Ode'.[33] Yes, 'le Théâtre' needs myth, not disparate, secular, familiar myths but one single, unifying myth: 'un, dégagé de personnalité, car il compose notre aspect multiple.'[34] This universal myth requires no physical place for its enactment, only 'le fictif foyer de vision dardé par le regard d'une foule!', a mental Holy of Holies in which 'aboutissent, dans quelque éclair suprême, d'où s'éveille la

---

[23] OC, 542.   [24] Ibid.   [25] Ibid.   [26] Ibid.   [27] OC, 543.   [28] Ibid.
[29] Ibid.   [30] OC, 544.   [31] OC, 546.
[32] OC, 544. Mallarmé's attempt to repulse the colonizing ambitions of (Wagnerian) music by asserting the priority of poetry is consciously presented in nationalistic terms as an ironic imitation of the contemporary Franco-German power struggle.
[33] OC, 544-5.   [34] OC, 545.

Figure que nul n'est, chaque attitude mimique prise par elle à un rythme inclus dans la symphonie, et le délivrant!'[35]

'Fable', 'Poème', 'Ode', 'Mythe', 'la Figure que nul n'est': what Mallarmé envisages is a form of mental drama in which the protagonist ('Type sans dénomination préalable'[36]) enacts a 'geste' with which each human observer can identify, a 'geste' in which the essential rhythms of human experience are contained and for which music is a necessary accompaniment rather than a mere 'juxtaposition' because it, too, in its 'principe même' (which Wagner's music fails to exploit) conveys those very rhythms:

Alors viennent expirer comme aux pieds de l'incarnation, pas sans qu'un lien certain les apparente ainsi à son humanité, ces raréfactions et ces sommités naturelles que la Musique rend, arrière prolongement vibratoire de tout comme la Vie.[37]

By means of this process of identification the contingency of the human condition is transcended through art: 'L'Homme, puis son authentique séjour terrestre, échangent une réciprocité de preuves. Ainsi le Mystère.'[38] Elsewhere Mallarmé states that *Hamlet* is the nearest one comes in the theatre to such an ideal drama;[39] but at the beginning of his essay on Wagner (thus illustrating at the outset as well as in his conclusion the high summit beneath which Bayreuth is merely 'à mi-côte'), Mallarmé singles out 'la Danse' as the best medium for the achievement of this 'Mystère', for the expression of the 'Idée': 'la Danse, seule capable, par son écriture sommaire, de traduire le fugace et le soudain jusqu'à l'Idée—pareille vision comprend tout, absolument tout le Spectacle futur.'[40] 'Un coup de Dés' will be Mallarme's own attempt to outdo both *Hamlet* and the ballet, his own 'total work of art'.

In his 'Rêverie' Mallarmé rejects Wagnerian opera for, in a sense, saying too much, for being too narratively particular; dance is purer, more 'total'. In 'La Musique et les lettres',[41] on the other hand, Mallarmé condemns music for saying too little: 'elle ne se confie pas volontiers', as he wryly puts it.[42] Here, having discussed the 'crise' provoked by *vers libre*, he goes on (as he will in the 1895 section of 'Crise de vers') to attempt to justify the status of 'les Lettres' in the light of the great claims currently being made for 'la Musique'. Why write? he wonders. Certainly not to 'represent' the world, not even to 'evoke' or 'suggest' its physical attributes, but rather to 'libérer, hors d'une poignée de poussière ou réalité sans l'enclore, au livre, même comme texte, la dispersion volatile soit l'esprit, qui n'a que faire de rien outre la musicalité de tout'.[43] 'Oui', he asserts famously, 'la Littérature existe et, si l'on veut, seule, à l'exception de tout'[44]—this because 'La Nature a lieu, on n'y ajoutera pas'[45] and 'Tout l'acte disponible, à jamais

[35] Ibid.   [36] Ibid.   [37] Ibid.   [38] Ibid.
[39] 'Hamlet' (in 'Crayonné au théâtre'), OC, 299.   [40] OC, 541.   [41] OC, 642–57.
[42] OC, 648.   [43] OC, 645.   [44] OC, 646.   [45] OC, 647.

et seulement, reste de saisir les rapports, entre temps, rares ou multipliés; d'après quelque état intérieur et que l'on veuille à son gré étendre, simplifier le monde.'[46] 'Saisir les rapports', 'simplifier le monde': once more the ambition to seize the rhythms of human experience and to distil them into one 'geste', one 'acte'; and once more the claim to be inventive, creative: 'A l'égal de créer: la notion d'un objet, échappant, qui fait défaut.'[47] Language is everything but the world, yet creates by revealing essential relationships within our experience of the world. Here Mallarmé comes close to reiterating what he had stated in his 'Avant-Dire' to René Ghil's *Traité du verbe* in 1886 and what he repeats at the end of 'Crise de vers':

A quoi bon la merveille de transposer un fait de nature en sa presque disparition vibratoire selon le jeu de la parole, cependant; si ce n'est pour qu'en émane, sans la gêne d'un proche ou concret rappel, la notion pure.

Je dis: une fleur! et, hors de l'oubli où ma voix relègue aucun contour, en tant que quelque chose d'autre que les calices sus, *musicalement* se lève, *idée* même et suave, l'absente de tous bouquets. (my emphases)

But music itself, though it shares 'une ambition, la même'[48] with 'les Lettres' (namely to express these relationships, this 'Idée'), falls short in its inability to name things. In Wagner's operas the 'tracé [...] des sinueuses et mobiles variations de l'Idée' is 'vain, si le langage, par la retrempe et l'essor purifiants du chant, n'y confère un sens'.[49] Thus music needs language to complement it, whereas language has no need of the physical accompaniment of music since it can incorporate the rhythms and 'sinuosity' of music within its own performance. Indeed when it comes to the separate performances of concert music and book-reading, Mallarmé makes it quite plain which he sees as requiring the greater intellectual effort:

L'un des modes incline à l'autre et y disparaissant, ressort avec emprunts: deux fois, se parachève, oscillant, un genre entier. Théâtralement pour la foule qui assiste, sans conscience, à l'audition de sa grandeur: ou, l'individu requiert la lucidité, du livre explicatif et familier.[50]

Here, in 'La Musique et les lettres', he is summarizing what he had said in his 'Avant-Dire' to Ghil's *Traité* in the passage which figures towards the end of 'Crise de vers' and which provides the perfect introduction to a study of the 'music' of 'Un coup de Dés':

Certainement, je ne m'assieds jamais aux gradins des concerts, sans percevoir parmi l'obscure sublimité telle ébauche de quelqu'un des poèmes immanents à l'humanité ou leur originel état, d'autant plus compréhensible que tu et que pour en déterminer la vaste ligne le compositeur éprouva cette facilité de suspendre jusqu'à la tentation de s'expliquer. Je me figure par un déracinable préjugé d'écrivain, que rien ne

---

[46] Ibid.   [47] Ibid.   [48] *OC*, 648.   [49] Ibid.   [50] *OC*, 649.

demeurera sans être proféré; que nous en sommes là, précisément, à rechercher, devant une brisure des grands rythmes littéraires (il en a été question plus haut [i.e. the advent of *vers libre*]) et leur éparpillement en frissons articulés proches de l'instrumentation, un art d'achever la transposition, au Livre, de la symphonie ou uniment de reprendre notre bien: car, ce n'est pas de sonorités élémentaires par les cuivres, les cordes, les bois, indéniablement mais de l'intellectuelle parole à son apogée que doit avec plénitude et évidence, résulter, en tant que l'ensemble des rapports existant dans tout, la Musique.

'Un coup de Dés' is Mallarmé's response to a 'mémorable crise' in the history of poetry provoked by the abandonment of traditional prosody by the *verslibristes* and by a composer's ambition to base the 'total work of art' on music rather than words. In 'Un coup de Dés' Mallarmé invents a new prosody and brings to its highest level of sophistication his lifelong attempt to write literary 'music'—'dans le sens grec, au fond signifiant Idée ou rythme entre des rapports'.

(c) *'Un coup de Dés' and its Readers*

> entre les feuillets et le regard règne un silence encore, condition et délice de la lecture.
>
> ('Mimique')

'Un coup de Dés' is a tantalizing work because we do not quite have a definitive text. Although Mallarmé published a version of it (what he calls 'un état') in the periodical *Cosmopolis* in 1897, he was prevented by the periodical's own format from carrying out all his intentions. What he needed (he says in the preface, or 'Observation relative au poème') was 'une pagination spéciale ou de volume à moi'. This he looked likely to achieve when the fine-art publisher Ambroise Vollard agreed to publish the poem in a text to be printed by the Imprimerie Didot and to be illustrated by Odilon Redon. As Mallarmé remarks in his letter to Gide: 'Le poème s'imprime, en ce moment, tel que je l'ai conçu; quant à la pagination, où est tout l'effet.'[51] Several proof versions of this edition survive, notably the set of proofs corrected by Mallarmé and now preserved at Harvard, the so-called Lahure proofs.[52] But Mallarmé died before the edition was published, and the project was then abandoned. Hence certain aspects of the proposed edition remain shrouded in uncertainty: in particular, whether it would have been looseleaf, and how and where Redon's illustrations would have been included.

---

[51] *Corr.*, ix. 172.
[52] Reproduced by Robert Greer Cohn in his *Mallarmé's Masterwork: New Findings* (The Hague, 1966).

The question of Mallarmé's intentions in this poem is made even more tantalizing by Valéry. He describes how on one occasion in Paris the poet read the poem aloud to him,[53] and how on a visit to Mallarmé at Valvins he saw the poem in proof and listened to 'ce grand homme *discuter* (au sens presque de l'algèbre) les moindres détails de position du système verbal et visuel qu'il avait construit, [...] vérifiant minutieusement le montage de cette figure en qui devaient se composer le simultané de la vision avec le successif de la parole, comme si un équilibre très délicat eût dépendu de ces précisions'.[54] But unfortunately Valéry offers no further information about 'tout ce profond calcul'[55] which had just been described to him.

Critics on the whole have tended to ignore this idea of a 'profond calcul' and have sought either to construct a poetic argument in the text or to champion its apparent incoherence in the name of higher things. Thus for Claude Roulet, for example, the poem is 'une Ode allégorique', in which 'Mallarmé y transpose la Fable du monde, telle qu'elle est définie dans la Bible et par le corps des croyances chrétiennes'.[56] Gardner Davies sees the poem predominantly as a rewriting of *Igitur* and subjects it to 'une explica- tion rationnelle' by carefully analysing its syntax and demonstrating a Hegelian dialectic at work whereby throwing or not throwing the dice finally amounts to the same thing.[57] Malcolm Bowie, on the other hand, rejects any allegorizing approach because 'At its crudest [...] it commits the double wrong of falsely embellishing the problem ['the human problem at issue is a simple one'] and falsely normalising the texture'. For him the poem is essentially 'an "inscape" of the anxious and intellectually questing mind', 'a model of the thought-process at large', 'an uncannily rigorous and clear- headed attempt to represent the sensations of contingency', and he goes on to give a subtle account of the dialectic of order and chaos which governs the text.[58]

Bowie's account minimizes the linguistic nature of thought, an aspect which is stressed by Bertrand Marchal in his *Lecture de Mallarmé*. For him Mallarmé is writing about the inability of the mind to go beyond language and how it dwells in a realm of 'fictions', the 'fictions' of language. There is no God, but rather a void beyond language, and the writer in writing is simply producing one of the millions of combinations of words

[53] *Œuvres*, ed. Jean Hytier (Bibliothèque de la Pléiade) (2 vols, Paris, 1957–60), i. 623.

[54] *Œuvres*, i. 625.

[55] Ibid. Cf. also Gide's comment (on 22 Nov. 1913) that 'Un coup de Dés' was born of '*la logique*': see his 'Verlaine et Mallarmé', *Œuvres complètes*, ed. L. Martin-Chauffier, Nouvelle Revue française (15 vols, n.p., n.d.), vii. 427.

[56] Claude Roulet, *Élucidation du poème de Stéphane Mallarmé: 'Un coup de dés jamais n'abolira le hasard'* (Neuchâtel, 1943), 12.

[57] Gardner Davies, *Vers une explication rationnelle du 'Coup de Dés': Essai d'exégèse mallarméenne* (Paris, 1953; rev. edn, Paris, 1992).

[58] Bowie, *The Art of Being Difficult*, 124, 119, 128, and 132.

which already (potentially) exist; he is merely activating one contingent set of relationships. He is no longer the Master, just a temporary passenger: 'L'abîme qui engloutit le Maître est l'image d'un langage tourbillonnaire déchaîné par la mort de Dieu, qui affole le sens et évacue le sujet humain.'[59] Poetry thus becomes a form of celebration, an aesthetic celebration of language, and the poet an anonymous 'desservant'—like a priest or a conductor with his back to us. The poem is 'une liturgie fictive de la beauté'.[60] Marchal's thesis is in effect an embellishment on Blanchot's view that the writer operates within an 'espace littéraire' and that 'Un coup de Dés', far from being a rewriting of *Igitur*, presents the poet with his 'dernière chance, qui n'est pas de vouloir annuler le hasard, fût-ce par un acte de négation mortel, mais de s'abandonner entièrement à ce hasard, de le consacrer en entrant sans réserve dans son intimité, avec l'abandon de l'impuissance'.[61] However, both these responses to the poem, like the readings of Kristeva and Derrida also, considerably undervalue Mallarmé's pursuit of mastery in 'Un coup de Dés'. For there is indeed a 'profond calcul' at work.

---

[59] *Lecture de Mallarmé*, 287.
[60] *Lecture de Mallarmé*, 288.
[61] Blanchot, *L'Espace littéraire*, 119.

2

The Quest for Prosody

> il ne s'agit pas, ainsi que toujours, de traits sonores réguliers ou vers—
> plutôt, de subdivisions prismatiques de l'Idée.
>
> ('Observation relative an poème')

(a) 'Versification', or the Cubic Alexandrine

> l'unique Nombre qui ne peut pas être un autre [...]

'Un coup de Dés' gives every appearance of having been composed at random, its text strewn across the page like dice along the baize, its words the flotsam from a shipwreck bobbing here and there on the waves of the turning pages. There is, of course, no conventional versification: no terminal rhymes (no fixed termini even, except for the last word, the 'point dernier qui le sacre' (23)),[1] and no metrical regularity. Nevertheless, in his preface, Mallarmé speaks of the poem's 'versification', of a 'prosodie, demeurant dans une œuvre, qui manque de précédents, à l'état élémentaire'. As we have seen, he speaks of his 'tentative' as having affinities with *vers libre* and the prose poem, and he claims also to have borrowed certain 'moyens' from concert music. Nevertheless, he maintains that his new mode of writing—'Le genre, que c'en devienne un comme la symphonie, peu à

---

[1] Whereas the text has no clear starting-point. The title-page begins it, yet 'UN COUP DE DÉS' on p. 3 might be seen as the first phrase of the 'poem' itself. Even on the title-page it is not the title which initiates 'Un coup de Dés' but the word 'POÈME', which is perhaps the 'true' title of the work (with 'Un coup de Dés' etc. a mere subtitle: cf. 'Prose (pour des Esseintes)'), a proud and brazen declaration of the text's status despite the absence of traditional prosody.

Throughout Part V parenthetical page references refer to 'Un coup de Dés'. The pagination is that envisaged by Mallarmé and proceeds from p. 1 (title page), p. 2 (blank verso of title page), p. 3 ('UN COUP DE DÉS'), and p. 4 ('JAMAIS [...] NAUFRAGE') to p. 23 ('fusionne avec au delà [...] un Coup de Dés') and p. 24 (blank verso). p. 12–13 of the text constitute the centrefold 'COMME SI [...] COMME SI'. Quotations reproduce capital/lower case and bold/plain variations but not differences in type size. The latter are indicated where of relevance to the argument.

peu, à côté du chant personnel'—'laisse intact l'antique vers, auquel je garde un culte'.

How, then, is 'Un coup de Dés' 'versified' and how, if at all, does it leave the 'antique vers' intact? Mallarmé's only explicit indication in the preface is that the blank spaces of the text, its most immediately striking feature perhaps, were required ('comme silence alentour, ordinairement') by the 'versification' and that he has sought to maintain a proportion of 2 : 1 ('je ne transgresse cette mesure, seulement la disperse') between blank space and printed text just as one might find, he seems to suggest ('ordinairement'), between a conventionally versified poem and the space within which it is customarily printed. It is not at all evident that Mallarmé has in fact observed such a proportion, but what his comment does confirm is that 'versification' involves spatial disposition and the physical dimensions of the text and that he is concerned to offer a novel and, as it were, distorted mirror-image of traditional prosody. Accordingly it becomes impossible not to acknowledge, in this poem about a hypothetical throw of at least two dice, that the 'profond calcul' governing the text is based on the number twelve.

This thesis, first advanced by Mitsou Ronat and complemented by the contribution of Jacques Roubaud in the almost definitive edition of 'Un coup de Dés' published in Paris in 1980, has had some opponents, notably Robert Greer Cohn and, to a lesser extent, Virginia La Charité, and so it may be helpful to rehearse the main points of the debate before going on to show further ways in which the number twelve (together with certain other numbers) accounts for an extensive range of formal and semantic patterns to be found in the text.

For Ronat the number twelve informs the text in the following ways:

(i) the poem consists of 24 pages, which constitute a printer's 'cahier' or signature,[2] and which correspond to the number of syllables in a couplet of alexandrines (a distich writ large);

---

[2] Virginia La Charité, in *The Dynamics of Space: Mallarmé's 'Un Coup de dés jamais n'abolira le hasard'* (Lexington, Ky., 1987), mistakenly takes issue with Ronat here. Because she believes that the text consists only of the twenty-one pages on which there is print, La Charité claims that 'Ronat misreads the text through her intellectual play with the number 12' and that her 'descriptions of the text are subsequently erroneous because she insists on basing her argument on 24 pages and the number 12' (p. 181 n. 8). Also, she claims, 'there is no mathematical system which is built on the number 12' (p. 127). Given Mallarmé's predilection for blank spaces, it is perfectly possible to envisage the blank pages (2, 4, and 24) as part of the text (e.g. as large spaces of silence into which, at first, the text tentatively introduces itself, and then, at the end, as the final 'authenticated' silence on to which the linguistic act gives). There is no evidence that 'Ronat misunderstands that a signature always consists of an even number of pages, usually four, and therefore that the printer had to use 24 pages or six signatures in order to accommodate a 21-page [*sic*] text' (p. 181 n. 8). As Ronat herself points out in her edition (p. 3), Mallarmé numbered the pages 1–24 himself and refers to this numbering in correspondence with his printer.

(ii) each page offers the potential space for a maximum of 36 lines of print, as evident on p. 10;[3]

(iii) including the title, counting lines spread across the double page as one, and 'en tenant compte des corps typographiques', there are 216 lines of print, which represents a quarter of the total potential area for print (24 pages of 36 lines offering 864 possible lines) or, if the text is envisaged as consisting of 12 double pages, a half of the potential area;[4]

(iv) if one takes the double page as a single unit and observes the traditional rules for counting syllables (while also counting each diaeresis as one vowel and 'enjambant le blanc dans le même corps typographique'), there are 1,224 syllables, or 'positions métriques', in the poem as a whole (including its title-page)[5]—i.e. a multiple of 12 and 24 (and therefore, one might add, of the very numbers in the total itself—12 : 24);

(v) turning to the typography of the text, Ronat further maintains—on the basis of having consulted 'un catalogue ancien de caractères, aux pages des Didot-Bodoni-Didones' for which, regrettably, she gives no reference—that in the Didot type style which Mallarmé had chosen (and in which the extant proofs are printed), the type sizes which he selected are also numerically significant. Allegedly, the main 'word-string' of the text ('*UN COUP DE DÉS JAMAIS N'ABOLIRA LE HASARD*') is in 60-point, '*POÈME*' in 36-point, '*MALLARMÉ*' and '*SI C'ÉTAIT LE NOMBRE*', etc. in 24-point, each of them multiples of 12;[6]

(vi) the dimensions of the printed text, as evident from the proofs but not subsequently observed until Ronat's own edition, are 27 cm × 18 cm for a single page or 27 cm × 36 cm for a double page (omitting the central margins), and these dimensions combine the divisors of 12 (1, 2, 3, and 4).

Mitsou Ronat's theory is a persuasive one (except possibly in the particulars of (iii) and (v)), and her emphasis on the proper dimensions of the

---

[3] I have not examined any proof copies of the poem myself, but that reproduced by Cohn in *Mallarmé's Masterwork: New Findings* confirms this. La Charité's contention that there are thirty-eight lines per page (*The Dynamics of Space*, 48) is not substantiated other than by her arbitrary decision to take 8-point type as that in which the major part of the text is printed (Ronat has 16-point). Given Mallarmé's great attention to the typographical layout of the text, she is wrong to argue that 'In establishing the space of *Un Coup de dés*, a reader may adopt any point size as his basis for analysis and measurement, as long as he takes into account the spatial dimensions and variations required by Mallarmé in the construct of his poem' (n. 12 on p. 182).

[4] I have been unable to reproduce her finding of 216 lines of print, reaching instead a total of 204 lines (by including the title-page and counting as one those lines which spread across the central margins *in the same typeface*). Ronat's calculation might be viable if certain lines in particularly large type were counted as occupying more than one line of print.

[5] This calculation is confirmed by the evidence.

[6] According to Ronat, the greater part of the text is in 16-point, and the 'small print' on pp. 18–19 in 10-point. She makes no comment on the lack of connection with the number twelve here but proposes instead the debatable thesis that the five typesizes may correspond to the five fundamental tones of French intonation ('quatre tons simples et un ton contrastif'; p. 4).

text (vi) was taken further in a review article by Jean-Claude Lebensztejn.[7] He points out that the edition for which Mallarmé had corrected the proofs shortly before he died[8] was to be a folio edition measuring 38 cm × 28.5 cm for a single page and thus 38 cm × 57 cm for a double page. Hence, not only would the area of printed text 27 cm × 18 cm have reflected the proportions 3 : 2 for a single page, the overall page size would have had the proportions 4 : 3 for a single page (or for the whole text when shut or folded) and 2 : 3 for a double page (or for the whole text when open or unfolded).[9]

These dimensions support the idea of what I have chosen to call the 'cubic alexandrine': like the two-dimensional classical alexandrine divided into two hemistichs, the three-dimensional 'Un coup de Dés' consists of six folded sheets (the fold being the equivalent of the caesura), thus twelve pages (either twelve 'spreads', i.e. double pages,[10] or twelve separate pages, each with its own recto and verso), or twenty-four sides (or 'pages' in the sense that a book has x number of pages), each page (in either sense) with (potentially) thirty-six lines of print, the whole containing 1,224 verse syllables. Were one to accept Ronat's calculation of 216 lines of text, then one could argue that the poem illustrates the mathematical procedure of 'élévation', with the fundamental 6 being successively raised to 6^2 (lines on page), 6^3 (lines in text), and 6^4 (total number of syllables). A study of the 'pages quadrillées' of the manuscript might further reveal that the squares of white space amount to 6^5.[11] And does not the poem itself 'relate' how 'une élévation ordinaire verse l'absence' (21)? A raising of ordinals confers structure upon empty space: it versifies the silence.

[7] 'Note relative au "Coup de Dés"', *Critique*, 36 (1980), 633–59.

[8] Printed by Didot and to be published by Ambroise Vollard with illustrations by Odilon Redon. As Lebensztejn notes, Mallarmé was averse to illustration: (see *OC*, 878: 'Je suis pour—aucune illustration, tout ce qu'évoque un livre devant se passer dans l'esprit du lecteur'), but an artwork for collectors and bibliophiles was the only way to finance the expensive project of printing 'Un coup de Dés' exactly as he wanted it. After Mallarmé's death the project was abandoned, probably by Vollard rather than Didot (see Lebensztejn, 'Note relative au "Coup de Dés"', 638), and there is at present no way of knowing how the illustrations would have been incorporated, whether the folio would have been looseleaf or stitched, or what type of paper would have been employed. Furthermore the moulds for the Didot font selected by Mallarmé have since been destroyed and the font recast, which makes a 'definitive' edition the more difficult (and expensive) to realize.

[9] Cf. *Le 'Livre' de Mallarmé*, ed. Scherer, fos. 39 (A)–41 (A) for evidence that Mallarmé thought in such terms. Ronat mistakenly argues (p. 4) that the dimensions described on fo. 39 (A) tally exactly with those of 'Un coup de Dés'.

[10] In his preface Mallarmé explicitly alludes to these double pages in terms of traditional versification, referring to 'une vision simultanée de la Page: celle-ci prise pour unité comme l'est autre part le Vers ou ligne parfaite'.

[11] Mondor refers to 'de grandes pages quadrillées' (*Vie de Mallarmé*, 795): in fact the manuscript consists of an exercise book measuring 33 cm in height by 50 cm in width (when open). I have not had the opportunity of consulting this manuscript, which is at present in private hands, and I am grateful to Professor Bertrand Marchal (who has been able to consult it once) for passing on these measurements to me.

Robert Greer Cohn's principal objection to this approach to 'Un coup de Dés' concerns 'l'évidente futilité de faire croire que cet homme de *lettres* par excellence (y compris la musique) ait subordonné cet investissement de toute une vie, au moment d'aborder une synthèse ambitieuse, à un jeu rudimentaire de chiffres'.[12] Coming from such an innovative reader of Mallarmé such an appeal to Romantic notions of 'literature' is surprising, and quite unMallarméan, and in any case there is far more than a 'jeu rudimentaire' at work here. But Cohn's more detailed objections merit further attention. He is right to point out, as Lebensztejn also does,[13] that the title of the poem has thirteen syllables, right also that not all the type sizes are multiples or divisors of twelve,[14] that Ronat's quotation from Scherer's edition of Le 'Livre' is inapposite,[15] and that her calculation (see (iii) above) of the proportion of print to blank space is at odds with Mallarmé's (admittedly not binding) remark in the preface about 'un tiers'. While Cohn's reason for excluding the title from the text of the poem itself is weak ('il y aurait une répetition lourde entre le titre et les premiers mots du texte'),[16] there is force, as will be seen presently, in his contention that twelve is not the only number to inform the text. Nevertheless, as Ronat points out in her reply to Cohn,[17] the number twelve is not just any old number but the metrical basis of the most prominent metre in the history of French poetry, and she is justified in asserting that 'le nombre 12 peut traduire à la fois une expérience de rupture et la volonté de prolonger la tradition qui caractérise l'aventure mallarméenne'. Mallarmé is outstripping the *verslibristes* in his departure from conventional versification and yet also surpassing his own most ambitious attempts to 'vaincre le Hasard' in his control of the poetic text.

The idea of a 'cubic alexandrine' is further supported by the evident analogy between an alexandrine and two dice, the significance of which is surprisingly underestimated by the participants in this debate. By abandoning the fixed form of the alexandrine Mallarmé has embarked on a perilous enterprise, and the two dice (the symbol of his new 'instrument' of versifica-

[12] 'A propos du *Coup de Dés*', *Critique*, 38 (1982), 92.

[13] 'Note relative au "Coup de Dés"', 651.

[14] If Ronat's numbers are correct, however, the type size ranges from 60-point to 10-point and is predominantly in 16 (=10+6), a number which might be said to combine the duodecimal and decimal numerical systems on which the dimensions are based.

[15] See above, n. 9.

[16] 'A propos du *Coup de Dés*', 93. One reason for regarding the words on the title-page as part of the poem as a whole is that Mallarmé specifically wanted them not to be printed on different paper from the rest of the poem (see Danielle Mihram, 'The Abortive Didot/Vollard Edition of *Un coup de Dés*', *French Studies*, 33 (1979), 52). A further reason is that these words contribute to the apposite total of metrical positions calculated by Ronat under (iv) above. And cf. also the use of 'Sainte' and other titles in the *Poésies* as integral parts of the verbal lacework of the text in question.

[17] *Critique*, 38 (1982), 276–7.

tion), each with its potential maximum of 6, may produce any combination between 2 and 12. Indeed with two dice there is 1 chance in 36 of a particular combination coming up, just as on each page of this text there are 36 lines in which a particular linguistic combination (a word, or group of words) may find itself situated. Moreover, were we to envisage the possibility of three dice, as a three-dimensional text might suggest (in that Mallarmé's spatial versification has to contend with three dimensions),[18] then the chances of any one combination coming up are 1 in 216; and if Ronat's calculation of the number of printed lines in the text is correct, then in the text as a whole there are 216 lines in which a particular linguistic combination may find itself situated. Since any particular linguistic combination will bring together some of the 24 letters of the (French) alphabet, the chances of any one letter appearing on any one of the 36 lines on the page is the same as the chance of any one line appearing in the text as a whole (24 pages of 36 lines). And the numbers on any one die add up to 21, the total number of printed pages in the text:[19] 21, itself a mirror image of 12. Finally, the two sides of a die add up to 7 (just as there is a pattern established between the recto and verso of a single page), and 7 is the most likely number to be thrown with two dice. The Septentrion (23), therefore, is the most probable constellation when the dice-words reach the empty spaces of the sky-page.

Rather like a computer monitor upon which the words, stricken by a 'virus', tumble down the screen, so the pages of Mallarmé's text display words falling like feathers in the wind, ripped from the wings of an alexandrine, floating seemingly free. 'Chance' (10) itself derives from 'cadere' (= to fall) and meant originally the 'manière dont tombent les dés' (Robert), and is thus synonymous with 'chute'. Deprived of its traditional supports the new Mallarméan line of verse will (s)tumble, 'chancellera' (10)—and yet, thanks to the spatial prosody, 'chance—ailera'. Chance (because the 'aile' of the alexandrine 'erra' from the path of regularity) will now itself lend wing to the poetic flight: and 'chancellera', will cancel—not only by abolishing the alexandrine but, in its etymological sense, by drawing an X or erecting a trellis. From the cancellation of traditional verse, an apparent act of 'folie' (10),[20] a new system of relationships will be born of chance itself, a new grid pattern to restore order to 'le Vers'—for example, the chiasmus that holds the entire 'Poème' in place: 'UN COUP DE DÉS / COMME SI / COMME SI / un Coup de Dés.'

---

[18] La Charité comments that the then popular game of hazard is played with three dice (*The Dynamics of Space*, 122).

[19] A point made by La Charité (*The Dynamics of Space*, 127).

[20] Cf. Mallarmé's famous comment to Valéry: 'Ne trouvez-vous pas que c'est un acte de démence?' (Valéry, *Œuvres*, i. 625). 'Dé-mence' indeed.

Far from Mallarmé's transposition of the alexandrine into a new spatial 'versification' being a 'jeu rudimentaire', it represents a subtle attempt to set up the essential tension which governs the text: that between chaos and order, or contingency and necessity. Moreover such numerical preoccupations have an ancient and respectable past, not least in Pythagoras and his theory of 'harmonia'. Central to this was the 'tetractys', the first four natural numbers (1, 2, 3, and 4) conceived of as being connected in various relations and from which can be constructed the harmonic ratios of the fourth, the fifth, and the octave. For the ancients this 'tetractys' was the 'harmonia' in which the Sirens sang, and Plato identifies this song with the music of the spheres in which the heavenly bodies move.[21] There will be occasion to look again at the 'torsion de sirène' (16) mentioned in 'Un coup de Dés', but for the moment suffice it to say that when 'le poète s'est efforcé de faire de la musique avec des mots',[22] he was seeking to create a siren song: a form of harmonious beauty that is both mythical in its elusiveness and dangerous in its luring of the poet's craft onto the rocks of irregularity and towards the consequent shipwreck of ordinary poetic pattern.

There is, of course, the comparable danger that the prospect of novel textual patterns will lure the reader into excessive recuperation. After all, the constellations themselves are but approximate patterns, and history records the different persons or objects with which they have variously been identified. The Plough is also a Great Bear and a Big Dipper. Moreover (for as long as we remain ignorant of the physics of the Big Bang), the stars just happen to be in those positions: the human desire for order has arranged them. Mallarmé's patterning of 'Un coup de Dés' preserves this precariousness, and the reader is caught up in the tension between chaos and order. Just as we may tentatively perceive certain visual shapes in the text: a ship capsizing or the dip of a bird's wing (6–7), a ship on an even keel (8–9), a solitary feather floating down (14–15), a decorative plume adorning the head (16–17), or the Plough itself (20–1, 22–3),[23] so too we may discern numerical patterns and yet wonder if they are really there. Nevertheless the recurrence of the number twelve does seem to point to a creative intelligence at work, as does (in ways to be discussed below) the insistent presence of the number seven.

As Ronat and several other critics have suggested, the typography of 'Un coup de Dés' constitutes an important aspect of its 'versification'. Mal-

[21] See G. S. Kirk, J. E. Raven, and M. Schofield, *The Pre-Socratic Philosophers* (2nd edn, Cambridge, 1983), 232–4.

[22] As stated in the note, probably written by Mallarmé, which the editors of *Cosmopolis* appended to Mallarmé's 'Observation relative au poème' on first publication (and reproduced by Ronat in her edition).

[23] Cf. Mallarmé's comments to Gide: 'La constellation y affectera, *d'après des lois exactes* et autant qu'il est permis à un texte imprimé, fatalement, une allure de constellation. Le vaisseau y donne de la bande, du haut d'une page au bas de l'autre, etc.' (*Corr.*, ix. 172; my emphasis).

larmé's own reference in his preface to 'La différence des caractères d'imprimerie entre le motif prépondérant, un secondaire et d'adjacents' points to an evident analogy with music and the use of the central word-string 'UN COUP DE DÉS / JAMAIS / N'ABOLIRA / LE HASARD' as a quasi-Wagnerian leitmotif. His suggestions that this difference 'dicte son importance à l'émission orale' and that the position of a word on the page is an indication of rising or falling intonation do not appear to have affected his own recitation of the poem to Valéry ('d'une voix basse, égale, sans le moindre "effet", presque à soi-même'[24]). Nevertheless there is no question but that type size, together with the choice of roman or italic, medium or bold, upper or lower case, are important ways of 'versifying' or 'stylizing' the linguistic material. According to Valéry indeed 'cette disposition typographique [...] était l'essentiel de sa tentative'.[25]

From Mitsou Ronat's edition and the so-called 'Lahure' proofs reproduced by Cohn it would appear that Mallarmé used five different sizes of type.[26] If 'par' (1) is printed in bold as its position on the title-page indicates that it might have been, then it is possible to count twelve variations of type in 'Un coup de Dés'.[27] Six of these variations are in bold type, six in medium; six are in upper case, six in lower case. Roman, accounting for seven variations, predominates slightly over italic: perhaps as the seven white keys predominate over the five black keys on a piano keyboard, perhaps also with the implication that in this text fixity of pattern (figured by roman) ultimately predominates over uncertainty (as figured by italic).

---

[24] Valéry, Œuvres, i. 623.

[25] Œuvres, i. 625.

[26] Whether or not they correspond to the numbers 60, 36, 24, 16, and 10 suggested by Ronat. The Dictionnaire de l'imprimerie, ed. Edmond Morin (2nd edn, Brussels, 1933), for example, gives no 60-point in its list of Didot (and other) typefaces (p. 60).

[27] Using Ronat's point-size for ease of reference, the twelve variations are as follows: (a) 60—bold roman upper-case: 'UN COUP DE DÉS / JAMAIS / N'ABOLIRA / LE HASARD' (3, 5, 11, 19); (b) 36—bold roman upper case: 'POÈME' (1); (c) 24—bold roman upper case: 'STÉPHANE MALLARMÉ' (1); (d) 24—bold italic upper case: 'SI / C'ÉTAIT LE NOMBRE / CE SERAIT (17–19); (e) 24—bold italic lower case: 'Un coup de Dés jamais n'abolira le Hasard' (1); (f) 16—bold roman lower case: 'par' (1); (g) 16—medium roman upper case: 'QUAND BIEN MÊME LANCÉ DANS DES CIRCONSTANCES / ÉTERNELLES / DU FOND D'UN NAUFRAGE' (5), 'SOIT' (6), 'LE MAÎTRE' (8), 'RIEN / N'AURA EU LIEU / QUE LE LIEU' (20–1), and 'EXCEPTÉ / PEUT-ÊTRE / UNE CONSTELLATION' (22–3); (h) 16—medium roman lower case: 'que / l'Abîme' (6) and most or all of the text on pp. 6–7, 8–9, 10, 20–1, and 22–3; (i) 16—medium italic upper case: 'COMME SI / [...] / COMME SI' (12–13); (j) 16—medium italic lower case: 'plume solitaire éperdue' (14–15) and all, most, or some of the text on pp. 14–15, 16–17, and 19; (k) 10—medium roman lower case: 'autrement qu'hallucination' (19) and other text on this page; (l) 10—medium italic lower case: 'issu stellaire' (18) and other text on this page.

La Charité (The Dynamics of Space, 48) argues for 'seven different type sizes' and '12 type variations' but does not list or illustrate them. Dee Reynolds suggests eight different typefaces, three of which appear both as roman and as italic, three as roman only, and two as italic only (with further upper/lower case variation): see David Scott, Pictorialist Poetics: Poetry and the Visual Arts in Nineteenth-Century France (Cambridge, 1988), 139 and n. 49.

The choices of particular variations are not hard to interpret, with size and boldness of type corresponding to the status of a particular linguistic combination on a sliding scale of importance from central leitmotif to incidental rider to the 'argument'. Roman characters seem to be associated with the certainty of assertion (especially in the various aphorisms which stud the text) while italic seems to be the typeface of hypothesis ('*COMME SI* / [. . .] / *COMME SI*').[28] As will be seen presently, the poem, while it 'évite le récit' as Mallarmé assures us in his preface, may be said to represent the hypothetical unfolding of an action which in fact never takes place. '*N'ABOLIRA*' (l. 11) is the pivot of this non-event (as befits the verb in a negative proposition): before it the Master (and the poem) contemplates the possibility of action (and its possible consequences); after it comes the result of the action, and an assessment of that result. The italics begin immediately after '*N'ABOLIRA*' and end with 'la neutralité identique du gouffre' (19); they represent a loss of control (as the doer awaits the result of his doing), both the tumbling of the dice and the (simulated) temporary dissolution of the poetic text.

As is well known, Mallarmé undertook close investigation of different typefaces before he finally chose Didot for 'Un coup de Dés'. Generally it is argued that he did so on aesthetic grounds, the Didot typeface being particularly elegant in its shapes and generous in its use of blank space within and between the characters.[29] It is also the case that Didot was renowned as a typeface for the harmony between its roman and italic type,[30] a feature which Mallarmé would have valued highly given his own attempt to 'orchestrate' roman and italic as the visual emblems of certainty and hypothesis, of order and chaos. Still more important to Mallarmé, however, may have been the legal and historical associations of Didot typography. For reasons to be discussed later, it was helpful to Mallarmé's purpose that Didot typeface should be the one generally used by contemporary officialdom,[31] but also he cannot have failed to be aware of the Didot family's especial claim to fame as typographers. For it was they, in the eighteenth century, who had rationalized the measurement of typeface by adopting Pierre-Simon Fournier's idea of measuring type size in 'points' and then basing the measurement on the French 'pied du roi'.[32] Didot divided a

---

[28] The traditional use of italics for the title is thus perhaps ironized, or 'enroulé[e] avec ironie' (13), as if the self-assertion of a title was at its least appropriate in this poem about the contingency of linguistic and poetic expression.

[29] See Mihram, 'The Abortive Didot/Vollard Edition of *Un coup de Dés*', 44.

[30] Ibid.

[31] The use of Didot typeface for official documents by the French administration is alluded to by Tibor Papp (Ronat edn, 25) and by La Charité (*The Dynamics of Space*, 96).

[32] Measuring 0.324 metres and its 12 'pouces' themselves divisible into 12 'lignes', the French 'pied du roi' was longer than the 'pied anglais' (0.305 metres). In 1723 a royal decree had established 10 1/2 'lignes' as the standard type size. See *Dictionnaire de l'imprimerie*, ed. Morin, 86, 192–3.

twelfth of the 'pied du roi', a 'pouce', into 72 'points', with 12-point (previously 'un cicéro') and 6-point (previously 'une nonpareille') being key point-sizes in the measurement of a page. 'Un douze', abbreviated to dz, is in fact the principal such measurement: hence, for example, Jean-Claude Lebensztejn's description of the print-area of a single page of 'Un coup de Dés' as being 27 cm × 18 cm or 60 × 40 dz.[33] Indeed the major complaint about the Didot system has always been its lack of fit with the metric system, yet it has persisted in use among printers precisely because its key number, 12, is divisible by so many whole numbers.[34]

Hence the number twelve is of significance to the poet-typographer as well as the poet-versifier, and Mondor's claim that the manuscript of 'Un coup de Dés' consisted of 'grandes pages quadrillées' may suggest that Mallarmé calculated the exact height and position of every letter of his text to the nearest dz. Of course such squared paper is what this French schoolteacher wrote on anyway, as do his successors and their pupils to this day; but there is every reason to believe that Mallarmé's 'profond calcul' would have exploited such squares, and that each character was given its place on the grid according to the least random of arithmetical calculations. Others may succeed even in reconstructing any such calculations, but for the moment it may be sufficient to note the evident analogy between Mallarmé's squared paper and the printer's 'chase' or frame for holding types—those cubes, or dice, which bear the characters.[35] In the printed version of 'Un coup de Dés' these lines and calculations haunt the blank spaces of the text like some ghostly prosody.

(b) The Shipwreck of the Alexandrine

naufrage cela direct de l'homme / sans nef / n'importe / où vaine.

Such is the 'versification' of 'Un coup de Dés', and this radical break with poetic tradition is one of the several allegories which are sewn into the semantic lacework of the text. Jacques Roubaud has suggested that 'LE MAÎTRE' (8) who is shipwrecked is Victor Hugo, the master of the alexandrine and traditional French prosody, and that the poem '"narre la catastrophe" littéraire que constituent la mort de l'alexandrin et l'avènement du vers libre'.[36] But this is too specific: the 'Maître' may just as well be

[33] 'Note relative au "Coup de Dés"', 640.
[34] See Dictionnaire de l'imprimerie, ed. Morin, 192.
[35] As La Charité notes, the frame—determining the dimensions of the text—is hammered into place by a 'coup de dés', after which 'Mobility of the printer's die is possible only through the variations of typefaces on the page' ('Mallarmé's Livre: The Graphomatics of the Text', Symposium, 34 (1980), 256). See also The Dynamics of Space, 111.
[36] Ronat edn, 2.

Mallarmé himself, whose poetic 'vaisseau' is breaking up under him and
who hesitates to throw the dice of his extraordinary *vers libre*. And, of
course, not Mallarmé himself as flesh-and-blood poet, but Mallarmé as
exponent and guardian of 'le Mètre': both poetic metre and measurement
itself. Accordingly, it is now proposed to read 'Un coup de Dés' as an
account of the 'shipwreck' of the alexandrine and the emergence of a new
prosodic shape from the midst of the textual spume.

The dice-words of 'Un coup de Dés' are thrown from the dice-box of a
'naufrage' (5), the 'naufrage' that is *vers libre*, and on pp. 6–7 we both see
(visually portrayed) and read of the storm-tossed craft of prosody seeking its
former equilibrium in the vertiginous, featureless whiteness of the page
('l'Abîme / blanchi / étale / furieux'). Like some wounded bird, the 'vers'
tilts madly down and onwards in search of its caesura and (beyond it) of the
other wing of its second hemistich ('plane désespérément / d'aile / la sienne /
par [. . .]'), until it meets the gutter of the folded page and begins to right
itself, to find a new kind of equilibrium. Its own particular 'mal de mer' has
been a 'mal à dresser le vol' (l. 7). As one might hasten to 'dresser les
vergues' (square the yard[-arm]s) or 'dresser la barre' (right the helm), so
the wing of poetic endeavour strives to control its flight as, in quasi-sexual
frenzy, it covers the spurting words ('et couvrant les jaillissements') and
skims the prancing waves of liberated language and turning page ('coupant
au ras les bonds'): hom. '"coupe" hante, aura/ora[le], les bonds'? 'coupe
hante! Or! Allez, bon!'? At any rate, the ship-wing of verse now finds upon
its arrival on the shores of this opposing page, this 'voile alternative',
precisely a new kind of canvas for a new kind of sailing and a wingspan
or prosody ('envergure') that is new in both its measurements and its
character. The two pages become as two hemistichs, the sails on a ship, or
the wings on a bird, and the potentially threatening shadow of the gutter
('l'ombre enfouie dans la profondeur par cette voile alternative [the right-
hand page]') is exploited like some buried treasure, contained (cf. 'résume')
and turned to account as the new caesura of a paginal alexandrine. Deep in
the shadows of the double page, 'très à l'intérieur', lies the mystery of this
new 'prosody', its hidden threads of gold (hom. 'traits à l'intérieur') lacing
the text together in a summary of itself ('résume'). And 'treize à l'intérieur'?
The alexandrine has sunk without trace, and we are left with the thirteen
syllables of the poem's title and its leitmotif. But, in the course of this double
page, the abyss that is *vers libre* has become at once the backbone of a bird,
the mast between two sails, and the hull of a craft that may yet remain
afloat ('la coque / d'un bâtiment / penché de l'un ou l'autre bord')—and the
shell of a bird's egg from which may hatch the poetic flights of the future.

Enter the Master/Metre on pp. 8–9, rising up ('surgi') like some unlikely
Venus from the waves. There he stands, sizing up the situation ('inférant'):
separated from traditional prosody ('hors d'anciens calculs') almost as if,

with age, he has forgotten the ropes, forgotten how to manage this kind of writing, this hand-work ('où la manœuvre avec l'âge oubliée')—for like some master of the golden dance (hom. 'hors d'anciens') who has let go of the barre ('jadis il empoignait la barre'), or some master printer who controlled his type with the 'barre' that divides the 'châssis' or 'chase', he the ship's master has let go of the helm and is now faced, as if by a conflagration of poetic metre, of metrical 'feet' ('cette conflagration à ses pieds'), with the featureless whiteness of a double page ('de l'horizon unanime') that lacks the fixed poetic form that previously allowed him to steer a safe passage. Now in his fist (and, homophonically, in the printer's 'points') there is the potential to stand up to the surrounding turbulence ('comme on menace un destin et les vents') and to cast into the 'tempête' of poetic upheaval that emblem of traditional prosody, 'l'unique Nombre qui ne peut pas être un autre', the alexandrine[37]—with the prospect that the splintering of the alexandrine can be redeemed by a re-enfolding of its number and divisors within the text such that order is restored and the storm safely and proudly weathered ('en reployer la division et passer fier'). To do so, he would need to become 'un autre / Esprit', the ghostly successor of the traditional prosodist who once ruled over 'l'empire de la passion et des rêveries' (as Mallarmé calls it at the end of the preface), and one who is pure mind (or, as the preface also has it, 'intellect').

The Master/Metre hesitates, wryly reluctant to present the spectacle of himself as an ageing follower of fashion, a hoary maniac who is a little old for such games, a pedant uneasy at the thought of seeing where the random waves of *vers libre* will take him ('plutôt / que de jouer / en maniaque chenu / la partie / au nom des flots'). The outstretched arm, ready for the throw, signals the imminence of his own death as the prosodist of yore (but not yet his rebirth as the prosodist of yaw): the words are there, ready, laden with the 'secret' of how they will eventually fall out, but that 'secret' is beyond his present knowing ('écarté du secret qu'il détient'; cf. hom. 'qu'il, dé(s), tient'). But one such wave of random *vers libre*—perhaps the titular aphorism itself, the poem's 'heading', in which one extra syllable subverts the principal metre of French verse—finally overwhelms his mind, and the acclaimed leader of the Symbolist school sinks, a subjugated greybeard ('un envahit le chef', 'le chef / coule en barbe soumise',), the very picture of modern man adrift on a stormy sea of political instability and loss of faith, man without a ship and man without a port, man without a church ('naufrage cela direct de l'homme / sans nef / n'importe / où vaine'). 'Ou

---

[37] Ronat takes this line, itself the one alexandrine in the text, as the key to her duodecimal approach. It should be noted, in anticipation of further readings of this passage, that the number is also 'unique' in that the unique result of the dice-throw—whatever that may be and yet which, once the dice have been thrown, cannot be other—is envisaged as already present as potential within the fist of the dice-thrower.

veine'? Perhaps he is lucky: he may by chance succeed. With the new 'spring
of the arch' (the 'retombée d'un mal à dresser le vol') hinted at on the
previous page and suggestive of the new architecture of his paginal pro-
sody,[38] of his concerted *vers libre*, he may yet reconstruct both a ship and a
nave, a 'bâtiment', in which he may once again be Master and have the
measure of his medium.

   But for this to happen he must, as so often in Mallarmé's poetry, die and
be reborn. On p. 10 we find, in a characteristic syntactic turnabout, that the
Master is hesitating *not* to open his hand and throw the dice-words: and
hesitating 'ancestralement', i.e. because of some atavistic urge to use words
rather than to sink into silence.[39] Though his head may have sunk beneath
the waves, uselessly filled with the redundant rules of his poetic heritage[40]
and seat of an intellect that may be powerless against chance, the clenched
hand ('la main / crispée / par delà l'inutile tête') could yet bequeath the
vanishing prosody to chance itself—a Janus ('quelqu'un / ambigu') that ever
was ('immémorial') and ever will be ('ultérieur')—to chance in the form of
vers libre, a hybrid genre ('ambigu'), part 'vers antique' ('immémorial') and
part latest fashion ('ultérieur'). For it is the 'démon(t)', the dice-mountain of
chance in a poetic never-never-land ('de contrées nulles'[41]), which has pre-
sented itself to the Master in this way, an anti-Parnassus. The old man and
his old art of verse ('vieillard vers', 'vieil art, vers') have now been
brought—from their own 'contrées nulles' of sterile adherence to worn-
out prosody—to this moment of supreme and final conjunction with prob-
ability/provability that is 'Un coup de Dés' itself. Like Igitur, the Master is
met with the challenge of finding a new form of 'preuve'.

   There emerges from this artistic 'death' (or encounter with contingency)
an heir, a childlike ghost ('ombre puérile'), Mallarmé's new 'vers' as man-
ifested in the writing of 'Un coup de Dés', a shadow of its former self. Like a
pebble smoothed by the sea ('caressée et polie et rendue et lavée'), this 'vers'
has also been rendered more supple by being freed from the rigid divisions
of the 'vieil art/vieillard', from the unyielding bones of the shipwrecked
alexandrine's invariable measures and the planks of former craft ('assouplie
par la vague et soustraite / aux durs os perdus entre les ais'). Like some baby
newly baptized ('caressé et polie et rendue et lavée'), this new-born 'vers' is
the issue of a frolic with chance ('né / d'un ébat'); be it the sea of metrical

---

[38] Cf. the use of the architectural 'trombe' in 'A la nue accablante tu': see above, Part IV,
Ch. 4.
   [39] Cf. 'La Musique et les lettres': 'Je me figure par un indéracinable sans doute préjugé
d'écrivain, que rien ne demeurera sans être proféré' (OC, 367).
   [40] Cf. the reference in 'Crise de vers' to 'le legs prosodique' (OC, 364).
   [41] 'Contrée' derives from Latin 'contrata' and meant originally a 'pays en face'. Here it
suggests the blank space on the opposing page, an emblem of the absence of fixed poetic form, a
space with 'traits nuls' and so without those golden threads of poetic lacework.

indeterminacy (as 'mère' of the child-'vers') using the ancient versifier ('l'aïeul') as its passive partner or the versifier seeking actively to combat this indeterminacy ('la mer par l'aïeul tentant ou l'aïeul contre la mer / une chance oiseuse'). Whichever the case, there has been a betrothal ('Fian-çailles') of indeterminacy and ancient artistry such as to promise an ima-ginary wedding-veil and the resurgent possibility of a new kind of 'Poème' or 'Fiction' ('le voile d'illusion rejailli'). The new canvas sail of pp. 6–7 becomes a new veil, a text born of the union between contingency and control; and such a veil, so tenuous and insubstantial that it seems to haunt its two progenitors like the merest phantom gesture ('leur hantise / ainsi que le fantôme d'un geste'), 'chancellera'—will both stagger uncertainly across the page and yet, lent wings by chance, bridge the chasm of the featureless page with a chiasmus (on the following double page, the centrefold and deepest 'abîme' of the text, and also across 'Un coup de Dés' as a whole). And the new 'vers' that is this veil 's'affalera'—will continue to slump to the bottom of each page for lack of a fixed poetic form, and yet, like a sail being lowered down a mast or a lifeboat into the sea (the principal sense of 'affaler'), will also descend the page as the result of a consciously controlled 'manœuvre' overseen by the master in charge of its 'chute', of this 'chance oiseuse' (10). For in the pulley at the top of the mast is the 'dé', the 'Plaque de cuivre percée d'un trou circulaire, qu'on adapte aux rouets des bois des poulies pour recevoir l'axe' (Littré).

A new sail, a new veil: collapse and control, 'folie'. The 'maniaque chenu' of the alexandrine has become the 'acte de démence' that is the new 'vers'. And, lest we forget: 'N'ABOLIRA' (11). This childlike, ghostly heir to ancient prosody cannot abolish chance itself: no art ever could or will, for the artefact always exceeds the intentions of its artisan. But it can always pretend, pliantly displaying itself in sinuous italic as a merely provisional hypothesis yet boldly declaring its capital ambition to try: 'COMME SI / [...] / COMME SI.' The chiasmus on pp. 12–13, this double page being the centre of the poem, announces the tentativeness and novelty of the enter-prise: 'COMME SI / Une insinuation simple'—'le vierge indice / COMME SI'. The new spatial prosody is based on the hemistichs of the alexandrine (each page, we almost hear, is 'comme six', as well as like the English 'sea'); and whether its presence is obscure or blatant, self-consciously reflexive or crudely evident in its tumble down the page ('Une insinuation simple / au silence enroulée avec ironie / ou / le mystère / précipité / hurlé'), here it is in this nearby vortex of the poem (in the centre of the central double page), a 'proche tourbillon d'hilarité et d'horreur'. Whether the 'folie' of this new 'vers' be a cause for mirth (on the part of a scornful observer or the exhilarated poet as 'clown hilare') or a profound sense of horror (the read-er's and/or the poet's) at such a vision of anarchy, the new prosody performs its balancing act, like some circus acrobat with two feet precariously poised on a horse's back ('voltige'), around the 'gouffre' of both chaos and the centrefold—neither falling into it, there to strew its words, nor avoiding its dangers by keeping to the outside of the page ('sans le joncher / ni fuir'), but cradling it as the unsullied emblem of the new poetics of space ('et en berce le vierge indice'), a virgin sign born of dice, in dice. Where the old 'vers' is tossed in the stormy waves of the page, now the new 'vers' gently rocks in the still centre of a maelstrom.

As the centre is left behind, the visual turbulence recommences, and the extreme imbalance of pp. 14–15 offers an inverse image of that on the double page preceding the less asymmetrical, chiastic centrefold. Following the shipwreck of the alexandrine, the lopsided dive of the bird, and the drowning of the old master, the one surviving 'indice' of the event (a clue but also the index-finger of the vanished hand, a 'digitus', a 'dé') is a quill (feather or pen), solitary and distraught ('plume solitaire éperdue'), lost in the void (hom. 'et perdue'), unless by chance encounter or fleeting contact some duodecimal and cylindrical object like a toque were to come up against it ('que la rencontre ou l'effleure uné toque de minuit'). The solitary quill needs the new structure of a three-dimensional alexandrine for the turbulence of the text to be controlled ('immobilis[é]') in a willed stillness quite different in value from the unyielding whiteness of the page that mocks the poet's art ('cette blancheur rigide / dérisoire'). The cube of the die gives way to the cylinder of the toque (and of the dice-box and the inkwell, each in its own way a 'toque de minuit'), as the poem, constructed of concentric circles—'enroulée avec ironie'—begins to turn back on itself and proceed to its end by mirroring, double page by double page, the drama of its preceding pages.[42] The quill needs the weft and warp of the new prosody, a black velvet texture creased (during this 'crise de vers') as if by the dark wrinkles of creative merriment brought on by this confrontation with mocking whiteness ('au velours chiffonné par un esclaffement sombre') or creased in vexation ('chiffonné') at this very mockery, at the 'esclaffement sombre' of the unrelieved blankness.

For it is by contrast with this very blackness of a midnight sky (and the constraints of the new prosody) that the virgin quill itself, a white object previously lost against a white background (and a prosodist bereft of formal context), can now assert its own 'blancheur rigide'. This quill—'dérisoire' in the paltriness of its challenge to the random chaos of *vers libre*—stands out,

---

[42] Thus, surrounding the centrefold, pp. 10–11 and 14–15 (similar page layout in mirror-image; account of a meeting, the conjunction of the 'vieillard' with 'probabilité', of the 'plume' with the 'toque'); pp. 8–9 and 16–17 (balanced certainties are swallowed up by the sea-page: 'l'unique Nombre qui ne peut pas être un autre' and '*Si*'); pp. 6–7 and 18–19 (experience of shipwreck in 'l'Abîme' and the 'gouffre' respectively: capsizing ship and falling feather); pp. 4–5 and 20–1 (impossibility of achieving pattern: 'JAMAIS', 'RIEN / N'AURA EU LIEU / QUE LE LIEU'); pp. 2–3 and 22–3 (the 'désir' and the 'Idée': 'UN COUP DE DÉS' and 'EXCEPTÉ PEUT-ÊTRE UNE CONSTELLATION'); and pp. 1 and 24 (the title-page and silence).

however exiguously, yet still sufficiently ('en opposition au ciel / trop / pour ne pas marquer / exigüment') for the old master's heir—born on the reefs upon which the alexandrine foundered ('prince amer de l'écueil')—not to don it as a feather in his cap (s'en coiffe') as if it were the alexandrine itself ('comme de l'héroïque'[43]). The 'irrésistible' whiteness of the page is captured by and in the whiteness of the quill but is no longer overwhelming. It is 'contenu': contained within the new prosody of space, the new three-dimensional alexandrine, by the young prince's slight but now creative ('virile') powers of intellect ('sa petite raison')—and ratio (in the calculated dimensions of the text). Like another Hamlet, whose traditional nineteenth-century costume included a black velvet toque adorned with a white feather, the young poet-prince, the new 'vers', is caught between the fear of action and the need for action, between silent consent to chaos or the murder of the *vers libre* that has usurped the throne of the murdered alexandrine,[44] followed by a reinstatement in new form of the ancient lineage of the 'antique vers auquel je garde un culte'. As p. 10 revealed, the new 'vers' seems to share Hamlet's 'folie' but, like Hamlet's perhaps, it is only simulated: for here the new poet-prince will contain the whiteness 'en fou-dre'. The print may appear to zigzag across the pages like random flashes of lightning accompanying the tempest that caused the shipwreck, yet this 'foudre' may be the thunderbolt of a new creator, the thunderbolt of Jupiter which, since Virgil, has traditionally consisted of twelve parts.[45] Or the 'foudre' on a coat-of-arms, four spears arranged to form a St Andrew's cross, a chiasmus, against a background of ascending and descending flames, of a 'conflagration' (8). The 'coup de dés' is also a 'coup de foudre',[46] 'Un coup de Dés' a heraldic shield to protect the poet and to bear his arms while the die is '*LANCÉ DANS DES CIRCONSTANCES / ÉTERNELLES*', in the timeless joust of poetic art.

Like some Hamlet mourning the drowned Ophelia, the young prince of prosody is, on the following double page, at once 'soucieux / expiatoire et

[43] 'Le vers héroïque' is a term applied to Greek and Latin hexameters and to the French alexandrine (Robert). As Littré notes, it was also applied to the decasyllabic line of the French medieval *chanson de geste*. Originally (*c.*1170) the alexandrine allowed for the possibility of thirteen syllables if it contained a so-called 'césure épique', i.e. a non-elided but otherwise mute e between the sixth and seven syllables: e.g. 'Quand prise eut Babylon*e* que tant eut désirée' (see Jacques Roubaud, *La Vieillesse d'Alexandre* (Paris, 1978), 7). 'Un coup de Dés', the title of which has thirteen syllables (but no 'césure épique'), also ends on a decasyllable, 'Toute Pensée émet un Coup de Dés', and might be said to be a latter-day *chanson de geste*.

[44] Cf. Roubaud's reference to 'l'assassinat de l'alexandrin dans les années 1870–1880' (*La Vieillesse d'Alexandre*, 10).

[45] Littré: 'Sorte de dard enflammé [...]; suivant Virgile il était formé de trois rayons de grêle, trois de pluie, trois de feu et trois de vent.'

[46] The erotic connotation is prepared for by 's'en coiffe' ('falls for', 'becomes infatuated with'), as if the new 'vers', the young prince, is intoxicated (a further sense of 's'en coiffe') with his new-found potency ('sa petite raison virile'). Cf. 'Victorieusement fui...'.

pubère'. The old art has sunk beneath the waves; and he—beneath the skies (hom. 'sous cieux'), still anxious (despite the contact with the 'toque de minuit' and the activity of his 'raison virile/en foudre': i.e. the discovery of the new prosody) and concerned to propitiate the wrath of the gods (evident in this violent storm) by an act of purifying art even though he has only just learnt of his new-found powers ('pubère')—falls silent ('muet'): even though his voice has broken (hom. 'mué') and he possesses the feather, the new instrument of writing, that has fallen from the wings of the former alexandrine, that bird that has changed, moulted ('mué'). The mute space which invades the upper regions of this double page is broken, after this moment of anxiety and doubt, by a laughing, triumphant assertion that the simulation of the old prosody in a new form ('*COMME SI* / [...] / *COMME SI*') is the right way forward. 'As if' has become 'but yes!', and the letters of *SI*[47] in their bold sinuous italic have become an emblem of the new spatial prosody itself.

For *SI* is like Baudelaire's 'thyrse', except that the central rod and the surrounding vine have been separated out. In Mallarmé's version, the *I* is the 'plume solitaire éperdue' with its 'blancheur rigide', erect and assertive against the surrounding turbulence; it is now 'La lucide et seigneuriale aigrette de vertige / au front invisible'. The 'plume' has become an 'aigrette', a decorative osprey feather either real or made of precious stones (pearls from the sea, or diamonds ['solitaire', later 'brillant']) or glass (verre/vers). It is 'lucide' because (etymologically) bright, shining white like 'une lucide', a particularly bright star in a constellation; and 'seigneuriale' as the adornment of the new young master, the new prince of prosody.[48] The solitary survivor from the giddy whirl ('vertige') of the shipwreck, this quill is also a 'vers-tige': the 'tige', or central scape of the feather, connecting the 'vers' on either side, a means of controlling *vers libre* within a unified structure. Worn on the forehead of an invisible head (the 'impersonal poet' become an instrument of prosody), it 'scintille' (like a 'lucide') with a lucidity, or sure knowledge of its purpose, which contrasts with the hoary mania of the old master and the 'folie' that this prosodic experiment was once thought to be.

Behind the *I*, as if in its shadow, stands the *S*: like the dimly perceived shape of a sinuous siren, briefly upright ('puis ombrage / une stature mignonne ténébreuse debout / en sa torsion de sirène'), as with the scales on the ends of its forked tail it impatiently slaps the rock nearby, trying

---

[47] In the proofs Mallarmé is insistent on the largest bold italic which the printer can supply. Note also that SI visually resembles a pairing of 5 and 1. By an irony of history the international system of standardized measurement formulated and agreed in 1960 is known by the acronym SI (Système International).

[48] Cf. Larousse under 'toque'. When Napoleon created his new imperial nobility, he revised heraldic symbols by replacing the 'casques' and 'couronnes' of ancient nobility with toques bearing a varying number of plumes. The most prestigious, for princes, was a 'toque de velours noir bordée de vair avec un porte-aigrette d'or surmontée de sept plumes blanches'.

desperately to remain erect ('debout / le temps / de souffleter / par d'impatientes squames ultimes bifurquées / un roc'). This siren is the source of the siren song that is the text itself, sinuous eddies of words swirling round the quill as it writes and held in place by the 'squames', or squares, of the manuscript page or the invisible 'squames' with which the spatial prosody shapes the poem. Quill and text, leitmotif and 'motifs adjacents', centrefold and spreading lines, the direct and the oblique, 'le mystère hurlé' and 'Une insinuation simple': *si* symbolizes 'Un coup de Dés' and, by the reflection of art, *is*.

(c) *Six or Seven?*

SI / C'ÉTAIT LE NOMBRE.

But another shipwreck is in prospect, for the young prince aboard his new 'bâtiment' of a spatial prosody based on the numbers six and twelve has been lured on to a rock by this siren song. 'Seigneurial', he thought to have found a new ancestral seat, to have created a new prosodic structure from the infinite possibilities offered by *vers libre* ('manoir / [...] / qui imposa / une borne à l'infini'). But the 'point dernier qui le sacre' is still some way off, and his new seat proves to be a 'faux manoir', an illusory place of rest upon which he founders and which vanishes into the mist ('tout de suite / évaporé en brumes'). For the number six is quietly but surely being replaced by the number seven.

As we move from pp. 16–17 to 18–19, '*rire que si*' becomes '*rire que si C'ÉTAIT LE NOMBRE*' and the laughter begins to sound ironic. To have been so sure (we hear) 'que six était le nombre', that six would have been *the* number to structure the contingency of *vers libre* (six folded sheets, twelve double pages, etc.). No, that novel prosody would still be contingent, would still be ('*CE SERAIT*') '*LE HASARD*'. (Here the hypothesis begun with '*COMME SI*' begins to end as roman type returns, proclaiming paradoxically the certain existence of chance.) For what if six were just one of several numbers structuring the text, what if seven is just as responsible for patterning the void? 'Rire que six! Sept est le nombre', though not precisely homophonic (cf. [sete] and [sɛte]), raises the possibility which is confirmed on the final page that the constellation of the text may be more akin to the seven stars of the Plough than to the double-six of an alexandrine. Instead of achieving the maximum with his prosodic dice-throw, perhaps the poet has merely thrown the commonest combination of all.

If this text is indeed a princely shield, then, by heraldic rule, it has the space for seven 'pièces honorables' of which the oblique line (or 'barre'

(9))[49] is one. If the function of this text is to make 'cette blancheur' (15) of the page legible by fragmenting the whiteness by means of print, then it (or rather the 'plume') is comparable with the 'solitaire' diamond (or prism) which breaks light into a spectrum of seven colours (cf. Mallarmé's reference in the preface to the 'subdivisions prismatiques de l'Idée'). Moreover 'cette blancheur' of the blank page may be divisible not only into twelve double pages but into 'cette voile alternative' (appropriately mentioned on p. 7), or 'sept voiles alternatives'. For this is an alternative way of reading the text. If the reader counts successively what is visible to the eye as he or she first approaches the folded text, opens it, and then closes it after pp. 22–3, then there are thirteen 'spreads': the first and last (which are strictly speaking 'half-spreads') being the single pages 1 and 24, the seventh being the centrefold. These 'spreads' (and 'half-spreads') would thus correspond to the thirteen syllables of the title, while the syllabic distribution of the title (6+7) might be seen as a display of the text's own move from the six of dicing possibility to the seven of stellar pattern in the Plough, from the evils of devilish contingency as represented by the number of the Beast (666) to the perfection traditionally symbolized by the number seven.[50] Since the centrefold belongs as much to one half of the text as to the other, a counting of the 'spreads' in each half leads not to two sixes (or hemistichs) but to the figure of seven twice ('sept voiles alternatives'), in other words a paginal sonnet. 'Sept, voile alternative': seven is the other sail of this poetic craft upon which the Master seeks to navigate the maelstrom. For if the central gutter is taken as the heart of 'quelque proche tourbillon', then the poem may be said to consist of the seven concentric circles of a textual whirlpool, or perhaps the seven heavens of antiquity swirling in some kind of cosmic whirlwind. In either case 'Un coup de Dés' comes to resemble a cylindrical sonnet, a sacred scroll (cf. 'enroulée avec ironie') of reflexive sevens.

Might the text also be offering us an alternative dance of the seven veils? Is it haunted by Mallarmé's preoccupation with Hérodiade, the symbol of beauty whose performance means the severing of a head, the 'death' of Mallarmé, perhaps here reflected in the drowning of the old master and the

---

[49] If one reads 'la barre / de cette [sept,] conflagration', the oblique becomes one of seven ways of structuring the conflagration which the 'blason' of the text threatens (as *vers libre*) to become. The oblique itself is precisely the direction of reading which, in a novel manner, insinuates itself in 'Un coup de Dés' between the traditional readings across and down the page.

[50] See John Sweet, *Revelation* (London, 1990), 14–15: '*Six* is the number of Antichrist, seven minus one, the number of imperfection, penultimacy and evil. Its fundamental inadequacy is expressed in its intensification, *six hundred and sixty-six, the number of the beast* [Revelation 13: 18]. *Seven* is four plus three, signifying completeness.' As Sweet further points out, 'Numbers in both Greek and Hebrew were represented by letters of the alphabet—a=1, b=2 etc. (they did not have Arabic numerals)—and so any word or name could be given a numerical value by adding up its letters, a procedure called *isopsēphia* or *gēmatria*.' Applying this procedure to the French alphabet, one finds that 'silence' may be represented as 67. (I am grateful to Professor Richard Griffiths for drawing my attention to Sweet's book.)

baptism of his successor? Does 'l'inutile tête / legs en la disparition' (10) recall the 'rupture franche' of the 'Cantique de saint Jean', itself a reminiscence of Igitur's 'dernière figure, séparée de son personnage par une fraise arachnéenne et qui ne se connaît pas'?[51] Such links may seem tenuous until the role of music is recalled ('Musique [...] au fond signifiant Idée ou rythme entre des rapports'), together with Mallarmé's comparison of the versification of 'Un coup de Dés' to 'subdivisions prismatiques de l'Idée'. For *si* is the seventh note on the musical scale and so called after the initials of 'Sancte Iohannes' following a nomenclature introduced by Guido d'Arezzo.[52] D'Arezzo's scale, which may or may not have its origins in Pythagoras and the 'tetractys',[53] consisted of six overlapping hexachords (diatonic series of six notes having a semitone between the third and the fourth). D'Arezzo's gamut was later increased to include a seventh note, thus creating the octave (defined as the interval between two notes that are seven diatonic scale degrees apart). Equivalent to the Greek 'harmonia', the octave was distinguished from other perfect intervals by Ptolemy in the second century by being given the name 'homophonia'.

The 'plusieurs moyens' which Mallarmé claims in his preface to have used in writing 'Un coup de Dés' 'sous une influence, je sais, étrangère, celle de la Musique entendue au concert', now begin to seem more pervasive than a typographical imitation of the Wagnerian leitmotif or even than the symphonic structure of theme and variation. Were silence to be seen as the two 'homophonic' terms of this text (before the text is opened, after it is closed), then 'Un coup de Dés' is a repeated octave within which two groupings of seven paginal 'spreads' constitute the individual notes. Hence at the very heart of the text, between the two series of seven notes or 'spreads', lies the silence of the centrefold's central gutter; and hence the poem's self-description as 'Une insinuation au silence'. And it is in the course of this centrefold (pp. 12–13) that the text is most evidently at sixes and sevens. '*COMME SI* [...] / *COMME SI*' raises homophonically the prospect of two sixes being thrown in symmetrical order, a maximal structuring of the text as cubic alexandrine. And this homophone insists on its presence throughout the double page in 'insinuation', 'silence', and 'précipité', being echoed in reverse in 'mystère' and 'indice', and looming visually in 'simple'. It is indeed 'irré*si*stible' (15), finally imposing itself as queen to Hamlet's prince

[51] OC, 439.

[52] D'Arezzo designated the individual notes of the scale (or gamut: 'gamme ut') by taking the initial syllables of the half-lines in a hymn to St John the Baptist which themselves each fell on successive notes of the diatonic scale: '*Ut* queant laxis / *Re*sonare fibris / *Mi*ra gestorum / *Fa*muli tuorum / *Sol*ve polluti / *La*bii reatum, / Sancte Iohannes'. 'Si', coined when the Aretinian scale was increased to seven, has since been superseded by 'ti'. 'Si' is also the first word in 'Les Noces d'Hérodiade'.

[53] See Kirk *et al.*, *The Pre-Socratic Philosophers*, 234. Pythagoras is traditionally credited with the invention of the diatonic scale (see Littré, 'gamme').

on pp. 16–17 in 'sirène' ('si-reine', 'sea-reine') and *si* itself. Yet even while '*SI*' proclaims the centrality of six as structuring agent throughout the text, the very emphasis on homophony calls attention to its aural potential and its other meaning as the seventh note of the scale. And there at the heart of the text, as six proclaims itself, seven tacitly counters it in literal quantities. '*COMME SI*' (twice), 'silence', 'mystère', 'quelque', 'horreur', 'voltige', 'gouffre', 'joncher': only 'simple', 'ironie', 'proche', 'autour', and 'vierge indice' offer resistance (by having six, not seven, letters). Word length momentarily (?) loses its contingency on this double page, as six and seven vie for supremacy; and on pp. 18–19 the sixes boldly have it, as '*C'ÉTAIT, LE NOMBRE, CE SERAIT, LE HASARD*' assert their numbers ($1+5, 2\times6, 2\times6, 2\times6$). Here is silent numbering, a strategy of silence, 'Une insinuation au silence': and of course in music there are seven types of that seven-letter word 'silence'.[54] As we turn the pages from first to last, the seven spreads followed by seven spreads of 'Un coup de Dés' orchestrate blank space in a sonnet of silence.

Returning now to the shipwreck of the new prosody on the rock of seven, we note that the 'prince amer ('à mer')', standing 'soucieux' (16), might turn his gaze from the whiteness of the sea-page beneath to the blackness of the night sky above (cf. 'cette blancheur [...] / en opposition au ciel'), might count the 'cieux' beneath which he stands and recall (as already suggested) the seven heavens of antiquity (each planet having its own 'sky'), and he might further recall the 'music' that these spheres are alleged to make.[55] Perhaps seven is the number by which chance can be vanquished, not six. The pubescent prince of the cubic alexandrine gives way now to a new-born prosody, 'issu stellaire' (18), an issue of the stars indeed since the 'lucide' has become separated from the 'aigrette' (which flutters lost and vanquished at the bottom of the page: 19) and now asserts its starry certitude, the knowing reverse of 'si', 'is-su'. But 'six', the number which had once seemed the means of conquering the contingent *vers libre*, did it exist as a sure mathematical means, or did it simply offer (as the italics suggested) a sketchy, illusory pattern born of the anguish brought on by the shipwreck of the alexandrine ('*EXISTÂT-IL* / autrement qu'hallucination éparse d'agonie')? Did it really provide a structure that had beginning and ending ('*COMMEN-ÇÂT-IL ET CESSÂT-IL*'), for it seemed to be denied the very moment it appeared ('sourdant que nié': the '*SI*' of *COMME SI* / [...] / *COMME SI*' being both a six and a seven) and seemed to be at once surrounded and set at nought ('et clos quand apparu') by the contingent scattering of the text

[54] 'La pause, la demi-pause, le soupir, le demi-soupir, le quart de soupir, le huitième de soupir, le seizième de soupir' (Robert).
[55] Cf. Aristotle's account of this, reproduced in Kirk *et al.*, *The Pre-Socratic Philosophers*, 344–5.

('quelque profusion répandue en rareté')? Did it even manage to add up, to constitute a mathematical pattern at all ('SE CHIFFRÂT-IL')—a single pattern would have sufficed to prove its worth ('évidence de la somme pour peu qu'une')—and did it even shed any light ('ILLUMINÂT-IL') in the darkness of that 'ombre enfouie dans la profondeur' (7) as it had once promised to do? (Perhaps a stellar seven is more likely to shed this light.) No, the prosody of the cubic alexandrine was as contingent as chance itself, neither more nor less so, just the same ('CE SERAIT / pire / non / davantage ni moins / indifféremment mais autant LE HASARD').

And so the quill that had thought in encountering the 'toque de minuit' to have immobilized the page now falls ('Choit la plume': while fondled like a fond hope by chance itself ('LE HASARD / Choit / la plume')), hanging in the air and tilting from side to side (like the wing and ship on pp. 6–7, the 'mirror-page' of pp. 18–19[56]), a 'rythmique suspens' as surviving 'indice' of the disaster ('sinistre') which has taken place. It sinks into the grave of the white page from which it had previously arisen, at the summit of the page (14), as an act of 'folie' (10), an emblem of the new prosody of space ('s'ensevelir / aux écumes originelles / naguères d'où sursauta son délire jusqu'à une cime'). But this 'cime', the height of optimism and the belief in a prosody and form of textual control that would conquer the contingency of *vers libre* and give structure to the page, has withered and faded (as the image of the 'plume' now fades from the poem) with the realization that number has not vanquished the unrelieved sameness of the blank page ('flétrie / par la neutralité identique du gouffre'). The 'horizon unanime' (9), when sea and sky merged in the tempest which assailed the old master, has now become once more the 'l'Abîme' of the double page, its whiteness stretching out on either side of the central 'gouffre' in immaculate tedium.

The italics of hypothesis now end, as the fond notion of a cubic prosody recedes, a 'voile d'illusion' (10) or a plume of spray that leapt from the crest of a wave to figure the beauty of a siren before falling back into the limitless ocean. But even as it fell, its 'rythmique suspens' (like the earlier 'coque / d'un bâtiment / penché de l'un ou l'autre bord': 7) suggests that instead of looking for a prosody which 'immobilizes' the text, some more mobile, dynamic figuration will perhaps achieve the patterning if the contingency of the *vers libre* is to be overcome, a possibility which is explored and finally asserted in the remaining two double pages of the poem.

'RIEN', we now learn on pp. 20–1, 'N'AURA EU LIEU / QUE LE LIEU': nothing will have happened, the hypothesis has vanished, contingency is still the problem, and the place and space of the page will simply have asserted its own irrefutable existence. No trace is left of this dramatic 'crise [de vers]' (even though, being 'mémorable', it is potentially recordable), or

---

[56] See above, n. 42.

maybe it was a typically futile human event that took place, something undertaken without any prospect of a result ('ou se fût / l'événement accompli en vue de tout résultat nul / humain'). The everyday gesture of a hand raised to write, to make the prosodic throw, is simply tilting / pouring absence ('une élévation ordinaire verse l'absence'); and the 'vers', far from espousing the rhythms of the frothing, tumultuous waves of the turning pages, is nothing but an inferior, random lapping of print ('inférieur clapotis quelconque') in which the empty act of writing disperses itself in fits and starts ('comme pour disperser l'acte vide / abruptement'). This was the act of writing that had aspired, by means of the 'fiction' of a 'Poème' ('par son mensonge') to found the shipwreck of the alexandrine on the new but, alas, insubstantial basis of the '*si(x)*' ('qui sinon [si non] / [...] / eût fondé la perdition') within the indeterminate reaches of the white page in which all reality or shape or significance dissolves ('dans ces parages / du vague / en quoi toute reálité se dissout').

Yet even as this sense of failure is expressed, the alternative, positive, prospect of poetry as a patterned absence makes itself felt. Mallarme's cherished 'RIEN' is a something, and 'se fût l'événement' can be heard as the more confident 'ce fut l'événement': an event accomplished with no prospect of a tangible result, a human event, the great achievement that is Art. The very assertion 'RIEN / N'AURA EU LIEU / que le lieu' spreads across the page like the seven words[57] of a Plough. This is no ordinary elevation, but a religious dedication of language in ordered 'verse':[58] a repeated raising of words (as we turn each page and see 'le Vers' begin again at the top in hope and aspiration and expectant flight).[59] 'Verse l'absence': 'vers, cela [est une] absence', but also 'vers cela absence'; it is an absence, as we have seen so often, because 'le Vers' does not seek to represent the 'réalité' beyond language; but also, we hear, 'le Vers' concealed absence. By weaving its word-lace it offers a semblance of 'musical' inter-connectedness which veils the gulf (as Baudelaire put it in 'Une mort héroïque') of the Absurd, which draws a 'voile d'illusion' over the void. And 'illusion', being derived from 'ludere', is a game: chance has been incorporated into the game of art, the 'Jeu suprême', just as chance as 'chute' has become the 'rythmique suspens du sinistre'.

And on the final double page of 'Un coup de Dés' comes the salvaging of hope from the wreckage of prosody: 'EXCEPTÉ / PEUT-ÊTRE / UNE CON-

---

[57] Counting 'N'AURA' as one. Cf. *Corr.*, iv. 292, where Mallarmé refers to 'C'est' as one word.

[58] 'Ordinaire' comes from the Latin 'ordinarius', meaning 'rangé par ordre'. 'L'ordinaire de la messe' is the term for those parts of the Mass which do not vary with the religious calendar, such as the raising of the Host or 'Elevation'.

[59] The upper reaches of each page are generally associated with height, flight, hope, control, and the lower reaches with shipwreck, fall, dissolution, and chance.

STELLATION'. Language raised to the level of the 'Vers' ('à l'altitude') occupies an 'espace littéraire' where the place of the page ('l'endroit' and 'l'envers', the recto and verso of the text) 'fusionne avec au delà'—establishes contact (like the 'vieillard/vieil art' with 'probabilité' and the 'plume with the 'toque') with a beyond, a realm of spatial and semantic suggestion or 'mystère' far removed from the everyday ('hors l'intérêt / quant à lui signalé / en général'). And this new fusion, or pattern, replacing cubic prosody (hom. 'fut six'),[60] operates 'selon telle obliquité par telle déclivité', the oblique and sloping disposition of the words upon the page. Attempts to overcome the contingency of *vers libre* by founding some static, immobile prosodic system on the alexandrine or the sonnet give way to the concept of a dynamic spatial prosody wherein the scattering of the 'vers' across the page figures chance itself and thereby conquers it. For as Blanchot notes: 'du moment qu'il y a corrélation précise entre la forme du poème et l'affirmation qui le traverse en le soutenant, la nécessité se rétablit.'[61] Putting this slightly differently, one might say that the one way to make *vers libre* stop appearing contingent is to make chance and the problem of writerly control the subject of the poem, its central 'Pensée'.

Where once the 'vers' of 'Un coup de Dés' resembled the flames of 'cette conflagration à ses pieds' (pp. 8–9), a holocaust of metrical feet in twice-seven 'spreads', and then the jagged lightning of a twelve-part thunderbolt, now it consists of 'feux', 'les feux du firmament'; and the word 'vers' makes its first individual appearance in the poem (cf. 'envergure', 'verse'). The 'vers': 'ce doit être / le Septentrion aussi Nord / UNE CONSTELLATION.' The 'vers' (hom. 'ce doigt', an 'indice' or index finger to replace the 'plume') must resemble the Septentrion (the Plough), which is also North (and traditionally 'indicates' the position of the Pole Star), a Constellation. The number 'si(x)', here wistfully recalled in 'aussi' (hom. 'oh, six') had led to the number 'sept' (via 'si' as the seventh note on the scale), and 'sept' now leads via the Plough to the idea of prosody as a stellar arrangement providing the guidance that every poet, like every Northern mariner, requires to save his poetic craft from the shipwreck of contingency.

This new prosody of scattered print may seem cold and forbidding, far removed from our usual expectations, forgetful of tradition and suggestive of the decadence and dilapidation which have now befallen the great metres of French poetry ('froide d'oubli et de désuétude'); yet not so much that it does not itself use the numerical calculations of traditional versification (as we have seen) and cannot still exhibit them in a pyrotechnical display of

---

[60] Cf. 'aussi loin qu'un endroit / fusionne avec au delà': at an altitude, 'au si (x), loin, qu'un (en droit) fusionne avec au delà'—a distant 'six' which one fuses (with), resulting in the 'au delà' of seven, or the constellation of the Plough in the sky.

[61] *Le Livre à venir*, 317.

virtuosity. Across the empty spaces of this sky-page, raised to higher status by art itself ('sur quelque surface vacante et supérieure'), it 'itemizes' word by word ('n'énumère': as on a new-born naked sea (hom. '[quelque surface] née, nue, mer')) the numbers six and seven as if they were the stars of a constellation ('le heurt successif / sidéralement / d'un compte total en formation'). For there in the disposition of the words is the shape of the Plough, both in the passage from 'EXCEPTÉ / à l'altitude' to 'aussi Nord' (or to 'en formation') and from 'veillant' to 'un Coup de Dés'; and there is the sideral evidence of six in the number of words in 'veillant / doutant / roulant / brillant et méditant',[62] as if this were the final death agony of the dice's six as illusory pattern (hom. 'six dés râle ment')—before, finally, the text ends ('avant de s'arrêter') with two phrases of seven words each ('à quelque point dernier qui le sacre', 'Toute Pensée émet un Coup de Dés'), the two Plough shapes on the page now condensed into two word-strings, both recalling that most sacred of poetic constellations, the Sonnet.

Spatial prosody here is not cold and sterile, but fiery and dynamic: the words and the 'vers' itself ever watchful, questioning, tumbling, shining like stars and reflecting on their own significance, a beloved diamond saying much (hom. 'brillant aimé dit tant'), before they cease their rolling at a final place, not a full stop [or 'point dernier'] but another aphorism (to go with the title and the leitmotif of the poem) which 'consecrates' its ending by bringing the text ('enroulée avec ironie') back to its beginning with the words 'un Coup de Dés'. The 'coup de Dés' of the title has now become a 'Coup de Dés', for the 'coup' in question is that which we have just witnessed and which now exists, not any old throw of the dice but this particular text, a linguistic throw of the dice. As Mallarmé explained in his letter to Gide, this poem has enacted the rhythms of its own subject: 'le rythme d'une phrase au sujet d'un acte ou même d'un objet n'a de sens que s'il les imite et, figuré sur le papier, repris par les Lettres à l'estampe originelle, en doit rendre, malgré tout quelque chose.'[63] The prosody of 'Un coup de Dés' flirts with the cube and the Plough as spatial analogues of the alexandrine and the sonnet before discovering its final identity in a fusion of form and content, an act of writing that is the writing of an act: 'Ton acte toujours s'applique à du papier.'[64]

[62] The five /ant/ being also 'completed' by 'avant'.
[63] See above, Introd. to Part V n. 2
[64] 'L'Action restreinte', OC, 369.

3

The Quest for Authority

LE MAÎTRE hors d'anciens calculs.

(a) Dicing with Data

> du hasard, qui ne doit [...] jamais qu'être simulé.
> ('Planches et feuillets')

So far, then, we have been able to see the pertinence of Mallarmé's account in the preface of the way in which his text operates. There is no conventional versification, rather 'un morceau, lyrique ou de peu de pieds'; the only 'nouveauté' (compared with *vers libre* presumably) is 'un espacement de la lecture'. The white space of the paper 'intervient chaque fois qu'une image, d'elle-même, cesse ou rentre, acceptant la succession d'autres': and indeed the preceding reading of 'Un coup de Dés' as an allegorical quest for prosody has revealed just this, as the images of the dipping bird-wing, the capsizing boat, the drowning master with arm upraised, the central whirlpool (or whirlwind), the solitary quill encountering a 'toque de minuit', the young prince, the siren standing in the shadow of an osprey feather, the feather sinking beneath the waves, and the emerging Plough have followed each other in turn. No 'real' event can be reconstructed from this sequence, no 'récit' of a traditionally representational kind, for the simple reason that the poem narrates its own evolution and calls up these images in turn as glimmering evocations of its own twists and turns. There is a 'mise en scène spirituelle exacte', a precisely staged enactment of the poet's combat with his medium—at the centre of which lies a 'fil conducteur latent' (one such thread has just been followed), and the 'subdivisions prismatiques de l'Idée' surface and vanish more or less closely interwoven with this 'fil' ('à des places variables'), even as the 'vraisemblance' of the 'Idée' (rather than any crude story of avian catastrophe or maritime disaster) dictates. The degree of blank space between the words or word-clusters ('cette distance copiée

qui mentalement sépare des groupes de mots ou les mots entre eux') be-
comes a kind of scansion ('semble d'accélerer tantôt et de ralentir le mouve-
ment, le scandant, l'intimant même selon une vision simultanée de la Page')
leaving us with the spectacle of 'cet emploi à nu de la pensée avec retraits,
prolongements, fuites, ou son dessin même'.

One would be wrong to think, however, that this poem is simply about
thought as the experience of mental wandering or that its main concern is to
represent the way in which thought is composed of central strands accom-
panied with varying degrees of relevance by subsidiary notions, qualifica-
tions, and afterthoughts. Or rather such a reading is convincing only if we
recognize that for Mallarmé thinking and writing are synonymous: 'penser
étant écrire sans accessoires, ni chuchotement mais tacite encore.'[1] The
poem's final constellation—'Toute Pensée émet un Coup de Dés'—reaffirms
the Mallarméan thesis, both by the capitalization of 'Pensée' (as in a writer's
published 'Thoughts') and by the verb 'émettre', that thought is a linguistic
act. Accordingly any 'pensée', be it a 'thought', an intention (e.g. 'j'avais la
pensée d'écrire un poème'), or an aphorism, is an encounter with the
contingency of language, however greatly cherished as an incontrovertible
truth (hom. 'Toute Pensée aimée, d'un coup, deux dés'). Each thought, in
this linguistic sense, is a chancy business, a throw of the dice, because all the
words come tumbling out, bearing all sorts of contingent characteristics and
potential interconnections which may well subvert or even flatly contradict
the 'intended' thought. Why indeed do readers of 'Un coup de Dés' never
read the final 'Pensée' as a reference to pansies? Could not this famous
aphorism be another way of saying: 'Je dis: une fleur! et, hors de l'oubli où
ma voix relègue aucun contour, en tant que quelque chose d'autre que les
calices sus, musicalement se lève, idée même et suave, l'absente de tous
bouquets'? Any thought is the linguistic seedbed of a thousand notions,
which the poet endeavours to orchestrate as one single 'notion pure', or
'Idée', in his poem. In 'Un coup de Dés' the combat with *vers libre* serves as
a paradigm of that greater struggle, the struggle with contingent language,
and the great originality of the poem is to display visually the disseminating
energy of words while yet silently weaving their myriad threads of potential
interconnection into a tapestry of heroic proportions. By now following at
least some of these threads—and this must necessarily be a painstaking
process—it will be possible to see just how determined the Master is to
remain a master still.

The seed of the 'Idée' that is 'Un coup de Dés' is 'dé' itself, which as in
'Prose (pour des Esseintes)' is literally inside the dehiscent 'word-pod' 'Idée'.
In its meanings of 'die' and 'thimble' it has two etymologies: respectively,
'datum' (from 'dare' = 'donner', 'jeter'), that which is given or already cast,

---

[1] 'Crise de vers', OC, 363-4.

and 'digitus' (= 'doigt'). Thus it summarizes the act of writing: a finger sews the contingent data of language together, like a hand throwing some dice. In its two meanings it is at once a cube and a cylinder: both of them three-dimensional, the one having six equal faces (cf. the 'cubic alexandrine') and the other 'enroulé' like an ancient scroll (cf. the seven concentric circles of this cylindrical sonnet). A 'dé' is also a protective piece of metal which sailmakers place in the palm of the hand, so that the sewn text resembles a canvas sail empowering the ship of poetic language and the poet its mas-ter[2]—and, being part of a pulley, the 'dé' is something upon which to hoist and lower the canvas of the text. It is also a thimble-like glass, so that 'un coup de dés' is a 'coup de verre/vers': intoxicated disorder may be the result, or 'salut' (a toast to poetry, and the poet's own salvation). Otherwise 'un coup de dés' is both 'une affaire qu'on laisse au hasard' and the result of a particular dice-throw, a circumstance and a result. The phrase also contains the order to sew and a unit of measurement: 'coude!' A 'dé' is moreover a printing term, being an engraved stamp for impressing a design or figure (as in coin-making or the embossing of paper). A gaming die and the stamp of authority.

One or more 'dés' are used in the game called 'le hasard' (from the Arabic 'az-zahr', and then Spanish 'azar', meaning 'die'[3]), the term 'le hasard' also denoting 'un coup heureux à ce jeu'—for example, six (though the word itself contains the obverse of this, 'as' (= the one on a die)). On the one hand, 'un jeu de hasard' is said of a game in which 'le calcul, l'habileté [. . .] n'ont aucune part' (Robert); on the other, it is a game played by established rules, a context of necessity in which contingency may express itself. In these etymological circumstances a throw of the dice is unlikely to abolish the die nor (in the strong legal sense of 'abolir' (e.g. 'abolir une loi, abolir un crime')) to annul the laws of the game, nor yet the laws of probability. A die is cast with the authority of the law.

'Un coup de Dés jamais n'abolira le Hasard': a die will never abolish 'l'azar', or as Jacques Roubaud suggests, 'lazare'.[4] The thirteen syllables of the title create a pressure to make 'Hasard' no longer aspirate, so that we may read the title-phrase as meaning that the linguistic throw of the dice will never abolish this extraordinary capacity of language to rise again from the death of reference and to create a new world of meaning. The English teacher in Mallarmé had no doubt anticipated Roubaud's suggestion (by hearing the mortality in a 'die') and tacitly taken it further with the thought

[2] Cf. also 'tenir le dé dans la conversation': = 'se rendre maître de la conversation et garder la parole' (Robert).

[3] Both Littré and OED record (under 'hasard' and 'hazard' respectively) William of Tyre's view that the Arabic word is derived from a castle in Palestine at Hasart or Asart. The die would thus originally be akin to the lordly ancestral seat evoked in 'Un coup de Dés'.

[4] See Ronat's edn, 10.

that 'a dying never will abolish the possibility of resurrection', for that is the message of 'Plusieurs Sonnets', 'Hérodiade', and many of Mallarmé's most important works.

And so the 'coup de Dés' is 'lancé' within 'des circonstances éternelles' of language: within dice-circumstances, a circus act to produces stanzas, and a tilting with the lance. 'Un coup de Dés' will prove to be the supreme 'vers de circonstance'. 'Lancé' derives from Low Latin 'lanceare', meaning to 'manier la lance', particularly during a joust or 'combat avec la lance et l'écu'. To throw the dice is to tilt at chance, and textual construction is the poet's shield, the words inscribed within in it like a heraldic coat-of-arms. It is also to launch a ship (whose sails are stitched with the protection of a 'dé'), and it is to communicate a verbal message (cf. 'lancer un appel, une proclamation, un arrêt'): communication is a hazardous journey. To be 'lancé' is to be drunkenly garrulous (from the 'coup de verre'); to be 'lancé' (of a textile) is to be woven according to a method whereby 'on fait usage de plusieurs navettes, et où chaque coup de trame n'opère, dans toute la largeur de l'étoffe, qu'un croisement partiel, suivi ou interrompu' (Larousse). What better description of 'Un coup de Dés': intoxicated gush, or a text with stitch-words (continuous or discontinuous) that never cover the whole width of the page?

The threads of the text can now be seen to stretch out in multiple directions. From a chancy launch we move at once to the 'naufrage' and the foaming sea;[5] from the lance and the textile that is 'lancé' we move to 'SOIT (hom. 'soie') / que / l'Abîme'. The shipwreck has a 'fond' (from 'fundus'= hollow), the bottomless, empty abyss of a language that has cast off from the shores of reference; yet this very void is a foundation (with the 'fond de la mer' being thus the deep (linguistic) potential of the medium upon which the craft has embarked), just as 'le fond de la voile' is the central part of the sail-text which is soon to be filled with the wind of polysemy. The white 'fond' (background) of the page is the basis (or 'dé' in the sense of a statue's plinth) for the 'bâtiment'[6] of the text; and since 'fond' also denotes the white spaces in fine art prints and the inner edge of a page, this 'hollow' background will indeed be Mallarmé's principal instrument ('un espacement de la lecture') in creating his paginal 'estampes' from the shipwreck of conventional typography and prosody. Newly baptized by the waters of the shipwreck (hom. 'fonts'), this original poem begins its life, haunted by the shadowy linguistic presence of a 'fonte' that has itself been shipwrecked and flung across the sea-page.

---

[5] The 'eau' and the 'rage' have already been noted in 'A la nue accablante tu': see above, Part IV, Ch. 4.

[6] 'Bâtir' derives from 'bast' (= bark) and 'besten' (= to weave bark), so that 'bâtiment' is originally a woven structure, either a hut or an article of clothing.

The 'fond' of this new textile is 'soie', no doubt spun by the 'ver à soie', a silk that will now be woven into the black velvet of the 'toque de minuit'. 'Fond' is also the term applied to the background of a heraldic shield, and 'abîme' (derived from the Greek 'abussos' meaning 'sans fond') is—as we know well from Gide—the centre of such a shield, 'en abîme' thus being the term for a heraldic emblem 'placée au milieu de l'écu sans toucher ni charger aucune autre pièce' (Larousse). Each word of Mallarmé's text thus resembles an isolated emblem 'placée en abîme', his whole gamble the first and only true 'mise en abyme'[7] (cf. 'coule en barbe sou[s], mise [,] / naufrage [,] cela' (9)). The pages on which this 'Abîme' occurs themselves figure this imminent catastrophe of words sliding irrevocably into the abyss of the central page-gutter never to be seen again.

As mentioned previously, 'la barre' (as the helm which the master is said once to have grasped) is also a heraldic term: namely, for two diagonal lines drawn across the shield and occupying a third of its width—which may remind us of Mallarmé's prefatory remarks about the 2 : 1 proportion of blank space to print and of his comparison of the text to a 'partition' (not only a musical score but the term for the divisions of a heraldic shield). When we encounter 'chef' (9), which is, like 'barre', one of the seven 'pièces honorables du blason', and 'nef' the heraldic term for ship, and 'foudre' (15) with its four darts arranged in a St Andrew's cross ('en sautoir'), and learn that 'furieux' (6), 'ombre', 'vol' (7), 'partie' (8), 'aigrette' (16), 'roc', 'debout' (17), 'clos', and 'sinistre' (19) are all technical heraldic terms, then it is clear that the quarterings on Mallarmé's 'grandes pages quadrillées' have been devised with masterly precision. 'Le Maître' is like a medieval 'seigneur', and even the 'point' at the end ('qui le sacre') may denote 'chacun des carrés de l'échiqueté' (Larousse): the final chequered square on his quartered paper. The writing of 'Un coup de Dés' may be a quixotic tilt of the lance, but the result will be a heraldic shield proclaiming the authority of a master 'dans ces parages du vague'. A 'parage' being originally the 'tenure de fief indivis entre frères' (Robert), it would seem that the prince (from 'princeps', the first or number one) of this poem rules over his double pages as over a dominion united despite the apparent separation of the pages (hom. 'sépara[ges]'; cf. 'sépare pages'). No wonder his rule is threatened by the 'sirène' (16), for does she not, like Hamlet's mother and stepfather, represent an unlawful coupling of 'sire' and 'reine'?

The silken threads of the heraldic 'abîme' thus lead far into the text, and similar labyrinthine adventure awaits the reader who pauses to reflect on the 'musique des mots' which composes 'Un coup de Dés'. In his preface, as we have seen, Mallarmé mentions a 'fil conducteur latent' running through

---

[7] Gide first used the phrase 'mise en abyme' as a term for literary reflexivity in 1893: see Lucien Dällenbach, *Le Récit spéculaire: Essai sur la mise en abyme* (Paris, 1977), 15.

the text, and the allegory of the quest for prosody has been traced as one such possible thread. Does he perhaps have in mind the word 'dé' itself? Already it has been possible to show some of the linguistic 'subdivisions prismatiques de l'Idée' which appear when one fractures the unity of the word 'Idée' and examines the spectrum of the resultant polysemy. 'Dé' alone provokes the major themes and images of the poem, the sea and the text, the cube and the cylinder, the ship and the sail. The binary aspect of the 'dés' with their consequent variety of possible numerical combinations prompts the reflexive account of spatial prosody; and the notional maximum (six or twelve) is orchestrated with this notional binarity in the number seven, being the sum of opposite sides or the commonest sum of two dice.

Accordingly the word 'dé' is placed in the text in a numerically significant pattern, occurring seven times in each half of the text. Thus: in the title, on p. 3, in 'DES CIRCONSTANCES' (5), 'désespérément' (6), 'au nom des flots' (8), 'écarté du secret qu'il détient' (9), and 'l'ultérieur démon immémorial' (10); then, in the second half, 'cette blancheur rigide / dérisoire' (15), 'son délire' (19), 'eût fondé' (21), and finally, in a great flurry on the final printed page, 'déclivité', 'désuetude', 'sidéralement', 'un Coup de Dés'. In this way the word 'dé', as a 'fil conducteur latent', weaves itself through the text and associates itself with the nodal points of the 'fiction' that is this 'Poème'. A dice-throw in the dicey circumstances of language; a desperate throw yet not excluding the hope that the 'dé' may prove a magnet (hom. 'dés: espère! aimant') to guide the poet-mariner across the 'dés flots' of language (just as the ever-visible Plough helps him to find the Pole Star); the secrets, or 'mystère', which the 'dés' of language are about to reveal; the death of the 'vieil art' of representational lyric poetry as the poet is led into a quasi-stellar 'conjonction' with probability by 'l'ultérieur démon immémorial', language itself (of immemorial antiquity, its original meanings indeed forgotten, yet the ulterior purpose of the poet)—the 'démon de l'analogie', language as an obsessive, subversive 'familiar' assailing the poet with homophonies and semantic links which threaten his every effort at authority.

Then, in the second half, 'dé' figures first as the mocking whiteness of the page ('cette blancheur rigide, / dérisoire') but, as with 'désespérément', there may be a positive note, for the homophonic presence of 'dé' as 'ris' and 'soie' and 'soir' creates a new constellation of hope. 'Ris' is the term for 'chacune des bandes horizontales des voiles, qu'on peut replier [...] pour diminuer la surface de voilure présentée au vent' (Robert), and one can readily imagine Mallarmé himself laughing inwardly as he sailed his boat along the Seine at Valvins thinking that the false etymology of 'rire' (as cognate with 'ridere'= to fold) allowed him to transform the mockery (and derisory undifferentiatedness) of the 'rigid' page into the folds of a silken sail at sunset. The 'démon de l'analogie' brought the text to the point of 'folie' (p. 10), and, as mentioned earlier, this is recalled on p. 19 by the evocation of the solitary quill as it sinks into the 'écumes originelles' from which 'naguères [...] sursauta son délire jusqu'à une cime'. Following the death of the 'vieil art', the poet as impersonal quill revelled in the delirium of homophony, the 'son' of language now released from the tyranny of univocity. This 'délire'—the dice become the ancient symbol of poetic art (hom. 'lyre')—allows the 'plume' to reach the heights of the 'cime': dead as a referential lyricist, the poet becomes more truly and essentially a poet, the 'plus me' (no longer 'me') becomes indeed 'plus me' (more 'me'),[8] perhaps 'si-me': so much 'me', at any rate 'sɪ'. The dice has become a seven-string lyre... and another heraldic emblem, the symbol of music.

This metamorphosis is echoed on the following double page when, during this moment of doubt and therefore, characteristically, in a passage which can be read in at least two ways, the play (or plashing) of language is described as an 'inférieur clapotis quelconque comme pour disperser l'acte vide / abruptement', a poetic act which otherwise 'par son mensonge / eût fondé / la perdition'. On the one hand the linguistic throw of the dice is an inferior use of language which, by its very obscurity, disperses the significance of the 'acte vide' constituted by the non-referential use of language, an act which might otherwise have been the basis for the very ruin, or 'perdition', of language. On the other hand, perhaps the apparent 'babble' that is Mallarmé's use of language threatens to dissolve the important and valuable, 'empty' act of non-representational language which might otherwise, precisely, have provided a solid basis within apparent linguistic incoherence. A dice-throw 'DU FOND D'UN NAUFRAGE' has become the 'dé' as potential 'fond' in these textual reaches 'en quoi toute réalité se dissout' (and, as homophony itself, 'se dit sous').

On the final printed page of the poem 'dé' occurs four times. 'Déclivité' (from Latin 'de'+'clivus'= slope) links the dice with the innovative, sloping 'scansion' of the text and its tilting typography (and by a possible false etymology with the cleavage of the page) which separates the two slopes of this dicey Parnassus (or 'dé-mon[t]'). 'Désuetude' evokes the prosody that has fallen into disuse, but the 'CONSTELLATION / froide d'oubli et de désuétude' suggests Mallarmé's new constellations of language which revive and incorporate the forgotten homophonies and etymologies of the 'démon immémorial'. 'Sidéralement' in turn evokes the death of representational language as a false death (hom. 'râle ment'), suggesting that the 'hallucination éparse d'agonie' (19) is a positive description of the text itself and a foreshadowing of this final evocation of its constellation of language by means of the number six and the word 'dé' itself—no doubt leaving the reader somewhat 'sidéré' by such sustained dicing with linguistic data.

---

[8] See Derrida, *La Dissémination*, 307.

Constellations offer dicey data too. According to some versions, the Greeks divided the sky into 60 constellations, which might suggest a parallel with the 60-point size in which Ronat claims the central word-string of the poem is printed. Larousse, on the other hand, gives 48: 12 in the Zodiac, 21 in the northern hemisphere, and 15 in the southern. In this case the point-size of 'POÈME' would be the relevant analogy. In either case it would be possible to see each point-size as a constellation, and the twelve different type variations employed within the text as analogous with the twelve signs of the Zodiac, especially as the sixth sign is Virgo, 'le vierge indice' (or Virgo in the dice of the Zodiac) of p. 13.[9] At the same time the five type sizes might be said to echo the five 'aspects' of a planet, while the notion of 'aspect' is reflected in the textual constellation of words in 'conjonction' (10; cf. 'rencontre' (15)) or in 'opposition' (15) or in a relation of 'obliquité' (23). The 'crise de vers' may be of astrological origin (from the superstitious belief that pathological, political, and other 'crises', or critical moments, are the result of planetary aspect), but it will be survived by the stellar or planetary patterns of the 'vers'.

The 'fil conducteur latent' of 'dé' leads via the duodecimal Zodiac to constellations, and to the particular constellation which, being made up of seven stars, represents the stellar outcome of a throw of the 'dés'. Accordingly the final printed page of 'Un coup de Dés' leaves us with the image of the Septentrion, the constellation named after seven 'triones' or oxen, and (by the British) called the Plough. Here Mallarmé returns to the word-patterning, central to 'Ses purs ongles...', in which the etymology of 'vers' (from 'vertere', to turn, and hence to plough; and 'versus', a furrow) produces the allegorical figure of the poet as ploughman, tilling the whiteness of the pages and leaving 'sillons' (or creases) of verse, 'sillons' to resemble that left also in 'Un coup de Dés' by the ship at sea. Each line of print furrows the page, just as each turning page opens to reveal a new furrow in its central fold. This agricultural allegory is woven into the poem by means of various nodal words, some of which being of vinicultural application evoke once more the vine of the 'thyrse'. For the abandonment of prosody is akin to the abandonment of the plough: 'la manœuvre avec l'âge oubliée' (the 'âge' being the beam of a plough), while the 'aile' which dips so precariously on p. 6 can mean 'the lame du soc de la charrue' (Larousse). The 'délire' (19) which this departure from poetic convention represents is etymologically a departure from a furrow ('de'+'lira'), while 'le heurt successif / sidéralement' is (in one of the senses of 'heurt') a 'mound, or watershed', the ridge[10] between each furrow upon which the words, star-

---

[9] Of the other signs only Aquarius (Verseau) appears to be (slightly) in evidence: cf. 'verse l'absence' (21).

[10] Also denoted by the word 'billon' present in 'tourbillon' (13). Thus the 'mystère / précipité / hurlé' of poetic language finds itself 'dans quelque proche tour—billon d'hilarité et d'horreur',

like, stand out against the uniformity of the field. Thus, in humble circumstances, 'une élévation ordinaire *verse* l'absence' (21).

Or a vineyard. The 'mémorable crise' (20) has taken place ('ou se fût l'événement': hom. 'ce fut l'événement'). The crisis has been both a 'fût' in its sense as the shaft of a plough and a 'fût' as the container of the wine, or product, of the ploughing—in fact of 'ces parages du vague' (21), since one sense of 'parage' is the 'labour donné aux vignes avant l'hiver' (Littré). This 'parage' has already been evoked on pp. 14–15 where one sense of 'sombrer' (= 'donner le premier labour [à la vigne]' (Littré)) allows one to read that 'une toque de minuit' immobilizes and, 'par un esclaffement', 'sombre / cette blancheur rigide'. Again the furrowed surface (cf. 'au velours chiffonné'). That the result of the dice-throw as act of ploughing should be 'clos quand apparu / enfin / par quelque profusion répandue en rareté' (19) suggests that the 'foudre' (15), or large cask, has been filled with the choicest vintage (grown perhaps on the 'bras [de vigne]' (8) or on the 'vergue' implied in 'envergure' (7)).

(b) 'Toute Pensée émet un Coup de Dés'

le fantôme d'un geste.

Such is the 'horizon unanime' of language,[11] and such the fusion of land and sea and sky in 'Un coup de Dés', that the vocabulary and images of ploughing interweave with the motifs of a bird's wing and a ship at sea. As the Master dices with his linguistic data, the discrete categories of human experience appear to dissolve into one, and each singular event threatens to become the shadowy, ghostly repetition of a primordial 'geste', of some essential 'rythme' of human experience. Indeed, as we shall see presently, each branch of learning into which human intellectual enquiry is traditionally divided—theology, law, mathematics, the natural sciences, etc.—seems to provide him with the same cryptic reply: 'Toute Pensée émet un Coup de Dés'.

Thus the poem charts the heavens and the sea simultaneously; and in this song of a siren, itself half-woman and half-fish (but originally half-bird), many words are neither fish nor fowl. The furrow becomes a wake, the ploughshare's wing the feathered instrument of flight; the 'aigrette' of bird

---

a ridge within some adjacent circle of the maelstrom-page, a 'billon d'or, heurt'. The etymology of 'bercer' (from 'vertere' (Larousse)) allows one to read 'et en berce le vierge indice' at the bottom of the page as a reprise of the image of white space being ploughed by centrefold-furrows.

[11] 'Horizon' derives from the Greek word for 'borner', so that poetic language is used to set limits to silence with words which are unanimously polysemic.

(and heraldic shield) might be an 'aigrette d'eau', plume as spume, just as the 'aile' might be the sail of a ship ('les ailes d'un vaisseau') or the wing of a 'bâtiment', itself a ship. 'Barbe', 'coque', 'envergure', and 'roc' (the mythical bird as well as rock) are all avian as well as marine, while 'barbe' and 'coque' have further piscatory (if not Piscean) senses.[12] The 'manoir' of a landlubber may evoke that nautical periphrasis 'le manoir liquide', while 'barre' is both the sandbar and the helm by means of which the Master seeks to avoid it—perhaps in the 'manœuvre' (9) known as a 'rencontre' (15) whereby the helm is set to counteract the current and prevent a circular motion. Similarly the text is dotted with terrestrial navigational aids which anticipate the Plough, 'amer' (as noun), 'feux', and 'indice' each having this technical sense of reference point or beacon. An apparently simple statement such as 'à quelque dernier point qui le sacre' (23) figures this 'horizon unanime' (or 'neutralité identique') that is the 'gouffre' of homophony—with 'point' (the centre of an expanse of sail), 'quille' (the keel in 'qui le sacre'), and 'sacre' (a type of falcon)—and thus obliquely sews together at the end of the poem the various motifs of sail and ship and bird. Against the sky ('ciel': 'si aile') the bird has flown, and we are left with the canvas of the text and the music of the spheres.

The injunction 'coude!' and the 'dé' itself as both thimble and sailmaker's palm-guard together spawn the several allusions to sewing and weaving which the text contains. This is, as we learn on the final page, a 'compte total en formation', and 'compte' is the word for the 'nombre de cent fils employés dans la largeur d'une pièce de toile' (Larousse)—as it might be, the number of centimetres (cf. 'le Maître/le Mètre') in terms of which the print-area (27 cm × 18 cm) and the dimensions of the paper upon which the poem is printed (38 cm × 57 cm) have been calculated. The disappearance of traditional prosody, suggested by 'legs en la disparition', may perhaps be heard (in the former, bequeathed pronunciation of 'legs') as the vanishing of a 'lé': a unit of width when measuring fabric, sail, or paper—an absence 'dans ces parages / du vague / en quoi toute réalité se dissout', where 'parage' has the sense of dressing or sizing cloth. 'Barre', likewise, is a measurement of cloth. An 'aile' is used in spinning (Littré) while an 'ais' serves in weaving silk, the 'S O I [E]' of this bleached textuality, the 'Abîme / blanchi / [...] / furieux', which bears the grotesque, apparently random motifs of print like 'furie', a type of Indian silk 'ainsi nommée des figures hideuses qui y était imprimées' (Littré). 'Chef', 'chiffonné', 'coque' (as egg-shaped loop of ribbon or embroidery), 'enroulée', and 'ras' each has an application in the lacework of the text; and the 'dernier *point* qui le sacre' (in fact the word 'Dés') is the final stitch that completes the seamster's

---

[12] Many words have alternative meanings as crustacean varieties, which Littré is particularly thorough in recording.

design. The 'velours' of the poem, the 'toque de nuit' (from 'tocca'= silk, gauze), has been completed, a 'voile d'illusion', a playful veil laid across 'toute réalité'. 'RIEN / N'AURA EU LIEU / QUE LE LIEU'; but 'un endroit / fusionne avec au delà'—the 'right' side of a fabric has achieved the power to evoke the 'mystère'[13] within and beyond language, an 'endroit' woven with 'a fil conducteur latent' twisted ('en sa torsion de sirène') on the spindle or 'fuseau' which glimmers fitfully in 'fusionne avec au delà'.

If 'dé' gives us this measured textuality (from 'thimble' and 'coude!'), its number 'six' gives us the 'si' of the musical scale (as discussed above). Resembling a musical score, the poem orchestrates the seven silences of the empty page with notes and bars ('barre', 'division' (9)), parts and tempi (8, 17), while 'LE MAÎTRE' as 'chef' (9) of the orchestra and master of the dance 'coule' (9)—executes, rather than sinks (cf. 'couler un pas de danse, couler plusieurs notes'). Various ballet steps ('retombé[e]' (7), 'écarté' (9)) evoke the golden dance introduced in 'hors d'anciens calculs' and later recalled in 'dans ces parages' (21: hom. 'danses et parages du vague'). The poem may offer a 'rythmique suspens' (19), a siren song to suggest the music of the spheres, but has it actually managed to 'authentiquer le silence': 'SE CHIFFRÂT- IL'? Has it reproduced essential rhythms or merely recorded the chaos of noise? A composed authority or 'son délire'? As already mentioned, 'Mystère', etymologically, is a shutting of the lips: thus, for it to be authentic, it must not be 'hurlé' (from 'ululare'= to hoot, screech, ululate) but 'muet' (16), not an owl but a swan, a 'cygne/signe'.

Thus the 'fil conducteur' of 'dé' leads via 'six' and 'si' to music: 'rire que SI'. The six is a seven, and not only because of the musical scale. Its very appearance on the page suggests a 'stature mignonne ténébreuse / en sa torsion de sirène', and 'mignonne' (in English 'minion') is the printer's term for 7-point type.[14] At the same time 'Si' is a chemical as well as a musical symbol, being the symbol for silicon (formerly known as silicium), the commonest element in nature after oxygen (the O, and 'eau', which corresponds to the blank space of the text). Number 14 in the periodic table, silicon is formed by 'cristallisation cubique', thus suggesting a text of seven concentric circles or fourteen 'semicircles' composed according to the pro-

---

[13] 'le mystère hurlé' (13) suggests both a 'mystère ourlé', and a 'mystère' that is 'hure' and 'lé' (or 'lai'): a width of text or paper (or a medieval lay) and the tousled head, the 'chef' which 'coule en barbe soumise', of the Master as decapitated St John the Baptist. In the absence of traditional prosody the 'aile' of 'le vers' shaved the page ('coupant au ras les bonds' (7)), but now, following the immersion of the old Master, 'pubère' (16) (from 'pubis'='hair') and 'velours' (15) (from 'villus'='poil') suggest that the former severed head has been succeeded by the new 'hairiness' of the 'prince', which then 'crowns' itself with the 'toque de minuit'. 'Pubère', the new prosody has arisen from (and is) 'quelque proche tourbillon [...] d'horreur' (from 'hérissement des cheveux'), a swirl of horripilation.

[14] In view of this one wonders whether the smallest type size in the poem (on the following double page) should not be 7-point rather than the 10-point which Ronat has proposed.

sody of the cubic alexandrine. Itself the principal component of glass ('verre/vers'), silicon derives etymologically, via silicium, from 'silex'= 'caillou'—'caillou' being in turn the source of 'calcul' and 'calculus'. 'SI' thus stands within 'Un coup de Dés' as a symbol of material existence achieved through calculation, the poem as printed matter brought into being by 'LE $NOMBRE$'.

In this way 'Un coup de Dés' begins to assume a quasi-scientific air; and as the alternative senses of words are explored, other ghostly 'gestes' emerge: for the poem displays at once a chemical event, a botanical specimen, and a physical phenomenon. Thus within language 'toute réalité se dissout' (21), and following this dissolution the signified either forms a precipitate ('le mystère / précipité') or remains in suspension, a 'rythmique suspens' (19) that has no preponderance of silicon and is characterized by a chemical 'neutralité du gouffre'. Words separate into particles of sound (by 'division' (9)) which may reassemble in a new fusion of sense ('fusionne avec au delà' (23)) that offers all the appearance of being non-compound, '*une insinuation* simple' (12; my emphasis).

Similarly, words or word groups are like the petals on a flower or branches on a stem ('ailes'), the 'tige' in 'voltige' (12) or 'vertige' (17) being the hidden poetic stalk of analogy that joins them or the centre of the double page on either side of which they grow. The preface mentions a 'partition', potentially the segment of a flower, and we find the 'barbe soumise' (cf. the beard of an iris) being replaced by the 'plume solitaire' ('solitaire' describing a flower on a stem with no lateral shoots) and then the triumphant 'aigrette' (16: 'la partie supérieure du calice') which subsequently falls defeated ('flétrie') after becoming 'une cime' (hom. 'cyme', meaning a flowering shoot' (19)). 'Page' itself is a botanical term for each side of a leaf, 'squame' a botanical scale, and the twisting of words in the tourniquet of poetic usage becomes the 'torsion' of this folded siren song and its 'squames bifurquées' as it follows the sunlike gold of poetic beauty through the Zodiac of its twelve double pages: 'le mouvement de torsion ou de pli est presque général dans les feuilles qui suivent le cours du soleil, et dont la page inférieure regarde toujours le ciel et la lumière.'[15] The pages of 'Un coup de Dés' bear the creases of poetic language in an irregular pattern (the botanical sense of 'chiffonné'), no doubt because even a 'pensée' may have its irregularities as it strives after perfect expression, an 'insinuation' which 'voltige autour du gouffre / sans le joncher (from 'jonc')' (12–13). The twofold nature of this botanically ambiguous specimen ('ambigu' (10))—part perfect flower, part creasing leaf—is thus akin to the lightning flash, the 'coup de foudre' which blazes from this linguistic storm: 'éparse' (19: from Old French 'espars'= shaft of lightning) or 'foudre', scattered spars of language and destructive

---

[15] Littré, 'torsion'.

thunderbolts, or the heraldic order of crossed darts. Electricity as chaos, electricity as creative order.

Precipitate or suspension, twisted leaves or perfect flower, thunderbolt or symbolic cross: the scientific world of 'Un coup de Dés' offers the same unresolved, electric, polarized tension as the die and the thimble. Is language a game of chance or the means to a textual authority? The faculties of *belles-lettres* and the natural sciences have reserved their opinion. What of mathematics? What of philosophy? What of theology? What of law? '*SI*' gave us silicon, from 'silex'='caillou'. The Master has abandoned the pebbles with which his forebears counted ('hors d'anciens calculs') and become a quartered page ('quadrillé' but also having four corners and, as folded sheet, four sides) which contains the secret ('écarté du secret'). The poet as grid encounters 'la probabilité' (10) in search of new combinations and, empowered by ratio ('sa petite raison virile' (15)) and language ('raison' being the equivalent of 'logos'), achieves a controlled raising of words to the power of *x*: 'une élévation ordinaire' (21).[16] Perhaps the calculation ('*C'ÉTAIT LE NOMBRE*') may not amount to anything at all—'*SE CHIFFRÂT-IL*' (where 'chiffre', deriving etymologically from 'cifra'= zero, and 'sifr'= vide), contains the prospect of nullity)—but even this nullity is 'évidence de la somme pour peu qu'une', a sum total and a summa, an authenticated silence: 'une élévation ordinaire verse l'absence' (21). The whole text offers the spectacle of a 'compte total en formation' (23), a sum total of linguistic possibilities being arrived at, a rythmical arithmetic producing a 'chiffre', a 'symbole', an 'Idée'. Indeed time and space, the two 'rhythms' which govern our lives and this text, have been translated into signals, navigational aids, as we may hear in 'quant à lui signalé' (23). For Kant (cf. hom. 'quant' and 'Quant au livre') was the philosopher who called time and space 'les deux quanta originaires de notre intuition' (Robert). Quantity has been measured with the silicon of words, the pebbles of a computation; and the text itself presents a set of accounts, a 'compte total', a poetic version of single-entry bookkeeping (one sense of 'simple'), a record of a 'Pensée'.

For 'pensée' derives from 'pendere', meaning to weigh and hence (because coins were weighed for their value) to pay. There has been an attempt, once again in Mallarmé's poetry, to transmute base language into gold by means of poetic innovation. Gone is the '[or] d'anciens calculs', and non-representational language slides across the page, seemingly out of control, and 'coupant au ras les bonds / très à l'intérieur résume / l'ombre enfouie dans la profondeur par cette voile alternative' (7). The 'ras' (as well as being a half-submerged reef) is the 'filière par laquelle on fait passer le lingot qui sort de l'argue', and 'l'opération du ras se nomme le dégrossi du trait'

---

[16] See above, Part V, Ch. 2 (*a*) and cf. Valéry's comment on the poem: 'Il a essayé, pensai-je, d'élever enfin une page à la puissance du ciel étoilé!' (*Œuvres*, i. 626).

(Littré). In the making of golden wire or thread (the 'trait'), the ingot is processed by a 'filière', in English a 'die'. Here the 'Abîme' of language (and prosody) is heard to be 'coupant les bons traits à l'intérieur, l'ombre enfouie, etc.': apparently in turmoil and sliding into the abyss, words are busy cutting golden threads, preparing to sew them together and thus capture the buried treasure of the 'mystère' by means of this alternative kind of canvas. Haunting this allegory of alchemy is a familiar, homophonic ('oral') story of resurrection: 'eau, râle, les bons traits'. Thus 'Un coup de Dés' is itself the 'filière' or die by which the ingot of language is transformed into the golden threads of a 'Pensée' that is worth its weight in gold.

In a new Trial of the Pyx, words are assayed in the scales of the opposing pages,[17] and even when it seems that these pages (and the figures) may never balance and that the pen is lost in a sea of nonsense, the pivot returns: 'plume solitaire éperdu / sauf que la rencontre ou l'effleure' (hom. 'sauf que là, rencontre, houle et fleur')—except that (with the connotation of safety) there is an encounter (cf. 'le point de rencontre des pensées', 'rencontrer'= 'avoir la même pensée qu'un autre'), a pivotal point in the text (cf. 'la roue du rencontre qui meut le pivot du balancier'), with the pivot's 'dé' holding the wheel of this 'rencontre'. From the original thirteenth-century meanings of 'rencontre' as 'coup de dés' and 'combat', the pivot of a set of scales becomes both 'le hasard, événement fortuit par lequel on se trouve dans telle ou telle situation, on rencontre telles circonstances' (Robert), and a medieval joust. And here on the wildly unbalanced spread of pp. 14–15 this struggle with chance is at once the 'houle' of the stormy sea and the flower of beauty, the chaos of language and a happy turn of phrase ('expression heureuse, juste'). And, once more, a heraldic device ('un rencontre'= 'tête d'animal vue de face'): perhaps the 'chef' of the 'maniaque chenu', or the severed 'hure' of St John.

Together with accountancy, its more humble offshoot, the faculty of mathematics thus has a familiar story to tell in 'Un coup de Dés'. The allegory of philosophy, too, suggests a similar tension between truth and 'mensonge' (21). Since 'Toute Pensée émet un Coup de Dés' and since thought and language are synonymous for Mallarmé, 'les ailes de la pensée' may be substituted for the 'wings' of the broken alexandrine and the wheeling wings of language in the narratives constructed above. Thought flows into words, submerses itself in language ('coule en barbe soumise': cf. 'couler sa pensée dans des mots'), as the superior mind, the 'Esprit [d'une grande envergure]', casts the immutable result of its cogitation ('l'unique Nombre qui ne peut pas être un autre') into the linguistic tempest ('Esprit / pour le jeter / dans la tempête / en reployer la division et passer fier'). This thought (as it might be, the simple notion of 'chance', the 'dé') undergoes a

---

[17] Cf. the sign of the Zodiac known as 'la Balance' (Libra).

metamorphosis in which 'raison' (reason, proportion, logos, logic) seems like 'folie' before emerging, 'petite raison virile', in the 'Idée' which is the poem as a whole with its myriad semantic relationships untying and retying the original 'notion' in a 'Pensée' that is less a thought than a symbol of beauty, a flower. Now intellectual activity, fully conscious of the currents and reefs of language, has become a watchful, self-conscious, Cartesian exercise in doubt and 'Méditations', a dynamic brilliance of mental/linguistic fireworks ('de feux'): 'veillant / doutant / roulant / brillant et méditant'.

As for theology, the poet is once more St John the Baptist (as already suggested), a head severed from the body in the name of beauty like language from its referents, and ready to be sanctified as the Precursor of a resurrection. At first the poet is 'sans nef' (9): without traditional prosody, without the sure conveyance of representational language, and without a church. And yet the 'Mystère' awaits, a sacred silence behind closed lips and waiting to be expressed, to be 'hurlé / précipité'—since the 'hure' (or 'tête hérissée') of St John has become both 'legs' and 'lai', and has fallen, the lay of the last prophet. The poem is akin to a simple religious ceremony (cf. 'insinuation simple' and 'office simple'), in which the mystery of the divine is celebrated as an act of expiation (16) as if to appease the wrath of language, a ritual which, like mathematical calculation, leaves no certainty ('ILLUMINÂT-IL') but which, like the raising of the Host, is a symbolic act whereby the everyday is consecrated: 'une élévation ordinaire verse l'absence'. As Christ is absent (if not transubstantiated), so 'toute réalité se dissout', but the poem as a Mass creates a presence that is divine. This 'événement accompli en vue de tout résultat nul' is here strictly 'humain' (20–1) not supernatural or miraculous, but in its completeness the poetic act nevertheless arrives 'à quelque point dernier qui le sacre' (23). The 'feux' on the final page are also the 'feux de saint Jean', beacons lit in celebration of St John's feast day and the summer solstice. The golden sun of language has reached its zenith, and the poem constitutes a new 'bâtiment' in which to glorify its beauty and its mystery, an architectural 'élévation' to rival the finest cathedral, an act of creation: 'SOIT'. From 'SOIT' to 'soi' to 'SI': a book of Genesis and a New Testament proclaiming the Mystery of the Word with all the power of the 'Livre'. For 'Un coup de Dés' would have the force of a legal document: 'Ton acte toujours s'applique à du papier'.

(c) *The Art of Insinuation*

Une insinuation simple / au silence.

At its centre 'Un coup de Dés' describes itself (or the event of which it is an account, or 'compte total') as *'Une insinuation simple / au silence'*. As noted earlier, 'insinuation' has two principal meanings, one more familiar than the other: an oblique speech-act, and a legal act of registration. The first sense is of evident application to the poem since etymologically it derives from 'insinuere', meaning to introduce by windings or turnings, by a 'sinus'. The obliquity of language itself, the appearance of the words on the page, the indirectness of the allegories tracing the quest for prosody and the chancy joust with language, all are nicely summarized in this sinuosity, of which 's1' is the emblem. Indeed the six syllables of the word[18] conjure with homophony in such a way as to evoke, or insinuate, the central numerical motifs of the text: 'une, ainsi, nue, à six, on', a unity of the six and the one. The 'sinus' is a foldlike cavity and thus synonymous with the 'fond', 'Abîme', 'gouffre', and 'ciel' (from Greek 'koilos'= hollow) which are all images of the empty spaces of the turning pages. At the same time it is the geometrical 'sine', originally the perpendicular from one end of an arc to a diameter through the other, now a ratio within a right-angle triangle, and thus a form of 'musical' relationship between cube and circle, square and triangle. The supplementary sense of the Latin 'sinus'= bay, and the use of the 'sinus' in compasses and navigational charts, brings 'insinuation' into the semantic orbit of the Septentrion 'aussi Nord' (hom. 'au sin. "or"'), with the 'sine' thus becoming the golden ratio of 'Un coup de Dés', a stellar sign.

The poem therefore consists of a 'rythmique suspens du *sini*stre', the wreckage of language being prevented from sinking by sinuous geometric pattern, and this pattern aspires to the authority of a registered act. The act, as we have seen, is an attempt to found a new prosody and also an encounter with linguistic contingency. Other acts can be discerned within the sinuous constellations of the text, each one 'le fantôme d'un geste'. As suggested earlier, the whole (hypothetical) event could be seen as a pure allegory of human enterprise: the initial 'to do or not to do', the maelstrom of unleashed consequences (in italics), the retrospective surmise as to whether anything has changed. This fundamental rhythm is accompanied by a movement from senescence through death to rebirth and growth and doubt, which stands as an emblem of some quintessential human experience of the passage of time: the father of the act is reborn as the heir to the act, the new owner of its consequences.

This particular movement or 'rythme' is figured in the language of pro-creation and the family. Round the virgin centre of the text (its 'vierge indice' (13)), the death of the Master ('cadavre' (8)) is accompanied by a process of (re)generation: from 'couvrant' and 'les jaillissements' (7) to the 'coque' (7); the 'conjonction' of the 'vieillard/vieil art' with probability is an 'ébat' of 'la mer/mère' and the 'l'aïeul' and leads to 'Fiançailles', while

---

[18] Littré stipulates this number explicitly (in respect of the word's use in verse).

'perdus' and the repeated 'tentant' homophonically suggest further familial relations ('père', 'tante'). Here language as homophony or pure sound (the 'son' of the Master),[19] freed from the constraints of reference, is now 'son[,] ombre puérile', the ghost of language rising like a child, 'caressée et polie et rendue et lavée', and 'soustraite / aux durs os perdus entre les ais' (hom. 'aux durs O perdus entre les É'). After a form of linguistic baptism and purification, Mallarmé's new polysemic 'vers' emerges, ready to be 'berc[é]' (13); and the 'son délire' (19) or 'son mensonge' (21) becomes the pubescent prince, an 'issu stellaire' (18).

The poem thus registers a birth, a marriage, a death—and a will, for it records the 'legs en la disparition'. This legal sense of 'insinuation' is reinforced in the poem by multiple evocations of the legal process. Itself a linguistic encounter with the laws of chance, the text is also a form of 'procès-verbal', or 'compte[-rendu] total', of the trial of language: indeed it attempts to 'dresser le vol' (or 'volume': 'le "fantome" d'un geste') just as one might 'dresser un procès-verbal'. 'LE MAÎTRE' (the poet as lawman) abandons the Bar of old ('jadis il empoignait la barre') and dispenses with the letter of the old laws before entrusting the 'Esprit [des lois]' to the tempestuous passage ('passer[,] fier') of new legislation. The old legal heading ('chef') sinks 'soumise' (hom. 'sous mise [en jugement?]') into the whiteness of this unlegislated page. But the old 'barre' is replaced by the quasi-legal text which 'chancellera': the sense of a grid (in cancelling with an X) and its application to the grill formerly placed between judge and public etymologically yielding the office of 'chancellor'. The 'Maître' is called to a new bar where language and poetry are in 'crise' (20)—etymologically, before the judge; and while the laws of chance cannot be abrogated ('N'ABOLIRA'), the text offers a clue ('le vierge indice') that in these particular 'CIRCONSTANCES' (5), however slight the evidence ('évidence de la somme pour peu qu'une' (19)), the apparently empty act (21: 'l'acte vide' [of non-representational language, of poetry, of this experiment in *vers libre*]) may have some authority. The patterning by sixes, initially represented but then undermined by '*SI*', seems to be a way to 'immobilise[r]' the text: that is, legally speaking, to 'convertir fictivement en immeuble' ('immeuble'= 'qui ne peut pas être déplacé'). Like the 'fiction' of the Poème, the law of the text tries to immobilize language as immovable construct. But this proves to be a 'faux manoir' (17); the 'cime' of looked-for achievement is now 'flétrie', or branded (by linguistic thunderbolts?) like a criminal; and the vision of the text as 'real estate', as captured 'thingness', vanishes into the mist ('ces parages / du vague / en quoi toute réalité se dissout' ('réalité: from 'réellité'= 'contrat rendu réel'; 'réel': from 'res, rem'). For the moment the Master's heir has an insufficient legacy: 'sa petite raison virile' ('portion,

---

[19] Cf. 'Une dentelle abolit': 'Filial on aurait pu naître'.

part virile'= an heir's lawful or equal share) cannot contain the void: 'RIEN N'AURA EU LIEU'.

Instead the text becomes like a constellation. Cold with the 'désuétude' of laws fallen into disuse, it is an apparently fixed pattern of moving word-stars upon a 'surface vacante'—a property 'qui n'a pas de maître' (Robert)—and it is this very vacancy (of language, of the 'acte vide') which is here being legally documented: 'une élévation ordinaire *verse* l'absence' as one might 'verser au dossier un document'. Verse is an act of registration, yet also an insinuation of absence: 'absence' being an important legal concept about which there is an extensive note in the Code civil and which concerns 'l'incertitude sur l'existence d'une personne qui a disparue'. Does the 'bâtiment' of the text exist, or is it some ephemeral configuration of seaspray? Is the Master missing, or can the hand that once was seen to 'menace[r] un destin et les vents' (8–9) now be seen as 'main'+'as', a 'manœuvre', a manual act of stellar writing, a text that achieves a patterned unity. It is the *place* of writing which can be seen to exist, even if the writer and the 'réalité' which he seeks to evoke, are absent. I can doubt everything but that I doubt: nothing is, but the exception to this rule (or law)— 'EXCEPTÉ [...] / PEUT-ÊTRE' (it *can be*)—is the very act of saying that nothing is. In the trial of language there is no case to answer ('non-lieu') because language is not seeking after some faithful representation of reality; but there is a place, a unit of linguistic activity, 'un endroit' and 'un en droit'. Thanks to the etymology of 'endroit' (originally the preposition 'endreit' meaning 'towards'), that place is 'le vers': 'vers / ce doit être / le Septentrion'. This poem, as we have already seen, is about language being language. As act of 'insinuation', 'Un coup de Dés' takes the substance of the linguistic case (the 'fond d'un naufrage') and sums up its inner mystery ('très à l'intérieur résume / l'ombre enfouie dans la profondeur'). The folds of language have caused it to be arraigned at this critical moment; and this 'crise' is 'mémorable' because it can be turned into a 'mémoire' (or 'procès-verbal') within the immemorial medium of language (the 'ultérieur démon immémorial') and its endless throws of the dice ('DANS DES CIRCON-STANCES ÉTERNELLES').

In these manifold ways 'Un coup de Dés' is '*Une insinuation au silence*', a single text obliquely introduced into the surrounding silence and a quasi-legal act of registration. As Mallarmé puts it at the end of 'Le Mystère dans les lettres' (with reference, as we have seen at the beginning of this book, to the *reader*'s encounter with the poetic text[20]): 'quand s'aligna, dans une brisure, la moindre, disséminée, le hasard vaincu mot par mot, indéfectible-ment le blanc revient, tout à l'heure gratuit, certain maintenant, pour conclure que rien au delà et authentiquer le silence.' The gratuitous white-

---

[20] See above, 'Devant la lettre: On reading Mallarmé'.

ness of the page takes on a significance when it becomes the space that represents the 'breaks' within language. This linguistic discontinuity, or polysemy—for example, that 'dé' is a means of both gambling and sewing—causes language to disseminate, shipwrecking univocity—yet the slightest of these gaps can, by means of poetic assembly, become the space in which threads are tied and 'musical' relations established, such that each gap is now the 'lieu' wherein 'le hasard [est] vaincu mot par mot'. As a result the once gratuitous blank space reappears 'indéfectiblement': unfailingly (because it is always there) but also without fail, or (etymologically) 'sans faille': the 'défaille' of linguistic incoherence has become significant unity which it is impossible to 'défaire', an authenticated silence full of the music of the linguistic spheres, space invisibly constellated. In this way the inability of language to represent the world ('rien au delà') liberates the reader from the potential doubt ('certain maintenant') caused by the false prospect that the text has one, true, unambiguous meaning and provokes instead a dynamic reading that might mirror the constellation of the text itself: 'veillant / doutant / roulant / brillant et méditant', in endless deferral, as the reader traces the golden threads back and forth across the poem. Words weave their sinuous way through the emptiness of the page, enacting a new authority for language. This 'insinuation' is 'simple' (in the legal sense of 'simple') because it resembles a notary act whereby 'l'original est remis aux parties, et seulement mentionné au répertoire de l'étude du notaire':[21] a written contract between language and meaning, now gone from the hands of the poet-notary and merely recorded in a table of contents. A self-sufficient 'insinuation'.

The text is ultimately indivisible, simplex, a 'notion pure', an 'Idée simple'; but the traces of language constitute the 'subdivisions prismatiques de l'Idée'. For the reader, as Mallarmé goes on to describe at the end of 'Le Mystère dans les lettres', the 'virginité' of the text, its self-sufficiency and wholeness as yet unsullied by the reader's gaze ('qui solitairement, devant une transparence du regard adéquat'), divides (like the hymen before dissemination) 'en ses fragments de candeur, l'un et l'autre, preuves nuptiales de l'Idée'. The single virgin space has been split up by words into patches of white space ('candeur' from 'candidus'= white) which, like bridal veils (or 'le voile d'illusion'), attest to the hidden couplings of language which are silently taking place within them and which comprise the 'Idée'. Each space contains a 'preuve', an 'Igitur', a silent proof of the necessary relationship between these words that have seemingly been cast upon the page like the dice from a dice-box. 'Un coup de Dés' ends by proclaiming that 'Toute Pensée émet un Coup de Dés'; 'émettre' (from 'emittere'= 'lancer hors de') entered French via legal terminology and in the sense of 'interjeter'. Every thought, thus, is an

<hr />

[21] See Robert, 'simple', II. 2°, and cf. 'brevet', 3°.

'interjection' as well as an 'insinuation' into the silence, but in 'le vers' such a thought is raised to the level of a superior throw or interjection, namely a symbol. For 'symbole' itself derives etymologically from 'sum/syn' and 'ballein', the Greek words for 'together' and 'throw', these words being at the origin of the Greek 'sumbolon', or 'Latin 'symbolus': a 'signe de recon-naissance', being an 'objet coupé en deux constituant un signe de recon-naissance quand les porteurs pouvaient assembler ['sumballein'] les deux morceaux' (Robert). In religious terminology a symbol is a creed or religious rite, doubtless because this creed or rite constitutes the means by which members of a particular faith recognize each other as being of that faith. The whole text of 'Un coup de Dés' constitutes a 'symbol' of this kind, being divided in half by the centrefold between pp. 12–13, and with each of its double-page spreads being similarly divided by the central gutter. The meet-ing of word-strings across these divides emblematizes the acts of linguistic conjunction which 'le vers' is effecting throughout the poem. At the same time the text is a statement—and the 'ceremonial' enactment—of a belief (however precarious), namely that the linguistic act can achieve pattern of a sort and in the totalizing manner implied by Mallarmé's credo that 'tout, au monde, existe pour aboutir à un beau livre'.

'Un coup de Dés' would seem to be offering an alternative to the Bible, rather as Hugo had sought to simulate the Old and New Testaments in his division of *Les Contemplations* into 'Autrefois' and 'Aujourd'hui'. As Mal-larmé puts it towards the end of 'Crise de vers': 'plus ou moins, tous les livres contiennent la fusion de quelques redites comptées: même il n'en serait qu'un—au monde, sa loi—bible comme la simulent les nations.'[22] The resurrection of the Master has already been noted and, briefly, the act of genesis. More especially there would seem to be a clear analogy with the five books of the Pentateuch, known in Hebrew as the 'torah'—a word meaning originally a 'throw' but coming to mean a body of accepted 'law', and in particular Mosaic Law, because the proposed laws have been cast before the people for agreement or disagreement. By being *Une insinuation simple / au silence enroulée avec ironie* this poem imitates the 'torah' itself, this being a 'rouleau de parchemin enroulé autour de deux baguettes, portant le texte du Pentateuque copié à la main' (Robert). 'Simple' in that it has only the single 'baguette' of its centrefold, this poem is nevertheless a sacred text of circular character worthy to be preserved in some secular equivalent of the 'armoire aux thoras' to be found in a synagogue. As Mallarmé suggested in the different context of his sonnet on Wagner: 'Enfouissez-le-moi plutôt dans une armoire'. He has buried his own 'moi', if not in an 'ar*moi*re', then at least in this 'ar*moi*rie', a heraldic text which proclaims the lineage and authority of its Master and which is yet more

---

[22] OC, 367.

sacred than the vellum manuscripts of a Wagnerian score. Mallarmé has abandoned the 'Hiéroglyphes dont s'exalte le millier' and from the 'clartés maîtresses' of his own text 'a jailli / Jusque vers un parvis né pour leur simulacre'. The 'vers' has become the 'endroit' for a form of musical 'simulacrum' which surpasses the 'sanglots sybillins' of Bayreuth.

Thus 'Un coup de Dés' is very much a 'fragment d'exécuté' of the 'Livre' which Mallarmé aspired to write throughout his poetic career. But the word 'fragment' which Mallarmé uses in the so-called 'Autobiographie' suggests that it might have been part of a larger work, as some prose poems or early versions of 'Hérodiade' were to be part of 'le Livre'; and indeed Mallarmé talks here of 'un livre, tout bonnement, en maints tomes'. Nevertheless it may be more profitable to envisage 'Un coup de Dés' as a self-sufficient, miniature version of the 'total' work which might have offered that 'explication orphique de la Terre' which the poet claimed as 'le seul devoir du poète et le jeu littéraire par excellence'. His account of such an 'explication'—or unfolding—applies well to 'Un coup de Dés': 'car le rythme même du livre, alors impersonnel et vivant, jusque dans sa pagination, se juxtapose aux équations de ce rêve, ou Ode'; and he would seem in it to have achieved the limited ambition which he describes to Verlaine:

je réussirai peut-être; non pas à faire cet ouvrage dans son ensemble (il faudrait être je ne sais qui pour cela!) mais à en montrer un fragment d'exécuté, à en faire scintiller par une place l'authenticité glorieuse, en indiquant le reste tout entier auquel ne suffit pas une vie. Prouver par les portions faites que ce livre existe, et que j'ai connu ce que je n'aurai pu accomplir.[23]

In this 'Autobiographie' Mallarmé sketches in his family background for Verlaine, remarking on the way in which he has branched out from its recent civil service tradition and renewed an earlier literary trend among his forebears:

Mes familles paternelle et maternelle présentaient, depuis la Révolution, une suite ininterrompue de fonctionnaires dans l'Administration et l'Enregistrement; et bien qu'ils y eussent occupé presque toujours de hauts emplois, j'ai esquivé cette carrière à laquelle on me destina dès les langes. Je retrouve trace du goût de tenir une plume, pour autre chose qu'enregistrer des actes, chez plusieurs de mes ascendants: l'un, avant la création de l'Enregistrement sans doute, fut syndic des libraires sous Louis XVI et son nom m'est apparu au bas du Privilège du roi placé en tête de l'édition originale française de Vathek de Beckford que j'ai réimprimé. Un autre écrivait des vers badins dans les Almanachs des Muses et les Étrennes aux Dames. J'ai connu enfant, dans le vieil intérieur de bourgeoisie parisienne familiale M. Magnien, un arrière-petit-cousin, qui avait publié un volume romantique à toute crinière appelé *Ange* ou *Démon*, lequel reparaît quelquefois côté cher dans les catalogues de bouquinistes que je reçois.[24]

[23] *OC*, 663.   [24] *OC*, 661-2.

Might it be that Mallarmé's final masterpiece allowed him to unite these two traditions? For what is 'Un coup de Dés' if not the 'enregistrement d'un acte'? May it not be that the poet who proclaimed his own 'death' and has been regarded as the very model of a post-modernist writer may have used the act of writing—in full, ironic awareness of his actions—to reassert his own position within a family tradition but in the new impersonal shape of a 'plume' tracing *'Une insinuation simple / au silence'*? Vigny's 'L'Esprit pur' begins with the poet's belief that, childless though he be, he has added lustre to the family name which will live on in his works:

> J'ai mis sur le cimier doré du gentilhomme
> Une plume de fer qui n'est pas sans beauté.

In 'Un coup de Dés' Mallarmé likewise has redesigned his heraldic crest and proclaimed his affiliation to a tradition of literary 'enregistrement' which has never known a more radical, more ambitious, or more complex attempt to express 'le Mystère dans les lettres'. His choice of Didot type, the 'official' civil service type style of the day, is the ironic stamp of authority whereby he announces his own accession to authorial power; but his actual death just before a first edition of 'Un coup de Dés' could be published on the basis of his corrected proofs provides a final, poignant commentary on the precariousness of this power. Like Hamlet, Mallarmé ended up acting out his own solitary drama, the doomed creator of a linguistic labyrinth that was almost complete:

mais avance *le seigneur latent qui ne peut devenir,* juvénile ombre de tous, ainsi tenant du mythe. Son solitaire drame! et qui, parfois, tant ce promeneur d'un labyrinthe de trouble et de griefs en prolonge les circuits avec le suspens d'un acte inachevé, semble le spectacle même pourquoi existent la rampe ainsi que l'espace doré quasi moral qu'elle défend, car il n'est point d'autre sujet, sachez bien: l'antagonisme de rêve chez l'homme avec les fatalités à son existence départies par le malheur.[25]

---

[25] 'Hamlet', OC, 300.

Conclusion

je me fus fidèle.[1]

In his study of Mallarmé's thought, *La Religion de Mallarmé*, Bertrand Marchal has presented a powerful and coherent case that the 'sujet, de pensée, unique' to which the poet refers in the short preamble to *Divagations* is none other than religion, and that the question of religion centrally informs all Mallarmé's thinking about poetry from 'Hérodiade' and *Igitur*, through *Les Dieux antiques* and the articles on music and the theatre, to the late prose writings on 'le Livre', the status of 'les Lettres', and the role of the poet in society. Not religion in any denominational sense, but 'la religion unique, latente':[2] the ways in which human beings have sought to come to terms with mortality and to explain the mystery of their situation within the universal scheme of things.

'Divinité' for Mallarmé denotes the human impulse to temper inner fears by projecting this existential anguish onto some external backdrop, there to sublimate it within a symbolic order. Nature itself provided the first such symbolic order, as the annual and diurnal progress of the sun mirrored the human experience of growth and decay. Cast down by its own ephemerality, the primitive mind beheld the 'Tragedy of Nature' played out at sunset and in the autumn, and drew strength from the recurrent prospect of a new dawn and the rites of spring: '"Notre ami le Soleil est mort, reviendra-t-il?" Quand ils le revoyaient dans l'Est, ils se réjouissaient parce que l'astre rapportait avec lui et sa lumière et leur vie.'[3] Thereafter the drama of existential anguish, of the perceived conflict between being and nothingness, of light and darkness, came to be symbolized at one remove in pagan and Christian religions, which, as Mallarmé read in the works of Max Müller and others, proliferated because of *philological* slippage, a 'disease of language'. Gods, be they pagan or Christian, are the figures or emblems of 'la divinité, inscrite au fond de notre être', their names but names, the

---

[1] From a letter which Mallarmé drafted three weeks before his death to Jean Bernard of *Le Figaro* in response to the latter's survey concerning 'l'Idéal à vingt ans' (OC, 883).
[2] *Les Dieux antiques*, OC, 1169.   [3] *Les Dieux antiques*, OC, 1169.

means whereby human beings may articulate their own 'divinité';[4] and in the course of time these articulations have gradually obfuscated the primordial 'rhythm' of experience of which they were originally the expression. With God dead, poetry can now offer at once a return to origins and a task for the future: 'La Poésie est l'expression, par le language humain ramené à son rythme essentiel, du sens mystérieux des aspects de l'existence: elle doue ainsi d'authenticité notre séjour et constitue la seule tâche spirituelle.'[5]

But how? In his separate readings of Mallarmé's poems (in the earlier *Lecture de Mallarmé*), Marchal recognizes the reflexive character of Mallarmé's poetic art and sees this art as a quasi-religious celebration of language within the void of a godless world:

Au contraire de certains romantiques dont les poèmes célébraient une vérité légitimée par Dieu [...], Mallarmé écarte l'idée même de vérité pour concevoir la poésie comme une [...] célébration esthétique du langage lui-même;

un simulacre de célébration (messe solaire ou apothéose stellaire) qui prolonge idéalement le geste vide d'une fictive épiphanie du monde.

In Marchal's account, Mallarmé sees language as a collection of myriad possibilities from which 'Le poète ne peut qu'actualiser, fût-ce au prix d'une vie, quelques combinaisons virtuelles. Au rêve de maîtrise succède le plaisir du jeu.'[6]

But such an approach substantially underrates the degree of Mallarmé's ambition and the scope of his achievement. The unity of thought which Marchal demonstrates in Mallarmé's discursive writing is matched by the singleness of purpose which is evident in the development of his poetic art. From approximately the 'Ouverture' onwards, that purpose was to enact *poetically*—that is to say, linguistically—the fundamental 'rhythm' of human experience epitomized by the passage of the sun and the cycle of response which it provokes, from the anguish felt as darkness falls, to the hope of salvation intimated by starlight and granted by the dawn, to the ensuing doubt. Will day always follow night? Shall the pattern hold? In the theatre of our universe this is the condition of uncertainty in which human beings, Hamlet-like, are condemned to live; this is 'la pièce écrite au folio du ciel et mimée avec le geste de ses passions par l'Homme'.[7] The function of poetry is to mime this drama, to enact this never-ending 'doute' in a linguistic 'Jeu suprême'.

---

[4] *Les Dieux antiques*, OC, 1185.

[5] *Corr.*, ii. 266 (to Léo d'Orfer, 27 June 1884). Mallarmé had been asked to provide a definition of poetry for a collection of such definitions.

[6] *Lecture de Mallarmé*, 287, 315, 288 respectively. Cf. Michel Foucault, *Les Mots et les choses* (Paris, 1966), 317: 'Mallarmé ne cesse de s'effacer lui-même de son propre langage au point de ne plus vouloir y figurer qu'à titre d'exécuteur dans une pure cérémonie du Livre où le discours se composerait de lui-même.'

[7] 'Crayonné au théâtre', OC, 294.

And, from the 'Ouverture' onwards if not before, Mallarmé's poetry does just this. Unfortunately the difficulty of his writing has meant that his readers have tended to experience the anguish of nightfall more acutely than the proffered splendours of stellar configuration, and so his work has spawned its own myth of 'glorious failure'. *Unfolding Mallarmé* has been an attempt to part some of the folds of darkness which this poet so knowingly applied, to explicate shapes—a constellation or a rainbow, a hyperbola, a cube, a scroll—and to trace the emergence of these configurations from the foam of linguistic contingency. For only if the extent of Mallarmé's 'mastery' is perceived can the status of this contingency be accurately assessed and the fundamental 'rhythm' of his writing—'le doute du Jeu suprême'—undergone both as he himself experienced it in the act of writing and as he wished his reader to experience it in the act of reading: an experience pithily summarized in his posthumously published notes as 'la grande aventure intérieure, ou [? où] on va savoir si quelque chose ou rien'.[8]

Mallarmé's own moment of truth—a glottal spasm—came on 9 September 1898, and he seems to have staged it as a solar drama in which the poet's sunset might be followed by a readerly dawn. Having suffered a severe choking fit on the preceding day, intimations of mortality appear to have prompted him to leave a copy of the unpublished 'Cantique de saint Jean' on his desk by way of a last testament.[9] His summer solstice[10] now past, he had felt the gathering folds of darkness in his bones:

> Le soleil que sa halte
> Surnaturelle exalte
> Aussitôt redescend
> Incandescent
>
> Je sens comme aux vertèbres
> S'éployer des ténèbres
> Toutes dans un frisson
> A l'unisson—

and he had begun to contemplate the prospect of an imminent 'rupture franche' (l. 13) as a baptism in the glacial waters of eternity. The first word of his projected *Poésies* became now also his last:

> Mais selon un baptême
> Illuminée au même

---

[8] *Le 'Livre' de Mallarmé*, ed. Scherer, f. 100 (A).

[9] The 'Cantique' is the only completed part of 'Les Noces d'Hérodiade' (except for the already published 'Scène'), and was perhaps therefore the last unfinished poem of which he wanted—during the summer months of 1898 when his health was poor—to leave a polished final version before he died.

[10] Marked (three days later) in the Christian calendar by the Feast of the Nativity of St John, the name-day for those baptized with the name of the saint who began Christian baptism.

Principe qui m'élut
Penche un salut[.]

'Ave' turns to 'vale': the poet bows his head in final salutation and antici-
pates that secular form of salvation which he had already proclaimed for
Gautier and Poe, Baudelaire and Verlaine. As this most terminal of rhymes
implies, he will at least—at last—be *read*: 'Tel qu'en lui-même enfin l'Éter-
nité le change...'—/lu/, (hom.) 'Tel, quand lu [...]'.

In 'Toast funèbre' and the 'Tombeaux', Mallarmé 'consoles' his fellow-
poets with this thought that their genius will shine forth more 'purely' after
their demise: death, as he informs the departed Verlaine, is but 'Un peu
profond ruisseau'.[11] A vain hope. As the example of the posthumous 'Mal-
larmé' shows, a writer's reputation is subject to no fewer vagaries during the
afterlife of posterity's perusal than it is during the living death of contem-
porary controversy and incomprehension. For, upon his last breath, the
myth of Mallarmé began, the myth of failure. Wedged into his blotter lay
a letter to his wife and daughter, asking them to burn his notes: 'il n'y a pas
là d'héritage littéraire, mes pauvres enfants [...] croyez que ce devait être
très beau.'[12] Following the comments to Verlaine about 'le Livre' in his
'Autobiographie' (1885), this parting shot only reinforced the notion that
the Master had been undertaking some extraordinary work and that death
had interrupted him. The myth took further hold the following year with
the publication of the Deman *Poésies*, where the poet refers to 'Beaucoup de
ces poèmes' as being 'études en vue de mieux, comme on essaie les becs de sa
plume avant de se mettre à l'œuvre'.[13] When in 1957 Jacques Scherer
published more than a hundred pages of surviving notes as *Le 'Livre' de
Mallarmé*, the myth seemed to some to be a myth no longer: here, as Scherer
proclaimed, was 'l'esquisse du Livre'.[14] Was it?

In discussing Mallarmé's conception of the 'Livre', one should always be
careful to distinguish between an object and an ideal. When he writes in the
'Autobiographie' of 'le Livre, persuadé au fond qu'il n'y en a qu'un, tenté à
son insu par quiconque a écrit, même les Génies',[15] he is referring to an ideal
of literature towards which all writers have been working, an ideal of 'pure
literariness' comparable with the original 'rythme' of which all subsequent
mythological representations have been a philologically 'fallen' version:
whereas when he refers to 'un livre, tout bonnement, en maints tomes',[16]
he is probably reiterating the ambition he had formulated in his letters to

---

[11] 'Tombeau', l. 14.

[12] Quoted in Mondor, *Vie de Mallarmé*, 801. Cf. Henri Mondor, *Autres Précisions sur
Mallarmé et inédits* (Paris, 1961), 250–1. For a more detailed account of Mallarmé's final
hours and the immediate aftermath of his death, see Millan, *Mallarmé: A Throw of the Dice*,
317–20.

[13] In his 'Bibliographie', OC, 77.   [14] *Le 'Livre' de Mallarmé*, ed. Scherer, p. iii.

[15] OC, 663.   [16] OC, 662–3.

Cazalis in the mid-1860s to produce an 'œuvre' in five or seven parts. No such work exists, but does that mean that Mallarmé failed to achieve his ideal of 'literariness'?

Briefly stated, Mallarmé's poetic career may be summarized as follows. During the first half of the 1860s he came to understand, through reading Poe and through a process of poetic experimentation, where his own originality as a poet might lie. Adopting Poe's definition of beauty as an 'effect', he came to see that beauty derives from the effect of 'necessity'. At the same time his own writing had shown him how little the poet writes the poem; how it is rather the poem—words themselves, and especially rhyme—which 'writes' the poet. Language tenders its threads of 'virtualité' for the poet to weave them into textuality. Within the poetic context a word, therefore, is not so much a representation of the world outside language as a response to other words, to the possibilities inherent in language itself. Thus any poem becomes first and foremost a display of its own genesis.

The complexity which the *knowing* orchestration of this reflexivity could generate is first manifested in the 'Ouverture' to 'Hérodiade', a poem which Mallarmé never published and which helped to precipitate the 'crisis' of 1866–71. Such complexity, Mallarmé appears to have decided, was more successfully controlled within the firm limits of the sonnet (in 'Sonnet allégorique de lui-même' and 'De l'orient passé des Temps'), but even here there was room for improvement. Thereafter, one may reasonably assume, this poet who was also a language-teacher spent some twenty years refining his knowledge of the 'virtualités' of the French language[17]—especially as these years saw the publication of the great dictionaries of Littré and Larousse—and at the same time periodically revising or composing a number of poems in the light of his discoveries. His 'Pursuit of Beauty' was a pursuit of the 'effect of necessity', and this was the ideal which he came to capitalize as 'le Livre'. Having ceded the initiative to words, his was now an art of combination, of 'Musique': every word, every aspect of every word, every aspect of the paginal context of that word, every verse-form, would need to be given a 'necessary' function within what he also capitalized as 'le Vers'. Hence the enormous time the process took; hence the comparatively small eventual output. During this 'interregnum' (as he calls it in the 'Autobiographie'[18]), when he had so to speak 'bracketed' the contemporary (bourgeois) world, he continued to 'travailler avec mystère en vue de plus

---

[17] Cf. Valéry: 'Parfois, considérant l'appareil neuf et délicieux de quelque endroit de ses poèmes, je me disais qu'il avait arrêté sa pensée sur presque tous les mots de notre langue. Le livre singulier qu'il a écrit sur le vocabulaire anglais suppose bien des études et des réflexions sur le nôtre' (*Œuvres*, i. 655).

[18] In 'L'Action restreinte' he uses the image of the railway tunnel which precedes arrival at a city-centre terminus, at 'l'édifice de haut verre [hom. vers] essuyé d'un vol de la Justice' (*OC*, 371–2).

tard ou de jamais et de temps en temps à envoyer aux vivants sa carte de visite, stances ou sonnets'.[19] Working *with* the mystery of language, as well as in mysterious silence, he indeed published the occasional 'visiting card'— 'Toast funèbre', 'Le Tombeau d'Edgar Poe'—but only in 1887, in the *Poésies*, did he finally call in person. Here, revealed, was the work of the poet whom Verlaine had newly brought to prominence in *Les Poètes maudits*.

Whereupon, in the third and last phase of his career, Mallarmé embarked on a further period of radical experimentation. As the younger generation of poets 'invented' *vers libre* and founded a school of Symbolism, their 'Master' quickly moved beyond the confines of the Petrarchan sonnet, of the alexandrine, and even of punctuation, as he sought to create new forms of 'necessity'—out of the octosyllabic sonnet, the heptasyllabic sonnet, and the Shakespearean sonnet, and out of the blank page itself. When he wrote 'Le Livre, instrument spirituel' for *La Revue blanche* in 1895, the future shape of 'Un coup de Dés' was clearly in his mind. Here, having established a contrast between 'le journal' and 'le Livre', he taxes the former with many shortcomings, including the 'monotonie' of its columnar layout, and he envisages a literary alternative:

Pourquoi—un jeu de grandeur, de pensée ou d'émoi, considérable, phrase poursuivie, en gros caractère, une ligne par page à emplacement gradué, ne maintiendrait-il le lecteur en haleine, la durée du livre, avec appel à sa puissance d'enthousiasme: autour, menus, des groupes, secondairement d'après leur importance, explicatifs ou dérivés—un semis de fioritures.[20]

The broadsheet newspaper—'étalée, pleine'—symbolizes blatancy and the crude necessity of unit costs, whereas in a poet's hands the folio sheet ('la feuille') might become the 'lieu' of a linguistic and typographical ritual wherein the beauty of poetic 'necessity'—of poetry in its etymological sense of 'fashioning', of 'fiction'—was at once 'anointed' and 'confirmed': here

les mots, originellement, se réduisent à l'emploi, doué d'infinité jusqu'à sacrer une langue, des quelque vingt lettres—leur devenir, tout y rentre pour tantôt sourdre, principe—approchant d'un rite la composition typographique.

Le livre, expansion totale de la lettre, doit d'elle tirer, directement, une mobilité et spacieux, par correspondances, instituer un jeu, on ne sait, qui confirme la fiction.[21]

As we have seen, 'Un coup de Dés' is such a 'lieu', an 'instrument spirituel' upon which the poet and reader may perform the 'music' of the 'Idée'. But *will* the reader perform this 'music'? As we have also seen, 'Un coup de Dés' is essentially about linguistic expression (and about thought as a form of linguistic expression): 'Toute Pensée émet un Coup de Dés.' What about the *reception* of such expression? As Bertrand Marchal has sug-

---

[19] *OC*, 664.   [20] *OC*, 381.   [21] *OC*, 380.

gested,[22] the question of reading is central to the allegory of 'Les Noces d'Hérodiade'; and the play on /lu/ provides support for his argument. Resplendently situated within the ill*u*mination of the Precursor's halo, the final homophone of the 'Cantique de saint Jean' calls on the reader to follow the saint's 'pur regard / Là-haut' (l. 20), to aspire to that 'transparence du regard adéquat' referred to at the end of 'Le Mystère dans les lettres' by which the 'virginité' of the paginal silence shall be 'divisé en ses fragments de candeur, l'un et l'autre, preuves nuptiales de l'Idée'. For only then will the reader's own pursuit of beauty be consummated: or, as Hérodiade herself puts it at the end of the 'Finale' in 'Les Noces d'Hérodiade':

il fallait
La hantise soudain quelconque d'une face
Pour que je m'entr'ouvrisse et reine triomphasse.

For all the seeming self-sufficiency of the Mallarméan text—'fait, étant'[23]—it shall remain a closed book, a sterile realm of glacial beauty, if it is not read. Having asked the Nourrice (in the 'Scène intermédiaire') to bring her the head of St John, Hérodiade seeks reassurance in 'Finale' that its white ('candid') stare (as suggested by its 'regard révulsé'), which seems to be concentrated on her physical beauty, is in fact gazing upwards to the ideal.[24] Since St John's dead lips cannot give her this reassurance, she wonders if a kiss[25] would extract 'l'arcane messéant / A dire excepté par une bouche défunte' (ll. 24–5) and thereby bring about a form of mystical union. Only by an act of silent orality shall this 'arcane' known to 'son pur regard' (cf. hom. '[le] son pur, regard') become the means to a 'rupture' no less 'franche' than the decapitation of St John or the mammary mutilation of the 'antique amazone' who has the last word in 'Mes bouquins refermés...' (and therefore in the posthumous *Poésies* as a whole). The 'hymen' of impenetrability that separates text and reader must be ruptured if poetic beauty is to triumph; and her lips, be they oral or vulval, must part in rhyme if the reader is to become privy to the 'arcane'—or, as the full title of 'Les Noces d'Hérodiade' has it, the 'Mystère'. By mouthing her homophonies, the reader shall know beauty: 'le rien de mystère, indispensable, qui demeure, exprimé, quelque peu'[26]—that 'Mystère' which, as it happened, was the last word in Mallarmé's farewell letter to his family.[27]

Although 'Les Noces d'Hérodiade. Mystère' invites us allegorically to imitate St John—that is, to turn our eyes from the beauties of the real,

---

[22] *Lecture de Mallarmé*, 62–6.   [23] 'L'Action restreinte', *OC*, 372.
[24] Cf. the reference to the poet's pact with Beauty at the end of 'Étalages': 'un pacte avec la Beauté qu'il se chargea d'apercevoir de son nécessaire et compréhensif regard, et dont il connaît les transformations' (*OC*, 378).
[25] Oscar Wilde's *Salomé*, in which this motif is first introduced, dates from 1893.
[26] *OC*, 370.   [27] See Mondor, *Vie de Mallarmé*, 801.

physical world and to gaze with 'ingénuité'—there is nevertheless no guar-
antee that we shall accept. If there is one constant which lends unity to the
various notes published as *Le 'Livre'*, it is Mallarmé's ambition to eliminate
this last residue of contingency by transforming the act of reading into a
quasi-liturgical ceremony in which the reader's 'response' will be as much a
necessary part of the 'office' as the responses of a Christian congregation. A
'carte d'invitation'[28] indeed will be issued to this secular ritual—or a 'billet'
to this verbal 'bal' or 'ballet'[29]—and the text ('le Livre', 'le livre', 'le
Mystère', 'l'Idée', 'le Drame', etc.) will be performed under the direction
of the poet/'opérateur' solely so that its intricate and knowingly calculated
'relationships' may be made manifest: 'Les Lectures n'ayant d'autre but que
de montrer ces rapports scientifiques.'[30] The kind of mathematical calcula-
tions posited earlier for 'Un coup de Dés' are here plainly in evidence as
Mallarmé seeks to unite the text (page, fold, line of verse, volume, print-run,
price), the reader (in groups of 9, 12, 24), and reading itself (single or
repeated, twice in a day, three times a year, or four, or five, or ten[31]) in an
arithmetical calculation of the strictest necessity. As though in a real theatre,
the performance will be illuminated by a 'lustre'—only here this 'lustre' will
be in a necessary verbal relation with the ancient 'lustrum' (or quinquennial
ceremony of purification) which Mallarmé's new rite may seek to simulate[32]
and in which the poet is himself one of the faithful: 'Je suis moi—fidèle au
livre.'[33]

   Gustave Kahn recalled meeting Mallarmé two years before his death and
hearing him talk about 'Un coup de Dés'—'que devaient suivre neuf autres
poèmes'.[34] Another 'livre', this time in ten volumes? Had death not inter-
vened, Mallarmé would doubtless have continued his pursuit of the ideal
'Livre', and there is every chance that any subsequent poems would have
been as intricate and original as 'Un coup de Dés'. They might even have
given effect to some of the intentions so inscrutably and so tantalizingly
recorded in his surviving notes. To this extent, therefore, Scherer is right to
claim that his edition reproduces 'l'esquisse du Livre'—but only if we
recognize that these notes would not all have led to one single 'Grand
Œuvre' but rather are the laboratory notes of a poet experimenting mentally
(as it were, 'writing aloud') on a whole range of possible ways of continuing
his lifelong struggle with 'le Hasard'. And had Mallarmé written even a
further twenty poems, he would doubtless always have claimed that he had

---

[28] *Le 'Livre' de Mallarmé*, ed. Scherer, fo. 48 (B). Cf. fo. 61 (B).
[29] *Le 'Livre' de Mallarmé*, ed. Scherer, fos. 60 (B), 72 (B), 80 (B), 102 (A)–107 (A).
[30] *Le 'Livre' de Mallarmé*, ed. Scherer, fo. 41 (A).
[31] *Le 'Livre' de Mallarmé*, ed. Scherer, fos. 64 (B), 68 (B), 82 (B), 91 (A).
[32] *Le 'Livre' de Mallarmé*, ed. Scherer, fos. 50 (B), 86 (B).
[33] *Le 'Livre' de Mallarmé*, ed. Scherer, fo. 35 (B).
[34] Gustave Kahn, *Symbolistes et décadents* (Paris, 1902), 24.

failed. For, as Valéry later observed, a poem is never finished: it is merely abandoned. And so too for Mallarmé. Each text is born of language itself, and could be perfected *ad infinitum*: 'un livre ne commence ni ne finit: tout au plus fait-il semblant.'[35] There is no failure in that.

But the myth persists. Despite Scherer's excellent analysis of Mallarmé's battle with contingency and the cogent way in which he relates the fragments of *Le 'Livre'* to Mallarmé's theoretical statements in 'Variations sur un sujet',[36] he can still argue that '"Un coup de Dés", qui est lui-même hasard, tente en vain de l'abolir'.[37] And a critic as subtle as Leo Bersani can still speak of 'Mallarmé's extraordinary surrender to the contingent'.[38] It has been the purpose of this book to dispel that myth, a myth which Post-structuralist readings of Mallarmé have simply perpetuated by seeing in Mallarmé's 'failure' a glorious recognition of the 'absence' to be found at the heart of a logocentric world. In proposing new meanings in Mallarmé's poetry and in presenting the development of his poetic art as a successful search for linguistic and textual mastery, I have chosen to stress certain dominant patterns of significance in each text. Other patterns have been knowingly—and doubtless unknowingly—omitted, while the 'effect of necessity' on which I have insisted is far from absolute. Even as my own reader may have been willing to hear some of the 'homophonic' readings which I have suggested, other homophonies will probably have interrupted the aural 'score' in a contingent and quite possibly ridiculous manner. But I have wanted to show that there are more patterns in Mallarmé than have so far met the critical eye; and that these patterns are invitations to explore further the mysterious universe of language itself. Above all I have endeavoured to show that Mallarmé meant what he said: he was, if nothing else, a man of his word.

In sum, Mallarmé was a fundamentalist. For him, a poet is a wordsmith, employing an everyday medium to transmute the hopes and fears of the human soul into a golden treasury of sound and meaning:

Le poète, verbal, se défie, il persiste, dans une prévention jolie, pas étroitesse, mais sa suprématie au nom du moyen, le plus humble conséquemment essentiel, la parole: or, à quelle hauteur qu'exultent des cordes et des cuivres, un vers, du fait de l'approche immédiate de l'âme, y atteint.[39]

'Religion' comes from 'religare'= to bind,[40] and Mallarmé is a 'religious' poet in that he binds words together into patterns which promise signifi-

---

[35] *Le 'Livre' de Mallarmé*, ed. Scherer, fo. 181 (A).
[36] See his introduction to *Le 'Livre' de Mallarmé*; and cf. Marchal, *La Religion de Mallarmé*, 495–548.
[37] p. xiv.
[38] *The Death of Stéphane Mallarmé* (Cambridge, 1982), 57.
[39] 'Plaisir sacré', OC, 389.
[40] Noted by Marchal, *La Religion de Mallarmé*, 28. Marchal briefly traces a historical move from religion as what binds human beings to God to religion as that which binds human beings to each other.

cance. Like Vulcan, the blacksmith husband of Venus, he forges homophony into the thunderbolts of rhyme, 'cette fulgurante cause de délice': and rhyme—the marriage of sameness and difference—sets the seal on the essential connectedness of all things and thus constitutes the 'divine' projection of a universal human aspiration:

Ainsi lancé de soi le principe qui n'est—que le Vers! attire non moins que dégage pour son épanouissement [...] les mille éléments de beauté pressés d'accourir et de s'ordonner dans leur valeur essentielle. Signe! au gouffre central d'une spirituelle impossibilité que rien soit exclusivement à tout, le numérateur divin de notre apothéose, quelque suprême moule qui n'ayant pas lieu en tant que d'aucun objet qui existe: mais il emprunte, pour y aviver un sceau tous gisements épars, ignorés et flottants selon quelque richesse, et les forger.[41]

By means of this 'fulgurance' the poem becomes a sacred, musical text which is seemingly independent of its individual creator and offers itself as an expression of this 'divine' aspiration by virtue of the very symmetry of its pages:

quel est-il: l'hymne, harmonie et joie, comme pur ensemble groupé dans quelque circonstance fulgurante, des relations entre tout. L'homme chargé de voir divinement, en raison que le lien, à volonté, limpide, n'a d'expression qu'au parallélisme, devant son regard, de feuillets.[42]

Forged within a framework—be it a sonnet or six folded sheets of paper—this 'lien' of intentional, 'limpid' interconnection is mirrored in the folds of the Book itself; and this folding (even in a newspaper) is thus, in a fundamental or etymological sense, 'religious': 'Le pliage est, vis-à-vis de la feuille imprimée grande, un indice, quasi religieux.'[43] In this way the folds of rhyme represent the barely parted lips of mystery, of 'le mystère dont on est au monde pour envisager la grandeur';[44] and the Book—like a casket—becomes the protective container of the mysterious, enfolded 'divinity' of humanity: 'défendant contre le brutal espace une délicatesse reployée infinie et intime de l'être en soi- même.'[45] Or a tomb: 'le miniscule tombeau [...] de l'âme.'[46] 'Âme'—from 'anima'= breath—denotes, in Mallarmé's 'fundamentalist' terminology,[47] the irreducible essence of human linguistic expression, the universal, physical 'soupir' shaped into words and 'perpetuated' in the tomb of the poetic text.

---

[41] 'Solennité', OC, 333.
[42] 'Le Livre, instrument spirituel', OC, 378.
[43] 'Le Livre, instrument spirituel', OC, 379.
[44] 'Le Genre ou des modernes', OC, 314.
[45] 'Le Genre ou des modernes', OC, 318.
[46] 'Le Livre, instrument spirituel', OC, 379.
[47] Cf. the playful analogies between writing poetry (by the 'expression' of words) and exhaling smoke in 'Toute l'âme résumée'.

But though the Book protects poetic pattern from the brutal infinity of empty space, it must needs—like the virginal Hérodiade—be penetrated by the metaphorical paper-knife of the reader's 'conscience':

Le reploiement vierge du livre, encore, prête à un sacrifice dont saigna la tranche rouge des anciens tomes; l'introduction d'une arme, ou coupe-papier, pour établir la prise de possession. Combien personnelle plus avant, la conscience, sans ce simulacre barbare: quand elle se fera participation, au livre pris d'ici, de là, varié en airs, deviné comme une énigme—presque refait par soi. Les plis perpétueront une marque, intacte, conviant à ouvrir, fermer la feuille, selon le maître.[48]

Almost 'scriptible' ('presque refait par soi'), the Mallarméan text thus remains 'lisible', controlled and enfolded by a Master. Fashioned in the absence of any other divine guarantor of truth than humanity itself, the Book bids us unfold its pages in a readerly performance which has the power to fill the existential void:

La merveille d'un haut poème comme ici me semble que, naissent des conditions pour en autoriser le déploiement visible et l'interprétation, d'abord il s'y prêtera et ingénument au besoin ne remplace tout que faute de tout.[49]

---

[48] 'Le Livre, instrument spirituel', OC, 381. Cf. La Dernière Mode: 'Solennités tout intimes, l'une: de placer le couteau d'ivoire dans l'ombre que font deux pages jointes d'un volume: l'autre, luxueuse, fière et si spécialement parisienne: une Première dans n'importe quel endroit' (OC, 718).

[49] 'Solennité', OC, 335.

Select Bibliography

1. THE WORKS OF MALLARMÉ

(a) Collected Editions

Œuvres complètes, ed. Henri Mondor and G. Jean-Aubry (Bibliothèque de la Pléiade) (Paris, 1951).

Œuvres complètes, vol. i: Poésies, ed. Carl Paul Barbier and Charles Gordon Millan (Paris, 1983).

Igitur, Divagations, Un coup de dés, ed. Yves Bonnefoy (Paris, 1976).

Œuvres, ed. Yves-Alain Favre (Paris, 1985).

Poésies, ed. Pierre Citron (Paris, 1987).

Poésies, ed. Lloyd James Austin (Paris, 1989).

Poésies, ed. Bertrand Marchal (Paris, 1992).

Correspondance, ed. Henri Mondor and Jean-Pierre Richard (vol. i), Henri Mondor and Lloyd James Austin (vols ii–xi) (11 vols, Paris, 1959–85) [Austin's supplements in French Studies, 40 (1986), 1–25; 41 (1987), 155–80; 44 (1990), 170–95; 45 (1991), 166–94; 47 (1993), 172–201; 48 (1994), 17–49].

Correspondance complète (1862–1871), suivi[e] de Lettres sur la poésie (1872–1898), avec des lettres inédites, ed. Bertrand Marchal (Paris, 1995).

Documents Stéphane Mallarmé, ed. Carl Paul Barbier et al. (7 vols, Paris, 1968–80).

(b) Individual Editions

Le 'Livre' de Mallarmé, ed. Jacques Scherer (Paris, 1957; 2nd edn, 1977).

Les Noces d'Hérodiade: Mystère, ed. Gardner Davies (Paris, 1959).

Un coup de Dés jamais n'abolira le Hasard, ed. Mitsou Ronat (Paris, 1980).

2. OTHER PRIMARY SOURCES

BAUDELAIRE, CHARLES, Œuvres complètes, ed. Claude Pichois (Bibliothèque de la Pléiade) (2 vols, Paris, 1975–6).

GIDE, ANDRÉ, Œuvres complètes, ed. L. Martin-Chauffier, Nouvelle Revue française (15 vols, n.p., n.d.).

HUYSMANS, KARL-JORIS, A rebours, ed. Marc Fumaroli (Paris, 1983).

POE, EDGAR ALLAN, 'The Philosophy of Composition', in *Selected Writings*, ed. David Galloway (London, 1967).

PROUST, MARCEL, 'Contre l'obscurité', in *Chroniques* (Paris, 1927), 137–44.

VALÉRY, PAUL, *Œuvres*, ed. Jean Hytier (Bibliothèque de la Pléiade) (2 vols, Paris, 1957–60).

3. WORKS OF REFERENCE

Dictionary of Scientific Biography, ed. C. G. Gillispie (16 vols, New York, 1970).

Dictionnaire alphabétique et analogique de la langue française, ed. Paul Robert (9 vols, Paris, 1985).

Dictionnaire de la langue française, ed. Paul-Émile Littré (4 vols, Paris, 1863–72; Suppl. 1877).

Dictionnaire de l'imprimerie, ed. Edmond Morin (2nd edn, Brussels, 1933).

Dictionnaire étymologique du français, ed. Jacqueline Picoche (Paris, 1990).

Dictionnaire étymologique et explicatif de la langue française et spécialement du langage populaire, ed. Charles Toubin (Paris, 1886).

Grand Dictionnaire universel du XIXe siècle, ed. Pierre Larousse (15 vols, Paris, 1866–76; 1st Suppl. 1877; 2nd Suppl. s.d. [1890]; reprinted by Slatkine, 17 vols, Geneva, 1982).

Princeton Encyclopedia of Poetry and Poetics, ed. Alex Preminger (2nd edn, London, 1975).

4. WORKS ON VERSIFICATION

BANVILLE, THÉODORE DE, *Petit Traité de poésie française* (Paris, 1872).

BECQ DE FOUQUIÈRES, LOUIS, *Traité général de versification française* (Paris, 1879).

DELAPORTE, VICTOR, *De la rime française* (Paris, 1898).

LE GOFFIC, CHARLES, and THIEULIN, ÉDOUARD, *Nouveau Traité de versification française* (Paris, 1890).

TENINT, WILHEM, *Prosodie de l'école moderne* (Paris, 1844).

5. CRITICAL WORKS

ABASTADO, CLAUDE, *Expérience et théorie de la création poétique chez Mallarmé* (Paris, 1970).

—— 'Lecture inverse d'un sonnet nul', *Littérature*, 6 (1972), 78–85.

—— 'Le "Livre" de Mallarmé: Un autoportrait mythique', *Romantisme*, 44 (1984), 65–81.

—— 'Stéphane Mallarmé: "A la nue accablante tu"', in Hartmut Stenzel and Heinz Thoma (eds), *Die Französische Lyrik des 19. Jahrhunderts* (Munich, 1987), 219–34.

ARTHUR, ROSS, 'When is a Word not a Word: Thoughts on Mallarmé's Sonnet en -yx', *Romance Notes*, 27 (1986–7), 167–73.

ASSAD, MARIA L., 'Mallarmé's "Hérodiade": A Hermeneutical Gesture', *Paragraph*, 12 (1989), 181–96.

AUSTIN, LLOYD JAMES, 'Mallarmé et le rêve du livre', *Mercure de France*, 317 (1953), 81–108.

—— 'Les "Années d'apprentissage" de Stéphane Mallarmé', *Revue d'histoire littéraire de la France*, 56 (1956), 65–84.

—— 'Le "Cantique de saint Jean" de Stéphane Mallarmé', *AUMLA*, 10 (1959), 46–59.

—— 'Mallarmé and the *Prose pour des Esseintes*', *Forum for Modern Language Studies*, 2 (1966), 197–213.

—— 'Mallarmé disciple de Baudelaire: *Le Parnasse contemporain*', *Revue d'histoire littéraire de la France*, 67 (1967), 437–49.

—— '"L'Après-midi d'un faune": Essai d'explication', *Synthèses*, 258–9 (1967–8), 24–35.

—— 'Mallarmé's Reshaping of "Le Pitre châtié"', in E. M. Beaumont *et al.* (eds), *Order and Adventure in Post-Romantic French Poetry. Essays Presented to C. A. Hackett* (Oxford, 1973), 56–71; reprinted in *Poetic Principles and Practice* (Cambridge, 1987).

—— 'Meaning in Mallarmé: Remarks on "A la nue accablante tu"', *Australian Journal of French Studies*, 16 (1979), 217–25.

—— 'The Indubitable Wing: Mallarmé's "Quand l'ombre menaça de la fatale loi…"', in *Mélanges de littérature française moderne offerts à Garnet Rees* (Paris, 1980), 1–14.

—— 'How Ambiguous Is Mallarmé? Reflections on the Captive Swan', in *Literature and Society: Studies in Nineteenth and Twentieth Century French Literature Presented to R. J. North* (Birmingham, 1980), 102–14.

—— *Poetic Principles and Practice: Occasional Papers on Baudelaire, Mallarmé and Valéry* (Cambridge, 1987).

BÉNICHOU, PAUL, 'La "Prose pour des Esseintes"', *Saggi e ricerche di letteratura francese*, 27 (1988), 27–58.

—— *Selon Mallarmé* (Paris, 1995).

BERG, R.-J., '"Le Pitre châtié" I et II, ou l'intertextualité problématique', *Nineteenth-Century French Studies*, 15 (1986–7), 376–84.

BERNARD, SUZANNE, *Mallarmé et la musique* (Paris, 1959).

—— *Le Poème en prose de Baudelaire jusqu'à nos jours* (Paris, 1959).

BERSANI, LEO, *The Death of Stéphane Mallarmé* (Cambridge, 1982).

BLANCHOT, MAURICE, *Faux Pas* (Paris, 1943).

—— *La Part du feu* (Paris, 1949).

—— *L'Espace littéraire* (Paris, 1955).

—— *Le Livre à venir* (Paris, 1959).

BOUGNOUX, DANIEL, 'L'Éclat du signe', *Littérature*, 14 (1974), 83–93.

BOWIE, MALCOLM, *Mallarmé and the Art of Being Difficult* (Cambridge, 1978).

—— 'Genius at Nightfall: Mallarmé's "Quand l'ombre menaça de la fatale loi…"', in Christopher Prendergast (ed.), *Nineteenth-Century French Poetry: Introductions to Close Reading* (Cambridge, 1990), 225–42.

BURT, ELLEN, 'Mallarmé's "Sonnet en yx": The Ambiguities of Speculation', *Yale French Studies*, 54 (1977), 55–82.

CAMPION, PIERRE, *Mallarmé: Poésie et philosophie* (Paris, 1994).

CARRON, JEAN-CLAUDE, '*Sainte* de Mallarmé: Poétique et musiques', *Kentucky Romance Quarterly*, 26 (1979), 133–41.

CHADWICK, CHARLES, *Mallarmé: Sa pensée dans sa poésie* (Paris, 1962).

CHAMBERS, ROSS, 'An Address in the Country: Mallarmé and the Kinds of Literary Context', *French Forum*, 11 (1986), 199–215.

CHAMPIGNY, ROBERT, 'The *Swan* and the Question of Pure Poetry', *L'Esprit créateur*, 1 (1961), 145–55.

CHASSÉ, CHARLES, *Les Clefs de Mallarmé* (Paris, 1954).

CHAUSSERIE-LAPRÉE, JEAN-PIERRE, 'L'Architecture secrète de l'"Ouverture ancienne"', *Europe*, 54 (Apr.–May 1976), 74–103.

—— 'Équilibres mallarméens', *Europe*, 54 (Apr.–May 1976), 161–70.

CHISHOLM, A. R., 'Mallarmé: "Quand l'ombre menaça . . ."', *French Studies*, 15 (1961), 146–9.

—— *Mallarmé's Grand Œuvre* (Manchester, 1962).

—— '"Don du poème"', *Essays in French Literature*, 3 (1966), 33–7.

—— 'Mallarmé and the Riddle of the Ptyx', *AUMLA*, 40 (1973), 246–8.

CITRON, PIERRE, 'Sur le sonnet en -yx de Mallarmé', *Revue d'histoire littéraire de la France*, 69 (1969), 113–6.

COHN, ROBERT GREER, *L'Œuvre de Mallarmé: Un coup de Dés* (Paris, 1951).

—— *Toward the Poems of Mallarmé* (Berkeley, 1965).

—— *Mallarmé's Masterwork: New Findings* (The Hague, 1966).

—— 'A propos du *Coup de Dés*', *Critique*, 38 (1982), 92–3.

Colloque Mallarmé (Glasgow, novembre 1973) en l'honneur de Austin Gill (Paris, 1975).

CORNULIER, BENOÎT DE, 'Remarques sur le sonnet "Le vierge, le vivace et le bel aujourd'hui" de Stéphane Mallarmé', *Studi francesi*, 22 (1978), 59–75.

COUFFIGNAL, ROBERT, 'Une catabase mallarméenne: Approches nouvelles du sonnet en -yx', *Littératures*, 20 (1989), 53–62.

CROWLEY, ROSALINE, 'Towards the Poetics of Juxtaposition: "L'Après-midi d'un faune"', *Yale French Studies*, 54 (1977), 33–44.

DÄLLENBACH, LUCIEN, *Le Récit spéculaire: Essai sur la mise en abyme* (Paris, 1977).

DAVIES, GARDNER, *Vers une explication rationnelle du 'Coup de Dés': Essai d'exégèse mallarméenne* (Paris, 1953; rev. edn, Paris, 1992).

—— *Mallarmé et le drame solaire* (Paris, 1959).

—— *Mallarmé et le rêve d''Hérodiade'* (Paris, 1978).

—— *Mallarmé et la 'couche suffisante d'intelligibilité'* (Paris, 1988).

DAYAN, PETER, *Mallarmé's 'Divine Transposition': Real and Apparent Sources of Value* (Oxford, 1986).

DERRIDA, JACQUES, *La Dissémination* (Paris, 1972).

DORNBUSH, JEAN, 'The Death of the Penultimate: Paradox in Mallarmé's "Le Démon de l'analogie"', *French Forum*, 5 (1980), 239–60.

DRAGONETTI, ROGER, *Études sur Mallarmé*, ed. Wilfried Smekens (Ghent, 1992), 49–71.

DUMAS, OLIVIER, 'Mallarmé, Platon et "La Prose pour des Esseintes"', *Revue des sciences humaines*, 126 (1967), 239–57.

FOUCAULT, MICHEL, *Les Mots et les choses* (Paris, 1966).

FOWLIE, WALLACE, *Mallarmé* (London, 1953).

FRANKLIN, URSULA, *An Anatomy of Poesis: The Prose Poems of Stéphane Mallarmé* (Chapel Hill, NC, 1976).

FREY, HANS-JOST, 'Spume', *Yale French Studies*, 74 (1988), 249–60.

FRIEDRICH, HUGO, *Die Struktur der modernen Lyrik* (Hamburg, 1956).

GAÈDE, ÉDOUARD, 'Le Problème du langage chez Mallarmé', *Revue d'histoire littéraire de la France*, 68 (1968), 45–65.

GENGOUX, JACQUES, *Le Symbolisme de Mallarmé* (Paris, 1950).

GILL, AUSTIN, *The Early Mallarmé* (2 vols, Oxford, 1979, 1986).

GOFFIN, ROBERT, *Mallarmé vivant* (Paris, 1956).

HUBERT, JUDD D., 'A post-Mortem on "The Penultimate"', *Substance*, 56 (1988), 78–86.

HUOT, SYLVIANE, *Le 'Mythe d'Hérodiade' chez Mallarmé* (Paris, 1977).

JOHNSON, BARBARA, *Défigurations du langage poétique: La Seconde Révolution baudelairienne* (Paris, 1979).

—— *The Critical Difference: Essays in the Contemporary Rhetoric of Reading* (Baltimore, 1980).

—— *A World of Difference* (Baltimore, 1987).

KAUFMANN, VINCENT, *Le Livre et ses adresses (Mallarmé, Ponge, Valéry, Blanchot)* (Paris, 1986).

KILLICK, RACHEL, 'Mallarmé's "Quatorzains"', *Essays in French Literature*, 19 (1982), 17–33.

KINLOCH, DAVID, 'Mallarmé and the Chinese Artist', *Romance Studies*, 14 (1989), 77–88.

KIRK, G. S., RAVEN, J. E., and SCHOFIELD, M., *The Pre-Socratic Philosophers* (2nd edn, Cambridge, 1983).

KRISTEVA, JULIA, *La Révolution du langage poétique: L'Avant-garde à la fin du XIXe siècle: Lautréamont et Mallarmé* (Paris, 1974).

KROMER, GRETCHEN, 'The Redoutable PTYX', *Modern Language Notes*, 86 (1971), 563–72.

LA CHARITÉ, VIRGINIA, 'Mallarmé's *Livre*: The Graphomatics of the Text', *Symposium*, 34 (1980), 249–59.

—— *The Dynamics of Space: Mallarmé's 'Un coup de dés jamais n'abolira le hasard'* (Lexington, Ky., 1987).

LEBENSZTEJN, JEAN-CLAUDE, 'Note relative au "Coup de Dés"', *Critique*, 36 (1980), 633–59.

LEES, HEATH, 'Mallarmé's Moire', *French Bulletin*, 51 (Summer 1994), 14–16.

LLOYD, ROSEMARY, *Mallarmé: 'Poésies'* (London, 1984).

LOWE, CATHERINE, 'Le Mirage de ptyx, implication à la rime', *Poétique*, 15 (1984), 325–45.

LUND, HANS PETER, *L'Itinéraire de Mallarmé* (Copenhagen, 1969).

LYOTARD, JEAN-FRANÇOIS, *Discours, figure* (Paris, 1978).

MARCHAL, BERTRAND, *Lecture de Mallarmé* (Paris, 1985).

—— *La Religion de Mallarmé* (Paris, 1988).

MAZALÉYRAT, JEAN, 'Note technique sur les sonnets de Mallarmé', *Littératures*, 9–10 (1984), 185–90.

MICHAUD, GUY, *Mallarmé* (2nd edn, Paris, 1971).

MIHRAM, DANIELLE, 'The Abortive Didot/Vollard Edition of *Un coup de Dés*', *French Studies*, 33 (1979), 39–56.

MILLAN, GORDON, *Mallarmé: A Throw of the Dice: The Life of Stéphane Mallarmé* (London, 1994).

MONDOR, HENRI, *Vie de Mallarmé* (Paris, 1941).

——*Eugène Lefébure: Sa vie, ses lettres à Mallarmé* (Paris, 1951).

——*Mallarmé lycéen* (Paris, 1954).

——*Autres Précisions sur Mallarmé et inédits* (Paris, 1961).

MOSSOP, D. J., *Pure Poetry: Studies in French Poetic Theory and Practice 1746 to 1945* (Oxford, 1971).

NOULET, ÉMILIE, *L'Œuvre poétique de Stéphane Mallarmé* (Paris, 1940).

——*Vingt poèmes de Stéphane Mallarmé* (Paris, 1967).

OLDS, MARSHALL, C., *Desire Seeking Expression: Mallarmé's 'Prose pour des Esseintes'* (Lexington, Ky., 1983).

POULET, GEORGES, *La Distance intérieure* (Paris, 1952), 298–355.

REYNOLDS, DEIRDRE, 'Illustration, Present or Absent: Reflecting Reflexivity in Mallarmé's "Sonnet en yx"', *Journal of European Studies*, 19 (1989), 311–29.

——'Mallarmé et la transformation esthétique du langage, à l'exemple de "Ses purs ongles"', *French Forum*, 15 (1990), 203–20.

RICHARD, JEAN-PIERRE, *L'Univers imaginaire de Mallarmé* (Paris, 1961).

——'Feu rué, feu scintillé: Note sur Mallarmé, le fantasme et l'écriture', *Littérature*, 17 (1975), 84–104 (reprinted in *Microlectures* (Paris, 1984)).

RIFFATERRE, MICHEL, *The Semiotics of Poetry* (Bloomington, Ind., 1978).

ROBB, GRAHAM, 'The Phoenix of Mallarmé's "Sonnet en -yx"', *French Studies Bulletin*, 24 (Autumn 1987), 13–15.

RONAT, MITSOU, 'Réponse à Robert Greer Cohn', *Critique*, 38 (1982), 276–7.

ROUBAUD, JACQUES, *La Vieillesse d'Alexandre* (Paris, 1978).

ROULET, CLAUDE, *Élucidation du poème de Stéphane Mallarmé: 'Un coup de dés jamais n'abolira le hasard'* (Neuchâtel, 1943).

SARTRE, JEAN-PAUL, *Mallarmé: La lucidité et sa face d'ombre* (Paris, 1986).

SAURAT, DENIS, 'La Nuit d'Idumée', *Nouvelle Revue française*, 1 Dec. 1952.

SCHERER, JACQUES, *Grammaire de Mallarmé* (Paris, 1977).

SCOTT, CLIVE, *Vers libre: The Emergence of Free Verse in France 1886–1914* (Oxford, 1990).

SCOTT, DAVID H. T., *Sonnet Theory and Practice in Nineteenth-Century France: Sonnets on the Sonnet* (Hull, 1977).

——'Mallarmé and the Octosyllabic Sonnet', *French Studies*, 31 (1977), 149–63.

——*Pictorialist Poetics: Poetry and the Visual Arts in Nineteenth-Century France* (Cambridge, 1988).

SMITH, HAROLD J., 'Mallarmé's Faun: Hero or Anti-Hero?', *Romanic Review*, 64 (1973), 111–24.

SOLLERS, PHILIPPE, *Logiques* (Paris, 1968).

SONNENFELD, ALBERT, 'Élaboration secondaire du grimoire: Mallarmé et le poète-critique', *Romanic Review*, 69 (1978), 72–89.

STAUB, HANS, 'Le Mirage interne des mots', *Cahiers de l'Association internationale des études françaises*, 27 (1975), 275–88.

STEINMETZ, JEAN-LUC, 'Le Paradoxe mallarméen: Les *Poèmes en prose*', *Europe*, 54 (Apr.–May 1976), 134–60.

SURER, PAUL, 'Explication de texte: "L'Azur"', *L'Information littéraire*, 19 (1967), 92–6.

SWEET, JOHN, *Revelation* (London, 1990).

TERDIMAN, RICHARD, *Discourse/Counter-Discourse* (Ithaca, NY, 1985).

THIBAUDET, ALBERT, *La Poésie de Stéphane Mallarmé* (Paris, 1926).

VAN LAERE, FRANÇOIS, 'Le Hasard éliminé: L'Ordonnance d'un livre de vers', *Synthèses*, 258–9 (1967–8), 107–12.

VERDIN, SIMONNE, *Stéphane Mallarmé: Le Presque Contradictoire* (Paris, 1975).

WATSON, LAWRENCE, 'Some Further Thoughts on Mallarmé's "Sonnet en -yx"', *French Studies Bulletin*, 27 (Summer 1988), 13–16.

Index